For Dick from Hugh
April, 1936

THE LEAGUE OF NATIONS
AND
THE RULE OF LAW, 1918–1935

MACMILLAN AND CO., Limited
LONDON · BOMBAY · CALCUTTA · MADRAS
MELBOURNE

THE MACMILLAN COMPANY
NEW YORK · BOSTON · CHICAGO
DALLAS · ATLANTA · SAN FRANCISCO

THE MACMILLAN COMPANY
OF CANADA, LIMITED
TORONTO

THE LEAGUE OF NATIONS
AND
THE RULE OF LAW
1918-1935

BY

ALFRED ZIMMERN

Montague Burton Professor of International Relations
in the University of Oxford
Fellow of New College

MACMILLAN AND CO., LIMITED
ST. MARTIN'S STREET, LONDON
1936

COPYRIGHT

TO

THE WARDEN AND FELLOWS

OF

NEW COLLEGE

PREFACE

A STUDY of the League of Nations must of necessity be a study both of forms and of forces. The reader of these pages will therefore find himself being carried forward from the one to the other and even, on occasion, being borne to and fro between them. What he must not, however, expect to find is an analysis of any of the particular problems, political, economic, social and, not least, psychological, which have formed the stuff and substance of international politics during the period under review. To have attempted to deal with all or even the most important of these would have required a series of volumes, while to have selected one or two of the chief would have been to set the whole work out of proportion.

There is a further reason for abstaining at this stage from the attempt, in a work of this character, to discuss individual problems, either in the political or the economic field. It is that all schemes or suggestions for dealing with them must be conditioned by one major consideration—whether or not, in some form or another, the rule of law, as we understand the term in this country, is to be established in the sphere of international relations. At the moment of writing, this question still awaits an answer. At times indeed, in penning these pages, I have been in doubt whether to employ the past or the present tense, whether I was writing a history of an experiment that had reached its conclusion or describing the early phases of a living and developing institution. If in this matter of style I have erred on the side of optimism, I trust that the reader will not feel that I have allowed it to colour the substance of the book or to affect the impartiality of the analysis.

My thanks are due to several friends who have been good enough to read portions of the book in proof or typescript, particularly to Mr David Hunter Miller, who has saved me from errors of fact in regard to the drafting of the Covenant. I must also acknowledge the permission received to publish the Memorandum reproduced on p. 196 and the following pages and to make use of other material referred to in Chapter III of Part II.

In order to make the book as serviceable as possible, I have limited the footnote references to works likely to be of help in a further study of the subject. The literature on the League of Nations is so extensive and various that the outstanding contributions to it may easily be lost sight of in the flood of superficial or propagandist material. In referring to actual League proceedings I have, generally speaking, abstained from giving references to the relevant League publications, thinking that serious students of the subject would be able to find their way about in them without detailed guidance.

A. Z.

New College, Oxford
October 21, 1935

CONTENTS

ix

CHAPTER IX

CHAPTER X

CHAPTER XI

PART III

THE WORKING OF THE LEAGUE

CHAPTER I

CHAPTER II

CHAPTER III

CHAPTER IV

INTRODUCTION

THE best way of approaching the study of the League of Nations at its present stage is to think of it as a particular method for carrying on relations between states. This method was devised at the close of the World War in the hope that it would conduce to a better understanding, particularly between the Great Powers, than had existed in the years before 1914.

Whatever else may be thought about the war, it cannot be denied that it involved a failure of the older methods, of what is often comprehensively called 'the old diplomacy'. The men who, in 1919, brought the League of Nations into existence aimed at providing machinery which would, so far as is humanly possible, prevent the recurrence of such a catastrophe. They did not indeed imagine that machinery would ever count for more than human motive or that the procedure enshrined in the Covenant would prove either fool-proof or knave-proof. But they were resolved to ensure that statesmanship in the post-war world should be provided with the best safeguards that could be devised to restrain reckless or criminal policies in international affairs and that, should a breakdown nevertheless occur, it should be in no way attributable to the lack of adequate machinery or to technical defects in its working.

The states which have adopted this new method of intercourse are 'members of the League of Nations'.

They include the overwhelming majority of the sixty-odd states which are eligible for membership. The few which do not form part of this company incur the disadvantage of being unable to make full use of the new League method. Several of them have, however, shown their appreciation of its value by arranging to make use of it for a number of purposes without assuming the obligations of direct membership. Broadly speaking, therefore, we may say that the new method has justified itself in the working and that there is every likelihood that it will become a permanent part of the political arrangements of mankind.

The fact that the founders of the League were, on the whole, successful in their plan of organisation makes it all the more unfortunate that their work should be mis-described in its English title. For 'the League of Nations' is a misnomer—a fact which has given rise to much confusion of thought in the English-speaking world. Neither the word 'League' nor the word 'Nations' is accurate. The term 'League', with its philanthropic and humanitarian associations, suggests common action by a band of crusaders and enthusiasts *against* some other party or group or cause. It implies a certain *exclusiveness*, derived from a common attachment to certain particular principles or doctrines. But the essential underlying idea of the League of Nations is its *inclusiveness*. It is a new method or model for *all* states and its membership is intended to be universal—is, so to speak, potentially universal. It is framed to be an all-embracing association. This is much more clearly expressed in the French term 'Society' (*Société des Nations*). Much misunderstanding as to aims and methods would have been prevented if this discrepancy between the French and English titles had been avoided. As it is, the English-speaking world must accustom itself to thinking of the League as being no less, and no more, than an all-inclusive association.

This leads us on to the second part of the title. Of what is this association composed ? What are its constituent units ? Both texts give the same answer— *Nations*. Both are mistaken. They both misrepresent the membership of the League. Here again is a fruitful cause of confusion.

The term 'nation' opens out a large theme for discussion, into which this is not the place to enter. But one thing is quite certain. The members of the League are not nations but states. Membership of the League has nothing whatsoever to do with nationality or nationhood. It is concerned simply and solely with statehood—that is to say with *political* status. This will be clear at a glance to anyone who consults the list of the actual members of the League. He will find there 'the British Empire' and 'the United Socialist Soviet Republics', which are certainly neither of them nations, in any sense of that word: and he will look in vain for other names, such as 'Scotland' and 'Wales', which should certainly find a place in any true 'association of nations'.

How was it that this strange mistake came to be made? It was not a pure oversight. At one of the early sittings of the committee which drafted the Covenant the Brazilian delegate, with characteristic acumen, pointed out that international law knew nothing of nations but only of states. But his protest went unregarded, the general view being that 'nothing was to be gained by modifying forms of wording consecrated by general usage in both languages'.[1] In other words, the majority of the members of the committee were

[1] Miller, *The Drafting of the Covenant* (1928), ii. 423.

under the sway of a particular political theory, according to which every 'nation' had a *right* to political independence, and they embodied this theory in the superscripture of the Covenant.

The theory in question is neither ancient nor universally accepted. It originated in Western Continental Europe during the latter part of the eighteenth century, its vogue being due to the particular conditions in that area.[1] It is, of course, a revolutionary theory: that is to say, to put it into practice, to make the political organisation of the world conform to it, would involve an upheaval of the existing political arrangements over a large part of the world. Since the committee was drawing up a plan providing for better means of co-operation between existing states, it was not at all within its province to concern itself with the problem of political organisation in general, with such questions as whether Great Britain should, or should not, be broken up into three national units or the Arab peoples, for instance, united into one. But through inertia, or the reluctance of 'practical' men to face an issue of far-reaching principle, the drafters of the Covenant let slip a rare opportunity for clearing out of the way a difficulty of long standing. Thus they carried forward into the post-war world one of the principal causes of confusion and conflict in the international politics of nineteenth century Europe.

However this may be, the League of Nations was never intended to be, nor is it, a revolutionary organisation. On the contrary, it accepts the world of states as it finds it and merely seeks to provide a more satisfactory means for carrying on some of the business

[1] On this see Macartney, *National States and National Minorities* (1934), esp. p. 99, and *La Nationalité et l'histoire* (ed. Koht: Paris, 1929).

which these states transact between one another. It is not even revolutionary in the more limited sense of revolutionising the methods for carrying on interstate business. It does not supersede the older methods. It merely supplements them. The old methods still go on, and were intended by the framers of the Covenant to go on, side by side with the new. We shall not therefore be able to understand exactly how the League of Nations has improved, or attempted to improve, upon the previous system until we have examined this in itself, in its pre-war form. The first part of this book will therefore be devoted to an inquiry into the pre-war system of relations between states.

But before attempting this task a further word of warning is needed.

We shall be concerned throughout with methods of co-operation *between states*, whether by means of the League or in other ways. This is only a very small part of the field of *international relations*. To understand international relations in their full extent involves not merely a knowledge of the relations between states but also of the relations between *peoples*. Moreover, it involves not merely a knowledge of the relations *between* peoples but a knowledge of the *peoples themselves*. Both these large subjects lie outside our present scope. But the reader should constantly bear them in mind; for without some general background of knowledge in these fields the study of methods will be unintelligible and may even be misleading and dangerous. The study of the relations between X and Y presupposes some knowledge at least of X and Y in themselves. The League of Nations is not a patent method of interstate co-operation applicable to all states at any moment of history. It is a particular

B

method which is being attempted at a particular moment of history when there are certain principal Powers with clearly marked characteristics and policies. The method of this book must be, in the main, a method of analysis: for what we are concerned with is a problem of political science. As we shall be studying this problem in the concrete and watching the attempts made to deal with it in particular circumstances, we shall be compelled at times to adopt the narrative form. But the record thus unfolded is not history: it is a mere episode against the background of history—unintelligible without a knowledge of the larger issues of policy involved and of the still larger problems of the relations between *peoples* and of the interaction of the cultures, traditions, attitudes, ingrained ways of thinking and feeling, which constitute the raw material of policy. None of this, of course, can be systematically set forth in these pages: it must be assumed rather than described. Nevertheless its influence will be apparent at many points in our analysis. Descartes, Burke and Jefferson were not members of the committee that drafted the Covenant of the League of Nations: but their ghosts were an active influence throughout its proceedings.

The student of the League of Nations should never forget that the existence of machinery for co-operation between particular governments provides little or no clue as to the nature or importance of the relations between the peoples of the states concerned. The existence of such machinery may in fact mean either of two quite opposite things. It may mean that there is *so much intercourse* between these peoples that it has become necessary to provide official intergovernmental machinery to regulate it. But it may equally well mean that there is *so little intercourse* between these peoples, and that what there is has been carried on under such difficulties, that private agencies have found it necessary to have recourse to public safeguards. In other words, the official machinery may be an index, either of a very intimate relationship or of the exact contrary. The Joint High Commission for dealing with questions arising out of the common frontier between the United States and Canada is an example of the former condition. The numerous treaties or so-called 'Capitulations' for the protection of European trade interests in certain economically undeveloped countries are an example of the latter.

What has just been said applies not only to the relations between particular countries but to international relations taken as a whole. This can best be brought out by two contrasted examples. Why, it may be asked, did the League of Nations survive the set-backs of the period following 1931—the flouting of its authority in the Far East and in the Chaco, the failure of the Economic and Disarmament Conferences and numerous misadventures of other kinds—whilst the Congress system, devised in 1815, broke down irremediably in 1823 when the British Government refused to make use of it for the affairs of Latin America? The answer is to be found in the increased volume of international intercourse which has made the League of Nations an indispensable agency for the life of the modern world. Thus even at moments when its political usefulness seemed likely to come to an end, at least for a time, it was hardly possible to contemplate the disappearance of the rest of its machinery.[1] But if we frame our question

---

[1] This issue was frankly discussed by the Foreign Minister of Norway in a speech in the Assembly on September 11, 1935, when the future of the League, as an agency for the prevention of war, was hanging in the balance.

in another way, we shall elicit a rather different answer. Why, we may ask, is there a central organisation at Geneva, with a dozen or more separate departments of business and a staff of a thousand officials, whilst the peoples of the British Commonwealth have no central organisation whatsoever to facilitate the transaction of their common affairs? The answer is certainly not to be found by comparing the volume of international business with the volume of business carried on between the members of the British Commonwealth. There is not proportionately *more* international business than there is intra-imperial business. On the contrary, there are proportionately very many more transactions between individuals living under British rule than between citizens of the fifty-odd states members of the League taken together. But intercourse in the former case is easy and natural and has therefore the less need for official machinery to control it. Interchange of teachers, for instance, has been going on for more than a generation without the assistance of an Imperial Educational Secretariat—not to speak of a central Ministry. The absence of such machinery, with its accompanying 'red tape', has been more than compensated for by the activities of voluntary bodies with the enthusiasm and initiative that they bring with them.

Voluntary and unofficial action in the international field is, for the most part, outside our scope. Nevertheless it is one of the principal elements in the whole international problem and its existence must be kept in mind by every student of the subject. Without the co-operation of voluntary agencies intergovernmental organisation can never proceed very far. It is not governments but peoples that give international relations both their substance and their particular tone.

One final reminder may be added. When the League is presented as a method or system of interstate co-operation it must never be forgotten that the amount and character of this co-operation are constantly changing—not only from year to year but in times of crisis even from month to month. The League of Nations has been neatly defined by a close observer as 'the maximum of co-operation between governments at any given moment'. There have indeed been moments within the last fifteen years when the available maximum was very small indeed—when therefore, for the time being, the League had almost ceased to exist as a going concern. Nevertheless its *organisation* remained unchanged: for an organisation cannot expand or shrink automatically according to the increase or decrease of the business entrusted to it. International trade, for instance, diminished in volume by two-thirds between 1929 and 1933: but this did not involve a corresponding diminution of the League's financial and economic organisation: on the contrary, it rendered this branch of the League's work even more necessary than before. In all that follows, then, the reader should remember that the external facts, the details of machinery and organisation, are not the essential facts for the understanding of the problems which the League exists to solve. The essential facts are in the realm not of machinery but of politics and psychology. They are reflected in the use made of the machinery and in the vicissitudes to which it is subjected. But the League as an organisation is only enlightening in so far as it points beyond itself to the forces in the mind of man upon which its own future and that of our present-day civilisation depend.

PART I

THE PRE-WAR SYSTEM

CHAPTER I

DIPLOMACY

THE established and traditional method of carrying on relations between states is by means of diplomats—that is to say, special agents representing one state in the capital of another.

The diplomatic system, in its present form, dates from the end of the European Middle Ages when the unity of Christendom was broken up by the consolidation of independent states recognising no political superior. Modern diplomacy therefore may be described as a system of intercourse between sovereign states or, in its most advanced form, between sovereign peoples.

But this modern system is only an adaptation of a practice which has existed from time immemorial between independent neighbouring communities. The ambassador of to-day is the successor of a long line of 'envoys', 'heralds' and other special agents going back to the time of primitive tribalism. The word 'diplomatic' itself bears the mark of classical antiquity, for the 'diplomat' is the bearer of a 'diploma' ($\delta\iota\pi\lambda\omega\mu\alpha$) that is, a folded or 'doubled' paper containing a confidential message.

In its modern form the system was slow to develop. Up to the end of the seventeenth century the diplomat was still generally a personage employed on a

13

temporary mission. Even Grotius regarded permanent legations as unnecessary. Thus the system as we know it to-day has less than three centuries of history behind it. But during these three centuries contacts between the principal states have multiplied to a degree and in a manner unimaginable to the men of the seventeenth century and the diplomatic system has been compelled, sometimes tardily, to adapt itself to these changes. Not the least of these have occurred during the present generation. In this chapter, however, we shall confine ourselves to the system as it functioned during the pre-war period.

The business of the Ambassador or, as he is called in all but the few leading capitals, the Minister, is to keep his government fully and regularly informed as to the conditions in the country to which he is accredited and the policy of its rulers and also to cultivate the best possible mutual relations.

These two separate but related tasks require a very special combination of qualities for their successful accomplishment. Herein lies the basis of what is, in its normal form, a profession and, at its best, little less than a fine art.

For his task as an informant an ambassador needs knowledge, curiosity, initiative, precision and, above all, judgment. For his task as an intermediary he requires sympathy, courage, tact, discretion and again judgment.

To pursue either of the two tasks at the expense of the other is to court failure. An ambassador who enlightens his government without winning the confidence of his hosts is of very limited value. An ambassador who, through excess of sympathy, has taken the colour of his environment may be worse than useless and become a positive danger. The perfect diplomat must be neither a mere intelligence officer nor a chameleon.

For the performance of this double task ambassadors and ministers are equipped with a small staff or 'official family'. In its post-war development this family, as we shall see, exhibits some peculiar features. Here we are only concerned with its traditional form. A pre-war British embassy included a 'Counsellor' and Secretaries of various grades, all trained in the same school as the Ambassador, together with a Naval and a Military Attaché. The two last-named held their appointments direct from the Admiralty and the War Office and made their reports to them. In certain cases they had at their disposal a sum of money to help them in drawing up their reports and this they were author-ised to spend upon informants on the spot. This system necessarily involved a kind of investigation which, at its best, was not easily compatible with the spirit of the rest of an Embassy's activities and, at its worst, might be a means of poisoning the relations between the two countries concerned.

Such, in very brief outline, is 'the old diplomacy'. Let us now attempt to assess both its qualities and defects.

The idea underlying the system clearly commands our sympathy. It is obviously desirable that every state in the world—that is, every independent political authority—should be officially linked with every other state. And it is equally desirable that, whatever other ties may be developed, these links should exist in the country and amid the people of the several states. It is the great merit of the diplomatic system that it intro-duces into the life of every political community an element of internationalism. It is a standing reminder of the existence of a wider world—a world not merely of things but of human beings—outside the state frontiers. It proclaims the principle of the *decentralisation of international relations*. Even if it were possible—which it is not—to concentrate the conduct of inter-state business in a single diplomatic metropolis, whether at Geneva or elsewhere, it would be highly undesirable; for under such conditions of centralisation it would be difficult, if not impossible, to maintain and develop the understanding between peoples upon which, in the last resort, the successful conduct of such business may depend. The diplomatic *milieu* has indeed often been held up to criticism and even to ridicule. Its great potential influence for good may be vitiated by social exclusiveness, dulled by routine, perverted by intrigue or frittered away in purposeless frivolity. But even at its worst those who frequent it enjoy the advantage of living in the midst of a genuine national society and its work is carried on under conditions less artificial than those of a centre where there are neither hosts nor guests and everyone is equally away from home.

The second great merit of the diplomatic system has already been mentioned. It has crystallised an important set of functions and activities into the rules and standards of a profession. Diplomacy, for all that is said against it, is an immense repository of experience. 'There is no profession', remarks one of the most skilled living practitioners of the art, 'which is more diverse in its calls than that of the diplomat. There is none in which there are fewer precise rules and more traditions, in which more perseverance is needed for success and yet success depends more on accidental circumstances,

none in which an exact discipline is more necessary and
which nevertheless requires for its exercise greater
firmness of character and independence of spirit.'[1]

Having assessed the merits of the diplomatic system, let us turn to its defects or, it would be fairer to
say, to its shortcomings: for most of them arise quite
naturally out of the conditions in which the diplomat
finds himself placed. The difficulty is not that his work
is badly done: it is that, even when it is well done, it
is not equal to the full task of promoting understanding between peoples. It does not fail: it simply
falls short. To adapt a famous phrase: 'Diplomacy is
not enough'.

The first shortcoming springs almost inevitably out
of the history and traditions of the diplomatic service.
It is the survival of the spirit of caste. As the personal
envoy of the monarch, the diplomat was originally
either a nobleman or a Court favourite, and these royal
or aristocratic associations have clung to the profession
in all the older countries, including our own. For over
half a century after the Civil Service as a whole had
been thrown open to equal competition, entrance into
the foreign service was guarded by a régime of special
nomination and by the requirement of an income of
£400 a year. These anomalies were abolished on the
advice of a Royal Commission which reported in 1914,
and, so far as our own country is concerned, the spirit
of aloofness engendered by the earlier system is rapidly
becoming ancient history. Nevertheless, looking at the
world as a whole and particularly at continental
Europe, no one would deny that the 'old diplomacy'
with its aristocratic bias has accomplished far less than

---

[1] *Le Diplomate*, by Jules Cambon, French Ambassador in Berlin,
1908–14 (Paris, 1926), p. 1.

C

might have been expected from such a universal system of *liaison* in promoting mutual knowledge and understanding between the peoples. One can go further and say that it has, in some cases, been a force in the contrary direction. It has often discouraged international movements inspired with sentiments different from its own. Sometimes it has done even worse: it has used the ease and grace of the aristocratic demeanour in order to exploit the sense of inferiority among the unprivileged. Thus, whether consciously or not, it has sowed the seed of snobbishness, that most infectious and international of modern social diseases.

The second shortcoming arises out of the nature of the profession itself. The diplomat, as such, has no full or first-hand equipment in any particular field, either of theory or practice, either of science or of public affairs. He is not a specialist. He is not one of those who know 'everything of something'. His business is to know something of everything—or, at least, of very many things—and, if he is to be regarded as a specialist at all, he is a specialist in *relations*, relations between individuals, between peoples, between problems, rather than a specialist in any particular subject at either end of the relation. In other words, he is an intermediary: his function is to be eternally Between. Under such circumstances, it is inevitable that the steadily widening range of international business and of the technical problems involved by it should put a severe strain upon the resources of the old-time diplomat. Sir Ernest Satow, who wrote his *Guide to Diplomatic Practice* during the war, after his retirement from the Service, might complacently rank 'good temper, good health and good looks', together with 'rather more than average intelligence', as the most necessary qualifica-

tions for a young diplomat, adding that science is 'not
necessary' and geography 'not of great value' and
omitting all reference to economics.[1] But it is doubtful
whether, even at that time, most of his colleagues
would have agreed with him. Be that as it may, it is
certain that the multiplicity of new contacts and problems has greatly altered the character and extent of
interstate business and has placed those responsible
for the conduct of diplomacy before an inexorable
dilemma—either to adjust the diplomatic system to
these new requirements or to find some other way for
dealing with them.

The third drawback is closely related to what has
just been said. The diplomat is not merely unspecial-
ised, but also, as a result of this, almost inevitably *non-
co-operative* in temper and outlook. The training and
experience of diplomacy do not fit a man to promote
co-operation between any particular element in his
own country and the corresponding element in another.
They merely fit him to understand and to promote, in
any foreign capital, the general interests of his own
country. This is perhaps best illustrated by a comparison. When a group drawn from any of the recognised
professions—doctors, teachers, chemists, engineers—
meets in an international Conference, everyone is conscious of a common professional tie underlying and
facilitating the proceedings. The members of the Conference are united by the possession of a common body
of knowledge and of a common outlook—perhaps even
a common practical purpose—resulting from that
knowledge. Very different is the atmosphere of a Conference of diplomats, however good may be the personal
relations between the individuals composing it. For

---

[1] *Guide* (first edition), i. 183-4.

diplomats are not, in the same sense, fellow professionals. They have no common theme, no common attachment to a science or an art. Their attachment is to their
own country and to its foreign service, on whose behalf
and under whose instructions they are acting. Thus a
Conference of diplomats, from the nature of the case, is
not a Conference of fellow professionals united in a
common cause, but a meeting of attorneys, each conscious of a separate purpose, their obligation towards
their client.

There is nothing blameworthy in this, any more than
the profession of an advocate or of a soldier is blameworthy. Cecil Spring-Rice, who sacrificed his life
through his exertions as a British diplomat during the
war, has described this sense of professional devotion
in verses which will live in English literature.[1] But it
is the tragedy of a noble profession that its technique
should not be one of co-operation but of individual
persuasion. The Between Man cannot be other than a
lonely figure.

The fourth and last criticism to be made against 'the
old diplomacy' is at once the most familiar and the
most serious. It is the connexion between diplomacy
and war, or, to be more precise, the use of the threat
of war by diplomats as the crowning argument in a
political discussion.

In order justly to assess this criticism, in so far as it
relates to diplomacy proper, it is, however, necessary
to make clear certain distinctions.

In the first place the reproach only attaches to a
very small proportion of those actually engaged in
diplomacy. It applies solely to the diplomacy of the

[1] They were fitly included in the Thanksgiving Service at St. Paul's
on May 6, 1935.

Great Powers and certainly not even to all of these.
Weak powers, for obvious reasons, do not conduct
their diplomacy at the sword's point—not even in
dealing with powers weaker than themselves. Strong
powers only do so when they are both strong and un-
principled—a combination which may not be unusual
but is not invariable. Thus the reproach should not be
levelled indiscriminately at the diplomatic system: it
does not arise out of the system itself but out of an
abuse of it. It is not that the diplomatic system as
practised by the smaller powers was unnatural, whilst
that practised by their larger neighbours was natural.
If we are to judge by numbers we must conclude the
reverse to have been the case. If so, what faces us is
not an indictment against the system as a whole, but
a problem. What means can be adopted to ensure that
the diplomatic system, as employed by the Great
Powers, shall be as free from abuse in this respect as
the diplomacy of the most respected of the smaller
powers? Thus stated, the question is reduced to
manageable proportions. We leave its discussion for a
later page.

The second distinction to be made is that between
the diplomat himself and those from whom he receives
his orders. When a diplomat presents an ultimatum,
whether open or concealed, it is not fair either to him
or to the system to saddle him with the blame. He may
or may not be in sympathy with the objects and
methods of his government: but in any case his government's objects are likely to be perfectly independent
of the particular methods adopted to pursue them.
There have no doubt in the past been ambassadors and
other diplomats who have used their individual influence in favour of war-like policies. But there have

been others who have worked, often under difficulties, in the contrary sense. It would therefore be a mistake to identify 'the old diplomacy' as such with policies of intimidation and provocation. The evil lies much deeper down—not in the agents but in their principals, and sometimes not even in them but in the policies which they inherited from their forerunners or in the ideas and ambitions of their populations and in their sense of what constitutes the greatness and glory of a people.

Let us turn therefore from the diplomat, serving his country abroad, to his home base, to the superiors to whom he is responsible and from whom, for good or for evil, his instructions are derived.

CHAPTER II

In earlier days the diplomat was the personal envoy of the sovereign. To-day, in all countries with a modern organisation, his activities are directed and controlled through a particular government department, usually known as the Foreign Office or Ministry of Foreign Affairs: in some countries, as, for instance, the British Dominions, the title 'External Affairs' has been preferred—with very good reason, for, as we shall discover, the old distinction between 'foreign' and 'domestic' questions no longer holds good. What used to be called 'foreign' affairs are in reality only domestic affairs in their external aspect. In the United States, the department responsible for external affairs is known as 'the Department of State', ranking above all the other departments and being entrusted with certain other duties which attest its pre-eminence.

The Foreign Secretary, or, to give him his full official title, His Majesty's Principal Secretary of State for Foreign Affairs, is the representative of the sovereign in his relations with other sovereigns. The work that he carries on, though subject, like all the rest of our public affairs, to the control of Parliament, is of a more delicate and confidential character than that of any other minister and was the last field in which not only the influence but the prerogative of the sovereign was strongly exerted, as the records of Queen Victoria bear witness. One evidence of this is the custom according to which treaties are drawn up in the names of sovereigns or other titular heads of states. This traditional practice, it may be observed in passing, has proved extremely convenient to the members of the British Commonwealth under post-war conditions, for it has enabled them to exercise their independence in foreign relations whilst maintaining the unity of the Commonwealth in the face of foreign powers.

The Foreign Secretary carries out his work by means of a threefold staff. There is, firstly, his own departmental staff in Whitehall. In addition to that there are two branches of what may be called 'out-door staff', the Diplomatic Service and the Consular Service. The Consular Service, which falls to be mentioned here, has had a distinct history of its own. The 'consul' was originally a representative of the foreign merchant community empowered to settle commercial disputes on their behalf with the government of the country. He was not therefore the representative of his sovereign and might even not be a citizen of the state on behalf of whose nationals he acted. In recent times, however, consular services have become more and more closely linked with the diplomatic system and this process has been carried further in Great Britain as a result of the war.

The work of a Foreign Office differs in kind from that of any other government department—except, in Great Britain, that of the Dominions Office, which may be described as a kind of family Foreign Office. A government official of the ordinary type *makes decisions* —or, to be precise, prepares the ground for decisions to be made by his official superior or by the Minister.

When the decision is made, whether it applies to a single case or to a million, it is executed, and the matter is generally closed. The men responsible for these decisions are therefore, in biblical language, centurions: the modern term for their characteristic attitude of mind and type of behaviour is 'bureaucrat'; and there are bureaucrats outside government offices wherever problems of large-scale administration bring the same qualities and defects into play.

The Foreign Office official is not a bureaucrat. It does not fall to him to make decisions which issue in the form of commands. He can give no orders: he can only endeavour to persuade. In other words, he is not an administrator but a negotiator; and his characteristic defects are therefore of a quite different order. If he is over-subtle, he becomes tortuous; if he is over-discreet, he becomes secretive and even mysterious; if he is over-patient, he becomes a confirmed procrastinator; if he is over-cautious, he ends in believing no-one and losing all hope of agreement on anything.

It needs a very special equipment to resist these influences, whether in a subordinate or in a chief. For the quality of mind required of a Foreign Secretary is even rarer and finer than that required of an ambassador. An ambassador's task is to sum up the situation at one particular centre. The Foreign Secretary's is to assimilate the reports of his agents and thus to survey the entire world-situation at any given moment, appreciating its dangers and realising the possibilities open for useful action. He must therefore acquire and cultivate a sense at once of the complexity and the simultaneity of international affairs. This is a severe demand: many professions develop a sense for the complexity of things and a capacity for unravelling them in detail: others, such as journalism, provide a constant sense of the variety and multiplicity of the world's problems. But to hold both in the mind at the same time and to add to that the practical gift which can use them as materials for the working out of a national policy is a very rare accomplishment. Foreign Secretaries, it may be said, are never born and, under modern conditions, are seldom perfectly made. There are few departments of public or indeed of any affairs where experience counts for so much.

This description of the character of the Foreign Secretary's work will be sufficient to explain why it is so difficult to apply to it the ordinary standards of control by Parliament and public opinion.

The parliamentary control of foreign affairs ranks with the problem of the Second Chamber as one of the standing dilemmas of modern democratic government. In the latter case the dilemma is familiar: if the Second Chamber, by its powers and composition, is strong enough to resist the government of the day, the result is deadlock: if it is not in a position to do this, it is difficult to ensure that it shall be able to do any useful work at all. The position as to the parliamentary control of foreign affairs is much the same. It is possible in theory to devise means for keeping members of Parliament sufficiently well informed for its judgment, not merely on matters of principle but on matters of detail and delicate appreciation, to be of value. That is, supposedly, the idea underlying the institution of Foreign Affairs Committees, such as exist, for instance, in both the French Chambers. But the defects of such an arrangement are obvious. The discussions of such a Committee will only be useful if its members are supplied with up-to-date confidential material. If this is done, with all the risks of leakage involved, the Committee becomes more than a parliamentary body. It becomes almost a second Foreign Office, and its chairman a second, that is to say, a rival, Foreign Secretary. The alternative course, to which the official mind is naturally more prone, is to withhold certain information—particularly information supplied, under conditions of confidence, by foreign governments or from other similar sources. In that case, the deliberations of the Committee must be of a general character and might almost equally well be carried on in the full House.[1]

It is clear, therefore, that the problem of parliamentary control cannot be solved by mechanical means. Experience shows that the value of debates on foreign affairs and the degree of their influence upon the policy of the Foreign Secretary and the Cabinet depend chiefly upon the number of men in the House who have a comprehensive and first-hand knowledge of international affairs. Such men, in the nature of the case, can never be very numerous, probably never numerous enough to man a respectably-sized Committee. But their influence will be out of all proportion to their numbers, particularly if there are among them members who have had official experience at home or abroad and, above all, one or more ex-Foreign Secretaries.

Still more difficult is the problem of bringing public opinion, in the broader sense, to bear on foreign affairs. Not only can the general public never be as familiar

---

[1] On the working of the French Foreign Affairs Committees see the first-hand account by Joseph Barthélemy in *La Conduite de la Politique extérieure dans les Démocracies* (Bulletins 3 and 4, 1930, of the Paris office of the Carnegie Foundation), especially the description of the Committee Room on p. 146.

with such problems in detail as with the ordinary issues of domestic politics: there is the added difficulty that the conditions involved are generally so remote from the experience of 'the man in the street' that he has no easy means of bringing his healthy common sense to bear upon them. Thus it is easy for him to divest himself, unconsciously, of his saving realism and to fall a victim either to the well-meaning appeals of the ignorant sentimentalist or to the artful wiles of unscrupulous propaganda.

The remedy here is not to mobilise sentiment against sentiment or propaganda against propaganda but to deepen and strengthen the foundations of general education. But, even at its best, as in the northern countries, public opinion will seldom be in a position to assert itself confidently upon the *details* of foreign policy. All the more necessary is it that it should gain a firm grasp on *principles*. We shall examine on a later page whether any issues of principle can thus be popularised and to what extent public opinion can thus be brought to bear on the problems of the post-war world.

We have touched on the question of secrecy. Something more needs to be said on this point.

There is more secrecy in foreign affairs than in domestic affairs for the simple reason that the Foreign Minister is not merely keeping his own secrets—which Parliament could, if necessary, compel him to divulge —but the secrets of other governments. A Foreign Secretary who told the House of Commons all that he knew would therefore very soon have little left to tell. He would dry up the sources of his information. But there is nothing necessarily reprehensible, or even dangerous, in secrecy in itself. Parish Councils do not

discuss in public the rival merits and personal qualifications of candidates for public positions. The *limits* of
secret discussion, in domestic as in foreign affairs, are
a matter for careful appreciation in each case. There
can, however, be no doubt that pre-war diplomacy
exaggerated the necessity for secrecy and underrated
the tonic value of fresh air in international discussions.
It was an accepted convention that international conferences should take place behind closed doors and
that thus the real obstacles to agreements between
governments should never be revealed to the public.
We shall see in the sequel how practice has recently
changed in this respect.

But if secret *discussion* is a matter for consideration
in each case, secret *agreements*, resulting from such
discussions, stand upon a very different footing.

In pre-war diplomacy secret treaties were a regular
and accepted feature. It was considered perfectly
legitimate and reasonable that rulers should engage
their peoples behind their backs. This tradition had
lingered on from the time when the peoples did not
count. Foreign policy was the prerogative of monarchs.
It was natural, therefore, for monarchs to make treaties
and for their peoples to be obedient in carrying them
out when called upon.

Even in the democratic countries the custom lingered
on, because they were tied up, in their international
dealings, with governments of the older type. The last
secret treaty negotiated by Great Britain in peace-
time was an agreement with Germany as to the
eventual disposition of the Portuguese colonies. This
was negotiated in 1913 and reached the stage of being
'initialled'—that is to say, completed for formal signature. But at this stage a difficulty arose. The British

Foreign Secretary was willing to keep it secret for twelve months after signature. The Germans wished it to be kept secret indefinitely. Thus the negotiations hung fire and were still incomplete in July 1914.

Closely allied to secret treaties are treaties concluded and then published without any opportunity of discussion by the legislature. In a democratic country this is a dangerous procedure, since, if the published engagement runs definitely counter to popular sentiment, it may provoke a vote of censure and lead to the fall of the government. The obligations of the treaty would then remain but in the altered atmosphere they would lose a good deal of their original value for the other party. But where the matters at issue make no strong appeal to public opinion a government can well afford to take this risk. An instance of this procedure was the conclusion and publication of the second Anglo-Japanese Treaty—that of 1905— by which Great Britain disinterested herself of the fate of Korea. This took place during the parliamentary vacation and was the work of a government which was known to be moribund at the time and fell from power a few weeks later. The treaty, however, remained and its effects duly worked themselves out.

But where popular assemblies are likely to be troublesome there are other available expedients. It is always possible for a particular administration to enter into obligations which are binding upon itself without assuming the form of a treaty. Two instances of the adoption of this type of procedure during the generation preceding the war have recently been brought to light—one in Great Britain and the other in the United States.

In 1887 Lord Salisbury, who was then both Prime

Minister and Foreign Secretary, entered into a secret understanding with Italy in regard to the Mediterranean. It was binding for so long as he was in power, but, perhaps in accordance with his calculations, it never needed to be brought into play. When Lord Rosebery succeeded him at the Foreign Office in 1892 he was informed of its existence. He refused to look at it and it passed into history.[1]

The other instance belongs to the record of the Far East. After the Russo-Japanese war President Theodore Roosevelt became convinced that the wisest policy for the United States was to allow Japan a free hand in that region. He therefore sent Mr Taft, then Governor of the Philippines, to Tokio, and the result of his conversation with the Japanese authorities was the drawing up, not of a treaty (which would have had to be submitted to the United States Senate, under the two-thirds rule) but of an 'Agreed Memorandum'. In this document, the existence of which was not even suspected at the time, President Roosevelt intimated that he would offer no objection to the Japanese annexation of Korea. Korea was duly annexed during President Roosevelt's term of office. Curiously enough, when Mr Taft succeeded him and was free to adopt a policy of his own, he did not follow so complacent a course.[2]

Enough has been said to show how, under the pre-war system, the Chancelleries were free to make engagements and counter-engagements, to promise war or to threaten war, and to commit their peoples in support of their policies. It is not within the scope of

---

[1] See *British Documents on the Origins of the War*, viii. 13.
[2] For the Agreed Memorandum see Charles P. Howland, *American Foreign Relations* (1930), iii. p. 42 ff.

this book to determine how far the catastrophe of 1914 was caused by these elements in the pre-war system, regarded purely from the point of view of machinery, and how far by the policies of individual governments and statesmen. But we shall describe in a later section the effort that has been made to remedy these defects in the working of the pre-war system and—to adapt a famous expression—to make the practice of Foreign Offices safe for the world.[1]

[1] There is a useful book on the British Foreign Office in the 'Whitehall Series' by Sir John Tilley and Mr Stephen Gaselee (1933). See also the historical sketch by Mr Algernon Cecil in vol. iii. of the *Cambridge History of British Foreign Policy* (1923) and, from the angle of the United States, DeWitt Poole, *The Conduct of Foreign Relations under Modern Democratic Conditions* (New Haven, 1924).

CHAPTER III

CONFERENCES

THE routine activities of Foreign Offices and diplomats during the pre-war period were from time to time interrupted by Conferences or Congresses.

The international Conference, with which the present generation is so familiar, goes back far into history. It is older than the sovereign state and its diplomatic system. It took shape, very much in its present-day form, in the later Middle Ages, the chief difference being that at that time the Papal Legate presided as by right. The account given by an ecclesiastical historian of the manœuvring between the parties at the Congress of Arras in 1435 reads almost like a description of contemporary happenings.[1] The first full-dress international Conference of post-mediaeval times was that which marked the close of the Thirty Years War and issued in the Peace of Westphalia. The reason why this document bore the name of a province rather than of a town lay in considerations of etiquette, themselves the aftermath of the religious conflict. These prevented the parties from meeting in a single centre and the delegations were therefore divided between the two neighbouring cities of Münster and Osnabrück.

[1] See Creighton, *History of the Papacy* (ed. 1897), ii. 293, and Van Vollenhoven, *Du Droit de Paix* (1932), pp. 15 and 45.

During the nineteenth century the word 'Congress' was ordinarily used for gatherings of exceptional importance and 'Conference' for lesser occasions. But since the more modest term became attached to the Paris gathering of 1919 the distinction has become obsolete and 'Conference' now holds the field.

In the old diplomatic system a Conference was needed when, for one reason or another, individual states found themselves unable to cope with a situation by themselves and thus felt the need for agreement with other states.

This need might arise in one of three ways.

The first and most obvious need for a Conference was at the close of a war. Apart from the actual negotiation of terms of peace, arising out of the result of the fighting, such an occasion always involved arrangements for the renewal of relations in various fields. In modern times these consequential matters have assumed a steadily increasing importance.

The second way in which the need arose would be the occurrence of some emergency calling for action by more than one state. In the pre-war period such emergencies were generally of a political character, such as a crisis in the Near East or some other region in which the interests of several powers were involved and were in danger of collision. The Berlin Conference of 1885 on tropical Africa is a good example of this type of gathering. Emergencies affecting the economic system as a whole, such as a grave depression, were not at that time, or indeed until 1933, considered to be a subject for a conference of governments.

The third set of cases arose when it was found necessary or desirable to attempt to draw up general rules for dealing with some particular problem of an international character. To use the language of domestic affairs, a Conference of this kind was summoned when a question was considered 'ripe' for international treatment.

But how, under the old diplomatic system, could a question be *ripened*? What means existed for pressing it forward up to the point where governments were ready to take the unusual step of summoning a Conference?

There were, broadly speaking, two ways in which this ripening process took place.

The first was through the pressure of public opinion, resulting from an agitation conducted by public-spirited private citizens. It was a movement of this character which led to the inclusion in the Treaty of Vienna in 1815 of the clause prohibiting the Slave Trade. This did not form the occasion of a special Conference but simply involved the use of an existing Conference for a humanitarian purpose extraneous to its main business. A more remarkable instance is the Geneva Conference of 1864 which drew up the first Red Cross Convention. This was directly due to the movement set on foot by Henri Dunant, a public-spirited citizen of Geneva, together with Tolstoi and others who had been shocked by the revelations as to the treatment of the wounded at the battle of Solferino in 1859.

But there was another road leading to an international Conference of the rule-making or law-making type. A problem or set of questions might have been under consideration by international bodies of an unofficial character and these discussions might have led to agreement as to the need for international rules and even to their formulation in draft form. In these cases governments might be persuaded to take the problem

into official consideration as 'ripe' for treatment. It by
no means followed, however, that agreement between
the experts or technicians necessarily led to agreement
between their governments. More than one Conference
has often been needed in order to secure the embodiment of the sought-for rules in a treaty or, as it is
generally called in such cases, a 'convention'. During
the latter part of the nineteenth century, when the
changes brought about by the Industrial Revolution
were beginning to reveal their full effects, Conferences
of this type became increasingly numerous. They resulted in a considerable volume of treaties or conventions in a great variety of fields. No less than 257
'multipartite international instruments' are enumerated
for the half-century between 1864 and 1914.[1]

Let us now attempt to form a picture of the working
of these international gatherings.

In the Middle Ages, as we have seen, a certain fixed
order was maintained in their proceedings through the
authority of the Papacy, whose representative occupied
the chair. This tradition lingered on, in its secular
form, for several centuries, the representative of the
Holy Roman Empire being recognised as entitled to
preside. But this shadowy personage disappeared in
1806, and in the course of the nineteenth century the
theory that Conference membership was limited by the
boundaries of Christendom was tacitly abandoned.
After the Crimean War Turkey was admitted, and by
the time that Japan had become eligible for membership the religious question was no longer even
thought of.

[1] Manley O. Hudson, *International Legislation* (Washington, 1931), i.
pp. xix-xxxvi. It is admitted, however, that some of these instruments
'proved to be abortive'.

Thus the nineteenth-century international Conference was a miscellaneous gathering of so-called sovereign states, equal in status but differing in experience, in outlook, in geographical and economic circumstances, and above all, in power. The one quality common to all, or almost all, was an extreme sensitiveness. The weak were apprehensive for their rights, the strong for their prestige, and both alike for their independence and the dignity attaching to it. These apprehensions were reflected in the instructions with which the delegates were furnished.

Thus forearmed, the members assembled to do business. But before business could be transacted there was a procedure to be arranged. It must be remembered that (apart from exceptions to be mentioned later) the pre-war Conference was complete in itself. Its machinery had therefore not merely to be wound up but actually to be constructed at the time. The experience of one Conference was rarely available for another, since the *personnel*, the place and the accompanying circumstances, often so important for the success of a meeting, would no longer be the same. We are familiar to-day with the idea that there is a technique of Conference. Books have been written upon it both in its domestic and its international aspect.[1] But to read the proceedings of a pre-war Conference of the usual improvised type is to discover that its members were moving about in 'worlds unrealised', encountering obstacle after obstacle and circumventing them as best they could with little help either from general rules or, in most cases, from particular experience.

[1] See especially Norman L. Hill, *The Public International Conference: its Functions, Organisation and Procedure*, 1929 (with useful bibliography).

These problems of procedure, when set down in black and white, may seem of very minor importance. In a homogeneous national gathering, however strong the conflict of opinion on particular issues, they would present little difficulty and, if need be, a majority vote would settle any or all of them satisfactorily and for good. But in an international Conference unanimity is the order of the day, and though questions of procedure, which must be decided one way or the other, are subject to voting, it is always desirable to avoid an open division because of the susceptibilities involved. It is under these conditions that a Conference, in which everyone is a 'foreigner' to everyone else, is called upon to elect its chairman, its 'bureau' or executive committee, and its secretariat: to adopt its rules of business and standing orders: to examine the credentials of the delegates: to consider and adopt or amend the draft agenda: to agree upon the exact wording of the questions at issue and to decide upon the order in which they shall be discussed: to consider whether it is advisable to break up the full Conference into Committees and, if so, to decide upon their composition and, in particular, upon the degree of representation to be accorded to the Great and Small Powers, and to those which are classed, or wish to be classed, in neither category: to deal with the numerous problems arising out of the language difficulty—which languages shall be recognised as official or, if that has been settled beforehand, the exact arrangements to be made for interpretation. Finally, there would be the ever-present problem of publicity. If the press is not to be admitted, how is it to be kept informed? If by an official summary, how is it to be drawn up and how is the editorial committee to be composed and controlled?

The bare enumeration of these questions is sufficient to reveal the possibilities of friction involved in them when they are being handled by a body of men unaccustomed to working together and untrained in the art—for it is an art—of international co-operation. It is no wonder that those who took part in these gatherings found that they put a severe strain upon their forbearance and good temper. 'The machinery of this Conference', reported Sir Edward Fry, the chief British delegate, at the close of the Second Hague Conference, 'has proved in a high degree dilatory and confusing: the right of individual delegates to waste the time of the Conference, the rights of the majority over the minority in the absence of unanimity, the power of a chairman to confine the discussions within due limits— these and many other questions demand solution before another meeting of the Conference can prove satisfactory.' Sir Edward Fry was a Judge and a Quaker, and thus doubly schooled in patience. The secretary of the delegation, in a private letter to a colleague at the Foreign Office, gives vent to his feelings in terser language. 'These last weeks', he writes, 'have passed in a state of perpetual flurry and tedious and invariably useless work.' The wonder is not that the pre-war Conference attained meagre results, but that, under such conditions, there were ever any results to show at all.[1]

---

[1] *British Documents*, viii. 296, 287. The conditions of the Paris Peace Conference, so vividly portrayed in Mr Harold Nicolson's diary, reproduced in his *Peace-Making*, were, of course, quite exceptional, if only because of the very large number of topics under consideration and the consequent unwieldy size of the chief delegations. The British Delegation alone numbered about 400, including clerical staff, and that of the United States was nearly as large.

CHAPTER IV

SECRETARIATS AND OTHER PERMANENT ORGANS

THE pre-war international Conference, as described in the preceding chapter, was clearly a makeshift capable of improvement. To the political scientist it immediately suggests the question: Why could not some permanent organisation be devised to secure continuity between successive Conferences and thus facilitate their organisation? The answer is that, in certain cases, a permanent organisation of this kind was actually set on foot. The experiments in this field form one of the most interesting features of the pre-war system. Not only do they refute the assertion, still constantly made, that the nineteenth century was a period of 'international anarchy', but they also constitute an index, remarkable in its precision, as to the degree of organised international co-operation which was practicable under the conditions at that time. That the nineteenth century proceeded so far as it did along this road and then found its progress blocked is due, not to the lack of organising ability in this field, but to deeper causes which we shall henceforward encounter more and more frequently in these pages.

The problem before modern civilisation is often stated in the following summary form. The Industrial Revolution has abolished distance and made the whole world one place. It has created a material internationalism. It remains, we are told, to transform this material internationalism into a political internationalism, to extend the control of government over the economic process set in motion by the Industrial Revolution.

Let us then attempt to watch the effort made—for it was made—to extend this international political control in the realm for which it would seem best fitted, that very realm of *communications* which exhibits the most characteristic achievements of the new industrialism.

I

During the half-century preceding 1914 forms of international organisation were developed in five different fields of communication: Posts, Telegraphs, Wireless Telegraphy, Railways[1] and Motor-cars. It will be sufficient for our purpose to deal only with the first three of these, and with these, of course, not in their technical aspect but from the point of view which interests us in these pages, the possibilities and limits of international organisation.

To the ordinary man in the twentieth century it seems little less than a Law of Nature that a letter stamped and addressed to a foreign country should reach its destination. He does not stop to remind himself that he is requiring a service from a foreign government and that that service would not be rendered if it were not provided for beforehand—in other words, if there did not exist an agreed regulation laid down in a treaty. Yet this apparent Law of Nature, like the adhesive postage-stamp which is its symbol,

---

[1] There were two separate organisations for railways, one concerned with freight transportation and the other with technical standardisation.

dates from less than a hundred years ago. We have only to cast back our minds a few generations to come upon a condition of chaos in postal matters similar to that which exists in some other fields of international relationship to-day.

The history of postal communications can be very broadly summed up as a record of competition between state and private systems for the conveyance of mails. Generally speaking, the state made its own arrangements, in the form of couriers, for its own postal matter, whilst merchants and others made use of private agencies. Sometimes, however, the public authority would give a concession to a private firm, such as the princely house of Thurn and Taxis, which enjoyed a postal monopoly for many generations in certain territories of the Holy Roman Empire.

Modern postal reform originates in the agitation carried on by Rowland Hill close on a hundred years ago. At that time postal rates in Great Britain were bewildering in their variety, ranging from fourpence for a distance of fifteen miles to a shilling for three hundred. Hill pleaded for a uniform cheap inland postage with a penny rate up to half an ounce and an extra penny for every additional half-ounce. Penny postage on these lines was introduced in 1840 and, contrary to the official estimates, proved an immediate and overwhelming success.

In Germany, the other country which is important for postal history, postal relations in the early nineteenth century were regulated by about a hundred different treaties between independent principalities. A first Postal Conference of all the German states, held in 1847, proved abortive; but in 1850 an Austro-Prussian postal union was formed, to which Bavaria,

Saxony and other states soon acceded. In the succeeding years a large degree of administrative unification took place in Germany, and when the German Empire was established in 1871 it was accompanied by the establishment of a single German postal system on modern lines.

Meanwhile these efforts at domestic organisation in Great Britain, Germany and elsewhere had paved the way, as national improvements so frequently do, for international action. At the suggestion of the government of the United States, acting under the influence of Postmaster-General Blair, an international Conference was summoned. It met in Paris in 1863, fourteen countries being represented. As so often at a first Conference, no immediate result was obtained: but the difficulties were explored.

After the Franco-German War the initiative was taken by the head of the new Imperial German Postal Service, Dr. von Stephan. At his instigation a Conference was summoned at Berne in 1874. Twenty-two states were represented, including the whole of Europe, the United States and Egypt. Stephan brought with him the draft of a Convention, and this found such favour that it was adopted by the Conference with only slight modifications.[1] Thus there came into existence in 1875 what was first known as the General Postal Union, re-christened in 1878 as the Universal Postal Union.

The Universal Postal Union has proved, both in its range and in its working, the most successful piece of modern interstate machinery. It is worth while, therefore, to look briefly both at the rules which it estab-

---

[1] The two texts will be found in Sly, *Genesis of the Postal Union*, International Conciliation Pamphlets, No. 233 (1927).

lished and at the way in which their carrying out is provided for. The rules laid down in the Convention are very simple—so simple that their operation has obliterated from men's minds the chaos which they superseded. They can be summed up under three heads.

First, for the purposes of the mutual exchange of correspondence, all members of the Universal Postal Union form one single territory. In other words, so far as the *conveyance* of mails is concerned, there are no frontiers. The citizens of every country which is a member of the Union have the right to make use, for their correspondence, of any means of transport used by any other country. The mail transport service of the world is thus pooled, as the reader can verify for himself if he will look up the mail announcements in the daily newspapers. Let it be noted in passing, however, that the pooling of facilities does not involve the amalgamation of administrative services. All that it means is that free intercourse has been established between them. The Universal Postal Union is not a postal Super-state. It is a very complete and intimate system of co-operation between independent postal administrations. It is, so to speak, a postal Free Trade Union.

Secondly, the Convention provides for a uniform maximum rate: this does not, however, rule out lower rates, such as exist, for instance, in Great Britain for mail to the United States.

Thirdly, there is no detailed accounting between administrations. Each administration retains the sums which it receives for postal matter dispatched by it. This arrangement replaced the older system under which the expenses for carrying each mail were divided between the countries through which it passed, with bewildering results.[1]

Let us now turn to the organisation of the Union. Here too the framers of the Convention were striking out new and interesting paths.

The Union is managed or, in other words, governed by the Postal Union Congress. This Congress is nothing else than a prolongation of the Conference of 1874. The Convention provides that it shall meet every five years. It held its jubilee meeting in London in 1929. The Congress is an extremely efficient body. In the light of what was said in the last chapter, two facts are significant. Its decisions are taken by majority vote and there is only one official language, French. Still more remarkable is it that, though the decisions of the Congress, like those of all international Conferences, require ratification by the governments, they are put into effect whether they have been ratified or not.

Why do the Foreign Offices put up with this affront? And why do outvoted minorities at the Congress not display their resentment or even threaten to resign from the Union? The answer is to be found in the nature of the service which the Union renders. It is at once *indispensable* and *completely removed from Power-politics*. The meaning of this last expression will become clearer in the sequel. Here it is enough to say that no state can ever afford to think about resigning from the Union. It would expose its citizens and its own official services to an inconvenience too intolerable even to be contemplated. That is why questions which, in another connexion, might form endless themes for acrimonious

[1] For the exception granted to Persia in 1906 to compensate for the conveyance of Bibles in bulk, not offset by the outward conveyance of Korans, see Woolf, *International Government* (1916), p. 129.

debate—such as the votes to be given to colonial
territories, the control over admission of new members,
such as Panama, the Soudan or Manchukuo, and many
more that could be imagined by meticulous diplomats
—are allowed to remain more or less dormant. In other
words, the Postal Union is equipped with a very special
reserve-power or 'sanction' of its own. Compliance with
the terms of the Convention, in fact, as a high authority
remarks, 'is ensured by the very real sanction that any
other course would make it impossible to carry on the
postal service'.[1] 'It is not unusual', remarks the same
writer, who appears to have scant regard for the mature
deliberations of the Chancelleries, 'for countries only to
ratify a particular Convention when it has already been
superseded by another'—that is, after an interval of
more than five years. It should be added in this connexion that Postal Union Conventions are not submitted to the ordeal of discussion by the United States
Senate. By an Act of Congress dating from 1872 the
Executive has general authority to conclude postal
treaties.[2]

A word must be said about the finances of the Union.
They cause little difficulty, as the expenses involved
are so slight—about £5000 a year on a gold basis. The
member states are divided into seven classes, their
contributions ranging from £300 to £15.

An interesting feature is the provision for compulsory
arbitration in the case of disputes arising out of the
interpretation of the Convention. Each party chooses
another member of the Union as an arbiter and the
decision is left to the two members thus chosen. In

---

[1] General (now Sir Frederic) Williamson, Director of Postal Services
at the G.P.O., London, in *International Affairs*, ix. (January 1930), p. 74.
[2] See Moore's *Digest* (Washington, 1906), v. 220.

1929 a difference of opinion between Greece and Jugo-
slavia was settled in this way by the Netherlands and
Switzerland.

Having examined the Convention, let us look at the
permanent organisation set up by it. If the reader
should chance to visit Berne, let him seek for the
centre of this complex and ubiquitous organisation of
which every post-office in the world may be considered
a branch establishment. Well outside the centre of the
town in a quiet street he will find an unpretentious
villa, of suburban type, with a plot of garden in front
and behind. Here, in No. 38 Schwarztorstrasse, the
work of the Union is carried on by a staff of some nine
persons, almost all of them Swiss. The office is watched
over by the Swiss Government—that is to say, by its
Political Department or Foreign Office—which makes
the appointments, fixes the salary scale and is responsible for other necessary arrangements.

The business of this office, or, to be more precise, this
international postal *Secretariat*, is twofold. It is, firstly,
a centre and clearing-house for information. In this
connexion it publishes a monthly journal, of which,
there are versions in four languages, English, French,
German and Spanish. Secondly, it prepares the Congress. The Director of the office is always the Vice-
President of the Congress, while the Assistant Director
is head of the Congress Secretariat. In this way the
smooth working of the Congress is ensured and the
difficulties spoken of in the previous chapter so far
as possible circumvented.

It must not, however, be imagined that these permanent officials impose their will on the Congress. All
that they do is to facilitate its proceedings by careful
technical preparation. One method adopted has been

the appointment of a *Preparatory Committee* representing a wide variety of countries in order to sift the proposals submitted to the Congress. Before the London Conference of 1929 no fewer than two thousand such proposals were sent in. These were ironed out by the Preparatory Committee, so that when the Congress met it had before it the Committee's analysis of the proposals made for each Article of the Convention—a business-like method of procedure well suited to what has now, in spite of its official governmental status, become something very like an international organisation of fellow professionals.

The reader may perhaps wonder why these arrangements have been described at such length. The reason will become clear in the sequel; for the success of the Postal Union has caused its methods to be taken as a model for much larger and more difficult undertakings.

II

The Post and the Telegraph are commonly associated together. Superficially regarded, their international organisation is very similar. Both early formed the subject of international Conventions, the Telegraph Convention dating from as far back as 1865. Both are served by a regular Congress with an almost worldwide membership. And each has its permanent secretariat at Berne. But in reality the history of their development exhibits the sharpest contrast. To turn from Posts to Telegraphs is to forsake the quiet haunts of professionalism and to be plunged into the vortex of Power-politics.

The reason for the contrast is to be found, of course,

in the nature of the service rendered in each case. The post is pre-eminently a social convenience. It is part of the everyday life of the individual modern citizen. It is one of the indispensable instruments of his welfare. The telegraph, on the other hand, in addition to its social usefulness, forms part of the technical apparatus of a modern state and, more particularly, of a well-equipped Great Power. Cables have often been described as constituting the nerve-system of a widespread empire. Their strategic value is indeed obvious. But they have a political importance, or, at least, a potential political importance, extending far beyond this. Command over a cable system involves commercial advantages of undeniable value. It facilitates the rapid transmission of news to particular centres and thus leads naturally to the quotation of world prices in terms of the currency of these centres. Moreover, for suspicious minds, these facilities are capable of being turned to unscrupulous uses. The power that controls a cable, like the power that controls a market, is free to exercise the arts of discrimination. It can censor messages, delay them and even distort them. The fact that such practices run clean contrary to professional etiquette is not in itself sufficient to allay suspicion, particularly at times of severe political tension or rivalry. Cables may thus be said to carry with them what may be called a 'power-economic value'; they form an important part of what has now become known as the 'war-potential'.

Thus it came about that, whilst the Telegraph Union, with its office in Berne and its regular Congress, was peacefully devising and maintaining regulations on the technical side of the traffic, providing for uniformity in apparatus, regular hours and scales of charge for

E

customers and other professional details, the telegraph itself became one of the battle-grounds of Power-politics in the period preceding the war.

The story is worth recording in outline, both because it illustrates what can go on behind the façade of an international agency and because, falling as it did outside the operation of Foreign Offices, it has not generally been set in its due place in pre-war political history.

During the nineteenth century, cable supremacy grew up, through British initiative and foresight, as a natural appendage to unchallenged British sea-power. The support of the Government was available for cable companies in securing permission from foreign governments to link up their cables with land telegraph lines. In addition to this, cable-operating became something like an all-British profession: as late as 1920, 95 per cent of the operators on the Atlantic lines were British subjects. Moreover, one of the chief raw materials used in making cables—gutta-percha—was for a long time a British monopoly. Thus by 1905 there were under the seas of the world 121,000 mile-lengths of British-owned cable, valued at £22,000,000.[1]

In 1894, six years after the accession of William II, the German Government began to stretch out its hands to secure cable-lines under its own control. A German company laid a direct cable from Emden to New York. It asked permission of the British authorities to land it at Porthcurno in Cornwall, so as to be in touch with the world-wide network of the British system, of which the Azores were an important link. To the

---

[1] For the above see the article by the Hon. George Peel, entitled 'The Nerves of Empire', with illustrative maps, in C. S. Goldman, *The Empire and the Century*, 1905; also, in critical vein, G. A. Schreiner, *Cables and Wireless and their Rôle in the Foreign Relations of the United States*, 1924.

astonishment of the mercantile community, which was not alive to the power-economic issues involved, the government of the day—a Liberal government—refused the German request. When the Germans then turned to the Azores, they again met with a refusal, since a British company had secured a monopoly concession in the previous year. We need not follow the further history of the German efforts in the Atlantic area. Only one fact is worth recording, because of its curious setting. In October 1911, 'a hundred days after the Agadir *coup*', a German cable for the first time touched land in France, at no less important a spot than the great naval centre of Brest. This was due to the fact that the French department concerned entertained relations with its opposite number in Germany of a far more cordial nature than those between the two Foreign Offices: and it was celebrated by a German publicist at the time as 'a public manifestation of the *rapprochement* between Germany and France . . . in the struggle against British cable supremacy'.[1]

But German activity assumed its most interesting form in the Pacific. At the close of the Spanish-American War Germany purchased from Spain the group of the Marianne and Caroline islands, now familiar to students of international politics as the region of the Japanese Mandate. Wishing to use this as a base for a cable system independent of Great Britain, she turned to Holland for co-operation. The result was the formation of what can best be described as an International Public Corporation—perhaps the first of its kind. However that may be, it is undoubtedly

---

[1] These details, and some of those in the following paragraphs, are taken from Lesage, *Les Cables soumarins allemands*, Paris, 1915. See especially pp. 85-9 and p. 156 ff.

one of the progenitors of a hybrid family—a cross between pure business and pure politics—of which there have been numerous later specimens.[1] The charter of this new enterprise, known as the German-Dutch Telegraph Company, contained the following provisions, which are interesting in view of later developments. Two-thirds of the members of the board of directors were to be either German or Dutch nationals. One German and one Dutch director were to be named by the respective governments. A delegate of each of the governments was to have the right of being present at all meetings of the board of directors and at the general meeting of shareholders. All provisions regarding rates and arrangements with other companies and other governments were to be submitted to the two governments. The head officers of all the cable stations were to be either German or Dutch nationals. In return for these elements of control the company received substantial government subventions. Its rate of profit was apparently subject to no limitation: as it turned out, its dividend varied between 6 and $6\frac{1}{2}$ per cent.

In 1914 the German-Dutch Telegraph Company owned over 4000 miles of cable, centred at the island of Yap, whence lines ran to the Celebes, to Guam—in the possession of the United States—and to Shanghai. At this point we must break off the story.

The third factor in communications, Wireless Telegraphy, need not detain us long, since its history falls chiefly within the post-war period: but a brief state-

[1] On this subject see Minost, *Le Fédéralisme économique et les sociétés à charte internationale*, Paris, 1929. See also *British Documents*, i. 45, where it appears that as early as 1897 Mr Joseph Chamberlain had put forward a scheme, on similar lines to that described in the text, for an Anglo-Portuguese Company to run the railway between Delagoa Bay and the Transvaal.

ment is necessary to complete the account of the preceding paragraphs.

The invention of wireless telegraphy struck a blow at the monopoly of the telegraph as a means of long-distance communication. It challenged the telegraph in three ways. Its plant was cheaper. It was independent of cable lines, with the political control exercised over them by superior sea-power. Moreover, it was also independent of monopoly products, such as gutta-percha. Its discovery therefore involved a political problem.

It was in Great Britain that wireless telegraphy was first developed on a commercial basis through the efforts of an Italian inventor, Guglielmo Marconi. The first British Company holding the Marconi patent was floated in 1897. For some years after that date an attempt was made to develop the new invention as a British monopoly, special consideration being reserved for Italy. The company, for instance, entered into an agreement with Lloyd's providing that the Marconi system should be exclusively employed at Lloyd stations, Lloyd's undertaking not to communicate with ships equipped with other systems.

This led, not unnaturally, to protests, which culminated in the summoning of an international Conference at Berlin in 1903. The Conference adopted a series of recommendations couched in very liberal terms. The British delegates, whose embarrassment can be read between the lines of the proceedings, reserved their assent.

After the failure of the first Conference, a second was summoned in 1906. By this time the attitude of the British Government had changed. It was willing to agree to the obligation to transmit wireless calls, emanating from any system, from coast to ship and from coast to coast, with priority for distress calls. It further agreed to the establishment of a permanent international bureau, to be installed in the International Telegraph Office at Berne. It refused, however, for the time being, to agree that messages might be transmitted by any system from ship to ship. This only became obligatory at the subsequent Conference which followed on the *Titanic* disaster.

During the pre-war period the possibilities of wireless telegraphy for ordinary commercial use were undeveloped. The invention that made this possible came at a later date. But its strategic value was fully recognised—not least by the German Government. In 1913 the Germans devised the idea of a world-wide system under German control, centring in a station at Nauen near Berlin. The idea was never realised: but when the German submarine cables were cut Nauen remained to Germany as a means for communicating with the outer world.

Here we must leave for the moment the subject which has led us into these by-paths—the attempt to establish international political control in the realm in which the material interdependence of the modern world is revealed in its most characteristic form, that of communications. The problem involved, it will have been realised, is more complex than would appear at first sight.

III

Permanent bodies were established during the pre-war period in a number of other fields. The bare enumeration or description of these efforts is not very instructive: for a statement of this kind does not explain why the endeavour should have been made in one field rather than in another: still less does it throw light on the actual inner working of the institutions described. The subject is, however, so important in its bearing on post-war development that space must be found for a brief mention of three further pre-war organisms, presenting particular points of interest.[1]

The first two concern rivers, one in the Old World, the other in the New. The Congress of Vienna in 1815 had laid down a rule about international rivers. An international river is a river which, either for the whole or for part of its course, runs between the territory of two or more states. The principle laid down in 1815 was that all rivers which flow between two states for any part of their course should be entirely free for navigation for commerce from the highest point of navigation to their mouth. In this way navigation on international rivers became a matter of world concern. But for a long time after 1815 no practical steps were taken to bring this concern to bear on any particular case. Agreements were indeed entered into between individual states as to rivers flowing through their territory, such as the Rhine, the Scheldt, the Elbe, the Weser, the Vistula and the Po, but no international machinery was set up to safeguard their observance.

[1] By far the most complete and revealing work on any of the bodies of this character is Asher Hobson, *The International Institute of Agriculture* (University of California Press, 1931). Mr Hobson was the United States representative on the governing body of the Institute from 1922 to 1929 and he has made full use of his official material and experience. It must not, of course, be taken as a correct account of the Institute in question at the present time; but as a description of the general conditions under which a body of that kind carries on its work it is invaluable. The best of the more general accounts are those by L. S. Woolf, *International Government*, 1916, already referred to, and F. B. Sayre, *Experiments in International Administration*, New York, 1919.

After the Crimean War, however, when Turkey had been admitted into the family of nations, the question of the Danube came under review. As a result it was decided to set up an international organisation. The European Danube Commission carried on its work as a Danube Conservancy, lighting and buoying the river, attending to problems of wharfage and dredging, during the half-century preceding the war. So far as can be judged, its work was well done—sufficiently well done for the system to be revived, with certain modifications, at the close of the war. But it did that and nothing more. It did not take root in the Danube territory and spread its influence into other fields. It looked efficiently after *things*: it kept the Danube flowing. But it meant little or nothing to the dwellers on its banks. It will live in history, not so much for any permanent benefit conferred on the Danubian region, as for having afforded an invaluable training-ground for the study of Balkan politics for one of the best-informed and most penetrating European publicists of the last generation. For it was as Secretary-General of the European Commission of the Danube at Galatz from 1893 to 1904 that Auguste Gauvain acquired the knowledge and the insight which made him in later years one of the leading influences in European affairs.[1]

Let us now turn to the New World. The boundary between the United States and Canada includes the longest water frontier in the world, extending from the Lake of the Woods, in the extreme west of Ontario,

[1] See Siegfried, *Notice sur la vie et les travaux de M. Auguste Gauvain* (Paris, 1933), pp. 9-10, where the political aspect of the Danube Commission is touched upon. From Galatz Gauvain passed to Berne, where he spent four years in the Railway Transport Office in a very different atmosphere.

to Cornwall on the St. Lawrence, sixty miles above Montreal. Across this frontier run vast economic interests affecting the daily life of millions of human beings. The diversion of water in one spot, for instance, may have incalculable effects upon living conditions or navigation elsewhere.

To deal with the intricate problems of this region there was set up in 1909, by the Boundary Waters Treaty, an International Joint Commission of six members, three from each country. The instruction given to the Commission by the treaty is both to *settle* and to *prevent* disputes. But in fact it has been able, with general consent, to go considerably beyond its original mandate. It has indeed acted, and very success-fully, as an arbitral body, having, up to 1931, decided sixteen cases, all but one of them by unanimous vote. But it has also developed imperceptibly into an ad-ministrative body, watching over the carrying out of its own decisions and handling local difficulties at the stage before they have become acute. It employs a local staff in various areas and has even established local boards of control. 'Whether the text of the treaty directly authorises the Commission to establish such boards itself', drily remarks a legal commentator, 'is not entirely clear. In practice the boards have been set up by the joint action of the two governments, taken in pursuance of advice contained in reports by the Commission.' In the same way, a board of engineers was set up to deal with a particular situation causing dispute at the Lake of the Woods. Further, four im-portant investigations have been undertaken through the Commission, one of which resulted in the drawing up of the well-known St. Lawrence Waterway Scheme.

It is thus that institutions *grow*—to use the familiar

British metaphor. But they only grow when they are planted in healthy soil. The activities of the American-Canadian Joint Commission are a testimony to the influence of two factors which are always free to operate when power-political influences are kept at a distance —the regional spirit and the professional spirit.[1]

IV

Our last instance is interesting because it illustrates the interaction between international and domestic politics, a connexion which always exists but which it is not always easy to track down. The story is that of the Sugar Commission.

It was Napoleon who initiated the production of beet sugar in Europe. During the nineteenth century it developed apace, being encouraged by subsidies in various countries, notably in France, Belgium and Holland. These subsidies were granted not only for production but also on export. The result was not only to cause damage to the cane-sugar countries, but also to injure the beet-sugar countries through their mutual competition. It was a clear case for international regulation. The suppression of the bounties was evidently in the general interest. It was equally evident that it could only be carried through by joint action.

Negotiations were opened in 1862. These led to the Sugar Convention of 1864 and to a second Convention in 1877. But the difficulties were not overcome, chiefly because there was no supervision over the execution of the Convention. Eventually in 1902, under the Brussels

---

[1] See H. A. Smith, *The Economic Uses of International Rivers*, 1931, who prints the text of the treaty setting up the Commission (p. 170 ff.).

Convention, resulting from a Conference in that city, a Permanent Sugar Commission was set up.

Under the Brussels Convention all the important beet sugar providing countries, fourteen in number,[1] together with Great Britain, as a large importer of sugar, agreed, for a period of five years, to abolish bounties and to prohibit and penalise the importation of bounty-fed sugar from other countries.

To the student of political science the Sugar Commission presents one feature of special interest. In spite of the fact that it dealt with questions involving important national interests, including the determination of tariff rates, it was empowered to take decisions by a simple majority vote.

The subsequent history of the Commission is instructive. It became an issue in the British General Election of 1906, which was fought largely on the question of Free Trade *versus* Protection. Free Traders espoused the cause of cheap sugar, both because it was a staple food of the masses and because it was a raw material of various industries, such as jam-making. The new Liberal government, pledged in this sense, therefore gave notice in 1907 of Great Britain's intention to withdraw from the Commission. Thereupon the Commission met and hastily drew up an 'Additional Act' to the Convention which was so devised as to give satisfaction at once to the British consumer and the British colonial producer. So the Commission secured a reprieve. But when the second five-years period expired in 1913, Great Britain, under the influence of the manufacturers and consumers, again gave notice of withdrawal and this time carried out her intention.

---

[1] This is the maximum figure: Russia did not come in till some years later.

Whilst doing so, however, she gave a pledge not to depart from the fundamental principles of the Convention by granting bounties on the export of sugar or a preference to colonial sugar. Thus the Commission was able to carry on without her.

The blow that eventually ended its existence came again from Britain, but through the influence of an opposite policy. In the closing months of the war the British Government announced its conversion to the principle of Imperial Preference, and it was in order to enable it to give a preference to cane sugar from the Colonies that, in September 1918, it gave notice of the withdrawal of its pledge: this proved the death-blow of the Commission. Thus in 1920, after long birth-pangs and a brief life of eighteen years, it passed quietly out of existence in the first year of the League of Nations.[1]

[1] For this episode see, in addition to the account in Sayre already mentioned, E. Halévy, *Histoire du peuple anglais au XIXme siècle*, *Épilogue*, vol. ii. (1932), p. 17; the U.S. Tariff Commission *Report on Colonial Tariffs* (1922), p. 815; Viner, *Dumping: A Problem in International Trade* (1923), pp. 178 ff.; and Fuchs, *The Trade Policy of Great Britain and her Colonies since 1860* (1905), pp. 79-100. It is an ironical commentary on the story of the Sugar Commission that since its demise the British Government itself should have embarked on the policy of subsidising the production of beet sugar in Great Britain.

CHAPTER V

TREATIES OF GUARANTEE

So far we have been mainly concerned with the Family of States as a whole. The diplomatic system, the conduct of foreign affairs, conferences and the permanent arrangements arising out of them apply indistinguishably to states of all kinds, irrespective of their age or size or wealth or strength. We have, however, already had occasion to notice that, in the actual working of these arrangements, considerations of relative power were an important factor. International relations in the nineteenth century were not in fact carried on between states enjoying an equality similar to that which every Englishman enjoys before the law. Whatever the legal position might be—and to this point we shall return—states were not, in actual practice, thought of as equals on the international stage: and they were not really treated as equals. Moreover, whilst the strong were not slow to proclaim their superiority, the weak, generally speaking, acquiesced in their inferior status, if not as imposed by a Law of Nature, at least as being an unalterable condition of the existing world-order. The system of international relationship, in other words, was dominated by considerations of Power. It was essentially a system of Power-politics. Its main driving force was supplied, not by all the states, great and small, but by the particular group known, characteristically enough, as *The Great Powers*.

We have now to examine the special form assumed by these power-political relations in the nineteenth century. But, in order to understand it, we must glance back for a moment to the preceding age: for it was in the seventeenth and eighteenth centuries that the technical problems of modern power-political organisation originated.

The nineteenth century has often been described as an age of 'international anarchy'. The expression applies much more aptly to its predecessor. The eighteenth century was the age of interstate libertinism *par excellence*, the age when sovereigns were least embarrassed by any scruples as to the use of their absolute power and when they had developed to the finest point the technique for its exercise. It is true that the idea of a common Christendom lingered on in a shadowy form, connected in the minds of thinkers, and indeed of respectable persons in general, with the idea of a divine order in the universe and therefore in interstate as in domestic social relations. But this pale and mechanical Deism had little or no influence on the foreign policies of sovereigns and their ministers. It is reflected—in so far as it is reflected at all—rather in the watchwords adopted to justify their acts than in these acts themselves. Every age has its appropriate form of hypocrisy, rendering homage to the superior notions of the day. In the eighteenth century 'Reason', transmogrified into 'Reason of State', was a convenient pretext for setting aside the moral law; 'Nature' was invoked for the rounding off of a frontier; 'order' served as an excuse for the spoliation of the weak; whilst 'equilibrium' and 'the Balance of Power', transferred from the laboratory of the scientist, were a convenient justification for the shifting play of alliance and counter-alliance. To compare the principles, as set forth by international lawyers, such as the pious and diligent Vattel, with the practice as recorded by historians is to realise that liberty is not the only ideal in whose name crimes can be committed. The interstate technique of the eighteenth century culminated in the partition of Poland, a deed which lay like a dull weight on the whole life of nineteenth-century Europe.[1]

The particular pre-nineteenth-century legacy with which we are here concerned is that of Treaties of Guarantee, a device traced back by historians to the seventeenth century, but particularly in vogue in the eighteenth.

What is a Treaty of Guarantee? The question has been asked on both sides of the Atlantic, in connexion with the League of Nations Covenant. A better way of approaching the problem is to inquire *who is the guarantor* of a treaty? The guarantor is, historically, a particular kind of mediator. The custom of acting as the guarantor of a treaty arose out of the practice of mediation. Two states or groups of states, who had been at war, invited some other state or states to help them in coming to terms. This led on to a further step. The mediator was begged to continue his good offices by undertaking the responsibility for ensuring that the terms of peace, which he had helped to bring about, were duly observed.

A guarantee, therefore, in this connexion is a guarantee for the proper execution of a treaty. It was a device adopted, in a world where mutual confidence was at a

---

[1] The best general account of the system of international politics in the eighteenth century is still to be found in the classical first volume of Albert Sorel, *L'Europe et la Révolution française* (1885).

minimum, for ensuring that a treaty should not remain a mere 'scrap of paper'. Vattel states the position with disarming candour. A Guarantee, he explains, in a chapter devoted to Securities for the Observation of Treaties, is one of the means of enforcing obedience to a treaty 'independently of the good faith of the contracting parties. When those who conclude a Treaty of Peace or any other Treaty are not absolutely confident of its observance, they ask to have it guaranteed by a powerful sovereign. The guarantor promises to uphold the conditions of the Treaty and to procure their observance. . . . A guarantee is a species of Treaty by which the guarantor promises assistance to a state in case it has need of it to constrain a faithless signatory to fulfil his promises.'[1]

The guarantor, it will be noted, is assumed to be a 'powerful sovereign', more powerful than either of the parties to the treaty which he guarantees. He is a species of patron or protector—a Great Power that has placed its strength at the service of Right, or at least of Treaty Right.

We shall see as our story proceeds how this notion of the guarantee of the powerful sovereign becomes intertwined with nineteenth- and twentieth-century international politics.[2]

---

[1] De Vattel, *Le Droit des gens ou principes de la loi naturelle* (1758), book ii. ch. xvi. § 235.

[2] On the subject of this chapter see the essay on 'Treaties of Guarantee' in J. W. Headlam-Morley, *Studies in Diplomatic History* (1930); also Oppenheim, *International Law*, i. 770 ff. (ed. 1928). It is interesting to note that the Prime Minister of South Africa, in seeking recently for a formula which would satisfactorily define the relationship between South Africa and Great Britain in the sphere of defence, adopted, whether consciously or not, a wording closely resembling that of Vattel. He described the Admiral at Simonstown as 'the highest representative of the fleet of our greatest friend and most powerful friend, Great Britain'. (See *The Round Table*, June 1935, p. 491.)

CHAPTER VI

THE CONCERT OF EUROPE

I

THE eighteenth century knew nothing of a 'European system'. Its international politics were atomic; its temporary combinations were based on narrow calculations of self-interest; and in the absence of any cementing common principles, either political or moral, the statecraft of the day took refuge in ingenious substitutes for confidence and good faith. For why should a 'powerful sovereign' prove more trustworthy than the weaker state against whom his protection was involved? The dividing line between the eighteenth and the nineteenth centuries, in international politics, is not the Napoleonic wars, but the French Revolution. It was the incredible spectacle of the new régime on the banks of the Seine which drew together the startled representatives of what then began to be regarded as an old order common to them all. When the French people rose and took the reins of power into their own hands, when the Sovereign French Nation, the first Nation in Arms of modern times, stood, enthusiastic and challenging, in the place of the Sovereign Monarch and his levies, a thrill of horror ran through the Chancelleries. The time had come, it was felt, to take common measures against a common danger.

The first official manifestation of this suddenly

awakened sense of European solidarity followed immediately after Louis XVI and Marie Antoinette had been brought back to Paris under arrest after their flight to Varennes. The Emperor Leopold addressed a circular to his fellow-sovereigns denouncing an act of violence which set the seal of illegality on all that had been happening in France and touched 'the honour of all the sovereigns and the security of all the governments'. He went on to propose that common measures should be taken 'to vindicate the liberty and the honour of His Most Christian Majesty and his family and to set bounds to the dangerous extreme of the French Revolution, the fatal example of which it behoved all the governments to suppress'. Here is the Holy Alliance in embryo.[1]

The coalition brought into being in 1791 was repulsed by the new Model Army of the Revolution on the field of Valmy in the following year. During the succeeding generation it passed through many strange vicissitudes which entailed an interesting process of cross-fertilisation between the old régime and the new. When the final victory over the warrior offspring of the Revolution was gained in 1815, the Holy Roman Empire had disappeared and the child of the Corsican was living in the Hapsburg palace in Vienna. But our concern is not with these matters. We have to watch the shape taken by the new European system at the post-war council table.

Should there be henceforward a European system? Or should the coalition be dissolved and the Continent relapse into the atomism of the eighteenth century? To this question there was a unanimous answer. A return to atomism was unthinkable. The forces abroad

---

[1] Sorel, ii. 229.

in Europe were far too dangerous, the threat to the established order far too formidable, for the coalition to be abandoned. The question, therefore, which remained to be answered was as to what form the European system should take. How should the war-time association be prolonged and adapted to peace-time conditions?

There was a natural and traditional answer. The Great Powers, who together had won the victory, should together 'guarantee' the peace—that is to say, should act as an associated group of 'powerful sovereigns' to ensure the observance of the peace treaties and to come to the assistance of any party to them who was confronted by a 'faithless signatory'.

This was the solution desired by the victorious Continental Great Powers—by Russia, Austria and Prussia—a solution for which they made constant efforts, in 1815 and the succeeding years, to win the assent of Great Britain. In pursuit of this object they made the most flattering offers. Thus, at one moment of the Congress of Aix-la-Chapelle, which was the principal battle-ground in these matters, the Tsar tried to work on the British eagerness for an efficient means for suppressing the Slave Trade, and for an extension of the Right of Search, by recommending a scheme for an international navy, presumably under British command. This was to be attached to a 'neutral', or, as we should say to-day, international 'institution'—a sort of International Union against Piracy—established by all the Christian states, with its headquarters in some suitable spot in Africa. At another moment there emerged the idea—sponsored, curiously enough, by the Prussian generals—of a European Army, centred at Brussels, with the Duke of Wellington as its commander-in-chief. 'A more ingenious device for keeping us in hot water could not have been invented' was Castlereagh's comment on this proposal.

The plan for a general guarantee took various forms. The Tsar, who, when he was seized of an idea, had no taste for half-measures, was anxious to secure a guarantee not only of the territorial provisions of the peace treaties, but also of the maintenance in power of the particular régime in each country at the time that the treaties were concluded. In modern language, he wished to make the world 'safe for' sovereign monarchs. Thus Castlereagh found himself at Aix-la-Chapelle confronted with a scheme by which 'all the Powers of Europe' would be 'bound together in a common league guaranteeing to each other the existing order of things in thrones as well as in territories, all being bound to march, if requisite, against the first Power that offended either by her ambitions or by her revolutionary transgressions'. In other words, the Tsar desired that not only the Great Powers but all the signatories of the treaties should assume the obligations of guarantors and that those obligations should be extended in scope to include interference in the domestic affairs of the parties.[1]

The idea of bringing in the weak as well as the strong to act as guarantors did not develop into a leading issue at the time. It is only worth mentioning in passing, with a view to future events. Nor need we consider in detail the Tsar's scheme for a guarantee against domestic revolution. As Castlereagh remarked, in a Memorandum drawn up for the Cabinet, the whole conception was, to say the least, premature. It 'must

[1] Webster, *The Foreign Policy of Castlereagh, 1815–1822* (1925), pp. 140, 464, 164, 148.

be understood', he wrote, 'as morally implying the previous establishment of such a system of general government as may secure and enforce upon all Kings and nations an internal system of peace and justice. Till the mode of constructing such a system shall be devised', he concluded, the idea of a collective guarantee was out of the question; since 'nothing would be more immoral or prejudicial to the character of government generally than the idea that their force was collectively to be prostituted to the support of established power without any consideration of the extent to which it was abused'.[1] Here is laid down a line of policy to which Great Britain held firm throughout the nineteenth century. To be compelled, by agreements concluded beforehand, to intervene in the domestic affairs of other peoples is a notion abhorrent to the British mind. It does not follow, as has been held in various quarters at various times, that such intervention is always to be deprecated. The theory of absolute non-interventionism is as doctrinaire in its own way as the Tsar's ingenious scheme for using the power of Britain to keep the Continental monarchs on their thrones.

But the real issue was the guarantee not against internal revolution but against external aggression. Would Great Britain act as one of the guarantors of the territorial provisions of the peace? Would she, in other words, guarantee the new frontiers, pledging herself to intervene by force in the event of their violation?

On this point, too, Castlereagh was immovable. His dispatches record his conversation with the Tsar on the subject. He based his argument on the responsi-

[1] Webster, p. 151.

bility of the directors of British foreign policy to the House of Commons and public opinion. The methods available to an autocratic monarchy, he told him, were not possible of adoption by a parliamentary government. If an emergency arose and the Cabinet considered intervention desirable, 'the only chance we had', he argued, 'of making the nation feel the wisdom of such a course, was to be free, at the moment, to urge the policy of so acting, not because we had no choice but as having a choice; that this determination would best provide for the public safety, in which decision the advantage of not separating from our Allies would be urged with effect in proportion as we were known to have a free voice in the course to be pursued'.

The fundamental incompatibility between the parliamentary control of foreign policy and a general system of binding guarantees could not be more clearly stated. The guarantee system, after all, did not originate under conditions of responsible government: nor was the soil in which it grew up morally congenial to peoples nurtured in Parliamentarism. When the Tsar and his colleagues asked Great Britain to join them in a general guarantee, they were demanding a far greater concession of principle to expediency than they could be expected to realise. It is not surprising that the Tsar, after listening to Castlereagh, remarked that these were new ideas with which he was 'very little familiar'. The experience of a century, as we shall see, did not add greatly to their familiarity in the minds of Continental statesmen.[1]

Before leaving the subject of guarantees it is worth while recording the classical declaration on the subject by Castlereagh's successor, which is valuable because

[1] Webster, p. 157.

of the light that it throws on a subject peculiarly liable to confusion, the difference between a guarantee and a defensive alliance:

The British government [wrote Canning in September 1823] will not, in any case, undertake any guaranty [sic] whatever, either of territory or internal Institutions. The scrupulousness with which England is in the habit of fulfilling her obligations makes it the more necessary for her not to contract them lightly. A guaranty is one of the most onerous obligations which one State can contract towards another. A defensive Alliance binds the Government contracting it to come to the aid of its Ally in case of an unprovoked attack upon his Dominions; and to make, in his behalf, every reasonable and practicable exertion—practicable in extent, and reasonable in duration. But it does not bind the assisting Government to the alternative of either a successful result, or an indefinite prolongation of the war. A guaranty, strictly construed, knows no limits either of time or of degree. It would be, unless distinctly restricted in that respect, claimable in a War commenced by the Power to whom the guaranty is given, as well as in a War of unjust aggression against that Power; and the integrity of the territory of that Power must be maintained at whatever cost the effort to maintain it is prolonged; nay, though the guaranteed Power itself should contribute almost nothing to the maintaining it. If . . . the engagement is to be restricted in these particulars, it would constitute a unilateral defensive Alliance, but it would cease to be a guarantee.

Canning did not prove strictly accurate in the prophecy—if prophecy it was intended to be—embodied in his opening sentence. The British Government did in fact consent, during the nineteenth century, in a few cases, to enter into guarantees of territorial integrity. The case of Belgium is, of course, the most important. Canning's words, therefore, require to be somewhat attenuated if they are to be regarded as the enunciation of a standing principle of British policy.

Perhaps their underlying idea is best formulated in the comment which Sir James Headlam-Morley appends after citing the passage from Canning. 'Never enter into a guarantee if you can possibly avoid it, but, if you do, then see to it that the obligation is made firm and precise and let there be no hesitation about honouring it.'[1]

II

The rejection of the plan for a general guarantee left the problem of the European system unsolved. What was there that could take its place? What method of association could be devised which, without involving the rigidity of a guarantee, would nevertheless be sufficient to prevent Europe from relapsing into atomism.

This was the problem for which the genius of Castlereagh found the solution. It can be summed up in one word—*Consultation*, or, if the Anglo-Saxon version be preferred, *Keeping in Touch*.

Before we examine the legal form in which this solution was enshrined, let us look at it for a moment, as Castlereagh and his Cabinet must have looked at it, from the standpoint of British traditions and interests. Britain, so they must have reasoned, is part of Europe. She has vital interests on the Continent, both of a general and a particular nature. She has a general interest, firstly in preventing the Continent from falling under the supremacy of a single ambitious

---

[1] Headlam-Morley, pp. 119-20. The British guarantee of Portugal and her colonial possessions originated in 1661. The arrangement then concluded was a curious blend of an alliance and a guarantee, for the guarantee is appended in a 'Secret Article' to a Treaty of Perpetual Alliance. See *British Documents*, i. 93-5.

power; secondly, in promoting the good government, welfare and prosperity of the European peoples. She has a particular interest, firstly, in preserving the independence of the Low Countries; secondly, in maintaining her superior sea-power in European waters. Under these circumstances, Britain could neither disinterest herself of Europe—the Napoleonic Empire afforded recent enough proof of this—nor could she tie herself too closely to the European governments, none of which was at that time inspired by a spirit akin to her own or congenial to British public opinion. What she needed, therefore, was a system which would give her a *right* to interfere in the affairs of the Continent, but without any corresponding obligation. Or perhaps it would be fairer, or closer to Castlereagh's thought, to say that she needed a system which would set her free to follow her own sense of duty in regard to Continental affairs, leaving her with a moral obligation but with no legal obligation.

However that may be, whether self-interest or moral obligation was the guiding thought, the solution adopted corresponded exactly with the British requirements. It was embodied in the preamble of the Final Act of the Treaty of Vienna.

Being now desirous [runs this momentous document] to embrace, in one common transaction, the various results of their negotiations, for the purpose of confirming these by their reciprocal Ratifications, they authorize their Plenipotentiaries to unite, in a general instrument, the regulations of superior and permanent interest, and to join to that Act, as integral parts of the arrangements of Congress, the Treaties, Conventions, Declarations and other particular Acts as cited in the present Treaty.[1]

[1] Hertslet, *The Map of Europe by Treaty* (1875), i. 211.

These words were a death-blow to eighteenth-century atomism. Their result was, to quote the words of Sir James Headlam-Morley, that 'the sanction for each one of the particular territorial arrangements was no longer merely a partial and separate treaty. They were endorsed by all the eight powers who signed the general act of Congress, and in this way became a recognised part of the *general European establishment*. . . . Each of the states concerned obtained a title for its possessions of the strongest and most formal character'—but without a guarantee.[1]

But there was a further result from this procedure. It did not merely strengthen the rights of all the parties, great and small alike, to the treaties. It conferred new rights upon the Principal Powers who set their names to the General Act. It gave them a Right to Consultation and a Right to Propose a Conference.

Since each of the Principal Powers was a party to the General Act, no modification could be made in any of the treaty arrangements covered by this envelope without their consent. Hence arose the right to Consultation. But if any of the powers, when consulted, objected to the proposed change, the natural procedure, as between sovereigns, would be for the question to be brought before all the Principal Powers. Hence arose the Right to Propose a Conference.

But the reverse of the medal was equally important from the British point of view. Under the new system, remarks Sir James Headlam-Morley, 'though each Power had the right to be consulted, it had complete freedom to determine whether or not it should assert this right, and there was no obligation on any one Power as against any other to intervene, as there

[1] Headlam-Morley, pp. 116-17. The italics are inserted.

would have been had a guarantee been given. The practical effect of this', the Historical Adviser of the Foreign Office goes on to say, from the point of view of a Power such as Great Britain, was most advantageous. 'The Government retained full freedom to come to a decision on every occasion when, by war or in any other way, an alteration was proposed in the arrangements set up at Vienna. If it was a matter in which this country was concerned, it could at once intervene and claim that it should be brought before a Conference, as was done, for instance, with regard to Belgium and Denmark. On the other hand, when a change was introduced which the Government considered desirable, as for instance, the unification of Italy, it was quite free to give its consent, as far as it was concerned, and it remained for other Powers who opposed the change to require that it should be brought before a Conference.'

The arrangement above described formed the basis of what came to be known as the Concert of Europe— a system of Rights without Duties, and of Responsibilities without Organisation, which carried the Continent, without a major war, through the great political developments and the still greater economic transformation of the century between 1815 and 1914.

It is beyond the scope of these pages to describe the working of the Concert in detail. It functioned very differently at different times. The original idea of Castlereagh was to use the Conference method as a means for circumventing the delays of diplomacy and for thus maintaining constant personal touch between the leading statesmen of Europe. It was with that object that he favoured periodical meetings, at frequent intervals, of the Great Powers or what has become

known as 'the Congress System'. Four such meetings
were in fact held after the conclusion of peace at
Vienna—at Aix-la-Chapelle in 1818, at Opava (Troppau)
in 1820, at Ljubliana (Laibach) in 1821 and at Verona
(after Castlereagh's death) in 1822, the Aix-la-Chapelle
Conference being, in the words of its latest historian,
'the first ever held by the Great Powers of Europe to
regulate international differences in time of peace'.[1]

Thus during Castlereagh's time of office there was
developed a habit of Conference between the Great
Powers at intervals considerably less infrequent than
those which have, during the last fifty years, separated
the meetings of the self-governing members of the
British Commonwealth. Castlereagh was indeed so
firm a believer in the value of the Conference method
that at moments he seems to have entertained an
exaggerated idea of the possibilities opened out by it.
'It is satisfactory to observe', he tells the Cabinet in a
dispatch from Aix-la-Chapelle, no doubt intended for
its education, 'how little embarrassment and how much
solid good grow out of these reunions, which sound so
terrible at a distance. It really appears to me to be a
new discovery in the European government, at once
extinguishing the cobwebs with which diplomacy ob-
scures the horizon, bringing the whole system into its
true light, and giving to the counsels of the Great
Powers the efficiency and almost the simplicity of a
single State'. But he had hard work to carry his
Cabinet with him. Canning, in particular, scented
danger in the plan. 'It will necessarily involve us deeply
in all the politics of the Continent,' he told his fellow-
members of the Cabinet, in language familiar to a later
age, 'whereas our true policy has always been not to

---

[1] Webster, p. 121.

interfere except in great emergencies and then with commanding force'—in other words, to despair of prevention and to reserve the whole effort for surgery.[1]

It is not surprising then that, when Castlereagh died, the method of *regular* conference should have passed away with him. Canning, who succeeded him, did not wish to continue it, was indeed thankful to see it lapse. If the truth must be told, he was not capable of continuing it. For the Conference method requires very special qualities in its practitioners. Not all Foreign Secretaries are articles of export, suited to Continental conditions. Still less can it be assumed that all are fitted for the very special conditions, both political and psychological, of the Continental market-place. Castlereagh knew what he was saying when, in his last interview with George IV, shortly before his death, he declared: 'Sir! It is necessary to say good-bye to Europe . . . no-one after me understands the affairs of the Continent'.

This cry from the heart reveals that Castlereagh was under no illusions as to the value of the Conference method apart from the personality of those who employed it. He would not have needed to be told that Conference without understanding is futile and that Conference without the will to understand, so far from being an improvement on 'the old diplomacy', may be the most fertile breeding-ground of war. Chairs and tables are not enough.

III

From 1822 to 1914 the Concert system continued without regular Conferences between the leading states-

[1] Webster, pp. 153, 147.

men. It functioned, as it was intended by British
statesmanship to function, intermittently rather than
constantly. It was a safety-valve rather than a working
arrangement or, to adapt the expression of Burke, the
medicine of Europe rather than its daily bread. But
as the years went on it could claim a large amount of
useful work to its credit throughout the area within its
scope, which extended from the Low Countries in the
West to Egypt and the Lebanon in the East. Thus,
though its standards were vague and opportunist, its
methods eclectic and its permanent organisation non-
existent, it nevertheless became the repository of a
tradition under which peace between the Great Powers
was a habit and a general war unthinkable.[1]

The authority which the Concert came to exercise is
well brought in a speech by Lord Salisbury during one
of the phases of the interminable Graeco-Turkish
question: 'If it had not been for the Concert of Europe
the Hellenic Kingdom would never have been heard
of. . . . I feel it is our duty to sustain the federated
action of Europe. I think it has suffered by the somewhat absurd name which has been given to it—the
Concert of Europe—and the intense importance of the
fact has been buried under the bad jokes to which
the word has given rise. But the federated action of
Europe—if we can maintain it, if we can maintain this

[1] There is no good book in English analysing the working of the Concert. A bald summary of the facts, beginning with the Greek crisis of
1821 and ending with the Lausanne Conference of 1923, is contained in
the long chapter entitled 'The Concert in Political Action' in Butler and
Maccoby, *The Development of International Law* (1928); Holland's *The
European Concert in the Eastern Question* (1885) is written from the standpoint of the international lawyer but is well documented. An excellent
account of the inner working of the Concert at a time of crisis, covering
two separate Conferences, is contained in R. W. Seton-Watson, *Disraeli,
Gladstone and the Eastern Question*, 1935. See also Dupuis, *Le Concert
européen et l'équilibre des puissances*, Paris, 1909.

legislature—is our sole hope of escaping from the constant terror and the calamity of war.'[1]

From the point of view of political science this language is doubtless more than questionable. If the Great Powers constituted a federated legislature, it was a hitherto unheard-of type of federation and, judged by democratic standards, a most unrepresentative body of law-makers. But this did not prevent it from remaining a serviceable instrument up to the eve of the Great War. The last Conference under the Concert was that held in London in 1912-13, after the second Balkan War, under the chairmanship of Sir Edward Grey. Of the authority of the Concert at this time the editors of the British documents remark: 'During the Balkan wars the Concert of Europe became a real thing. It failed to prevent the smaller Powers from going to war; it succeeded in making peace possible between the Great Powers. . . . For once Europe was a reality.'[2]

The working of the Concert System, with the drawbacks incidental to its merits, was never better illustrated than during the twelve days of its death-agony. By an ironical turn of fate, its very flexibility, which had been its chief recommendation in British eyes, was now turned against Great Britain. It was Continental statesmanship which now held stubbornly to what has been called 'the policy of the free hand'. It was the Germans and Austro-Hungarians who refused to come into Conference, whilst the British Foreign Secretary made effort after effort to overcome their reluctance.[3]

[1] *Times,* March 20, 1897, quoted in Westlake, *International Law,* (2nd ed., 1910), i. 322.

[2] *British Documents,* ix. part ii. p. vi.

[3] On this, in addition to the collections of documents, see especially Grey's own reminiscences (*Twenty-Five Years* (1926), i. p. 314 ff.). The

The final stage of the abortive negotiations is worth analysing in some detail, for it fixes the exact point which the old system had reached before the opening of the discussions centring round the idea of a League of Nations.

On July 29, 1914, the German Chancellor, in an interview with the British Ambassador, tried to persuade Great Britain to pledge herself to remain neutral during the coming struggle—as she had remained of her own free will during the wars of 1864, 1866, 1870 and on other occasions. His effort, in other words, was to secure a guarantee of a character precisely the opposite of that which Continental statesmen had so often tried to press upon Great Britain. This time it was a *guarantee of non-interference,* a self-imposed ordinance of renunciation, a sort of British Monroe Doctrine eschewing Continental entanglements. Sir Edward Grey's answer was inevitable. He restated the traditional policy of 'the free hand'. 'We must preserve our full freedom to act as circumstances may seem to us to require in any development of the present crisis.' But to his refusal of the German Chancellor's offer he added a positive suggestion. 'If', he continued, in memorable words, 'the peace of Europe can be preserved and this crisis be safely passed, my own endeavour would be to promote some arrangement to which Germany could be a party, by which she could be assured that no hostile or aggressive policy would be pursued against her or her allies by France, Russia and ourselves, jointly or severally. I have desired this, and worked for it, as far as I could, through the last Balkan crisis

German Government justified its refusal of a Conference by describing it as a 'Court of Arbitration' on Austria-Hungary, thus introducing, or rather imputing to Great Britain, a legal notion quite foreign to the tradition of the Concert.

and, Germany having a corresponding object, our relations sensibly improved. The idea has hitherto been too Utopian to form the subject of definite proposals, but if this present crisis, so much more acute than any that Europe has had for generations, be safely passed, I am hopeful that the reaction and relief that will follow may make some more definite *rapprochement* between the Powers more possible than was possible before.'

What was this Utopian idea that lay in the background of the British Foreign Secretary's mind? *An improved and organised Concert.*[1]

IV

We have now to look briefly at the defects or limitations of the Concert system, regarded apart from the particular policies of its members.

The first point to be noted is that already referred to on a previous page.[2] It was a system confined to the Great Powers.

What is a Great Power? Many definitions might be framed in answer to this question—definitions according to which Sweden would figure as a greater power than Russia; Holland, irrespective of her colonies, than Germany; and China, irrespective of her size and population, than Japan. But such valuations would

---

[1] *British Documents*, xi. 185, 193. How 'Utopian' this had hitherto been thought is well illustrated by Grey's own comment on the dispersal of the Ambassadors' Conference over the Balkan Question in August 1913: 'It did not occur to any of us to suggest that we should be kept in existence as a Conference, as a body ready to be called together at any moment, to which future Balkan or indeed any troubles between the Great Powers might be referred' (Grey, i. 275).

[2] P. 74.

G

not fit into the system of international politics as history has known it hitherto. For realistic purposes—that is to say, for the political scientist seeking to analyse the world as he finds it—the definition must be drawn up in what the philosopher cannot but regard as brutal terms. A Great Power—we must conclude from the evidence before us—is a power that is in a position to apply more pressure than the majority of states in order to make its will prevail. The test, in other words, is not according to the relative degrees of virtue or happiness or culture or any other kind of well-being or quality of living but one of force—force raised indeed above the brute stage by the application of intelligence, discipline and scientific method, but nevertheless, in essence, a material rather than a spiritual manifestation.

By this standard Athens was a Great Power, not because she gave birth to Aeschylus and Sophocles, Thucydides and Aristophanes, Socrates and Plato, but because she repulsed the Persian invader on the field of Marathon—a victory due, let it never be forgotten, to superior armament.

> The flying Mede, his shaftless broken bow,
> The fiery Greek, his red pursuing spear.

Byron's lines remind us that it was not heroism alone but heroism wedded with intelligence which preserved our civilisation in its cradle from suppression by the hordes of Asia. Would the genius of Athens have flowered as it did had a foreign garrison remained quartered on the Acropolis and Attica become part of a Persian satrapy? To ask the question is to realise that the relationship between the two forms of 'greatness'—what may be called the qualitative and the

power-political—is not so remote as some social
thinkers would have us believe.

If we pursued these reflections further they would
perhaps lead us to the conclusion that there is nothing
inherently evil in political power, as such, nor in an
international system the constituent units of which
are 'Powers'. To make the contrary assumption is to
allow oneself to be led down a blind alley. Human
activities, whether international or domestic, can never
be organised or controlled by purely spiritual agencies.
Whether we like it or not—and few of us enjoy paying
our taxes—we have Caesar constantly with us and
he will always demand his due. The issue before the
student of international politics is not the issue between the spiritual and the material, between Quality
and Force, but the more realistic one as to how and
to what extent Caesar's own motives can be purified
and moralised. In other words, the problem of international politics is not the elimination of the conception
of Power, but its transformation—we may even say its
sublimation—through the influence of the notion of
moral responsibility. We can watch this process working itself out in the life of individual communities,
where, in the domain of domestic policy, the state is
becoming less and less an agency of pure power and
increasingly an agency of the common welfare. Its
policemen are no longer thought of simply as embodi-
ments of the mailed fist but rather as friends of the
public: its 'inspectors' are not mere detectives but
guides and advisers. It is not unrealistic to conceive
that a corresponding process could take place in the
realm of international politics. If such a development
should reach its completion, some states would still be
found stronger than others—for equality is not of this

world—but there would no longer be *Great Powers*. There would only be *Great Responsibles*.

From this vision of the future let us return to the nineteenth century.

In 1815 there were five Great Powers—Great Britain, France, Austria, Prussia and Russia. Italy was admitted into the favoured circle after the Crimean War. In 1871 Prussia became Germany. Finally, to carry our story forward, Japan became recognised as a Great Power as a result of the Anglo-Japanese Alliance of 1902 and her successful war against Russia in 1905, whilst the United States emerged as a Great Power after the Spanish-American War of 1898 and, under the energetic leadership of President Theodore Roosevelt, took part, alongside with the powers of the European Concert, in the Moroccan Conference of 1906.

The result of this division of the Family of States into classes, the Great and the Less-than-great, has been undeniably unfortunate. It has been bad for the morale of both sides. Under the Concert system, as peeps out from the words of Lord Salisbury quoted above, the Great Powers developed the characteristic defects of oligarchy and special privilege. They were tempted to be arrogant, aloof and secretive. Regarding themselves as the self-appointed guardians of the interests of the smaller states, they enjoyed the powers of what would to-day be called a Mandatory but without either the fixed obligations or the publicly recognised responsibility. The smaller states, on the other hand, fell into the faults incidental to their inferior status. Unable to make a positive contribution to the political life of Europe, they tended to cultivate a nagging and unhelpful spirit, inclined to be at once servile and self-righteous. We shall see in the sequel

how these attitudes and the intellectual habits and
doctrines resulting from them have persisted into the
post-war period.

The second great defect in the working of the Concert arose from the fundamental differences of political
outlook between its various members. For the majority
—for Russia, for the Austria of Metternich and the
Austria-Hungary that succeeded it, for Bismarckian
Germany—the Concert represented what it represented
to the Continental statesmen of 1815, a combination of
the forces of Order and Divine Right against the ideas
of 1789, against what Bismarck always called 'the
Revolution'. It was for them a dyke against the ever-
present danger of a raging flood from the West. To
British minds, attuned neither to Revolution nor to
Counter-Revolution, this whole conception was anti-
pathetic. Moreover, apart from the particular principles
involved, what was a dyke but a device for letting
water pile up and so postponing and thus intensifying
the eventual trouble? They therefore tended to regard
the Concert rather as a sluice-gate for allowing the
water to flow through gently than as a barrier against
its passage. The contrast between these two doctrines
and attitudes runs through the whole century of the
Concert. Intertwined with it is the record of France
with her 'Revolutionary Tradition', variously exemplified in the Bourgeois Monarchy, the Second Republic,
the 'Liberal Empire' and the Third Republic, and of
Italy from the days of Mazzini the Prophet and
Garibaldi the Liberator to Crispi and Giolitti, the
friends of the Central Empires.

The third important limitation under which the
Concert suffered was geographical. It covered only a
very small part of the world. It was confined to Europe

and the Near East—roughly speaking, to the area of the old Roman Empire with a north-eastward extension. No doubt this region, which seems so small when looked at on a globe, was by far the most important centre of international politics at that time. It was the seat, at once, of the world's predominant civilisation, of its chief political power and of its principal riches. Everything outside it, for men like Metternich and Bismarck, was a mere colonial accessory, a provincial appendage unworthy of the attention of metropolitans. These limits had been fixed when Canning in 1823 had prevented the monarchs of the day from interfering to suppress revolution in Latin America and, unnatural as they were, they had been adhered to until they came to be regarded as in the nature of things. It was not until the last quarter of the nineteenth century that European statesmanship began to chafe within its Continental shell and to stretch out impatient fingers towards regions beyond its grasp.[1] To that oceanic world, the world that the Concert never knew, it is now time to turn.

---

[1] During the Fashoda crisis of 1898 the idea cropped up in some of the Continental Chancelleries that the Anglo-French controversy over the Upper Nile valley ought to be laid before the Concert 'as an offshoot of the general Eastern question'. This well illustrates the growing uncertainty as to the political limits of 'Europe'. See *British Documents*, i. 175-6.

CHAPTER VII

As the globe is divided into two hemispheres, so the
world of nineteenth-century international politics was
divided into two regions, each with a political system
of its own. But, unlike the hemispheres, they were of
unequal size and the connexion between them was not
kept open. The affairs of Europe were under the
control of a close corporation of Great Powers. Her
system was oligarchical. The overseas world, on the
other hand, was under the control of a single power.
It was not a divided and fumbling oligarchy but a
firm, straightforward and competent monarchy. A
benevolent Britannia ruled the waves.

British sea-power in the nineteenth century was
exercised so silently, yet so efficiently, with so complete
a mastery yet with such characteristic reserve—a
reserve as characteristic of the Service as of the people
—that it is only in retrospect that its full significance
and, still more, its undeveloped potentialities are
coming to be realised. Even to-day there is no adequate
record of its contribution to the international politics
of the time. How indeed could this be either summarised in its results or described in the making? For the
essence of the Navy's achievement lay, not in what it
performed but in what it prevented, not in its own acts
and accomplishments but in its influence over the acts

87

of others. It was a major factor underlying every diplomatic negotiation in the oceanic world—and in many of those outside it—a factor that could never be assessed with precision but which could always be counted on, if need be, to turn the scales. If its weight was seldom actually thrown in, it was because those who had it at their command, true children of the nineteenth century, believed in the virtue of sparing use, both in the economy of force and in the economy of advertisement. But both were available when they were needed. The British Navy carried out, under nineteenth-century conditions, tasks for which in some quarters appeal is to-day being made to an 'international police force'. It kept the seas open for traffic and closed for pirates, made the 'Open Door' a reality and, so far as international law allowed, suppressed the slave trade and rescued its victims. Thus, to use the words of a naval historian, 'The White Ensign became the token of equal rights for all, a pledge of the brotherhood of all mankind'.[1]

---

[1] Callender, *The Naval Side of British History* (1924), p. 237: this is a good general sketch of the subject, but it is far from adequate on the political side, especially in its treatment of the nineteenth century. *The Cambridge History of British Foreign Policy* is equally unsatisfactory in this respect. The best recent treatment of the subject is contained in the books of Professor Admiral Sir Herbert Richmond, especially *National Policy* and *Naval Strength* (1928). Mahan's writings, which had so much vogue in the years before 1914, have not stood the test of time. He failed, for instance, to appreciate the new and formidable potentialities of sea-power in an industrialised world, with industrialised military systems.—For the prolonged diplomatic wrangle with other powers, including the United States, on the use of their flags to cover slave-ships, see the *Cambridge History of British Foreign Policy*, ii. p. 235 ff. Readers may be grateful, in this connexion, to be referred to the Prelude in *John Brown's Body* by Stephen Vincent Benét (New York, 1929).—There was, of course, a reverse side to the medal shown in the text. The power of the Navy was sometimes abused, both by governments and local commanders. One such instance, not forgotten in Japan, was the bombard-

If we leave the subject at this point it is because, for the political scientist, there is nothing more to record. The oceanic monarchy functioned without international machinery. It was a national instrument, primarily concerned with the carrying out of national policies, to which, almost by accident, it fell also to discharge international duties indispensable for the world. With the policies of the British Government we are not concerned in this study. But the duties we shall encounter later, when the question of their discharge, in altered conditions, comes under our review. For the benevolent despotism, like the oligarchy, reached its end in the Great War.

ment of Kagoshima in 1863, the details of which will be found in the *Cambridge Modern History*, xi. 845, and in Lord Salisbury's *Essay on Foreign Policy*, 1905 ed., p. 173 ff.

CHAPTER VIII

THE BREAK-THROUGH

WE have examined the double-barrelled system under which the international politics of the nineteenth century were conducted. But we shall not understand the problems with which the framers of the League of Nations Covenant were confronted unless we have clearly in mind the circumstances of the immediate pre-war period, when these arrangements were already undergoing a process of disintegration. For, appropriately enough, it was just during the last few years of the nineties that the system which we have been describing as that of the nineteenth century passed into a new phase. There was a change of conditions—one might almost say of the political climate—in both spheres, the Oceanic and the European.[1]

In the oceanic world British sea-power found itself confronted, not indeed with rivals, but with young and enterprising partners in the shape of two new Great

---

[1] For the sudden change of 'climate' in England round about New Year's Day 1896 see Garvin, *Life of Joseph Chamberlain*, iii. 92-3. But as late as 1901, Lord Salisbury denied that the policy of isolation involved any real danger to Great Britain or British interests. See his memorandum in *British Documents*, ii. 68: 'it would hardly be wise', he wrote, of a proposal that Great Britain should join the Triple Alliance, 'to incur novel and most onerous obligations, in order to guard against *a danger in whose existence we have no historical reason for believing*'. (Italics in the original.) The editors of the British documents date the change from 1898.

Powers. Both the United States and Japan, as we have
already observed, entered the lists in that capacity just
about that time. Their appearance coincided with a
grave preoccupation in British minds due to events in
quite a different quarter. The troubles in South Africa
and the diplomatic by-play with which they had been
accompanied on the Continent had led British statesmen to wonder whether it was safe to continue the old
system of the free hand in Europe together with an un-
supported naval supremacy overseas. These anxieties
were accentuated by the determination of the rulers
of Germany, the strongest military power on the Continent, to embark upon a career of sea-power. As a
result, Britain began to look round for companions—
perhaps it would be fairer to say, junior partners.
Negotiations were entered into with Germany but,
through no fault on the British side, they proved abortive. Soundings, equally without result, were made
regarding the possibilities of British-American co-
operation in the Far East. Eventually, in 1902, an
alliance was concluded with Japan. Later, in 1904, a
comprehensive understanding was reached with France
on a number of outstanding issues, laying the foundation for a close association with her in Continental
affairs. We have not here to appreciate the substantial
issues of policy involved in this re-orientation. We are
only concerned with its bearing on the system of the
grouping of the powers. This can be briefly stated.

The Anglo-Japanese Alliance, formed in 1902 and
renewed and extended in 1905, brought to an end the
period of sole British mastery of the Pacific. Viewed
in its strategic aspect, it enabled Great Britain to
diminish her forces in the Far East and to concentrate
a greater strength in European waters. The effect of

the European re-orientation was more complex. The disturbing factor here, as has been said, was Germany's bid for sea-power, not indeed for supremacy (though the word was sometimes whispered) but for a naval equipment so substantial as to cause serious annoyance—and more than annoyance—to the traditional mistress of the seas. What Germany, in fact, was doing—whether her rulers fully realised it or not—was to strike at the barrier which had since 1815, indeed since Trafalgar, divided the two regions of British external activity into something like water-tight compartments. By seeking to break through from the Continent into the ocean Germany worked on Great Britain like a magnet, pulling her in her turn towards the Continent. What had been two separate spheres of policy, for which two distinct methods and attitudes had been employed, were now merged by imperceptible stages into one—though the significance of the change was not realised at the time and still less was an appropriate new method worked out for dealing with this new situation.

Thus it was that, when the war came, it was not a Continental war, as in the Crimea, or an overseas war, as in the Transvaal, but a World War, a world in both realms, a double-barrelled war, requiring effort and sacrifice in proportion to the vastness of its scale and the complexity of its character.

The effort of British policy in the nineteenth century had been, if possible, to prevent war and, when this was not possible, to localise it. The war of 1914 was a contradiction of this standing principle. It was the demonstration that, as international politics had developed since the turn of the century, a war between Great Powers could no longer be compartmentalised.

It was a break-through, in the grand style, of the forces of disruption, carrying away in their path barriers that had held for a hundred years. Could peace be established on an equally world-wide basis, with a sweep as majestic and all-embracing? That was the problem set for statesmanship by the events of 1914.

CHAPTER IX

INTERNATIONAL LAW

WE have now reached 1914. But before we proceed further we must turn aside to describe the intervention of a new factor which will henceforward be a constant influence in the development of our analysis. We have to introduce and to characterise International Law.

For anyone trained in the British tradition, the term 'International Law' embodies a conception which is, at its best, confusing and at its worst exasperating. It is never law as we understand it, and it often, as it seems to us, comes dangerously near to being an imposture, a *simulacrum* of law, an attorney's mantle artfully displayed on the shoulders of arbitrary power. It is this deep-lying difference between the British and the Continental outlook on the subject of International Law, and of law generally, which has been at the bottom of much of the detailed controversy of the last twenty years. It is this which has led to words and notions such as 'right', 'justice', 'order', 'security' and even 'peace' becoming storm-centres of international politics, or to change the metaphor, missiles flung at one another by the obstinate occupants of two sets of intellectual trenches, stoutly constructed out of ancient political and social materials on either side. It is therefore advisable at this point, if only for the sake of avoiding the need for constant explanation at later stages, to attempt to define the customary British approach to this whole subject.

A satisfactory political system, in British eyes, is the offspring of a harmonious marriage between Law and Force. In our own country we take this fortunate union for granted. It is the essence of what we call British constitutionalism. By it is ensured the working of two processes, separable in theory for the analysis of the political scientist, but inextricably blended in practice, the observance of the law and the constant and steady development of the law, or, to use the language of post-war controversy, 'sanctions' and 'peaceful change'. Thus the judge, the legislator and the executive throughout its range, from the Prime Minister to the policeman, form interdependent parts of a single system.

This constitutional system does not function because it is wound up from outside or impelled from above. Its driving force is supplied from within. It derives its validity from consent: and its energy is constantly renewed and refreshed by contact with public opinion. It is the popular will which the legislator is seeking to embody in appropriate statutes. It is the popular will which the judge is engaged in interpreting and the policeman in enforcing. All three are performing what is felt to be a *social* function. They are adapting the organisation of the State, which is the most continuous and potent agency of social service in the community, to the permanent and changing needs of Society.

Seen as a part of this larger whole, law may be defined as social habit formulated into regulations. When these regulations, or any part of them, are felt to be anti-social—no longer in accordance with the general sentiment of the day, or even repugnant to it—

they are changed. Thus the notion of law and the notion of change, so far from being incompatible, are in fact complementary. The law is not a solid construction of dead material, a fixed and permanent monument: it is an integral part of a living and developing society created and transmitted by men—more like a tree than a table of stone. And it is because it is felt to have life in it, to be living with and through the society which it exists to serve, that it commands men's respect, their obedience, their loyalty and, if need be, their self-sacrifice.

Circumstances may indeed conceivably arise when this process of organic growth and peaceful change is arrested. Resistance may be offered to it by decaying and disintegrating elements within the society. The life of the tree may be obstructed by dead wood within or by parasites from without. In such a case, the organism, as we have described it, ceases to function. The constitutional system breaks down. What ensues is Revolution—in other words, War within the Society, Social War.

There is a school of thought which maintains that Social War is the chronic condition of mankind, that there has never been a harmonious society such as has been outlined in the preceding paragraphs, that constitutionalism is a figment of the imagination of liberal thinkers. We need not inquire into the truth or falsehood of their analysis as applied to societies in general, whether in the past or the present. All that we are concerned with here is to point out that British constitutionalism, the product of two and a half centuries of continuous and unbroken political and social development, is based upon the opposite assumption. It assumes the existence of a law-abiding society as the natural environment and necessary condition for the operation of law. This has never been better stated, in summary form, than in a brief essay which that great master of constitutional theory and practice, Lord Balfour, wrote towards the close of his life, after a considerable experience of the controversies of Geneva. 'Our alternating Cabinets', he there remarks, 'though belonging to different Parties, have never differed about the foundations of society. And it is evident that our whole political machinery presupposes a people so fundamentally at one that they can safely afford to bicker; and so sure of their own moderation that they are not dangerously disturbed by the never-ending din of political conflict. May it always be so!' [1]

Turn now to 'International Law'. What do we find? A situation almost exactly the opposite of what has just been described.

To begin with, where are we to look for the rules and obligations of International Law? We shall not find them embodied in the habits or the will, still less in the affections, of a society. The peoples of the world know little of them. International Law is remote both from their hearts and their minds. If we wish to discover where it is enshrined we must search the libraries. Its rules are recorded in books—in a succession of treatises extending over some three or more centuries.

When did these books begin to be written? Precisely at the time when the ancient constitution of Western Christendom had been disrupted, when respect for its authority in public affairs had disappeared and when, in the void thus created, there had supervened

[1] Introduction to Bagehot, *The English Constitution,* in the World's Classics edition (Oxford, 1928), p. xxiv.

sovereign states whose rulers gloried in their emancipation from the obligations of membership in a common Christian society and a Christian constitutional system.

International Law, in fact, is *a law without a constitution*. And since it is not grounded in a constitution, it lacks the possibility of natural growth. Unconnected with a *society*, it cannot adjust itself to its needs. It cannot gather itself together by imperceptible stages into a system. There is in fact, whatever the names used in the books, no *system* of international law—and still less, of course, a code. What is to be found in the treatises is simply a collection of rules which, when looked at closely, appear to have been thrown together, or to have been accumulated, almost at haphazard. Many of them would seem to be more appropriately described as materials for an etiquette book for the conduct of sovereigns and their representatives than as the elements of a true legal system.

The reason for this is very simple. The rules of international law, as they existed previous to 1914, were, with a few exceptions, not the outcome of the experience of the working of a world-society. They were simply the result of the contacts between a number of self-regarding political units—stars whose courses, as they moved majestically through a neutral firmament, crossed one another from time to time. The multiplication of these external impacts or collisions rendered it mutually convenient to bring their occasions under review and to frame rules for dealing with them.

The clearest evidence that modern international law was developed as a means for regulating external contacts rather than as an expression of the life of a true society is the large amount of space devoted to rules to be observed in time of war. Under a constitutional system the occurrence of social war is indeed not excluded: as we have seen, it always remains an ultimate possibility. But what would be thought of a statute-book nearly one-half of which was devoted to regulating the procedure of revolution? The fact that, from Grotius onward, so large a part of the labours of international lawyers has been expended on what are quaintly described as 'the laws of war' throws a glaring light on the inner contradiction which has vitiated the working of 'the Law of Nations'.

Why then, it may be asked, if international law, when its contents are analysed, turns out to be little more than a decorous name for a convenience of the Chancelleries, has it come to exercise any influence as such? How has it acquired such authority as it undoubtedly possesses in many quarters? Wherein consists the intellectual and moral ascendancy attained by Grotius and his successors? What is the secret of the appeal made by 'the Law of Nations' and of the hold which it has secured over men's minds, if not in Britain, at least in wide circles throughout the Continent? To answer these questions would be to write a lengthy chapter of the history of European thought. Put in a sentence, the explanation is that, since thought, like Nature, abhors a vacuum, men found in the conception of 'Natural Law', of which the international lawyers made use, a substitute for the Christian Law of the Middle Ages and for the Roman and Stoic Universalism which preceded it. 'Natural Law' was indeed not the law of a human society nor the command of an actual government. But it supplied a spiritual need. A great modern jurist, ex-President of the Permanent Court of International Justice, has compared it to the 'working hypothesis' of the scientist and described it as a 'temporary bridge' to carry men's minds across from mediaeval to modern conditions. Maine, writing before the necessity for an international constitutional system had become evident, uses harsher language. He calls it an eighteenth-century superstition—'a superstition of the lawyers' seized upon and promulgated by 'philosophers', 'in their eagerness to escape from what they deemed a superstition of the priests'.[1]

So far as the international lawyers themselves are concerned, Maine's criticism in the passage cited is less than fair. In spite of the misleading title of their subject, they have generally been fully conscious of its limitations. They have not needed to be reminded—in fact they have frequently had occasion to remind others—that the lawyer, whether on the bench or in the study, is not a statesman, still less a prophet. It is not for him to preach the need for a wider social consciousness or to propound practical solutions for the problems involved by the material interdependence of the modern world. His task arises at a later stage. It is a task of formulation, clarification and interpretation.

It is unfair to the men of the robe to set them in the forefront of the procession of history or to put watchwords in their mouths which lead men to claim from them more than they can give. It is their misfortune, not their fault, that the confusions and perplexities of

---

[1] Max Huber, *Die soziologischen Grundlagen des Völkerrechts*, 2nd ed. (Berlin, 1928), pp. 34-5; Maine, *Ancient Law*, chap. iv. (Routledge ed., p. 74). See also Barker, translation of Gierke's *Natural Law and the Theory of Society* (1934), p. xxxiv ff., and the lecture by Troeltsch in the same volume, p. 201 ff.; Brierly, *The Law of Nations* (1928), pp. 9-18; Cassirer, *Die Philosophie der Aufklärung* (1932), chap. vi., esp. p. 319 ff., and the present writer's paper on 'International Law and Social Consciousness' in the Grotius Society Transactions, vol. xx.

our time should have excited false hopes and led to a revival of superstition and even to the promulgation of what may not unfairly be described as substitute-religions in legal trappings—the adoration of the wig and gown.

CHAPTER X

THE HAGUE CONFERENCES

I

On August 24, 1898, the world was astonished to learn that the Tsar Nicholas II of Russia, through his Foreign Minister Count Mouravieff, had issued a circular letter to the principal governments denouncing war and the burden of armaments and proposing the summoning of a Conference on the subject.

We know to-day that the plan for a Conference originated, not in the idealism of the Russian monarch —though that was genuine enough in its own way— but in the difficulties of his Finance Minister Count Witte, who was unwilling to find the money for bringing the Russian artillery up to date. Two years before, the Russian consul at Buda-Pesth had been present as an observer at the annual Conference, held in that city, of the Inter-Parliamentary Union, an association composed of individual members from the parliaments of numerous countries. A discussion had taken place on the reduction of armaments by international agreement and the Russian observer had made a report on it to his official superiors. It was to the ideas in this report that Count Mouravieff had recourse as a way out of his colleague's perplexities.

The Conference met at The Hague and was in session from May 18 to June 29, 1899. It was a remarkable occasion, a sort of prologue to the Geneva meetings of the post-war era. For it brought together on a common platform representatives of three schools of thought who had for years past been working separately, approaching the problems of international politics from their own particular angle. At The Hague the Diplomats, the Lawyers and the Humanitarians or Pacifists—the latter term began to be used shortly after this date—came together for the first time. It was the dress rehearsal of Open Diplomacy. The Diplomats did not relish it. 'The shoal of telegrams, reports of proceedings of societies, hortatory letters, crankish proposals and peace pamphlets from America continue', wrote Andrew D. White, the United States Ambassador in Berlin, leader of the United States delegation at the Conference. If even the patience of this veteran Liberal and retired University president was ruffled, the feelings of the professionals may be imagined. 'The Conference', wrote Count Münster, one of the German delegates, 'has attracted here the political riff-raff of the whole world, journalists of the worst sort like Stead, baptized Jews like Bloch, woman peace agitators like Frau von Suttner, who gave a big dinner yesterday to the Russian delegation, Madame Salenko, etc. All this riff-raff (there are Young Turks and Armenians collaborating with them and socialists also) is openly working under Russian protection.'[1]

Such being the atmosphere of the Conference, it was hardly to be expected that its achievements would be considerable. The Tsar's message had proposed two topics for discussion—the reduction of armaments and

[1] For the above references see Halévy, *Épilogue*, i. pp. 60-61. The best short account of the Pacifist movement is Beales, *The History of Peace* (1931), with bibliography.

the peaceful settlement of international disputes. On the first of these—the real purpose of the meeting—the Conference proved a complete failure. Nothing whatever was achieved, save the expression of pious hopes. Seen in the light of the experience of Geneva, this is not surprising. The Russian Government indeed seems to have had no conception of the technical difficulties of the problem which they were casting into the arena. Not so the acute mind of Mr Balfour, who happened to be taking Lord Salisbury's work in the Foreign Office at the time. His first comment, in a dispatch to the British Ambassador at St. Petersburg sent a few days after the Tsar's original message, is worth quoting in its entirety for its almost uncanny foresight in formulating issues which have become familiar in the discussions of the last fifteen years.

The Marquess of Salisbury to Sir C. Scott.

FOREIGN OFFICE, *August* 30, 1898

Do you suppose Russian Government have thought out their own plan and have any definite scheme to lay before a Congress? Is the Congress to be allowed at the instance of one or of a majority of the Powers to discuss existing causes which might lead to hostilities, *e.g.* Alsace-Lorraine, Constantinople, Afghanistan, Egypt? Are armaments to be fixed according to area, population, or wealth or all three? Is the defensibility of a country or the reverse to be taken into account and if so who is to be the judge of it? If any country refuses to disarm, are the other countries to go to war with her in the interests of peace? These are not questions which you should press on Count Mouravieff without further instructions, but if informally any light could be thrown on them it would be desirable.

A. J. B.[1]

---

[1] *British Documents,* i. 215. Compare the Admiralty statement on p. 224.

Mr Balfour was no doubt unaware of the comment of Castlereagh when he was confronted with a similar scheme from the Tsar of that day, a personage even more cloudy than his successor. 'It is impossible not to perceive', he wrote, 'that the settlement of a scale of force for so many Powers, under such different circumstances as to their relative means, frontiers, positions and faculties for re-arming presents a very complicated question for negotiation; that the means of preserving a system, if once created, are not without their difficulties, liable as all states are to partial necessities for an increase of force; and it is further to be considered that on this, as on many subjects of a jealous character, in attempting to do too much, difficulties are rather brought into view than made to disappear.' [1]

Castlereagh's arguments 'put an end to serious discussion of the question' by the Congress powers. But the difficulties revealed at the first Hague Conference did not daunt those who, following the lead of the Tsar, had fixed on armaments as the principal target for crusaders in the field of international politics. A further attempt was made at the second Conference in 1907, with equal unsuccess. Then came the war—brought about, be it said in passing, not by competition in armaments but by political rivalries of which mounting armaments were the consequence and outward expression. It was in the summer of 1918, on the further shore of the Atlantic, as we shall see, that all-round 'disarmament', to give it its popular name, was again brought out into the arena of practical statesmanship. [2]

[1] Webster, p. 98.

[2] On the difficulties in which British Liberals involved themselves in 1907 by attempting to combine advocacy of 'disarmament' with the maintenance of British naval supremacy see Halévy, *Épilogue*, ii. p.

With the road to its major objective blocked, the first Hague Conference allowed itself to be diverted to the discussion of the 'laws of war'. It was agreed to apply the Red Cross Convention of 1864 to naval warfare and a Declaration, which reads strangely in the light of later events, was drawn up 'prohibiting the use of asphyxiating or deleterious gases'.

The main work of the Conference, however, as of that of its successor in 1907, was in the field of the peaceful settlement of international dispute.

Its proceedings on this subject cannot be made intelligible without a brief preliminary survey.

II

We saw in the last chapter how sovereign states, self-regarding though they were, became compelled, through their impacts upon one another, to enter into mutual engagements. Amongst these impacts there was a class or category which could be described as 'disputes'. A dispute, as between states, is a difference of opinion on a matter of policy which has not been overcome by the ordinary methods of diplomacy. Such a situation might lead, under the pre-war system, to war, in which case force would achieve for one of the parties what it had not been able to achieve by persuasion. But it might equally well happen that neither party desired to resort to force. In that case, since ordinary methods had failed, some extraordinary way of dealing with the matter must be found. This is the origin of Arbitration.

215 ff. and Woodward, *Great Britain and the German Navy* (1935), p. 103. So far as European waters are concerned, this inconsistency was continued into the post-war period.

The method of arbitration has its roots deep in history. It can be traced back to the Oriental monarchies and it was a familiar feature in the life of the Greek city-states. It was practised in the Middle Ages, in forms adapted to the conditions of the time, and was taken up again between the sovereigns of the post-mediaeval era. But its history in modern times dates from the year 1794, when it was applied to a dispute, or rather a series of disputes, of a particularly serious character, including the fixing of a frontier.

The initiative in this step forward in the use of arbitration came from the two English-speaking powers. The peace treaty following the War of American Independence had left several outstanding questions unsettled, including the boundary line between Canada and what a few years afterwards became the United States. Twelve years later, in 1794, largely through the activities of the United States Minister in London, John Jay, a treaty was signed between the two countries providing for the settlement of these questions by arbitration. The method adopted in the Jay Treaty was the setting up of Mixed Committees composed of an equal number of members chosen by each of the parties, with provision for an additional member, or super-arbiter, chosen by the members themselves in case of disagreement. The system adopted in the Jay Treaty gave excellent results. By 1804 all the outstanding questions were satisfactorily settled. Moreover, apart from the relations between the two countries concerned, the widening of the scope of official international relations by the use of this new method proved of permanent value. It had shown the helpfulness of supplementing the technique of diplomacy proper by bringing in new elements. The Mixed

Commission provided an opportunity for using the services both of *experts* and of *lawyers*—that is, of persons equipped with special knowledge not available to the ordinary diplomat and of persons with experience of the ordinary law and with an outlook akin to that of the judge.

Thus the Jay Treaty proved the forerunner of a large and steadily increasing number of cases submitted to arbitration in the course of the nineteenth century. It is, however, noticeable that the use of this method appealed particularly to the English-speaking countries and, in a lesser degree, to France: reasons of prestige, no doubt, prevented the autocracies from running the risk of an adverse decision.[1] Even in the English-speaking countries, however, the authorities preferred, as a general rule, to make use of the new method for questions of minor importance. There was a tendency to let larger questions lie dormant rather than to stir up feeling by submitting them to an arbitral decision. Thus the Oregon Boundary question—on which American public opinion expressed itself in the slogan 'Fifty-four Forty or Fight'—after lingering on for forty years, was eventually settled by direct negotiation in 1846, but a minor dispute which arose out of the

---

[1] The figures for the use of arbitration in the period between the Jay Treaty and 1914 are as follows:

Great Britain	. 71	Germany .	. 15*
U.S.A. .	. 69	Russia .	. 3
France .	. 33	Austria .	. 2
Italy .	. 19	Japan .	. 2

* Largely disputes between individual German states.

(from Politis, *La Justice internationale* (1924), p. 35). These figures are confined to the Great Powers: fuller details will be found in de Lapradelle and Politis, *Recueil des arbitrages internationaux*, Paris, 1905 (vol. i.) and 1923 (vol. ii.). There is a great increase in the figures for the second half of the century.

working of that treaty was submitted to arbitration.

All the more noteworthy was it that, in 1871, after long and complicated negotiations, the dispute arising out of the privateering activities of the *Alabama* and other vessels, which had caused intense irritation between the two countries throughout the previous decade, was submitted to an arbitral body. The *Alabama* case forms a landmark in the history of arbitration, both because of the political importance of the issue involved and because it led to the setting up of the first international tribunal of modern times. The tribunal consisted of one representative of each of the two parties together with three outsiders, a Brazilian, an Italian and a Swiss, chosen by their respective governments. The *Alabama* case gave a fillip to the movement in favour of arbitral methods and an increasing number of bilateral treaties providing for the use of these under particular circumstances were concluded during the succeeding quarter of a century. This tendency was strengthened by a movement emanating from the lawyers themselves. In 1873 there was formed an international association, a sort of academy, limited to the more eminent members of the confraternity, known as 'the Institute of Internatioual Law'. This body set itself at once to the task of interpreting the experience hitherto obtained in the field of arbitration and of clarifying it for future use. As early as 1875 it adopted and published a set of model rules for arbitral tribunals which, coming as they did from a body many of whose members were the habitual advisers of governments in these matters, attained considerable authority.[1]

---

[1] This document is conveniently reprinted in an appendix to Politis, *La Justice internationale*, Paris, 1924.

III

Such was the background against which the first Hague Conference faced the second item on its agenda —the peaceful settlement of disputes. Here, in contrast to the problem of disarmament, the conditions were ripe for a move forward.

Progress was achieved in two directions. The first was the setting-up of what was called the Permanent Court of Arbitration at The Hague. The title (as so often in this record) is misleading. What was done was to provide a *permanent framework for* ad hoc *tribunals*, which, as a great jurist remarked shortly afterwards, was a much wiser and more practical measure at that stage than the setting up of a Permanent Court.[1] This framework consisted of a body of rules, a list of suitable arbitrators available for the choice of the parties and a permanent office or secretariat for the keeping of archives and the receipt of applications and other correspondence.

The rules were inspired by the Institute scheme already referred to. Their underlying principle is stated in the opening words: 'International arbitration has for its object the settlement of differences between states by judges of their own choice, and on the basis of respect for law'. The wording makes it clear that the states, in their sovereignty, are free to choose their own arbitrators. What is being set up, therefore, is not a Court, as we understand it, but a temporary body, different in each case, and composed according to the inclinations of the parties. On the other hand,

---

[1] Louis Renault in his noteworthy preface to vol. i. of de Lapradelle and Politis, 1905.

the reader will have noted how the phraseology of law has here insinuated itself into the arbitral process. These *ad hoc* arbitrators are described as 'judges' and their duty is to settle the dispute 'on the basis of respect for law', a phrase which may be interpreted either narrowly (as referring to the rules of international law) or broadly (as meaning peaceful settlement as opposed to warfare). These ambiguities we shall have occasion to encounter again.

How was the list of suitable arbitrators arrived at? Through the choice of the governments. The Hague Convention lays it down that 'each Signatory Power shall select four persons at the most, of known competency in questions of international law, of the highest moral reputation and disposed to accept the duties of Arbitrators'. The persons thus selected are called 'the Members of the Court'. The constitution by treaty of this highly qualified, if widely scattered, body of potential arbitrators has proved more useful than was foreseen by anyone in 1899. The Convention provided that each party was to select two arbitrators from the list and that these four would then choose a fifth.

The permanent machinery set up was of the simplest character. A 'Secretary-general' and a miniature staff sufficed: in 1933 it consisted in all of five persons, all of them Dutch, though they might, of course, have been drawn from any of the signatory states. But even a miniature organisation requires supervision, and for this an important principle was adopted. Its management was entrusted to a Permanent Administrative Council, composed of the diplomatic representatives of the signatory powers accredited to the Netherlands Government—in other words, to a Committee of Diplomats.

It may be convenient at this point to describe briefly how this new institution worked in practice. Four cases were brought under it between 1899 and the second Hague Conference in 1907; eleven, including one of considerable political importance between France and Germany, between 1907 and 1914. Three cases have so far come before it in the post-war period, when, as we shall see, its opportunity for usefulness has been considerably circumscribed.[1]

The second direction in which an advance was made at the first Hague Conference was in defining and facilitating methods of intervention by third or outside parties in disputes between states.

In discussing the origin of the practice of arbitration we saw that it was adopted by sovereign states on their own initiative and to suit their own self-regarding convenience. We described them as planets proceeding on their own courses in a neutral firmament. But the firmament of international politics is not an uninhabited void. It is peopled by other states and their citizens. It is, at least in embryo, a community. The outbreak of hostilities between any two powers cannot leave other states unaware or indifferent. Thus it is natural for them on their side—or for some amongst them, who are in the best position to do so—to take an initiative of their own with a view to bringing the conflict to an end. To such initiatives international lawyers have attached the names of 'Good Offices' and 'Mediation'.

But to offer 'good offices' or 'mediation' as between two sovereign states engaged in settling a 'private'

---

[1] The best account of the Permanent Court of Arbitration is to be found in the first part of Manley O. Hudson, *The Permanent Court of International Justice*, 1934. For the details of organisation see p. 7 ff.

quarrel by force of arms was liable, under the traditional system, to lay a third party open to the charge of impertinent interference. It was this point that the Hague Convention took up. It placed the practice of mediation upon an agreed basis. In other words, it recognised the principle that an outbreak of war between two states was a matter of legitimate concern for all other states and provided certain facilities for their intervention. The exact point reached, as regards this intervention, under the two Hague Conventions can best be made clear by quoting the opening articles of the section dealing with 'Good Offices and Mediation':

In case of serious disagreement or dispute, before an appeal to arms, the Signatory Powers agree to have recourse, as far as circumstances allow, to the good offices or mediation of one or more friendly Powers.

Independently of this recourse, the Signatory Powers deem it expedient [the 1907 text adds 'and desirable'] that one or more Powers, strangers to the dispute, should on their own initiative and as far as circumstances may allow, offer their good offices or mediation to the States at variance.

Powers, strangers to the dispute, have the right to offer good offices or mediation, even during the course of hostilities.

The exercise of this right can never be regarded by either of the parties at variance as an unfriendly act.

The part of the mediator consists in reconciling the claims and appeasing the feelings of resentment which may have arisen between the States at variance.

The duties of the mediator are at an end when once it is declared, either by one of the parties to the dispute, or by the mediator himself, that the means of reconciliation proposed by him are not accepted.

Good offices and mediation, undertaken either at the request of the parties to the dispute or on the initiative of Powers, strangers to the dispute, have exclusively the character of advice and never have binding force.

I

The acceptance of mediation cannot, unless there be an agreement to the contrary, have the effect of interrupting, delaying or hindering mobilisation or other measures of preparation for war.

If mediation takes place after the commencement of hostilities the military operations in progress are not interrupted in the absence of an agreement to the contrary.

One other achievement in this field lies to the credit of the Hague Conferences. They devised and developed the technique of Commissions of Inquiry. The initiative in this matter came from one of the Russian delegates, M. de Martens, a most diligent worker in the field of international law. His suggestion was that there was room, in connexion with disputes, side by side with arbitral bodies of the now familiar type, for bodies of a purely fact-finding character. As a result, the 1899 Conference included in the Convention provisions for the appointment of 'International Commissions of Inquiry' and declared that it was 'expedient' that they should be made use of in disputes, 'involving neither honour nor vital interests', 'arising from a difference of opinion on points of fact'.

The adoption of this scheme proved unexpectedly fortunate. For in 1904 a serious dispute, turning precisely upon such a point of fact, arose between Great Britain and Russia when the Russian fleet, passing through the North Sea on its way from the Baltic to the Far East, fired on a number of British vessels fishing on the Dogger Bank. For a few days indignation and excitement in Britain were intense; but on a suggestion from London the Tsar took the initiative in proposing the use of the new machinery and the inquiry led to the award of substantial damages to the injured parties. It led also to considerable improvements in the procedure for such Commissions in the revised Convention of 1907.

Apart from this, the work of the Second Conference can be passed over in a few words. The years between 1899 and 1907 were a time of steady deterioration in international relations. The South African War, the Russo-Japanese War and the gathering of the European powers into two sharply divided camps had made the achievements of the first Conference seem very small in retrospect. The second Conference was due to the initiative of President Theodore Roosevelt, after his successful intervention as a mediator in the Russo-Japanese War. Its actual summoning, however, was left to the Tsar. Its labours were mainly devoted to the subject of the 'laws' of naval warfare. It adopted a convention, much acclaimed by pacifist opinion at the time, prohibiting the bombardment of unfortified cities and ports by naval forces. It attempted to set up an International Prize Court to replace the national tribunals which had hitherto had the duty of applying the rules of international law on this subject. But the attempt broke down as, for obvious reasons, it was difficult to arrive at an agreement on the principles according to which the proposed court should function. A special Conference was held later, in 1908, to try to clear up this problem. It led to the drawing up of a declaration, known as the Declaration of London, on the vexed subject of 'contraband of war'. This provoked a controversy in Great Britain between those who favoured arrangements based on Britain's probable neutrality in future wars and those who looked forward to her needing to put out her full sea-power as a belligerent. As a neutral, Britain's interest would be to encourage non-interference with cargoes: as a belligerent her interest would be in the opposite sense. A debate in the House of Lords, ending in a vote hostile to the Declaration, turned the scales and the Declaration was not ratified by the Government.[1]

Two other activities of the 1907 Conference must be briefly mentioned. An attempt was made to establish a Permanent Court of International Justice, with a regular bench of judges. But, mainly owing to the presence of the Latin American states (who were invited in 1907 for the first time), no agreement could be reached on the method of appointment of the judges.

On the other hand, the Conference was more successful in a minor field—the regulation of the use of force for the recovery of contract debts. This was a problem which particularly affected the Latin American states. They came to The Hague mindful of the combined blockade of Venezuela in 1902 by the fleets of Great Britain, Germany and Italy, for the recovery of certain debts owing to their nationals. Dr. Drago, the Argentine Foreign Minister had already in that year, in a dispatch to the Argentine minister at Washington, sought to make use of the Monroe Doctrine as a safeguard against outside interference of this kind. His idea had been taken up by the Third Pan-American Congress held in Rio de Janeiro in 1906 and was brought on thence to the Hague. 'A public debt', so ran the formula, 'cannot give rise to the right of intervention: much less to the occupation of the soil of any American nation by any European power.' The Conference refused to accept the 'Drago Doctrine' in this form, but adopted an intermediate

---

[1] See Halévy, *Épilogue*, ii. p. 214 ff., an article in *The Round Table*, March 1912, and Guichard, *The Naval Blockade, 1914-1918* (English translation, 1930), p. 16 ff.

solution ruling out armed intervention until after the
debtor country had either refused arbitration or failed
to carry out the arbitral award. In this way a considerable success was achieved for the principle of
arbitration: for, in effect, debtors would be almost
compelled to make use of it in the circumstances envisaged by Dr. Drago.

IV

Before we leave this subject one question remains to
be answered. Why was none of this machinery put into
motion in 1914? The answer is that, on the side of one
of the parties, there was not the willingness to make
use of it. In such circumstances the most perfect
machinery is powerless. The machinery available for
use in 1914 was not perfect. But it was sufficient for
the immediate purpose.

There was indeed no need in 1914 to employ any of
the expedients described in this chapter. The method
of the Concert by itself would have been enough. It
was in virtue of the Concert, of her rights derived from
the Final Act of the Treaty of Vienna, that Great
Britain intervened at the beginning of the crisis. Those
rights were not dormant. They had never been so
strongly asserted as in Mr Lloyd George's Mansion
House speech during the Agadir crisis of 1911. It was
casting a red herring across the trail for the German
Secretary of State for Foreign Affairs to characterise
Sir Edward Grey's proposal of a Conference as a suggestion for a Court of Arbitration.[1] There was no

---

[1] *British Documents*, xi. 128 (July 27): the German Chancellor's
expression was 'Areopagus' (p. 164: 'an Areopagus consisting of two
Powers of each group sitting in judgment on the two remaining Powers').
See also Grey, *Twenty-five Years*, i. 319-20.

question of a Commission of Inquiry. As for mediation, it was already provided for, so far as the European Great Powers were concerned, under the Concert system.

There was, however, one Great Power which needed the authority provided by the Hague Convention in order to mediate without incurring the charge of uncalled-for interference. This was the United States. On July 29, 1914, the Secretary of State informed the British Government of his readiness to tender his good offices, as provided for in the Convention. Sir Edward Grey could only tell him that 'hitherto all suggestions of mediation in the dispute between Austria and Serbia, which was at the root of the European difficulties, had been refused'. Early in August, after hostilities had broken out, the United States Senate passed a resolution requesting the President once more to use his good offices. On this occasion the President made his approach direct to the King, as one official head of a Hague Signatory Power to another. Mr Walter Hines Page, the United States Ambassador in London, to whom it fell to deliver the message to His Majesty, has left an account of his interview on that occasion. The King was broken-hearted but helpless. Things took their course as though the Hague Conference had never met. It was not lack of machinery which permitted the war to break out. The war-making forces simply swept the machinery out of their course. Not that machinery is valueless—far from that—but it is not the determining factor. The determining factor is *the will to co-operate*.[1]

[1] On the above see *British Documents*, xi. 169, 229, 292; and the index, p. 384, under 'Germany: Mediation', where the relevant references are conveniently collected. Also Hendrick, *Life of Walter Hines Page* (1922), p. 309 (one volume ed:).

CHAPTER XI

OUR description of pre-war conditions will not be complete without an account of certain events which took place in the United States following on the Hague Conference of 1907.

Methods for the peaceful settlement of international disputes had always been a matter of special interest to the government and people of the United States. The principle of arbitration, as we have seen, was bound up with the carrying-out of the treaty which consummated their independent status, and they had made constant use of it throughout the nineteenth century. It was natural, therefore, that progressively minded leadership in the United States should look for possibilities of advance in this field.

In 1909 President Taft succeeded Theodore Roosevelt at the White House. Taft was a jurist by training and a man of high ideals and noble purposes. He was eager to signalise his tenure of the Presidency by manifesting some striking advance by the United States along the road indicated by the Hague Conferences. He was, in fact, to adapt an expression used of Mr Gladstone, 'a lawyer in a hurry'.

The line of advance which Taft planned was that of *compulsory arbitration*. To make clear the issues involved in this we must once more interrupt our narrative in order to make a wider survey.

I

We have already noted that, as a result of the *Alabama* arbitration, there was a great increase, in the closing quarter of the nineteenth century, in bilateral arbitration treaties—that is, treaties between individual countries providing means for the peaceful settlement of their mutual disputes.

These treaties represented an advance on the method adopted for the *Alabama* case. On that occasion an *ad hoc* treaty had been made between Great Britain and the United States, dealing with that one particular issue. But this led to the natural question: Why not make a general treaty, apart from the circumstances of each particular case, providing means for peaceful settlement? Why not create a *framework*, as between any two countries, in order to facilitate the settlement of their mutual disputes if and when they occur? This could be done, for instance, by setting up joint boards of arbitrators or conciliators ready to act when called upon.

This need, however, was to some extent met by the Hague Convention of 1899, which provided a *general framework*, with facilities not for the use of two particular countries but for all countries who cared to sign the convention. Thus we already see, at this stage, what became much more important under post-war conditions, the distinction between *bilateral* and *multilateral* arrangements for peaceful settlement.

Once embarked on this bilateral method a further

question soon suggested itself to the legal mind. Why
should the framework remain bare and empty? Why
should it not, at least to some extent, be filled in?
Why not clothe the skeleton with at any rate a minimum of flesh and blood? In other words, why not
discover some *class of disputes* which the two states
would *promise in advance* to submit to the procedure
provided in the treaty?

But *what class* of disputes, the diplomats would immediately ask, would it be safe to hand over, *en bloc*,
to an arbitral body? The lawyers had a ready answer:
legal disputes. But what is a legal dispute? Here the
Hague Convention came to the rescue. In providing its
general framework for arbitration it had made a recommendation as to its use. 'In questions of a legal nature,'
so runs the Article, 'and especially in the interpretation or application of International Conventions,
arbitration is recognised by the Signatory Powers as
the most effective and at the same time the most
equitable means of settling disputes which diplomacy
has failed to settle.'

Here is what may be called a minimum definition of
a legal dispute. If nothing else can be agreed upon to
be a legal dispute, *at least* a dispute as to the interpretation or application of a treaty comes undeniably under
that description. This provided a starting-point for the
process of clothing the skeleton. It began to be customary to include in bilateral arbitration treaties a clause
providing that disputes arising out of the interpretation or application of that particular treaty should
be submitted to arbitration. And from this it was but
a step to extend the practice to 'legal disputes' as a
whole. Thus it became common to provide for the
settlement by arbitration 'of differences which may

arise of a legal nature or relating to the interpretation of treaties'—that is, not of that particular treaty but of all treaties between the two parties in question.

But at this stage the diplomats took alarm. The lawyers with their foibles were entering upon dangerous ground. Who could foresee what issues might not be involved in the interpretation of the letter of a treaty, perhaps concluded by a political negotiator careless in his use of legal terms? Moreover, who was to decide whether a dispute was 'of a legal nature' or not? To leave that decision to the arbitral body might lead to disagreeable surprises. Thus the Foreign Offices, watchful of the interests of their countries, felt it necessary to provide against the possible danger involved by the promise to submit to arbitration any *class* of dispute, however innocent in appearance. They did this by the introduction of a safeguarding formula. This was generally conceived in some such terms as these: 'provided that they (the differences to which the pledge to arbitrate is applied) do not affect the vital interests, the independence or the honour of the two Contracting Parties and do not concern the interests of third parties'.

It will be perceived that this proviso is so drawn up as to cover exactly the questions out of which serious controversies and hence wars are most likely to arise. In other words, the diplomats would not allow the lawyers to *bind* their countries to arbitration on a *class* of questions involving the issue of peace and war. In fact, they were determined, in spite of the lawyers, to treat arbitration as a secondary convenience and to keep its use firmly under their own control.

It was this control, this hedging in by the diplomats of the field of compulsory arbitration, which President

Taft was determined to resist. Before, however, we examine the means that he adopted, let us set out clearly the issue of principle involved.

What President Taft was anxious to do was to apply to disputes between states the same procedure *at every stage* as is applied in disputes between individual citizens within a state. He looked forward to the establishment of a Judicial System for the Family of States and his practical proposals were designed as a first step to that end. There is no doubt that this was his objective, for he states it quite clearly in a book written after he had retired from office and published on the eve of the war. The language that he there uses is so remarkable, especially as coming from a man who had been Chief Executive of a Great Power, that the crucial passage must be quoted in full:

'The ideal that I would aim at is an arbitral court in which any nation could make complaint against any other nation, and if the complaint is found by the court to be within its jurisdiction, the nation complained against should be summoned, the issue framed by pleadings, and the matter disposed of by judgment. It would, perhaps, sometimes require an international police force to carry out the judgment, but the public opinion of nations would accomplish much. With such a system we would count on a gradual abolishment of armaments and a feeling of the same kind of security that the United States and Canada have to-day which makes armaments and navies on our northern border entirely unnecessary.' [1]

It is difficult to read these lines without a feeling of

[1] *The United States and Peace* (1914), p. 131. The passage quoted is the conclusion of a chapter entitled 'Arbitration Treaties that Mean Something'.

dizziness. It is not that the ideal at the back of the writer's mind, the establishment of a Rule of Law for the world, is either unworthy or unattainable. It is that the method of procedure is—no other word seems appropriate—so topsy-turvy. It is as though the ex-President or, to call him by a title far more fitting for his equipment, the Chief Justice of the Supreme Court of the United States, were looking out into the future through a microscope attached to the end of a telescope. The essential factors are ignored, or introduced airily by the way, whilst the unessential or the consequential is placed in the centre of the picture. Mr Taft's vision is concentrated on a bench of judges, modelled, no doubt, on the Supreme Court of the United States. Before them are haled the mighty of the earth, the Great Powers in all their haughtiness. They are given a fair trial, according to the recognised American or Anglo-Saxon procedure, and 'the matter is disposed of by judgment'. But the losing party is recalcitrant. He is not inclined to pay the penalty. So the judge looks round for the sheriff and the sheriff requisitions the services of the 'international police force', whilst 'the public opinion of nations' manifests its approval. And *then*, when this 'system' has been for some time in operation, the world will enjoy security and armaments will dwindle to North American proportions.

It is obvious, of course, in the light of later events, that President Taft, in his whole approach to the problems of international politics, was beginning at the wrong end. His 'ideal', closely examined, is not a world community living under the rule of law. It is a fraction of a system of World-government set up in a void. It is a Judicature without a Legislature, with

only so much of an Executive as is needed to enforce
the decisions of the Bench, and with no social system
or social consciousness to rest upon. The Bench of Mr
Taft's imagination would have no law to administer.
It would not even be *part* of a constitutional system.
It would be an array of wigs and gowns vociferating in
emptiness.

II

In the light of this wider strategy it is not difficult to
understand the actual proposals put forward. President
Taft and his Secretary of State Mr Knox set as their
immediate objective the conclusion of two general
arbitration treaties—one with Great Britain, whose
Ambassador at that time was James Bryce, the other
with France. The special feature of these draft treaties
was that they contained *no reservations whatsoever*. The
parties agreed to submit *all* disputes not settled by
diplomacy to the specified procedures.

What were these procedures? The first, through
which all disputes were required to pass, was a Joint
High Commission of Inquiry. This was to be specially
constituted for each occasion and was to consist of six
members, three nominated by each side.

This Commission was modelled on the Hague body
of this type, which had proved so useful in the Dogger
Bank incident. But its functions were significantly
enlarged. It was no longer to be confined simply to
fact-finding. It was to be 'authorised'—the precise
words are too important not to be quoted—'to examine into and report upon the particular questions
or matters referred to it, for the purpose of facilitating
the solution of disputes by elucidating the facts and

to define the issues presented by such questions and *also to include in its report such recommendations and conclusions as may be appropriate'.*[1] Here are indicated two further duties beyond the elucidation of the facts of the dispute—the duty of *appreciating* or *interpreting* the facts and that of *drawing conclusions* from them, in the form of recommendations. The limits of 'inquiry' were thus substantially enlarged. On the other hand, the Commission was not allowed to go a step beyond the advisory function. Its members were to be in no sense arbitrators. Its reports, so runs the text, 'shall not be regarded as *decisions*[1] of the question or matters so submitted, either on the facts or on the law, and shall in no way have the character of an arbitral award'.

Nevertheless, on one all-important point the Commission was to be allowed to take a decison. This was no less than the question as to whether a particular dispute was, or was not, of a legal character. If five of its six members were in agreement as to the legal character of a dispute, their opinion was binding and the matter went forward from the Joint High Commission to a body of arbitrators. In that event, the decision of the arbitrators was final. There was no escape from it.

Disputes not thus declared to be of a legal nature went no further than the Joint High Commission, whose recommendations might or might not be adopted.

It will be seen that, under this scheme, Mr Taft attained his object. He had broken down the impermeable hedge set up by the diplomats and made it possible for one class of disputes to reach an arbitration board without the appeal to 'honour' or 'vital interests' in individual cases. It was a narrow pathway that was thus opened by the five-to-one majority

---

[1] Italics inserted.

on the High Commission. But the Foreign Offices would no longer control the entrance gate.

It is an unusual thing for a lawyer, with an outlook like that of Mr Taft, to be the Chief Executive of a Great Power. In that position he was able to overrule the diplomats—at any rate on his side of the water. It might therefore fairly have been expected that he would have been allowed to take this first modest step to the distant goal of his judicial paradise—all the more so as the British and French governments had decided to stifle the misgivings of their respective Foreign Offices. But relief came to the hard-pressed diplomats from an unexpected quarter. The United States Senate rallied to their rescue. When the draft treaties reached the Foreign Relations Committee of the Senate, where Henry Cabot Lodge was already entrenched, they were riddled with reservations. Immigration, State debts, the Monroe Doctrine all figured in the record. The treaties emerged from the Senate in so emasculated a form that their author decided to withdraw what was left of them. He was not the man to sponsor a make-believe.[1]

III

After the Lawyer, the Orator. In 1913 Woodrow Wilson became President of the United States with

---

[1] It should be noted that the draft treaties did not actually speak of 'legal' but of 'justiciable' disputes. This was a term of American jurisprudence which Mr Taft adopted deliberately for use in the international field. (See *The United States and Peace*, pp. 106-7.) It is defined in the treaties as meaning 'capable of judicial solution by the application of the principles of law or equity'. For a thoroughgoing criticism of the distinction between legal and non-legal issues see Lauterpacht, *The Function of Law in the International Community*, 1933.

William Jennings Bryan as his Secretary of State.
Mr Bryan, however, was not only an orator but a
politician. Thus, having evolved his own peace treaties,
he was able to see them through the Senate. And the
treaties in question were not, like Mr Taft's, a mere
meagre brace but a whole bevy, some thirty in all. Let
us examine their contents.

The Bryan treaties were not, strictly speaking, arbitration treaties. They contained no provisions for
arbitration at all. They were simply treaties for the
setting up of standing International Commissions of
Inquiry. The two parties to each treaty agree to establish such a Commission, composed of five members.
Each side chooses one national and one non-national,
and the fifth member, also a citizen of a third state, is
chosen by common agreement between the parties.
The treaties were concluded for a period of five years:
they were, however, to remain in force at the end of
that time subject to a twelve-month's notice of withdrawal from either side. Many of them are still in force.
There is, however, continual difficulty in preventing the
ranks of the Commissioners from becoming depleted.[1]

As in the case of the Taft treaties, all disputes of
every kind not settled by diplomacy are submitted to
Inquiry. Moreover, perhaps as a help to the weaker
party in a diplomatic negotiation, the Commissions
were empowered to offer their services, should their
members be unanimous, even *before* the failure of
diplomatic negotiations. But they were not empowered
to do more than to issue a report, normally before the
end of twelve months. The parties were not bound to

---

[1] In 1926 only three of the thirty treaties had their Commissions
properly constituted and in 1930, when the United States side was
complete, only six. See Sir John Fischer Williams in *International
Affairs*, x. 336 (May 1931).

act upon it. On the contrary, they remained at liberty to take such action as they might 'think fit'.

Here was no attempt to secure *decisions* on matters on which, according to the diplomats and the Senate, decisions might be disagreeable or dangerous. Hence the easy passage of the treaties. On the other hand, they contained certain novel features.

One of these was the introduction of a so-called 'cooling-off period' or 'moratorium for war'. The parties pledged themselves not to go to war for a period of twelve months, while the dispute was under inquiry. The idea behind this provision was that, since wars were the product of passion and 'hot blood', the year's delay would promote appeasement, so that at the end of the time the matters at issue would yield to reasonable treatment. We shall encounter again this optimistic theory, together with the devices of Inquiry and Delay with which it is associated.

Mr Bryan was, however, not satisfied with these merely negative provisions. As a crusader for disarmament he wished to find some way of embodying this theme also in his treaties. He therefore inserted in some of them a provision for an Armaments Truce or Holiday. The parties agreed 'not to increase their naval and military forces during the inquiry, except in the event of an increase becoming necessary owing to danger emanating from a third power'. But this proposition seemed to the Senate too dangerous— or perhaps merely too inconvenient; at any rate, it disappeared before ratification. The draft treaties in which it had been inserted were those with Salvador, Guatemala, Panama, Honduras and Persia.

Nevertheless Mr Bryan did not altogether fail in his attempt to secure recognition for the principle of

K

disarmament. Two treaties, those with France and
Sweden, contained provisions empowering the Commission to recommend the taking of precautionary
measures designed to maintain intact the rights of the
parties pending the conclusion of the Commission's
report. This idea, as we shall see, was destined to bear
fruit at Geneva.[1]

IV

Mr Bryan became Secretary of State on March 4,
1913. His treaties were drafted and negotiated during
the next twelve months. Then came the business of
securing signatures and ratifications. Thus in July 1914
he was busily engaged in what may be described as the
process of autograph-hunting. He was pressing foreign
powers to expedite the stages of his work of peace. He
did not allow events on the other side of the Atlantic
to divert him from his task.

Arrangements had been made in the early part of
July for the British and French treaties to be signed on
the same day, and signature was only delayed for a
few weeks for the document to be communicated to
the Dominions. Much happened during those weeks:
but the two treaties were duly signed early in September. On August 17 Mr Bryan sent a telegram to Berlin.
Eighteen treaties, he said, had been ratified by the
Senate on the previous Thursday: four more would
follow in a few days. The British and French treaties
were due for signature at an early date. Would not the
German Government follow suit? 'It would', he added,

---

[1] A useful analysis of the provisions of the Bryan treaties will be found
in Vulcan, *La Conciliation dans le droit international actuel* (Paris, 1932),
pp. 26-32.

'be a great triumph in diplomacy if it could be so arranged that the treaty with Germany could be signed on the same day as the British and French.' But the German Government's attention was concentrated on other 'triumphs'. Less circumspect, or perhaps less long-suffering, than the British and French Foreign Offices, the Germans turned a deaf ear to the suggestion. Four days later, on August 21, a curt message was received from the United States Embassy in Berlin: 'Sorry to report no hope peace treaty'.

Thus it came about that, during the two controversies which were carried on simultaneously between Washington and London and between Washington and Berlin throughout the two following years and more, Great Britain enjoyed the benefit of the year's respite provided by the Bryan Treaty, whilst the United States was free to declare war at any moment on the German Government, which she eventually did. This consideration undoubtedly influenced the authorities in Washington, both civil and military, who were directly concerned with British-American relations. But it exercised no influence whatsoever on the general situation. For the public on either side of the Atlantic the treaty was non-existent. Had the controversy on neutral rights been so handled by the British Cabinet as to inflame American feeling to the point of demanding a rupture, it is, to say the least, extremely doubtful whether the provision for the 'cooling-off period' would have stood the strain. Mr Bryan, it must be remembered, left office in 1915.

But it is the correspondence with the Belgian Government which throws the most vivid light on this strange encounter between the self-centred Crusader and inexorable Reality. On September 15, 1914, Mr

Bryan telegraphed to the United States Minister in Brussels, Mr Brand Whitlock — a name that will always be remembered in Brussels — the following routine dispatch:

'We have just signed treaties with Great Britain, France, Spain and China. These, with the twenty-two previously signed, connect this Government with more than two-thirds of the population of the globe by peace treaties which provide for investigation in all cases before hostilities can be commenced. Please say to the sovereign to whom you are accredited that this Government will be pleased to make a similar treaty with him.—W. J. BRYAN.'

'The sovereign', though Mr Bryan had overlooked the fact, was not in Brussels. King Albert was elsewhere, and otherwise engaged. Two months therefore elapsed before the telegram could be answered. The Minister preferred to send it by mail, in the diplomatic bag, so that it was not received in Washington till December 7. Here is the document in the form in which it is reproduced in the recently published American State papers:

File No. 711,0012/593.

The Minister in Belgium (Whitlock)
to the Secretary of State.
(No. 12)

AMERICAN LEGATION
BRUSSELS, *November* 16, 1914
(Received *December* 7)

MY DEAR MR SECRETARY,
Referring to your telegram of August 17, 7 P.M.,[1] expressing the hope that the Belgian Government would be prepared to sign a treaty similar to that already negotiated with the Netherlands Government, I beg to transmit herewith enclosed for your

[1] Evidently a communication previous to the routine telegram of September 15.

information, copy of the correspondence on the subject with the Belgian Government.

While, previous to the war, the Belgian Government had shown interest in these treaties, it was, upon the outbreak of hostilities and during its subsequent movement from place to place, so overtaxed and hurried, that, as the Minister for Foreign Affairs said, he had not the time for the calm and careful consideration which he would feel obliged to give to a matter of such a character.

In view of the circumstances I have not insisted further and shall not again take up the matter unless you desire me to do so.

I am (etc.),

BRAND WHITLOCK

This admirable specimen of the traditional forms of the Old Diplomacy, in all its reserve and correctitude, may fitly conclude our survey of the pre-war system.[1]

[1] For the documents referred to in the above paragraphs see *Papers relating to the Foreign Relations of the United States* (1914, Supplement: 'The World War'), pp. 3-11.

PART II

THE ELEMENTS OF THE COVENANT

CHAPTER I

THE WAR-TIME LEAGUE

IN July 1914, as we have seen, Sir Edward Grey was looking forward to an *improved Concert of Europe*, an idea which he said had hitherto been 'Utopian'. In 1919 the British and other governments adopted a plan, in the shape of the League of Nations, which was an improved Concert of Europe and very much more besides. The reason for this remarkable change of outlook, this rapid stride forward in political thinking, this revolution in the estimate of what was both practicable and desirable, is to be found in the war.

'War', said the Greek historian over two thousand years ago, 'is a forcible teacher.' The Great War taught the world the lesson of interdependence. It taught it by two methods at once. By its destructiveness, by its overthrow of all that had hitherto been regarded as stable in international politics, it compelled men to seek for new and surer forms of organisation. And at the same time by the associated effort which it called out for its own purposes it provided working models for the peace-time machinery of the future.

Our first task, then, is to examine these models: for unless we have them before our eyes we shall not understand what was in the minds of those who set themselves to the later task. It must never be forgotten that the Covenant was drawn up by men filled with the recent experience of the war. It affected different minds in different ways: but it deeply affected them all.

The war, seen from the angle of the student of political machinery, was a vast international enterprise—an enterprise, that is, carried on simultaneously by a number of independent governments. It was inevitable, therefore, that very soon the need should be felt for some method of collaboration more efficient for war purposes than the normal diplomatic machine. The problems involved were at once too *numerous*, too *varied*, too *technical* and too *urgent* to be disposed of in this way. A new and more expeditious technique was called for. The device adopted in the field of high policy was that of *Conference between heads of governments*. Thus in July 1915 there took place the first of a series of such special Conferences, arranged in order to secure a decision on a particular problem or set of problems. Those present at these Conferences were the British and French Prime Ministers together with the other Ministers specially concerned.

But something more was soon found to be needed. In January 1916, therefore, Mr Asquith put forward to M. Briand, the French Premier, the proposal that these special Conferences should be given a regular organisation. He suggested that there should be a standing inter-Allied Committee composed of the Prime Ministers and such other Ministers and experts as were needed, with a secretariat of its own. In other words, he wished to bring into existence a body composed of Prime Ministers, other Ministers, generals, admirals and civilian officials in key positions.

The origin of this proposal is not far to seek. It was modelled on the British Committee of Imperial Defence.

The Committee of Imperial Defence dates back to

the year 1895. It took its rise from the custom, which
still continues, of appointing special Committees of the
Cabinet to consider and report on particular questions.
In 1895 it was decided to institutionalise, or make permanent, one of these Committees—that concerned
with problems of defence. It was provided with a regular membership, composed of the Prime Minister, the
Secretary of State for War, the First Lord of the
Admiralty and their chief professional advisers. After
the South African War, in 1904, this Committee was
revived and reorganised by Mr Balfour. It was given
the title of 'The Committee of Imperial Defence' and
provided with a permanent secretariat. Its membership
was at the same time enlarged to include representation
from the India Office and the Colonial Office. During
the Imperial Defence Conference of 1909 and the Imperial Conference of 1911, the Prime Ministers of the
Dominions were invited to join the Committee, as had
indeed been in Mr Balfour's mind already in 1904.

Thus in 1914 there existed in Great Britain *a standing
body on which the responsible Ministers of a number of
governments were accustomed to sit together.* Moreover,
this Committee included professional advisers or experts, and it was equipped with a permanent secretariat.

We have here a combination of two of the forms
of international organisation that we have already
examined—the European Concert and the Postal
Union. In so far as the Committee of Imperial Defence
was a Committee containing representatives of several
governments, it resembled the Concert: but it was *a
Concert with a Secretariat.* In so far as it was a Committee composed of the professional advisers of several
governments, it resembled the Postal Union Congress,

which, as it will be recalled, quickly developed a permanent secretariat of its own.

Mr Asquith's plan was not adopted in the form in which he put it forward. The standing body was created, but without a secretariat. The new system was first put into effect at a Conference held in Paris in March 1916. On this occasion the Prime Ministers of Great Britain, France, Italy, Belgium and Serbia were present. They did not, however, themselves thresh out the military problems together with the group of professionals. This, no doubt, was felt to be too difficult a procedure. What actually happened was that the meeting of the Prime Ministers was *preceded* by a meeting of their respective professional advisers, the General Staffs. Here we have, in germ, the distinction between the League of Nations Council and its subordinate Advisory Committees.

During the first ten months of 1917 no less than eleven such Conferences were held. The experience thus gained led later in the same year to the adoption of Mr Asquith's original suggestion in a more highly developed form. There was set up a body known as the 'Supreme War Council', composed of two representatives from each of the countries concerned—the Prime Minister and one colleague—with a body of professional advisers to assist it. This group of professionals was provided with a secretariat.

Thus there came into existence, for problems of high policy, a standing international Conference supported by a regular working body of experts. Here was, in fact, *a Postal Union organisation for high policy*. This was an advance on anything that had ever been attempted in the nineteenth century. The coalition against Napoleon never enjoyed the services of a

Committee of military advisers, still less a secretariat. Nor did the Crimean allies. Nor did the Concert of Europe throughout its laborious handling of the 'Eastern Question'.

From this to the appointment of a generalissimo, in the person of Marshal Foch, was an easy step: for there now existed *a body capable of appointing him*.[1]

Thus it was that, during the closing period of the war, it became common to speak of 'the Allied League of Nations'. The statesmen responsible for the war-time organisation had little time to spare for thought on the problems of the future. They did not consciously think out the relationship between war-time and peace-time organisation, still less consider how the transition should be made from the one to the other. But, in Great Britain at any rate, where experience is always accepted as the best of guides, the notion became prevalent during the last year of the war, especially in governing circles, that somehow or other the lessons of

---

[1] The facts made use of in this chapter are largely derived from the paper entitled 'Diplomacy by Conference' read by Sir Maurice Hankey, Secretary of the Committee of Imperial Defence from 1912 and of the Cabinet since 1916, to the British Institute of International Affairs in November 1920 and published in *The Round Table* in March 1921. For the origin and development of the Committee of Imperial Defence see Sir Maurice Hankey's article in the *Army Quarterly* for July 1927, and Lowell, *The Government of England*, i. 104-5. Strictly speaking, the Committee consists of 'the Prime Minister and such persons as he chooses to ask to assist in the deliberations'. In practice, its composition, under the Prime Minister, now includes the Lord President of the Council, the Chancellor of the Exchequer, the Secretaries of State for Home Affairs, Foreign Affairs, Dominions, Colonies, India, War and Air, the First Lord of the Admiralty, the Chiefs of Staff of all the three defence Services and the Permanent Head of the Treasury, as the head of the Civil Service. When there is anything affecting the Empire as a whole the representatives of the Dominions are asked to attend. Between March 1934 and March 1935 the number of Committee and Sub-Committee meetings held was 237 (statement by the Prime Minister in the House of Commons on March 14, 1935, amplified, as regards the Home Secretary, on August 2, 1935).

the war-time organisation must be made use of for what had by now become the hope and watchword of millions—the League of Nations.

We have now to see how this idea took shape in another field of war-time effort.

CHAPTER II

IF the regular diplomatic machine proved unequal to the demands of the war in the sphere of high policy, the strain was felt even more severely in the domain of economic organisation. Here the need for a new technique was apparent from the first days—one might almost say the first hours—of the war. Problems incapable of solution on the old lines began to press in upon the authorities on every side.

One of the first of these was sugar. Three-quarters of the sugar imported into Great Britain in 1913 came from Germany and Austria-Hungary. What was to happen to this food of the poor when relations with these lands were broken off? Here was a problem which the Manchester School opponents of the Sugar Commission had never envisaged.[1] There was nothing for it but for the Government to take steps to ensure the

---

[1] In this connexion the Report, published in 1905, of the Royal Commission on the Supply of Food and Raw Material in Time of War makes interesting reading. Speaking of the supply of foodstuffs in time of war, it remarks that there is 'a certain advantage to us in the fact that the supplies of our principal foodstuffs are drawn in a greater proportion from foreign countries than from British possessions'. This curious conclusion is arrived at through the calculation that 'the more numerous the neutral Powers supplying our wants the less probable is the violation of International Law by our enemies'. There could hardly be a clearer illustration of how inconceivable a *World War* was to the pre-war generation in Great Britain—and indeed everywhere. The *localisation of war* was taken for granted. See Cmd. 2643 (1905), p. 59.

sugar supply of the country. Thus by August 20, little over a fortnight after the declaration of war, there had come into existence, under a Government which would indignantly have rejected the appellation of Socialist and under a Departmental Minister trained in the Manchester School, a central body charged with the duty of buying, selling and otherwise controlling sugar. It concealed the unorthodox character of its operations under the title of 'Royal Commission on Sugar Supplies'. Elsewhere, it might have been named 'the Sugar Commissariat'. It bought sugar from the British West Indies, Cuba and Java, arranged for its distribution through the wholesalers and fixed the prices for the retailers, who, under this arrangement, soon became little less than government agents, selling sugar on the public account for a fixed commission. It was a system easy to enforce. The 'sanction' lay in the fact that there was only one channel of supply. If a retailer was found to be overcharging, his sugar was cut off.

This arrangement, first applied to sugar, was extended, as need arose, to other commodities, such as wheat, meat, fats, oilseeds and metals. A similar method of control was established for the whole range of supplies purchased for the War Office—wool, flax, jute, hemp, leather and so on. Manufacturers, wholesale traders, shopkeepers and consumers throughout Great Britain became accustomed to this 'war-time Socialism'.

But it was impossible that this system should remain purely national in scope: for this would simply have left the door open for a ruinous competition between the purchasing governments. International organisation was urgently called for. Thus before the end of August 1914 there was set up a body called the

Revictualling Commission, better known under its French title—*Commission Internationale de Ravitaillement*, or C.I.R. Its duty was to pool the purchasing of the Allies. For this purpose it was composed of representatives of the different Allied buying departments. These departments, it need hardly be said, did not include the Foreign Offices. They did, however, include a large proportion of the *Government departments other than the Foreign Offices*.

We cannot here follow the growth of inter-Allied economic organisation between August 1914 and November 1918. For our purposes it is sufficient to say that out of the C.I.R. there was developed a number of separate inter-Allied Committees for particular commodities. By November 1918 there were in existence twenty such boards or Committees (known as 'Programme Committees') covering between them almost the whole range of imported commodities. They were, in fact, to use the language of the U.S.S.R., International Commissariats, and, as in Russia during the Five-Years Plan, their strength consisted in their control over purchasing power. The Allied peoples at that time had plenty of money, but only a limited amount of goods.

There was, however, this difference between the two situations. In Russia the limiting factor was the control exercised by the home government over purchasing power. Under the Five-Years Plan Soviet Russia was, so to speak, blockading herself. But in the Allied countries during the war the limiting factor, due to the submarine blockade and the huge military needs, was shipping space. Hence the pivot of the whole war-time economic organisation was the Shipping Commissariat or, to give it its orthodox name, the Inter-Allied

L

Maritime Transport Council or A.M.T.C. Its control over all the other Programme Committees was derived from one simple fact—its power to give or withhold shipping space.

Never before has the world been under so complete a control of its economic life as during the latter part of the war. The loose and private international economic organisation, which had grown up in the nineteenth century and had come to be taken for granted, was suddenly torn asunder and cast aside. Its place was rapidly taken by two highly organised governmental systems, covering between them almost the entire globe. The extent to which neutrals and other powers distant from the main scene of fighting were drawn into the Allied economic system is well illustrated by the fact that during the closing months of the war 90 per cent of the sea-going tonnage of the world was under the control of the Allied governments —in other words, of the Allied Maritime Transport Council, which allocated their cargoes and arranged their voyages.

Let us therefore now examine how this supreme economic body, this Commissariat of Commissariats, was actually organised.

The A.M.T.C. consisted of eight members, two from each of the Principal Powers—Great Britain, France, Italy and the United States. These members were persons of ministerial rank. The two British members were the Minister of Blockade, Lord Robert Cecil, as he then was, and the Shipping Controller. The French members were the Ministers of Commerce and of Food.

But Departmental Ministers, especially in war-time, are busy persons. The Council, therefore, only met at infrequent intervals. Its daily work was carried on by a staff of officials resident in London—or rather by four separate staffs, each remaining organically related to its own parent department. This composite organisation was supervised and 'welded into one' by a body of four persons, known as the Allied Maritime Transport Executive. It was composed of the departmental officials at the head of the British, French and Italian divisions of the staff, together with an American delegate, the British member (Mr J. A. Salter, as he then was) being at once *Chairman of the Executive* and *Secretary of the Council.*

This small body was the central hub of the Allied war-machine. From it went forth, daily and hourly, decisions which closely affected the interests, the needs and, above all, the daily habits of individuals over a large part of the world. And here too, under the impact of experience, were being hammered out conclusions as to the possibilities and limits of interstate co-operation which could have been arrived at in no other way. It was no accident that, when, a few months later, the Secretariat of the League of Nations came to be formed, three out of the four members of the Transport Executive, Mr Salter, M. Monnet and Signor Attolico, transferred their experience and driving power to its service. Let us therefore briefly analyse the working of this new war-time administrative machine.

The Transport Executive was a body of men which, as the term 'Executive' implies, made *decisions.* Those decisions were made *together*—that is, by persons representing four different governments, sets of interests, attitudes of mind. 'One of the most vital lessons of international administration', remarks Sir Arthur Salter, 'is that, in any difficult or complicated subject-matter, policy is adjusted much more easily if it is adjusted *in the actual process of formation*. If each of four separate countries considers a problem with international reactions from its own point of view, develops a national policy, begins to give it expression in administrative arrangements, fortifies it with Ministerial decisions and Cabinet authority, adjustment will prove almost impossible. Four rigid and developed policies will confront one another. . . . But if the national points of view can be explained while they are still developing, if policies can be brought into contact while they are still plastic and still unformed, agreement will be easier and probably better. Given the proper personal relations, many things can be explained which would never be put on paper or stated in a formal meeting.' On the Transport Executive, such relations existed: professional association grew into personal friendship, and in this way there was developed a system of *organic co-operation* between independent governments which was something quite new in the history of international relations.

How new it was, and how important were the consequences which flowed from its discovery, can best be understood if we ask ourselves whether the administrative problem set by the war could not have been solved along other lines.

There were two other possible ways of solving it. One was the way of *isolation*, the other was the way of *centralisation*.

Adopting the principle of isolation, each government might have worked out its own arrangements independently. This would have been much easier in the early stages. Each of the four plans would have looked very well on paper. But their independent functioning in an interdependent war would have caused much friction. This friction could have been dealt with by arbitration or conciliation or some other device for 'the peaceful settlement of disputes'. It is unnecessary to explore this road further. For war-time purposes it was a blind alley.

The other alternative would have been for each of the Allied governments to have surrendered its independence for the time being to an economic generalissimo or an international Committee of Public Safety with full powers to conduct that side of the war as it thought best, whatever the effects of the decisions taken upon the lives and fortunes of their peoples. That method, too, was impossible for the Allies. The Central Powers came nearer to its adoption, but the resistance thus aroused in Austria-Hungary was no unimportant factor in the break-up of the Hapsburg monarchy. Thus the only practicable policy, in the world as it now is, was the middle course—neither isolation nor centralisation but co-operation. It was in fact *during the war*, not after the war, that the choice was made between the *inter-state* and the *super-state* principle as the basis of the post-war effort for a 'new order'.

'The international machine', writes Sir Arthur Salter, 'was not an external organisation based on delegated authority. It was the national organisations linked together for international work and *themselves forming the instrument for that work.*' These words, based on experience, on experience of the most crucial kind, spell the doom of the vague dreams of world-government that were current in certain 'advanced' circles in the nineteenth century, and of which cobwebs still linger in some old-fashioned minds to-day. For 'the Parliament of Man, the Federation of the World' the war taught us to substitute the notion of organic association between independent, self-governing and co-operatively minded peoples. Democracy and centralisation do not belong to the same order of ideas. They are, in essence, as incompatible as freedom and slavery. That is why the Secretary of the Allied Maritime Transport Council, who happened also to be a political thinker of rare insight, looking back on his war-time experience, said of the League of Nations, in words which must have come as a surprise to some of his readers, that while *morally* it was 'a great effort of faith', it was '*administratively a great effort of decentralisation*'. When we come to examine the details of the Geneva organisation, with the devising and setting in motion of which he had so much to do, the full meaning of his words will become apparent.[1]

[1] See J. A. Salter, *Allied Shipping Control*, 1921, especially pp. 179 and 255 and the whole of Part V. The italics in the quotations given in the text are not in the original. See also *Dwight Morrow* by Harold Nicolson (1935), ch. xi., esp. p. 224.

CHAPTER III

WE have seen that, in Great Britain, the idea of the League of Nations had become associated with the system of international co-operation brought about by the war. Here, it was felt, was a practical going concern. Somehow or other its experience and momentum must be made use of for the post-war 'new order'. We have seen also how, on the economic side, this international co-operation had been developed along organic lines into something far more comprehensive and effective than had ever been attempted under pre-war conditions. What was more natural than that British minds, with their dislike of paper constitutions and fancy schemes and their respect for the accomplished fact, should fix on this as the natural starting-point for the ordering of the post-war world?

It must be remembered that, during the closing period of the war, especially after the entry of the United States, the machinery described in the last chapter had been fulfilling a double purpose. It had not only been supplying the armies and rationing the Allied peoples. It had also, under carefully devised safeguards, been rationing the neutral peoples adjacent to the blockaded area. From the administrative point of view, therefore, there was nothing either unduly novel or insuperably difficult involved in the idea of transforming what was now functioning as an Allied war-supply and blockade machine into an international machine for post-war economic reconstruction.

It was in the late summer of 1917, when the full effect of the United States' participation in the war was making itself felt, that these ideas began to take shape. On August 25, under the ominous title of 'A World Famine', an article appeared in *The New Statesman* bearing unmistakable marks of the hand of Mr Sidney Webb. It pointed out that the world after the war would be more or less 'in the position of a beleaguered city'. 'Some forty or fifty millions of European workers', now in arms or engaged in war trades, numbering with their dependents 'possibly one in twelve of the entire population of the globe', would need, immediately on the cessation of hostilities, to be provided either with work or subsistence; but there would not be enough foodstuffs or industrial raw materials to go round. There would therefore be the gravest risk of famine and revolution. Under these circumstances 'no government, belligerent or neutral,' the writer continued, 'will feel able, the morning after Peace has been declared, to dispense with the extensive controls that it has had to exercise over importing, exporting, manufacturing and distributing', and these national controls would need to be linked together through an international control. He then went on to propose the 'extension and transformation' of the existing inter-Allied machinery, suggesting that, in its enlarged form, including both neutrals and ex-enemies, it should be placed 'under the management of the Council of the League of Nations—or whatever may be the title of the Supernational Authority in which this war must issue'. And the article ended with the watchword, 'No cake for anyone until all have bread'.

The policy thus outlined was adopted by the Conference of the Socialist and Labour Parties of the Allied Nations which met in London a few days later and was widely advocated, especially in Great Britain, during the last year of hostilities.[1] It even found its way into the British Ministry of Propaganda and formed the subject of one of the resolutions adopted at the Inter-Allied Conference on Enemy Propaganda which met in London on August 14, 1918.[2]

Meanwhile the whole subject had been under the consideration of the Foreign Office, which, in August 1918, brought it to the attention of the Cabinet, or

[1] The resolution adopted at the Socialist and Labour Parties Conference was in the following terms: 'That in view of the probable world-wide shortage, after the war, of exportable foodstuffs and raw materials, and of merchant shipping, it is imperative, in order to prevent the most serious hardship, and even possible famine, in one country or another, that systematic arrangements should be made on an international basis for the allocation and conveyance of the available exportable surpluses of these commodities to the different countries in proportion, not to their purchasing powers but to their several pressing needs; and that, within each country, the government must for some time maintain its control of the most indispensable commodities, in order to secure their appropriation, not in a competitive market mainly to the richer classes in proportion to their means, but systematically, to meet the most urgent needs of the whole community on the principle of "no cake for anyone till all have bread"'.

[2] The Propaganda Conference resolution is given in Campbell Stuart, *The Secrets of Crewe House* (1920), p. 183. A more definite statement to the same effect was made by the Minister of Propaganda, Lord Northcliffe, under his own signature in an article which appeared in *The Times* of November 4, 1918: 'The cessation of hostilities', he wrote, 'will leave the world short of food, short of transport, short of raw materials. The machinery that has regulated these during the war will have to be kept in action beyond the war. Food will have to be rationed, transport will have to be rationed, raw material will have to be rationed. It is a world problem that can be settled only on a world basis.' See also the essay, dating from September 1917, reprinted in the writer's *Nationality and Government* (1918), p. 278 ff.

'War Cabinet' as it was at that time. As a result, the Foreign Office was instructed to prepare a detailed plan. This was drawn up in the ensuing weeks, after consultation and conference with representatives of all the Departments concerned, and circulated to the Cabinet on October 21. It proposed that during what was called the transition period—that is, the period between the end of the fighting and the conclusion of the final peace treaty[1]—the whole inter-Allied organisation should be maintained and the national controls on which it was based strengthened in order to prevent private purchases in primary markets. It went on to declare that 'the adherence of our present enemies to these controls must form one of the conditions of the peace preliminaries'. 'The adherence of neutrals', it was added, 'must also be secured and the machinery of the blockade must as rapidly as possible be superseded by the system of control administered by the inter-Allied organisation.'

It may be well to pause at this point to consider the implications of this scheme. It was not a plan for a League of Nations. But it aimed at creating conditions under which—and under which alone, as it was believed—the League of Nations, as a political organisation, could be set up with any hope of immediate success. It was, in fact, in the words of the Foreign Office document, 'the inevitable corollary of the whole idea of a League of Nations as it is beginning to take form both in the United States and in this country'. It would have set before the peoples, from the moment of

---

[1] It must be remembered that at this time it was expected that there would be two peace treaties, as in 1814 and 1871—a Preliminary Peace and a Final Peace. It was not foreseen that the Final Peace would be negotiated during an Armistice renewable at monthly intervals.

the firing of the last gun in the war, an example of international co-operation for a peaceful and beneficent purpose, touching them closely in their daily lives and activities. In such an atmosphere, with such a working model before their eyes, the elaboration of the political machinery and functions of the League of Nations would no longer have seemed a visionary enterprise provoking doubt and scepticism in practical minds. Indeed, it is tempting to speculate on what might have followed from the successful working of such a scheme. Certain it is that the new states and the new régimes in the old states, such as Germany, would have started on their careers under very different economic and psychological conditions from those which they had actually to face, and that this would have had a powerful influence on the whole subsequent development. One affirmation at any rate can be made without fear of contradiction. If the peace, as is so often said, was lost, its first great defeat, perhaps its greatest defeat of all, was suffered not in the Peace Conference itself but during the days and weeks immediately following the Armistice, when the economic forces were allowed to slip out of the control of statesmanship.

But this is to anticipate. We must return to watch the fortunes of the scheme put forward by the Foreign Office to the War Cabinet. Its vicissitudes can be traced in documents published by the United States Government. Already on October 15, 1918, the Commercial Adviser of the British Embassy in Washington, writing to the Counsellor for the Department of State, Mr Polk, set forth, on behalf of the British Government, the main lines of a proposed policy of post-war economic reconstruction and invited the co-operation of the United States. He pointed out the danger of 'industrial dislocation, the result of which would be social unrest, which might in turn delay for an indefinite time the re-establishment of the peaceful international relations which it is the object of the War to safeguard and secure', and urged that the Associated governments were 'under a moral obligation, in the interests of the Associated peoples, to carry on during the period of reconstruction that co-operation in the economic sphere which is being developed as a result of war conditions'. He added that the British Government was constantly being pressed to make a statement as to its post-war economic policy, but that it was 'strongly felt' that this should not be done until after a 'full and frank exchange of views' with the Allies and particularly with the Government of the United States. No reply seems to have been made to this communication.

Meanwhile events were moving forward with giant strides. The German Government had asked, not for a Preliminary Peace but for an Armistice, which would necessarily involve the continuance of the blockade. The question therefore arose as to how the needs of the people of the blockaded area were to be supplied during the period of the Armistice. This is the subject of a long dispatch cabled from Paris to Washington on October 30 by Mr Joseph Cotton, the representative of the United States Food Administration in Europe. He communicated the terms of a resolution approved by the British and French Foreign Offices which would next day be submitted to the War Council. Colonel House, the United States representative on that body, had no instructions and a decision at Washington was urgent, since, so the dispatch concludes, 'we cannot over-emphasise the need for prompt action'.

The resolution, on which the British and French governments were agreed, was to the effect that there should be included in the Armistice terms a provision placing the merchant marine of the Central Powers under the direction of the Allied Maritime Transport Council, and laying it down that such supplies of food or other commodities as might be allowed to the Central Powers should be obtained through the existing Allied organisations. Mr Cotton sent also a lengthy commentary explaining the need for the adoption of this policy and emphasising the 'entire dislocation' which would ensue if the Allied controls were abandoned. Similar messages were sent to the heads of the War Trade Board, the War Industries Board and the War Shipping Board at Washington.

No answer was received from Washington in time for the War Council meeting, and therefore no provision was made in the Armistice terms for the surrender of the German ships. On November 8 a reply was eventually received from Mr Hoover, to whom the decision had been turned over by the State department and, presumably, by the President. Its tenor was emphatically and indeed brutally negative, or perhaps it would be more correct to say, self-regarding. 'This government', so ran the message, 'will not agree to any programme that even looks like inter-Allied control of our resources after peace. After peace, over one-half of the whole export food supplies of the world will come from the United States, and for the buyers of these supplies to sit in majority in dictation to us as to prices and distribution is wholly inconceivable. The same applies to raw materials. Our only hope of securing justice in distribution, proper appreciation abroad of the effort we make to assist foreign nations,

and proper return for the service we will perform will
revolve around complete independence of commitment
to joint action on our part.' And the dispatch went on
to suggest that the right way of handling the problem
was 'to organise a duplication of the Belgian Relief
organisation', the Allies being represented on it in proportion to 'the actual resources in food, money or
shipping that they had for its support'.

Mr Hoover's argument, which, as we now know, was
the product of the working philosophy of a lifetime, is
no doubt theoretically defensible. But what made his
inveterate individualism, at this of all moments, to say
the least, most inopportune was that it bore no relation
whatsoever to the actual conditions which had immediately to be faced—and faced not by shopkeepers,
or even philanthropists, but by statesmen. It led to the
immediate break-up of the Allied economic organisation, followed by prolonged negotiations for the setting up of his proposed new body. But by the time
this was in action in February 1919, insufficiently
equipped with a personnel accustomed to corporate
work, three crucial months had been lost and the
situation had undergone an irretrievable deterioration.[1]

[1] For the above see *Foreign Relations of the United States* (1918, Sup-
plement I: 'The World War') (1933), i. 612-17; Salter, *The United States of
Europe*, p. 22 (Memorandum of May 1919); Eustace Percy, *The Responsibility of the League* (written in the second half of 1919), p. 61 ff.; Salter,
Allied Shipping Control (1921), pp. 219-22 and 323-30. Mr Winston
Churchill (in *The World Crisis*, 1929, v. 20-21) has related how on Armistice
Night he urged on the Prime Minister 'that we should immediately . . .
rush a dozen great ships crammed with provisions into Hamburg', and
that Mr Lloyd George 'balanced the project with favouring eye'. As to
the conditions that resulted from Mr Hoover's 'No', one piece of evidence
must suffice. On January 17, 1919, Dr. Alonzo Taylor, who was the
representative of the United States Secretary for Agriculture on the War
Trade Board, passed through Paris on his return from a journey in

By then the first draft of the Covenant of the League
of Nations had been drawn up—but under conditions
very different from those which might have prevailed
had Mr Hoover been co-operatively minded or had
President Wilson's political idealism been matched by
an understanding of economic realities.

Central Europe and called on General Bliss, a member of the United
States Peace Delegation. Here is General Bliss's account of his report:
'Dr. Alonzo Taylor says that one community may be starving while
another has plenty of food, but the embargoes and seizures of railway
transportation by the different governments prevent the food from
being distributed. He says that he did not see a single potato on the
market or on the table at Vienna, although millions of bushels of them
were to be obtained in Hungary. Each state seizes the former imperial
government rolling-stock in order to build up its own railway equipment.
Bohemia cuts off the supply of coal for Vienna; the Yugoslavs refused
transport of flour to Vienna until they could get salt. He says that there
is absolute and universal social disintegration' (Palmer, *Bliss : Peace-
maker* (1934), p. 367). See also Mr. Hoover's own retrospective account,
in an essay on *The Economic Administration during the Armistice*, contributed to House and Seymour: *What Really Happened at Paris* (New
York, 1921). This throws no light on what happened *before* Paris, but
gives details which explain his concern for the interests of the American
farmers and his fear of 'dictation' by the buyers of their products.
Food production in the United States had, in fact, been stimulated by
the promise of prices double those of food-producing areas more remote
from Europe.

CHAPTER IV

SOME UNOFFICIAL SCHEMES

THE events recorded in the last chapter made it clear in London that the problem of the establishment of a League of Nations must now be considered in and for itself. There could no longer be any question of adapting the war-time organisation to peace-time needs and thus of introducing the League of Nations to the peoples of the world as a going concern, actively engaged on tasks of reconstruction. This evolutionary conception had now to be put on one side. What President Wilson asked for, what he had taught the peoples to ask for, was something entirely new, a revolution in the management of the world's public affairs, a system, an outlook, a dispensation different from those which had prevailed during the nineteenth century and had ended by plunging humanity into the greatest of all wars.

It was in these circumstances that, immediately after the Armistice, as a part of the general re-allocation of duties in preparation for the forthcoming Peace Conference, certain members of the staff of the Foreign Office were directed to study and put forward proposals on the League of Nations.

The task with which they found themselves confronted cannot be understood without a survey of the material then at their disposal.

160

The League of Nations had by that time been a topic of discussion for over four years. If most of this had been vague and inconclusive, couched in the language of aspiration rather than of political science, nevertheless some solid work had been done, both officially and unofficially, on both sides of the Atlantic. The findings reached in these studies were for the most part (though not, as we shall see, in every case) available to the British authorities, as indeed, generally speaking, to the public.

I

Soon after the outbreak of the war groups had been formed in Great Britain and the United States to study what may be called the problem of war and peace. There were two separate study groups in Great Britain. One was centred round Lord Bryce and Mr G. Lowes Dickinson: the other was set up by the Fabian Society, its most active member and draftsman being Mr Leonard Woolf. In the United States the most prominent members of the group were ex-President Taft and President Lowell of Harvard.[1]

In June 1915 the United States group came before the public with a set of definite proposals and an organisation, named 'The League to Enforce Peace', was established to promulgate them. The Bryce group did not form a similar organisation of its own; but it was

---

[1] A well-documented record of the activities of the American group has been published by one of its original members, Mr Theodore Marburg, *The Development of the League of Nations Idea*, New York, 1932. The material relating to the groups as a whole is collected in L. S. Woolf, *The Framework of a Lasting Peace*, 1917. The Fabian material is given in a more complete form in Mr Woolf's other book, referred to on p. 45 above.

in the same year that a number of active spirits in close sympathy with the ideas of the Bryce group formed what was known as the League of Nations Society. A study group was also formed in Holland and entered into relations with the British and American groups.

The members of these groups were inspired with one leading idea, which was indeed not only an idea but a sentiment—*Never again*. What was occurring before their eyes was not only unexpected: for most of them it had been inconceivable. It ought not to have happened. It ought not to *have been able to happen*. It must not happen again.

With the exception of the Fabians, therefore, whose outlook was somewhat different, these groups devoted their efforts to devising plans *to prevent the next war*. The term League of Nations did not bear for them the meaning to which we have become accustomed, that of an *everyday institution*, part of the working machinery of the world. They thought of it as a sort of fire brigade, an emergency arrangement to be prepared beforehand in view of the next crisis. And its 'members' were not the governments and peoples of the world engaged in regular co-operation. They were simply a group, larger or smaller as the case might be, of signatories of an improved Hague Convention for the Pacific Settlement of Disputes.

Nevertheless, curiously enough, as it seems to us in retrospect, obsessed though the framers of these various schemes were with the horror of war, none of them provided for its *abolition*. None of them proposed that war, following the slave trade, should cease to be a recognised and legitimate practice in international relations. None of them *prohibited* recourse to war, still less treated it as a crime or a common nuisance, to be visited with appropriate penalties. All of them, unable to shake themselves free from the powerful tradition of international 'law', left the door open for states to settle their differences by force if other means proved ineffectual. All that they proposed were certain *safeguards* designed to make resort to this ultimate expedient less rapid and less likely.

It was their concentration on the future—not the end of hostilities or the signing of peace but the more remote future of the next international crisis, not To-morrow but the Day After To-morrow—which enabled these groups to co-operate in spite of the fact that, of the three countries in which the research was being undertaken, two were at the time neutral and one was a belligerent.

The American plan took the form that might have been expected from its chief sponsor, whose mind was still moving in its pre-war groove. It may be described as the Taft treaties with a penalty clause attached. All 'justiciable' questions were to go to a judicial tribunal 'for hearing and judgment'. The Court thus set up would be empowered to decide as to whether a given case was justiciable or not. Thus the five-to-one majority of 1911 was swept away and a bare majority substituted. Moreover, entrance to the hall of judgment was no longer to be controlled by a body of laymen— the Joint High Commission of the 1911 treaties—but by the bench itself.

All other disputes not settled by diplomacy were to go to a 'Council of Conciliation'—not, however, for decision, only for 'hearing, consideration and recom-mendation'.

Next came the penalty clause or sanction. Since this is the most important part of this American plan and

that from which Mr Taft's organisation drew its name
—the League to *Enforce* Peace—it is best to quote it
textually: 'The Signatory Powers shall jointly use
forthwith both their economic and military forces
against one of their number that goes to war, or com-
mits acts of hostility, against another of the signatories
before any question arising shall be submitted as
provided in the foregoing'.

This is two steps beyond the position of the Taft
treaties, which did not provide directly for the prevention of war. The first step was that taken in the Bryan
treaties, which contained the obligation of Inquiry and
Delay, but no provision for enforcing it. Here are
Inquiry and Delay together with Enforcement or Sanctions. Here, moreover, is the first mention of the
employment of 'economic force' as a form of penalty
separable from 'military force'.

The last of the four short articles provides for the
holding of Conferences 'from time to time to formulate
and codify rules of international law'. Such rules are
thereafter to 'govern in the decisions of the Judicial
Tribunal' 'unless some signatory shall signify its dissent within a stated period'. By casting on the governments the burden and odium of openly dissenting from
the rules thus adopted by this new international
legislature—for that is what, in effect, this 'Conference' would be—Mr Taft was trying to make a short
cut to his judicial paradise. This was not the last of
the attempts made by well-meaning and ingenious
draftsmen to hustle the world forward into the 'new
order' and to circumvent the slow-moving processes
of democratic parliaments and electorates.

To whom were these arrangements to apply? To the
members of the League of Nations. Who were to be

the members of this League of Nations? On this point the American group found it difficult to make up its mind. The League could not be confined to the Great Powers. That would be to offend against the legal doctrine of the Equality of States. Moreover, it would be disagreeably reminiscent of 'the old diplomacy', 'the Balance of Power' and other un-American notions. On the other hand, there were obvious difficulties about opening the League to all states, small or great, civilised or uncivilised, respectable or disreputable. The result was the adoption of an ingenious compromise in which one can see legalism at grips with considerations both of a realistic and of an ethical order. It was decided to admit all the Great Powers—the six in Europe, Japan and the United States—together with a select number of others. There were to be all the secondary European states, with the exception of the Balkan States and Turkey, together with the Argentine, Brazil and Chile. It was not, therefore, to be a very American League. Memories of the Second Hague Conference, where the Latin-American voting *bloc* was unduly conspicuous, had rather stifled Pan-American sentiment.[1]

II

Let us now turn to the Bryce scheme, not forgetting that its chief author, as British Ambassador in

[1] Marburg, ii. 725, i. 35; see also ii. 703, where Mr Andrew D. White is quoted as saying 'that the presence of the South American countries at the Second Hague Conference was a mistake and that Europe was loath to call the Third Conference by reason of their prospective presence'. In the 'Victory Programme', adopted on November 23, 1918, the proposal, however, is that 'the nations associated as belligerents in winning the war' should be original members of the League (*Taft Papers on League of Nations* (1920), p. 2).

Washington in 1911, had been closely associated with Mr Taft's proposals at that time.

In its published form the plan of the Bryce group dates from two years later than that of the League to Enforce Peace and it is much more detailed. Whereas the American plan consisted of only four short articles, the Bryce plan, which was drawn up in the form of a draft treaty, contained twenty. Nevertheless it can be briefly described, for it was on the same general lines. It was a project dealing with disputes and providing certain safeguards against war.

As regards justiciable disputes, it followed the American plan. They were to go to an international bench, which would also decide as to whether a given dispute was justiciable or not. But the Bryce plan went further and mentioned the Court by name. It was to be the 'Court of Arbitral Justice proposed at the Second Hague Conference', or, failing its constitution, the existing Permanent Court of Arbitration.

Non-justiciable disputes were to go, as in the American plan, to a 'Council of Conciliation'. But it was to be a very different body from that contemplated by the Americans. Lord Bryce and his associates conceived of it as a standing group of experienced public men qualified to deal with problems which baffled the regular working diplomat and his official superiors. It was to be a large body, composed of representatives of all the signatories, the Great Powers having three representatives each and the others at least one. They would be appointed by the respective governments and would hold office for a fixed term of years. In the words of the memorandum accompanying the draft treaty, 'the composition of the Council should enable its members to take a more impartial, comprehensive and international view (of questions submitted to them) than diplomatists have hitherto shown themselves inclined to take and to suggest a radical settlement rather than a mere temporary compromise, likely to be broken as soon as some Power is ready to risk war'. In fact it was to be an Areopagus of elder statesmen.

The Council, of course, would not be given power to impose its views. Its decisions would not bind the governments. They would simply be presented to the world as 'the views of an international body as to that solution of an urgent problem that is most in accordance with equity and the general interest'. But the Council would be allowed great latitude in its activity. When 'from any cause within its knowledge, the good relations between the signatory Powers are likely to be endangered', 'whether or not any dispute has actually arisen', it is empowered 'to make suggestions' and even, 'if it considers it expedient to do so, to publish such suggestions'.

It was further provided that the Council might sit in public or in private, as it thought fit, and that it might appoint Committees, not necessarily composed only of its own members.

The provisions against resort to war were on the American lines but more precise. The parties agree 'not to declare war, or to begin hostilities or hostile preparations' either (1) *before* the submission of the dispute to arbitration or to the Council, or (2) within twelve months after such submission, or (3) within a period of six months after the award or report of these bodies. Here again we have Inquiry and Delay but not absolute Prohibition.

The sanctions clause also follows the American plan.

Every signatory power is obliged, if the foregoing provisions have been violated, 'forthwith, in conjunction with the other signatory Powers, to take such concerted measures, economic and forcible [the wording here is curious], against the Power so acting as, in their judgment, are most effective and appropriate to the circumstances of the case'.

But one question remained over with which the American scheme had failed to deal. What was to be done if any power failed to accept or carry out either 'the award of the arbitral tribunal' (this British scheme does not say 'the judgment of the Court') or the recommendations of the Council? At this point Lord Bryce and his associates recur to the method of the Concert. The signatory powers undertake 'at a Conference forthwith to be summoned for the purpose' to 'consider, in concert, the situation which has arisen' and 'what collective action, if any, it is practicable to take' in order to carry through the award or recommendation. Here is an important advance in the working of the Concert. Instead of merely enjoying the *right* to ask for the summoning of a Conference, the powers are to bind themselves beforehand, in certain circumstances, to agree to the immediate summoning of a Conference. This is the first introduction of the principle of the *Consultative Pact*.

No provision of this kind was included in the American scheme. The Americans feared that, if an old-style Conference of the powers were allowed to appear at the end of the vista, the parties would be less likely to accept the recommendations or award at the earlier stage. The Elder Statesmen would be overshadowed by the Foreign Ministers and their authority correspondingly diminished. In this, as we shall see,

the American attitude resembled that of the Scandin-
avians. Their outlook on this point, in fact, was a
survival from the days when the United States was a
Small State.[1]

The British scheme, on the other hand, omitted the
American reference to the codification and development of international law. It merely expressed the hope
and expectation that this work would be carried on by
the Hague Conference, which should be given a regular
organisation, with provision for meetings at regular
intervals.

Finally, the Bryce scheme disposed of the difficult
question of membership of the League or, to use the
language of the Bryce memorandum, admission into
'the Union', by limiting it, at least at the outset,
to the Great Powers and any other *European* state
which might wish to join.

III

The plan put forward by the Fabian Society differed
in important respects from the two just described. In
so far as it covered the same ground—the settlement
of disputes—we need not analyse it in detail. Its chief
contribution in this field was its precise and formidable
list of possible economic penalties or sanctions, ranging
from special export duties to complete non-intercourse.[2] But its main interest lies in the fact that it
was the work of lively minds determined not to be
confined to what may be called the rut of The Hague
and ready to break fresh ground.

[1] Marburg, i. 34 (letter from Marburg to Bryce).
[2] *The Framework of a Lasting Peace*, pp. 116-17.

The scheme that thus emerged was characteristically Fabian both in its apparent moderation and in its resourcefulness. It attempted to apply the principle of the Inevitability of Gradualness to international politics. Thus it explicitly disclaimed the notion that what was required was anything new and revolutionary. 'All that will be immediately practicable *can be presented* [the phrase is characteristic] as only a more systematic development of the rapidly multiplying Arbitration Treaties of the present century and the conclusions of the two Conventions at The Hague.' 'Only on some such lines', the introduction to the Fabian draft treaty goes on to say, 'can we reasonably hope, at this juncture, to get the governments of the world to come into the proposed agreement.'

As it turned out, this gloomy estimate of what the governments would be prepared to accept was completely belied by the event. But it is only fair to its authors to recall the fact that it was written before the war-time organisation had assumed anything like its final shape.

In domestic affairs, the Fabian policy had been to move towards the complete abolition of the capitalist system through a succession of stages, each following almost imperceptibly from the last. The essential matter, in tactics of this kind, is to discover where to begin—at what point to insert the thin end of the persevering wedge. So far as capitalism was concerned the Fabians had found this in the municipal sphere, in what was known as 'gas and water socialism'. In their planning for a World Order they found it in the Universal Postal Union. If the Postal Union Conference had worked successfully for the best part of two generations, why, they asked themselves, should not this type of organisation be extended over the whole field of international affairs? Here was the natural starting-point for the process of what may be called 'gas and water internationalism'.

This underlying idea is openly expressed in the pre-amble to the Fabian draft treaty, which speaks of 'facilitating the development of such joint action as is exemplified by the Universal Postal Union'. But when the framers of the scheme found themselves faced with the problem of how their glorified Postal Union Con-ference was to be organised and what work it was to be given to do, their ingenuity was sorely taxed. The Postal Union, as we noted, has succeeded in its work because that work is both indispensable to every-day modern life and wholly removed from Power-politics. To adapt its machinery so as to enable it to conduct international affairs as a whole involved a multitude of problems. The Fabians faced them with their customary cold audacity; but the result proved somewhat elaborate. Out of the single World-Parlia-ment of the Postal Union there came forth a 'Council Sitting as a Whole', a 'Council of the Eight Great Powers', a 'Council for the States other than the Eight Great Powers', a 'Council for Europe' and a 'Council for America'. We need not follow these complications. They are interesting chiefly as a foretaste of the dis-cussions aroused some fifteen years later when M. Briand attempted to graft his plan for European Union on to the already existing organism of the League. At the time when they were devised they were more suggestive than helpful.

There were, however, two new features in the Fabian scheme which were of real practical importance.

In the first place, thanks to the masterly analysis

of Mr Woolf already referred to,[1] it drew attention to the existing international administrative agencies and offices and to the possibility thus opened up for coordination and development. And, secondly, its concentration of functions in the glorified Postal Union Conference proved a serviceable means for building a bridge between the lawyers and the diplomats, or, if this may be mentioned already at this stage, for transferring to Geneva a large part of the machinery and the business, or at least the potential business, of The Hague.

For the Fabians, anxious to make the fullest use of their glorified Postal Union Conference, empowered it to deal with 'non-justiciable' disputes—that is to say, broadly speaking, with the really important and dangerous disputes. 'The Council' (this was the name adopted for the body composed of representatives of all the 'constituent States', or, as we should say, the members of the League)—so runs the draft scheme— 'may itself invite the parties to lay any such question, difference or dispute before the Council, or the Council may itself take any such matter at issue into its own consideration'.

Thus the settlement of such disputes is thrown squarely on to a body where the Great Powers have the predominant influence. In this the Fabian scheme differs not only from the Taft plan but also from the Bryce scheme with its irremovable board of elder statesmen. The Fabians provide more scope for the Foreign Offices and the cabinets, and therefore, under the democratic régime, for parliaments, electorates and public opinion. Their International Council or glorified Postal Union Conference is thus designed to fulfil a

---

[1] Pp. 45 and 161 above.

double function. It is both a legislature and a sort of tribunal, having taken over from The Hague the whole of its machinery of Inquiry and Conciliation.

Certain other points in the Fabian scheme are worth noting. It provided for an International Secretariat, 'permanently open for business': the framers were evidently thinking of something on the modest scale of the Berne bureaux. And it laid it down that no treaty should henceforward be valid unless it had been communicated to the international authority. The task of registration was conferred, not upon the Secretariat, but upon the Registry of the International High Court set up to deal with 'justiciable' disputes. Finally, it is worthy of remark that the Fabian scheme deliberately leaves the armaments problem on one side. 'National disarmament', says the memorandum, 'is left to come about of itself, just as the individual carrying of arms falls silently into desuetude as and when fears of aggression die down before the rule of the law.'

CHAPTER V

A HOUSE OF LORDS DEBATE

ONE other unofficial pronouncement commands our attention. On March 19, 1918, a debate took place in the House of Lords on the League of Nations. It was introduced along familiar lines by Lord Parmoor, who asked the House to 'approve the principle of a League of Nations and the constitution of a Tribunal, whose orders shall be enforced by an adequate sanction'. In the course of the discussion Lord Lansdowne, the only ex-Foreign Minister in the House, whilst pleading for an improvement in the machinery for conducting foreign affairs, took occasion to issue a warning on the subject of disarmament. 'I believe', he said, 'that this question of disarmament is one of enormous difficulty and I think it would be a mistake to link it too closely with that of a League of Nations.' It was necessary first to find 'means of assuring international peace': then 'disarmament would follow almost automatically'.

But by far the most interesting speech in the debate came from Lord Parker of Waddington, one of the Lords of Appeal. He delivered a frontal attack on the whole doctrine of the Taft school and proposed an alternative approach. 'One thing only I fear,' he said, 'and that is that the movement in favour of the League of Nations runs some risk by reason of the fact

174

that its advocates are in somewhat too great a hurry. They are devoting their attention to the details of the superstructure rather than to the stability of the foundations.' He pointed out that 'schemes for an international tribunal and an international police force' were based upon a false analogy between municipal and international law. 'Every sound system of municipal law, with its tribunal and organised police, is a creation of historical growth, having its roots far in the past.' In the international sphere the condition was wholly different, and 'if we attack that part of the problem at first', he said, 'I have very serious fears that the whole structure that we are trying to build may fall about our ears. It is a very serious matter to ask great nations in the present day to agree beforehand to the arbitrament of a tribunal consisting of representatives of some two dozen or three dozen states, many of whom may be indirectly interested in casting their votes on this side or on that.'

The only sound course was to recognise that law-abiding sentiment as between states was still only in the embryonic stage. The right method of approach was to discard all secondary issues and to concentrate on mobilising sentiment and opinion against war itself, as anti-social conduct, a crime of violence against the community. 'There have been periods', he said, 'in the history of nations when in the absence of legal tribunals, in the absence of an organised police force, the sense of mutual obligation, which lies at the root of every legal system, has been so strongly developed that an act of violence done to the person or property of one member of the community has been resented as a wrong to all its members. In such a case neutrality is impossible. It is a disgrace, a crime. The hand of every man is against the wrongdoer. He becomes an outlaw. No-one may feed him or succour him or assist him to escape. Everyone must join in his arrest and punishment.' 'To this strong sense of mutual obligation', he went on, 'we owed in this country what is known as the "hue and cry", long regarded as an effective deterrent against crimes of violence. From it arose on the other side of the Atlantic that system of communal justice which, however rough and ready, contributed so largely to the establishment of law and order in the Western part of the American Continent. From it legal tribunals and an organised police force will readily develop. Without it no reign of law is possible.'

Was the time ripe for applying the principle of the 'hue and cry' to international affairs? Lord Parker believed that it was. His proposal for a League of Nations was therefore a very simple one. It was the constitution of what he called 'a League of Peace', the members of which would 'recognise that war, from whatever cause, is a danger to our common civilisation' and would 'join in a joint and several guarantee of every other member of the League against any act of war' from outside, and, *a fortiori*, from inside. And he proceeded to develop this conception in a series of concrete propositions, dealing with the details of the new 'hue and cry', which it is not necessary to par-ticularise here.

Here is new doctrine, and (despite its criticism of the 'lawyers in a hurry') radical doctrine. We are here on a track very different from any of those which we have hitherto been following in our analysis. We are not slipping furtively into the world-community on the heels of the Postal Union with its 'gas and water internationalism'. Nor are we being wafted thither in a lawyer's pipe-dream, convinced that all that is needed is to establish international institutions on a site already prepared. Nor, on the other hand, are we imprisoned within the pre-war system of state-sovereignty, reduced to devising expedients for softening the impacts between states, each with its own social system and the sense of obligation arising from it. Still less are we proposing to use the guarantee as an old-fashioned device for enabling a weaker state to enjoy the precarious protection of a stronger. Lord Parker's guarantee is not a guarantee given to one sovereign by another. It is the embodiment of a sense of solidarity, of common interest in the restraint of violence, transcending the boundaries of states great and small. It is not designed to bring the world community into existence: communities do not spring to birth by the adoption of paper obligations. It assumes that *the rudiments of a world-community—but only the rudiments*—are already in existence. It assumes that the vast majority of ordinary men and women, at least among the civilised peoples of mankind, have discovered by experience that war is an anachronism in twentieth-century life: that they are united in desiring to eliminate it from international politics as a common nuisance: and that they are therefore ready, individually, to co-operate with the public authority in stamping it out when there is danger of its occurring. On that basis of *embryonic world citizenship* Lord Parker builds a structure more firmly grounded, if less imposing, than that of the legalists. It is *the organisation of the hue and cry—and nothing more*.

Perhaps an analogy may help to make clear how citizenship, in the only true sense of the word, takes its

N

origin in this rudimentary sense of common responsibility for public order. Let us transport ourselves to ancient Athens, the community to which the Western world owes the twin conceptions of Liberty and Law, and to the moment in Athenian history corresponding to that in which the civilised world finds itself to-day. The problem was to accustom men to accept a wider authority than that of the household and the clan. Solon met it by turning every Athenian into a policeman—that is, by making every Athenian feel and act up to his responsibility for the administration of justice, feel it as a duty he owed, not as an individual to a friend in need, to a partner or an ally, but as a citizen of a free state. For he realised that it is only where men are jealous for the maintenance of justice that the freedom of the individual can be permanently secured. Thus when Solon was asked which was the best protected city, he had a ready reply: 'The city where all citizens, whether they have suffered injury or not, equally pursue and punish injustice'.

CHAPTER VI

THE PHILLIMORE REPORT AND THE FRENCH PLAN

AFTER this necessarily rapid survey of the chief un-official schemes available for study in November 1918 we can turn to the more official material.

I

Early in 1918, acting on a suggestion put forward by Lord Robert Cecil soon after he became a Minister in December 1916,[1] the Foreign Secretary, Mr Balfour, had appointed a Committee 'on the League of Nations'. Its composition is significant. The Chairman, Sir Walter (later, Lord) Phillimore, was a Judge noted as an authority on International Law. Of the six other members, one, Professor Pollard, was a consti-tutional historian; two, Sir Julian Corbett and Dr Holland Rose, were naval historians; whilst the three others were senior and outstanding members of the Foreign Office staff, Sir Eyre Crowe, Sir William (now Lord) Tyrrell and the Legal Adviser Mr (now Sir Cecil) Hurst.

The Committee's terms of reference were conceived along the line of the unofficial schemes. They were not asked to suggest a new system for conducting inter-

[1] On this see Noel-Baker in *Les Origines et l'œuvre de la Société des Nations*, ed. Munch (Copenhagen, 1923), ii. 17.

national affairs at the end of the war. They were to concern themselves with safeguards against the next. They were directed 'to inquire, particularly from a juridical and historical point of view, into the various schemes for establishing by means of a League of Nations, or other device, some alternative to war as a means of settling international disputes' and, if they thought fit, 'to elaborate a further scheme'. The League of Nations, it will be observed, is regarded simply as a 'device' for circumventing resort to war in a crisis, not as a regular working institution.

The Committee reported on March 20, 1918, and a copy of its report was communicated to President Wilson.

The 'Phillimore Plan' which emerged from this curiously composite body was an unsatisfactory hybrid. The officials succeeded in checking the juridical inclinations of the Chairman: but the Chairman and his colleagues were clearly in no mood to consider far-reaching political alternatives.

The plan takes the form of an 'Alliance', not of a 'League'. Nothing is said as to its composition: but, since relations with non-members are discussed, it is clearly not thought of as universal.

What were the engagements entered into between these 'Allies'? They were a modified and expurgated edition of the unofficial schemes. Since we are here dealing with what was subsequently embodied, with very slight alteration, in the Covenant, it is better to quote textually.

'Each of the Allied States (being the parties to the Convention) agrees with the other Allied States collectively and separately that it will not go to war with another of the Allied States:

'(*a*) Without previously submitting the matter in dispute to arbitration or to a Conference of the Allied States, and

'(*b*) until there has been an award or a report by the Conference' (there is a proviso at this point, to deal with cases of 'continuing injury', which we need not reproduce), 'and also that it will not go to war

'(*c*) with another of the Allied States which complies with the award or with the recommendation (if any) made by the Conference in its report.'

Here are Inquiry and Delay, as in the unofficial schemes. Here are the now familiar safeguards against war, without absolute prohibition. The Committee's report gives a frank statement of the reasoning behind these recommendations. The existence of two loopholes is recognised. One is the possibility that the 'Conference' will not be able to agree on a recommendation, thus leaving the door open for war. 'We are in great hope', says the report, the Foreign Office members no doubt grimly assenting, 'that this event will be rare.' The other loophole is that the party dissatisfied with the award of the Conference may refuse to comply with it. In that event the recalcitrant party would be bound, by the terms already cited, not to go to war with its opponent: but it might hold to its position without going to war and defy the authority of the Conference. In such circumstances the Allies are simply bound *not* to go to war with the party which is obedient to the Conference. In other words, the report hesitates to recommend that collective action shall be taken in order to *enforce* the recommendation. 'We have felt a doubt', it says, 'whether states would contract to do this and a still greater doubt whether, when the time came, they would fulfil their contract.'

Thus the Sanctions clause of the Phillimore plan is only operative when one of the above three provisions has been violated—when a state has resorted to war (1) without Inquiry, (2) without Delay or (3) against a state which has accepted an award or report.

But though the application of the Sanctions clause is thus carefully circumscribed, its contents are formidable and bear the marks of war-time experience. 'We have desired', so runs the report, 'to make it (the Sanction) as weighty as possible. We have therefore made it unanimous and automatic and one to which each state must contribute its force without waiting for the others, but we have recognised that some states may not be able to make, at any rate in certain cases, an effective contribution of military or naval force. We have accordingly provided that such states shall at the least take the financial, economic and other measures indicated in the Article.'[1]

The Article in question must be quoted textually, for it is, with a slight difference of wording, the Sanctions article, the famous Article XVI, of the Covenant:

'If, which may God avert, one of the Allied States should break the covenant contained in the preceding Article, this State will become *ipso facto* at war with all the other Allied States, and the latter agree to take and to support each other in taking jointly and severally all such measures—military, naval, financial and economic—as will best avail for restraining the breach of covenant. Such financial and economic measures shall include severance of all relations of

---

[1] The reference here is clearly to the smaller European states who had remained neutral during the war but would, it was expected, become members of the League of Nations or 'Alliance'.

trade and finance with the subjects of the covenant-breaking State, prohibition against the subjects of the Allied States entering into any relations with the subjects of the covenant-breaking State, and the prevention, so far as possible, of the subjects of the covenant-breaking State from having any commercial or financial intercourse with the subjects of any other State, whether party to this Convention or not.'

But what is this 'Conference' which will have charge of the dispute during the period of Inquiry and Delay? On this point the Committee had recourse to a curious expedient. The Phillimore Conference is a conference of diplomats in the most complete sense of the term. It is not a Conference of Foreign Ministers. Neither is it a Conference of Elder Statesmen along the lines of the Bryce plan. It is an Ambassadors' Conference. Here is the essential part of the Article. It must be textually reproduced: for, dispatched across the Atlantic, it became the backbone of President Wilson's plan:

'The seat of the Conference shall be at X, the convener shall be the Sovereign or President of the State of X and his representative shall be President of the Conference. The Allied States shall be represented at the Conference by their diplomatic representatives accredited to the State of X.'[1]

The sense of this becomes clearer when we turn its algebra into arithmetic. For X read 'Berne' or 'The Hague'. We realise then that the proposed machinery is that already in use for the Postal Union Bureau at

[1] The relevant article of the House Draft of July 16, 1918, is as follows: 'The Ambassadors and Ministers of the Contracting Powers to X and the Ministers of Foreign Affairs of X shall act as the respective delegates of the Powers in the League of Nations. The meetings shall be held at the seat of government of X, and the Minister for Foreign Affairs of X shall be the presiding officer.'

Berne and for the Administrative Council of the Permanent Court of Arbitration at The Hague.[1]

In justification of this proposal the Committee explained that they had been 'much impressed by Lieutenant-Colonel Sir Maurice Hankey's memorandum and address to us, in which he pointed out the great advantage arising from constant mutual intercourse between the representatives of nations'. But they clearly did not understand the essence of Sir Maurice Hankey's thesis on the subject of 'Diplomacy by Conference'. There is all the difference in the world between the results to be expected from a Conference of Ambassadors and from a Conference of Foreign Ministers. Sir Maurice Hankey's object was to *promote* constant mutual intercourse between 'principals', not to *utilise* the experience already existing in the diplomatic corps. No doubt, however, even in the spring of 1918, after nearly four years' experience of the war, it was difficult for men trained in the Foreign Office tradition to realise that Foreign Ministers, under the new conditions, would no longer be chained to their desks or confined to the routine of week-days and week-ends. It had not occurred to Sir Edward Grey in July 1914 to take the train for Vienna or Berlin. How then could a Conference for which, as the Committee observed, 'speedy action would be required' be otherwise composed than of persons to be found at a particular spot?

We have left to the last the more strictly juridical side of the Phillimore plan. Here the Committee saw to it that Mr Taft's ideas should be firmly resisted. There is a strict adherence to the non-committal language of the Hague Convention:[2]

[1] See pp. 47 and 111 above.   [2] See p. 121 above.

'If a dispute should hereafter arise between any of the Allied States as to the interpretation of a treaty, as to any question of international law, as to the existence of any fact which, if established, would constitute a breach of any international obligation, or as to the nature and extent of the reparation to be made for any such breach, if such dispute cannot be settled by negotiation, arbitration is recognised by the Allied States as the most effective and at the same time the most equitable means of settling the dispute.' This gave the Foreign Office—and the Cabinet and Parliament behind them—all that they needed. Their hands remained untied. They were free to adopt any procedure that they might think best in any given case. They had not surrendered their power of discretion in incalculable circumstances to an authority outside their own constitutional system, their own Realm of Law.

It was no doubt due to the foresight of the legal members of the Committee that there were added to the report two closing provisions, under the heading 'Conflict of Treaties', which are important enough to be quoted textually:

'The Allied States severally agree that the present Convention abrogates all treaty obligations *inter se* inconsistent with the terms hereof, and that they will not enter into any engagements inconsistent with the terms hereof.

'Where any of the Allied States, before becoming party to this Convention, shall have entered into any treaty imposing upon it obligations inconsistent with the terms of this Convention, it shall be the duty of such State to take immediate steps to procure its release from such obligations.'

II

The Phillimore Report was duly dispatched to Washington. But by November nothing was authoritatively known in the Foreign Office as to President Wilson's own plan for the League of Nations, of which he had now become recognised as the principal champion. The only available text on the subject, apart from pronouncements on particular problems, such as disarmament and 'equality of trade conditions', was Point XIV of the Fourteen Points of January 1918. This ran as follows:

'A general association of nations must be formed under specific covenants for the purpose of affording mutual guarantees of political independence and territorial integrity to great and small states alike.'

Here was an entirely different approach, an eighteenth-century approach—*guarantees*. Where did it spring from? What did it signify? It was impossible to say. President Wilson's mind on this subject was a mystery.

III

One other official document was available.

In July 1917 M. Ribot, then Prime Minister and Minister of Foreign Affairs, had appointed a Committee of leading French authorities to consider the problem of the 'Society of Nations'. It consisted of fourteen members, the Chairman being M. Léon Bourgeois, an ex-Prime Minister who had been leader of the French delegation at The Hague in 1907, and the two Vice-Chairmen being M. Jules Cambon, late Ambassador in

Berlin, and Admiral Lacaze. The Committee reported in June 1918 and its report was sent to the Foreign Office. It was also, of course, presented to the League of Nations Commission at the Peace Conference, where we shall meet it again.[1]

M. Bourgeois' scheme may be described as a stiffer edition of Mr Taft's. Like Mr Taft's, it is juridical in character: but it is more rigid in its arrangements both for the promulgation and for the enforcement of the law. In fact it closely resembles Mr Taft's *ideal*—international police force and all.[2] How surprised he must have been to see his distant vision brought down to earth in this fashion under the sponsorship of one of the most powerful governments in the world.

Legal disputes, under this French plan, are to go before 'an international tribunal', a full-dress judicial bench. All other disputes, together, apparently,[3] with the determination as to what is a legal dispute—here M. Bourgeois is more realistic than Mr Taft—come before a body composed of 'responsible ministers or their delegates'—in other words, the governments, with the Great Powers preponderating. This body will both *decide* the dispute and *ensure the execution* of its decision. Enforcement is provided for in case of need, by 'Sanctions' of various kinds, the enumeration of which takes up a good part of the document. Sanctions may be diplomatic, juridical, economic and, last but not least, military. These last are entrusted to a permanent international General Staff, which determines what contingents are to be called upon from the

---

[1] It is reprinted in Bourgeois, *Le Pacte du 1919 et la Société des Nations* (1919), p. 197 ff., and in Miller, *The Drafting of the Covenant*, ii. 238 ff.

[2] See p. 123 above.

[3] The wording on this point might have been made clearer.

individual members of the League, who are under the obligation of 'holding them at its disposition'.

Here are no loopholes left, either as regards decision or enforcement. Both Law and Order are perfectly provided for. And that is all. As the report observes: 'The League of Nations has not for its object the establishment of an international political state. It proposes nothing more than the maintenance of peace by the substitution of Right (*droit*) for Force in the settlement of conflict. Peace through Right—*La Paix par le Droit*—is its watchword.

Only on one point does the logic of this French (or should we say, Roman) project flinch. What is to be the membership of the Society of Nations? The very name suggests universality. Universality therefore would be the natural solution: 'the League of Nations', says the memorandum with a studied vagueness which is almost British, 'is universal in tendency'. But would this be *practical*? Can all nations be trusted to be equal to the duties of so responsible an association? The memorandum concludes that it is better to limit membership to 'nations constituted as States and provided with representative institutions permitting them to be considered as themselves responsible for the acts of their governments'. M. Bourgeois, like President Wilson, believed that, in an unregenerate world, it was best to begin with a restricted membership in order to make the world safe *at least* for democracy.

CHAPTER VII

A FOREIGN OFFICE MEMORANDUM

WE have examined the material available for study at
the Foreign Office in November 1918. Let us now see
how the problem presented itself to the advisers of the
British Government.

They were faced at one and the same moment both
with a condition and a theory. The condition was the
breakdown, or rather the extinction, of the system
under which relations between the powers had been
carried on throughout the nineteenth century. The
theory was 'the League of Nations', a high-sounding
phrase which had won the allegiance of millions but
to which very few attached any meaning in terms of
definite machinery or practical action. Both the condition and the theory called for immediate decisions—
the condition because, on the morrow of the Armistice,
the world's affairs required to be carried on and some
guiding principle was urgently required; the theory
because the peoples were crying out for a League of
Nations and the ruler of the most powerful state in the
world was about to cross the ocean to back up their
claims. There was thus both a void to be filled and an
ideal to be realised. Something had to be done to replace the Concert of Europe and the loose co-operation
established by the Final Act of the Treaty of Vienna.
And something had to be done to bring 'the League of

Nations' down from the clouds.

It was in some such mood as this that the memorandum printed at the end of this chapter was penned.[1] It was an attempt to meet both the demands of the moment, the practical and the idealistic. It met the former by proposing an improved Concert of the Powers. It met the latter by sifting the various proposals put forward and forming them into a comprehensive whole, thus constituting 'a League of Nations system'. In this system place was found for the scattered elements of pre-war international organisation, which were thus to be co-ordinated under a central authority and brought under more direct supervision by the governments and electorates. Thus the new system would consist of two main features: *arrangements for regular conference* and *collective treaties*.

The new Conference system was consciously inspired by the model of the War Council. But there entered into it also the thought of the British Imperial Conference. This system of regular meetings between governments, established long before the war, had not only stood the strain of war conditions but had emerged greatly strengthened, with a fine record of work to its credit. Diplomacy by Conference had proved its value during the war. And was not the war itself due, at least in large measure, to the absence of a system of regular Conference under the Concert of Europe? Did not the catastrophe become inevitable from the time that the European powers formed themselves into two

---

[1] In the first half of November 1918. The writer embodied the same ideas in an article contributed to the December issue of *The Round Table*. See *The Prospects of Democracy* (1929), where this article is reprinted (p. 165 ff.).

sharply divided groups, the Triple Alliance and the Triple Entente, each with its own system or, at least, habit of consultation? And was not this division, which hardened so rapidly into opposition, due to the absence of any obligation to come to sit regularly at a common table, under conditions permitting of frank and friendly discussion? Could not arrangements be devised which would make it morally impossible for a state, or a group of states, to remain apart and drift into an attitude of suspicion and bitterness?

This was the reasoning which led to the proposal for a *standing interstate Conference*, equipped with a permanent secretariat. As a regular working body the Conference, it was thought, would consist of the Great Powers, who would meet annually for a frank interchange of views, acting as a sort of executive Committee of the whole body of the members of the League. The larger gathering would meet at more infrequent intervals, possibly, like the British Imperial Conference, every four or five years.

Here we have the germ out of which the 'Council' and the 'Assembly' of the League were within a few weeks to develop. But as the draftsmen of the Covenant at Paris did not all of them understand, still less approve, the conception underlying the Foreign Office memorandum it is important that this should be clearly understood before we trace the later development.

The Council of the League was devised to be an *improved Concert*—improved in four ways: (1) by the provision of regular meetings; (2) by the equipment of a permanent secretariat; (3) by the enlargement of its area to include the whole world, and not Europe alone, as in the nineteenth century; and (4), last but not least, by becoming part of a world organisation composed of all or at least the overwhelming majority of states and being thus associated with a world-wide system of international co-operation. It was not to be merely an improved organisation of Power. It was to be a point of convergence between Power and Law. It was to be the inauguration of a Rule of Law under the guardianship of the powers, great and small.

What form was the Rule of Law to take? The simple form of a *guarantee of peace* or, in other words, the formulation, in a collective treaty or covenant (President Wilson had already used the word), of the principle of the Hue and Cry. Uneasy about the old-fashioned interpretation given by President Wilson to the term 'guarantee', which limited it to political independence and territorial integrity, whilst leaving the door open for war, the memorandum insisted that the essential issue was to associate all the peoples in the task of ensuring peace and restraining resort to violence. This 'simple guarantee', 'together with a statement of principle', was to be embodied in the Covenant. It would be accompanied by the arrangements for regular conference already described and the Phillimore Committee provisions for the peaceful settlement of disputes. These, it will be remembered, did not exclude resort to war after the process of Inquiry and Delay had been exhausted. In this new framework resort to war would be ruled out, and disputes which had not been settled would simply remain in suspense. On the other hand, the sanction provided for in the Phillimore plan would be attached to the new guarantee.[1]

Thus the League of Nations system, like the Athens of Solon, would be based on a firm foundation of order

[1] See p. 182 above.

and social solidarity. It would be, in the real sense of the words, a Society of States, and not only of states but of peoples.

We have now to see what it was proposed to erect on this foundation. Or, to change the metaphor, we have to see what streams were to converge in this new international channel. We have followed the course of three such streams—the Concert, the Hague and the type represented by the Postal Union. All three are provided for in the draft and associated with the new machinery of Conference.

The gulf between Power and Law is to be bridged by making the improved Concert responsible for 'the existing Hague organisation with any additions or modifications which may seem desirable'. Thus the new League Conference, a body composed of responsible statesmen, would concern itself directly with the Commissions of Inquiry and other devices set up at the Hague Conferences. The legalists, no doubt, would dislike it, but it was felt to be the best way of making the Hague machinery, so secluded in the years before the war, a factor that really counted in international politics.

At the same time the League system was to act as the connecting link between the various agencies, such as the Postal Union, set up by pre-war treaties. The new Conference would control and supervise their activities and they would be required to report regularly to it through the Secretariat.

Thus the Secretariat would have a double function. It would be deeply involved in high politics through its association with the improved Concert; and at the same time it would be a kind of central watch-tower for every kind of official international co-operation. In

o

this capacity it would be a *Secretariat of Secretariats*. The Secretariat of the Postal Union at Berne, for instance, would go on unchanged: but there would be a kind of super-Secretariat at Geneva, through which the work done at Berne and elsewhere would be reported to the larger and smaller Conferences—what are now known as the League Council and Assembly—and so linked up with other similar activities and made better known to the world.

Moreover, this concentration of international activities under the League would, it was hoped, stimulate activities, both official and unofficial, for the study of international problems. Some possible fields for such research are indicated in the memorandum. It is perhaps worth while singling out for special mention the suggestion for the study of the colour problem by a body on which Japan and India would be represented. This, it was thought, would be the best way of dealing with the *prevention of war*, as a long-distance problem, as contrasted with the short-distance problem of *restraining resort to violence*. For, in the long run, what was required was team-work among internationalists—that is, between men and women accustomed 'to look at problems from the point of view of the world as a whole'. Here is a foreshadowing of what later became known as 'the League Spirit'.

Shortly after this memorandum had been printed as a departmental document Lord Robert Cecil, who had on November 22 resigned from his position in the Government owing to his disagreement with it over the Welsh Church Bill, accepted the Foreign Secretary's invitation to take charge of the small League of Nations section in the department. Having examined the available material, he selected the memorandum as a basis to work from and asked that a summary should be prepared of the *organisation* that was envisaged in its proposals. This was done and there was added to it an outline of the Phillimore proposals for the prevention of war, which were only alluded to in the memorandum. The guarantee of peace, together with many other points, was not included in the shorter document. It was not a matter which required *organisation*, but an *obligation* to be included in the Covenant. This 'brief conspectus of League of Nations organisation', as it was described at the time, was the 'Cecil draft', familiar to students of the Covenant since 1919.[1] It was submitted to Lord Robert Cecil on December 14 and by him to the War Cabinet on the 17th. It was then taken to Paris, where on January 1 it was shown to Mr David Hunter Miller, President Wilson's Legal Adviser, together with a paper by General Smuts.

At this point the British and the American proposals confronted one another. From this confrontation there emerged the 'Hurst-Miller draft' which President Wilson placed on the table and succeeded in making the accepted basis of discussion at the first meeting of the League of Nations Commission of the Peace Conference on February 3. It is necessary therefore at this point to go back to the origins of President Wilson's draft. But before doing so something must be said about the Smuts memorandum.

---

[1] The Cecil draft was first published in the autumn of 1919 in the report of the hearings of the United States Senate Committee on Foreign Affairs (Senate Document No. 106, p. 1163). It is there described as 'Bullitt Exhibit No. 1'. It was later republished in Miller, *The Drafting of the Covenant*, ii. 61, where it is, rather misleadingly, placed *after* the Smuts memorandum.

A MEMORANDUM PREPARED FOR THE CONSIDERA-
TION OF THE BRITISH GOVERNMENT IN CON-
NEXION WITH THE FORTHCOMING PEACE
SETTLEMENT

THE LEAGUE OF NATIONS

ALTHOUGH the actual establishment of a League of Nations
cannot take place till a later period of the peace discussions, it
must, nevertheless, be to some extent a governing factor even
at this stage, since it will eventually supply the framework into
which the detailed arrangements of the settlement will be
required to fit. The following outline is put forward in the hope
and expectation that conditions on the continent of Europe
will render some arrangement of the kind possible before the
representatives of the various Powers at the Peace Conference have concluded their labours.

The establishment of what has come to be described as a
League of Nations would seem to divide itself into two parts:

1. Actual treaties and agreements of a collective character
   concluded by the civilised States of the world as a result
   of the Conference arising out of the war.
2. Arrangements for regular conference between these States
   in order to maintain, and as opportunity offers to extend,
   the understanding thus arrived at.

I. *Treaty Provisions*

The following points would seem to arise in connexion with
the treaties:

I. *Their Period of Validity.*—Since the League of Nations
involves associated action by the various States without any
derogation of their sovereignty, it is important to emphasise
the principle that the ultimate political responsibility for the
treaties and for the policy underlying them rests with the Parlia-

ments and peoples of the contracting Powers. Long-term, and
a fortiori permanent, engagements would be in contradiction to
this, and would tend to make the electors neglectful of their
obligations. Had the Belgian Treaty been renewable at regular
intervals the position in July 1914 would have been clearer. It
is suggested that the whole series of treaties should be for a
period of ten years only. This would provide useful opportunities at regularly recurring intervals for the amendment and
extension of obligations, or, should public opinion in any
country set in that direction, for their denunciation.

Probably, however, the actual guarantee of *peace* on which
the League is founded should be a permanent engagement and,
in this case, that simple guarantee, embodying the provisions
agreed upon for the pacific settlement of disputes and for
regular conference, together with a statement of principle,
should be embodied in a separate treaty.

II. In accordance with President Wilson's First Point, the
contracting Powers would bind themselves to make public any
treaties and understandings between one another or between
a member of the League and any one or more States outside the
League. Such treaties and agreements should be registered with
the secretariat of the Inter-State Conference mentioned below.

III. The obligations entered into should be clear and explicit
and capable of control and scrutiny by the other members of
the League. This axiom would seem at first sight to rule out:

(*a*) Any definite arrangement for the limitation of armaments according to an agreed scale, since the term armament defies accurate analysis, and the development of
commercial aircraft in the near future will still further
blur the distinction between implements of war and
instruments of peaceful intercourse.

(*b*) Provisions designed to limit the weapons or methods by
which war can be carried on. The experience of many
centuries, confirmed by the events of the war, shows that
such provisions have generally tended to favour unscrupulous Powers as against their opponents. We should
aim at embodying in the League of Nations Treaty only
such of the rules relating to war as have been observed

during this war by the Allies even when violated by the enemy, *e.g.* respect for the lives of non-combatants at sea.

IV. President Wilson's Fourteenth Point speaks of 'specific covenants for the purpose of affording mutual guarantees of political independence and territorial integrity to great and small States alike'. The question arises whether a specific guarantee to that effect should be embodied in the settlement. Recognition of the political independence of the contracting Powers is implicit in a treaty compact, and their territorial integrity is equally implied by the fact that the numerous geographical provisions embodied in the treaties will be endorsed by all the signatories. It may be doubted whether it would be wise to go further and to select the political independence and, in particular, the territorial integrity of the signatory States as matters requiring a specific guaranteeing clause. Such a guarantee would seem to imply that the frontiers of the signatory States, as they stood at the signing of peace, were regarded as being unalterable under all circumstances. It has indeed been frequently stated by Allied statesmen that it is one of our objects, in the forthcoming peace, to rearrange the map of the world in such a way as to lay the foundations of a durable peace. But it would be unwise to interpret this too literally, or to let it be implied that under no circumstances will a boundary be hereafter altered except by agreement between the States concerned. It should be remembered:

(*a*) That it is impossible to predict the changes in the composition of the population of any given area which may be brought about by migration or economic developments, or the political problems which may result from such changes.

(*b*) That, so far as State boundaries are determined by national feeling, the sentiment of nationality is still undeveloped over a large part of the world, while in Eastern Europe and Western Asia it is in a condition of such ferment that the boundaries fixed in such regions by the Peace Conference must be a matter of special concern to the Powers for many years to come, if only in the interests of racial and religious minorities. It is in fact only in quite a small number of cases, where geography and national sentiment speak with unmistakable authority, that boundaries can be regarded as in all circumstances unalterable. The Pyrenees are the best instance of a fixed geographical frontier and the Northern frontier of the United States of a fixed political frontier; but there are hardly any land frontiers, even in Western Europe, the alteration of which can be ruled out as, politically speaking, inconceivable; thus the frontiers of Switzerland and of Holland, to take two relatively stable neutral States, when looked at closely, reveal possibilities of readjustment in every direction. The Dollart coast, Zeeland, Limburg, Schaffhausen, Savoy, Vorarlberg, Ticino might any of them, by a turn of the political wheel, become international questions.

On the other hand, as already stated, it is essential that the provisions of the treaty should be clear and explicit, and it is dangerous to burke what will be a burning question, *i.e.* whether territorial integrity is or is not implicit in the treaty compacts, and whether the League is pledged to intervene against forcible transfers of territory and alterations of boundaries. It seems preferable, therefore, to exclude such a guarantee from the permanent treaty suggested under Section I above, but to include it, even though its inclusion may be otiose, in the individual treaties concluded for the brief period suggested above. This point is closely connected with the rights of minorities dealt with in the immediately following section.

V. *The Rights of Minorities.*—Efforts will doubtless be made to embody provisions in the treaty safeguarding the rights of racial, religious and other minorities and, further, to interpret the doctrine of 'national self-determination' as entitling such minorities, if they can claim to be nations, to present their case to the Peace Conference and to subsequent Inter-State Conferences. On both these points the best course would seem to be to leave as much discretion as possible in the hands of each of the Associated Powers. It would clearly be inadvisable to go even the smallest distance in the direction of admitting the claim of the American negroes, or the Southern Irish, or the Flemings or

Catalans, to appeal to an Inter-State Conference over the head of their own Government. Yet if a right of appeal is granted to the Macedonians or the German Bohemians it will be difficult to refuse it in the case of other nationalist movements. There is ample experience to show that attempts to dictate to an independent Power, by treaty provisions, a detailed policy of toleration and racial and religious equality in regard to education, worship, appointments to the public service, etc., is foredoomed to failure. The alternative policy of trusting members of the League to be true to their professions, and of offering them counsel and assistance in carrying them out, is likely to create a much more favourable atmosphere. The best course would seem to be to abstain from laying down any detailed treaty provisions as to the government of States which, like Czechoslovakia, are recognised as fully sovereign, but, where circumstances really absolutely require it, as in certain cases in the Balkans, to insert a general provision or *voeu*, embodying the principles of toleration and equality before the law, or guaranteeing special rights such as those relating to language, schools, etc. The conditions thus indicated would then become a mandate to the sovereign Power concerned as from the League, but instead of making this a starting point for perpetual haphazard interference by the 'Concert of Europe', as in the past, the treaty providing for a mandate of this kind in a particular case should provide also for the appointment of a commission of investigation to examine into the application of the general terms of the treaty. Such a commission should deliberate and report to the sovereign Power and should have the right to publish any such report.

If we adhere, in the treaties themselves, so far as possible to the doctrine of non-intervention in internal affairs we shall be on stronger ground in dealing with Governments which make propaganda in foreign countries a leading feature of their policy. We have to look forward to a period when Bolshevism—or the religion of the international class war—will be a prominent factor in European policy, and may at any time seize the reins of power in States which are, or desire to become, members of the League. We ought to lay it down in set terms that Governments which promote propaganda subversive of the Government of their neighbours are outside the pale of the League's membership. We can base our attitude here on the principle laid down in President Wilson's speech of March 5, 1917: 'The community of interest and of power upon which peace must henceforth depend imposes upon each nation the duty of seeing to it that all influences proceeding from its own citizens meant to encourage and assist revolution in other states should be sternly and effectually suppressed and prevented'. (The application of this to the activities of Irish-American Republican organisations will not be overlooked.)

VI. *Equality of Trade.*—Point Three of President Wilson's terms consists of an expression of opinion in favour of the removal of all economic barriers and of a definite provision for the establishment of an 'equality of trade conditions' among the members of the League of Nations. The first clause cannot be embodied in the treaty; it may be regarded rather in the light of a term of reference to any international bodies charged with economic functions. The second clause can probably be interpreted to mean the establishment of a universal system of most-favoured-nation treatment between the contracting Powers on the analogy of the system which prevailed over a large part of Europe in the two decades following the Cobden Treaty of 1860. The embodiment of this provision in the treaty is open to several difficulties:

(a) It involves a change in the American interpretation of most-favoured-nation treatment. At present, under decisions of the United States Supreme Court, most-favoured-nation treatment is held in that country to be compatible with reciprocity arrangements which discriminate against third powers. Thus the existing treaties between the United States on the one hand and Brazil and Cuba on the other offend against the principle of equality of trade conditions. It will be impossible to enact a universal most-favoured-nation system in the treaty until agreement has been arrived at as to the meaning of the term, and until existing American practice, which has hitherto enjoyed the support of the Republican party, has been brought into harmony with the policy advocated by the President.

(b) It is doubtful whether a universal most-favoured-nation system would be convenient for the newly liberated peoples of Eastern Europe. Such a system would make it impossible for any country to enter into a commercial alliance or customs union with its neighbours, and would therefore compel such countries to enter into political unions or federations. In the existing state of opinion in Eastern Europe it is doubtful whether Bohemia, Poland, Hungary and other countries in a similar position will desire to forgo their new-won sovereign independence; yet they may be driven by economic necessity into close relations of some kind with their neighbours.

(c) Most-favoured-nation treatment is in any case not enough to establish an 'equality of trade conditions', and it is to our interest to press for a more complete recognition of the implications of that phrase.

Whilst therefore some provision to this effect should be embodied in the treaty, sufficient to safeguard the contracting Powers (except in certain cases agreed upon) from the more obvious forms of discriminative treatment, the whole subject should be referred for more detailed investigation to an International Commission.

The question of access to the sea for inland states, claimed for Poland and Serbia in the Fourteen Points and more generally for all great peoples struggling to be free in the speech of January 22, 1917, arises under this head. It is suggested in a separate memorandum that the best way of meeting this need will be to establish a number of special commissions for certain scheduled ports and their hinterland routes and to place all these commissions under the general authority of a permanent Transit Commission appointed by and responsible to the Inter-State Conference.

VII. The treaty should give precision to the idea of the responsibility of the civilised States to the more backward peoples. Trusts or, to speak more precisely, charters should be drawn up for the various territories for whose future government the signatory Powers have to issue a mandate, and particular areas handed over to individual States who would be responsible to the League for the discharge of that mandate. Arrangements of this kind will require to be made for tropical Africa, for the Pacific Islands and for Western Asia.

VIII. As regards the settlement of disputes we should take our stand on the scheme laid down in the Phillimore Report and should support the embodiment of provisions to this effect in the general treaty referred to in Section I above.

II. *Arrangements for Regular Conference*

1. The organisation of the machinery for regular conference would seem to grow naturally out of the existing consultations at Versailles. The fundamental principle of the League would be that it is a meeting of Governments with Governments, each Government preserving its own independence and being responsible to its own people. The simplest way of perpetuating the existing meetings would be to provide that the Foreign Secretaries of the Great Powers (Britain, France, Italy, Japan and the United States with Germany and Russia when stable constitutional governments are established there) should meet annually for a frank interchange of views, and that the Foreign Secretaries of all the signatory Powers should meet at less frequent intervals, possibly every four or five years. In this way the Great Powers would stand out as being, what in fact they are, a sort of executive committee of the whole body of sovereign States. This arrangement would serve as an inducement to smaller Powers, such as the Scandinavian and Western Slav States, to form political unions such as would entitle them to rank as first-class Powers.

The public should be kept informed as to the range of subjects discussed at such meetings, and, as in the case of the Imperial Conference, a report of the proceedings with confidential matter omitted should subsequently be issued. This body would be known as the *Inter-State Conference*, and should be provided for in the general treaty of the League.

2. There would be an International Secretariat, the general

secretaryship being held in rotation for a period of several years' duration by a member of one of the Great Powers.

3. This secretariat would act as a channel of communication to the Inter-State Conference for all activities undertaken by international bodies under the supervision of the Inter-State Conference. Such activities would fall into three classes:

(i) *Judicial.*—The existing Hague organisation with any additions or modifications which may seem desirable would be placed under the authority of the Inter-State Conference, the independence of the judges or conciliators being secured by the method and terms of their appointment.

(ii) *International Administrative Bodies.*—There are a large number of existing bodies engaged in performing international functions in accordance with treaty arrangements. A list of them is given in Oppenheim, *International Law*, vol. i. 612 ff. They range from the Postal Union to the International Seismologic Association. These bodies at present work in isolation, and they are, moreover, very various in their composition. The conventions under which they work should be embodied among the treaties guaranteed by the League, and they should be required to report regularly to the Inter-State Conference through the secretariat.

It will, no doubt, be found necessary to set up a certain number of new bodies of this kind. These would seem to fall under two heads: (*a*) bodies performing local functions, such as the Danube and other Transit Commissions; (*b*) some of the existing inter-Allied bodies called into existence for war purposes may have to be retained in the form of international bodies. We must be guided here by the experience of the transition period, but the concentration of commercial and industrial power brought about by the war, and the general trend towards the development of international syndicates exercising large political influence may make it necessary for the League of Nations to undertake very considerable obligations in order to counteract the private power of such corporations. It is too early to make suggestions under this head, but this is probably the side of the League's work which will excite the greatest public interest, and on which its success and failure in the public mind will chiefly depend in the first lease of its existence.

4. *International Bodies for Study and Inquiry.*—The chief dangers to the world's peace in the future arise in connexion with problems which are not at present, and will perhaps never be, ripe for judicial determination. The League of Nations will be incomplete unless it sets on foot arrangements by which such problems can be discussed from different points of view in an atmosphere of study and detachment. It would therefore seem desirable to institute a number of permanent standing commissions to watch, discuss, and make periodical reports upon problems which involve contentions and dangerous issues, or a discussion of which is desirable in the interests of civilisation as a whole. The following possible classification of such subjects is suggested:

(i) *Justice,* covering the group of problems already dealt with in small part by the Slave Trade Treaty of 1841, and the White Slave Traffic Agreements of 1904 and 1910.

(ii) *Health.*—The question of preventing the spread of disease during the period of demobilisation is likely to be a very actual one, and may require special regulation. There are a number of existing conventions dealing with cholera, plague and other health questions, but the whole subject is in need of further inquiry and administrative development. Advance should be easy in this field, as there would seem to be no ground for divergence of interest between the Powers.

(iii) *Industrial Conditions.*—A demand will certainly arise both from America and from Germany for a stiffening of the existing provisions under the Berne Convention of 1906. The time is probably ripe for a certain step forward, but progress will be impeded for some time to come by the low standard of administration in practically every country except Britain and Germany. A standing commission of investigation into this whole subject, including the question of administration, would be of the greatest value.

(iv) *Finance and Currency.*—A body of experts approaching this difficult group of subjects from the point of view of the world as a whole will probably be able to make valuable recommendations on problems with which it is difficult, if not impossible, for individual Governments to deal separately.

(v) *Transit*, land, sea and air. As suggested in another memorandum, a permanent International Commission on this subject may be required to supervise the activities of various local Commissions established to secure free access to the sea for inland populations, in accordance with President Wilson's speech of January 22, 1917. It would probably be most convenient for this body also to undertake systematic inquiry into the large group of problems opened out under this head. Such problems as the fair adjustment of freight rates on main lines of communication by sea and land, and the working-out of the rules of the air would fall within its scope.

(vi) *Conservation of Resources.*—Although several treaties exist for the preservation of animals in Africa and elsewhere, no means exist at present for enabling the world to know whether or not it is wisely husbanding its animal, vegetable and mineral resources. A body or bodies similar to the Mineral Resources Board proposed for the British Empire in the report of the Dominions Royal Commission would seem capable of performing very useful service in this direction.

(vii) A Commission of investigation has already been suggested in connexion with the question of equality of trade conditions. Amongst the questions on which this body would be asked to give advice and make recommendations, 'dumping' may be specially mentioned.

(viii) The problem of the relation between the various races of mankind, in particular what is known as the colour problem, should be kept under permanent review by a body on which representatives of Japan, and of India and possibly of other races concerned, would sit side by side with European representatives. In questions where varying standards of life are involved, this body would no doubt confer jointly with the Industrial Commission.

(ix) A separate Commission should be appointed to deal with the problems of the Tropics, including the whole tropical region of Africa.

It should not be difficult to secure a strong personnel for these Commissions, both on the practical and more theoretical side, provided that the status and pay are made sufficiently attractive. The association in this work of some of the best brains from a number of different countries should promote a process of political invention which may be of very great service to civilisation. Experience shows that internationalism, which may be defined as the habit of looking at problems from the point of view of the world as a whole, can best be developed in an atmosphere of this kind.

III. *Arrangements for Popular Discussion*

President Wilson laid stress in his Mount Vernon speech on the formation 'of an organised opinion of mankind'. It would seem desirable to establish some body which would serve as a medium for the formation and expression of such a body of opinion. If this is not done, the Socialist International, which has, as it were, a vested interest in international opinion, will cover the same ground with unsatisfactory results. The best expedient would seem to be the institution of a periodical Congress of delegates of the Parliaments of the members of the League, meeting perhaps every four years. The delegations of this Congress might be chosen on a proportional system from amongst the various parties in the national Parliaments. The assignment of numbers to individual States will be a difficult problem, but since the votes taken will not be binding, British interests will not be greatly affected by it, and in any case it is desirable for educational reasons that the more backward countries should be substantially represented. The defect of large congresses is generally that they devote their time to debating academic resolutions. In this case, however, a regular staple of discussion will be afforded by the reports of the Inter-State Conference and of all the different international bodies, issued through the secretariat. The discussions would therefore in part be concerned with practical matters of business, and only in part with general questions. The Congress would embody its conclusions in recommendations which would be referred back to the sovereign Parliaments: and if, as is to be expected, much of its work were done through Committees, many of its recommendations on practical matters might secure or approach unanimity. The authority which it would wield would, of course, be purely moral, and would greatly depend on the degree of education in the various countries and on the atmosphere of their public life; but it could hardly be a hindrance and might prove to be a real help to the Inter-State Conference, on which the main burden of the work of maintaining the unity and welfare of civilisation would fall.

CHAPTER VIII

THE SMUTS PLAN

ON December 16 General Smuts, who had been for some time a member of the Imperial War Cabinet, wrote the foreword to an essay which was published very shortly afterwards under the title *The League of Nations: a Practical Suggestion*. It had, he explained, been 'hastily written at the last moment, and amid other pressing duties, in view of the early meeting of the peace conference'.

In its main lines, the plan put forward in the essay adheres to the standpoint and reinforces the argument of the Foreign Office memorandum. In some cases the actual wording is closely followed. In this respect General Smuts rendered a service to the advocates of a realistic League by supporting them with the whole weight of his authority as soldier, statesman and philosopher, and it may be added, with the persuasive power of his pen. In his opening words he ranges himself definitely against the Day After To-morrow School, who regarded the League simply 'as a means of preventing future wars'. In his eyes it was primarily to be 'a great organ of the ordinary peaceful life of civilisation', 'part and parcel of the common international life of states', 'an ever visible, living working organ of the polity of civilisation'. 'Its peace activity must be the foundation and guarantee of its war-power.'

Thereupon he proceeds to outline the main features of the Foreign Office memorandum. The League will not be a super-state but a 'permanent conference' between independent governments for 'joint international action in certain defined respects'. It will do its work through a 'general conference' which is to meet 'periodically' and a smaller body 'which will be the Executive and carry on the ordinary administration of the League'. This smaller body should also deal with disputes, on the lines of the Phillimore plan, as adopted by the Foreign Office memorandum. The suggestions for a League Secretariat and for the work of international administration and inquiry are modelled closely on the memorandum. There is, however, no mention of an inquiry into the colour problem.

But on certain points the Smuts plan diverged from the memorandum and these changes proved to be of far-reaching importance.

In the first place, the guarantee of peace was omitted. General Smuts had not a sufficient belief in the social solidarity of the civilised world to regard the Hue and Cry as practical politics. Like the Phillimore Committee, therefore, he leaves open a gap for war after the resources of Inquiry and Delay have been exhausted.

In the second place, he was greatly concerned with the future of the German colonies, especially in Africa. The memorandum had proposed that 'the treaty' (that is, the Covenant) 'should give precision to the idea of the responsibility of the civilised states to the more backward peoples' and that 'particular areas should be handed over to individual states who would be responsible to the League for the discharge of that mandate'. General Smuts warmly espoused the idea of placing territories for whose welfare the League was responsible under the rule of individual governments. 'Joint international administration,' he said, obviously referring to certain idealistic proposals put forward in Labour circles, 'in so far as it has been applied to territories or peoples, has been found wanting wherever it has been tried. It has worked fairly well in international business arrangements of a limited scope, such as postal arrangements, the Danube Commission and similar cases. But in those few cases where it has been tried in respect of peoples or territories it has not been a success. The administering personnel taken from different nations do not work smoothly or loyally together.' The experience of the Congo Free State was evidently in his mind.

But when he comes to enumerate the territories which should be placed under mandate in this way his argument takes a surprising turn. He proposes to exclude the German Pacific and African colonies from the scope of the new mandate system. The reason given is that they are inhabited by 'barbarians who not only cannot possibly govern themselves, but to whom it would be impracticable to apply any idea of self-determination in the European sense'. They must therefore be treated 'as a special case falling outside the scope of the principles applicable to the European and Asiatic communities' to whom alone the mandate system was applicable. Nothing more is said in the essay therefore about Africa and the Pacific. Instead, however, a scheme is worked out—or rather, lightly sketched—for making the League the 'reversionary' of the Russian, Austrian and Turkish empires. 'Europe is being liquidated and the League of Nations must be the heir to this great estate. The peoples left behind by the decomposition of Russia, Austria and Turkey are mostly untrained politically; many of them are either incapable of or deficient in power of self-government; they are mostly destitute and will require much nursing towards economic and political independence.' In plain English this was a proposal that the four Western Powers—Great Britain, the United States, France and Italy, together with Japan and Germany 'as soon as she has a stable democratic government' —should become responsible for the government of Eastern Europe, Western Asia and Asiatic Russia. The hope that these territories might be 'nursed' economically had already had to be abandoned when the proposal was made. As to its political and psychological implications, perhaps they can be disposed of by the mention of four names—Masaryk, Pilsudski, Lenin, Mustapha Kemal. It is not surprising that no more was heard of this scheme for diverting the mandate system from a plan for the betterment of backward peoples to something not very far removed from a twentieth-century Holy Alliance.

The third deviation from the memorandum was the change made in the title and composition of the *interstate Conference*. General Smuts re-christened it as 'the Council of the League' and increased its numbers by four additional members who were to take their places by rotation from two panels, one consisting of 'the important intermediate powers below the rank of Great Powers' (Central Russia, Poland, Hungary, Turkey and Greater Serbia—all in his mandated area— are mentioned in this connexion), and the other comprising all the other minor states in the League. The 'Council' would thus consist of two classes of members; the Great Powers would be 'permanent members', the other four members would be temporary.

This change of name and modification of membership and terms of tenure might seem a comparatively
slight readjustment of the original scheme; but to
anyone with experience of European politics it must
have been clear that these alterations would have
an important effect upon the working of what was
bound in any case to be a very delicate experiment.
To bring the whole body of states together in a
periodical Conference was one thing: to find a satisfactory means for the participation of some of them
in the work of the smaller executive Committee was
quite another. Moreover, the difficulty was intensified by a provision that voting on the Council should
not be by unanimity. In compensation, however, it
was to be heavily weighted: three adverse votes would
be sufficient to prevent the adoption of a resolution—
more than a two-thirds majority. This proposal was all
the more curious in view of the isolated position in
which South Africa has sometimes found herself at the
Imperial Conference. It undermined the whole basis of
the League as previously laid down and had evidently
not been fully thought out.

The last important deviation from the memorandum
was the introduction of the problem of armaments and
the prominence assigned to it. Three points were
selected by General Smuts for discussion: the abolition
of conscription and of conscript armies, the limitation
of armaments and the nationalisation of munitions
production. Of these he regarded the first as 'by far
the most important', adding that owing to the 'volume
of public opinion' behind it, it would be the most easy
of the three to carry through. Conscription should be
replaced by 'a simple militia system on a scale of

numbers and service agreed upon by the League', or by volunteers. As to the limitation of armaments, General Smuts realised that this would involve trying to find an answer to 'two conundrums': 'What are armaments?' and 'On what principle can one weapon of destruction be valued against another of a different kind?' Nevertheless he proposed that, *after the abolition of conscription*, the League Council should 'determine what direct military equipment and armament' was 'fair and reasonable' for the new militia or volunteer armies. As for the manufacture of arms, he proposed that all such factories should be nationalised and that their production should be 'subject to the inspection of the officers of the Council', which was also to be 'furnished periodically with returns of imports and exports of munitions of war into or from the territories of its members and, as far as possible, into or from other countries'.

All these three proposals regarding armaments, as we shall see, were to be taken up at the Peace Conference.[1]

---

[1] It should be remembered that at the time when the Smuts memorandum was written the abolition of conscription was a battle-cry in a British General Election then in progress. The 'volume of public opinion' referred to was, therefore, British opinion. Continental opinion on this subject was very different owing to the traditional association between democracy and the principle of 'the nation in arms', as against the ascendancy of a professional military caste. See p. 65 above. This mistake made by General Smuts and others in regarding compulsory military service rather than the political power of professional soldiers as 'the taproot of militarism' proved a serious hindrance to their understanding of post-war conditions on the Continent. For an acute American criticism of the memorandum see Miller, *The Drafting of the Covenant*, i. 34-5.

CHAPTER IX

So far we have been watching the development of the idea of the League of Nations in British minds. We have kept President Wilson in the background because, as has already been said, there was no means of knowing in London what form of organisation he had in view or how he intended to clothe the political ideas that he was so eloquently setting forth and associating with the project of a League of Nations. We have now to retrace our steps in order to watch how the idea of the League of Nations took shape in the mind of the man who will live in history as its founder.

Strangely enough, we shall find ourselves carried first to Latin America. For, just as, for the British Foreign Office, the Covenant was conceived as an improved and enlarged Concert of Europe, so for President Wilson the Covenant was an improved and enlarged Monroe Doctrine.

President Wilson was the son of a Presbyterian minister of Scotch-Irish descent; and he was born in Virginia and brought up in Georgia. Thus two strains of political thought were early implanted in his tenacious mind—the missionary zeal of the Covenanters and the devotion of the Southern Democrats to Popular Sovereignty or self-determination. Enthusiasm for the political regeneration of mankind was uneasily

215

yoked with a stern insistence on the maintenance of the rights and liberties of individual states and peoples. Thus Internationalism and Democracy shared his allegiance. There was no necessary incompatibility between the two. But their respective spheres needed to be carefully delimited. It was because this task was not undertaken, because President Wilson never fully thought out his political philosophy and brought its elements into harmony, that confusion ensued.

President Wilson came to power in March 1913 determined to inaugurate a new era in the foreign policy of the United States. There was to be 'a New Freedom' abroad as well as at home. In concrete terms this meant that in dealing with weaker powers the United States would not act as the agent of business interests or bolster up tyrannical governments against the wishes of the peoples concerned. Thus immediately on his accession to power he withdrew the government's support from a proposed 'six-power' loan to China and took the first steps leading towards the independence of the Philippines.

But it was with Latin America and with the interpretation of the Monroe Doctrine that his mind was chiefly occupied during the first year of his Presidency. His aim was to use the Monroe Doctrine as a means for counteracting the fear of an ascendancy of the United States in Latin America and for bringing about a partnership or association of American States for the advancement of democracy in world affairs. This reinterpretation of the Monroe Doctrine he expounded to the world in a speech at Mobile, Alabama, on October 27, 1913, and proceeded to illustrate, under great difficulties, by his policy towards General Huerta, the dictator of Mexico.

Then came the war. For Wilson, as for his friend
Colonel House and for most Americans, it signified the
moral bankruptcy of the Old Continent with its rival
ambitions and age-long hatreds. But for Wilson and
House it signified also, more specifically, the bankruptcy
of European diplomacy, resulting from the lack of an
organised system of international co-operation. The
ingenious mind of House had been playing with the
possibilities of such a system during two visits that
he had paid to Europe in the spring of 1913 and in the
early summer of 1914. His thoughts revolved around
the notion of an agreement between the United States,
Great Britain and Germany for the development of
'the waste places of the world'. The outbreak of the
war, which seemed to delay indefinitely the application
of such ideas to Europe, threw him back on the creation
of a system of international co-operation in North and
South America. On December 16, 1914, he suggested to
Wilson that he should 'formulate a plan to be agreed
upon by the republics of the two continents, which in
itself would serve as a model for the European nations'
when the time came for making peace.[1]

The rest of the episode is best told in House's own
words:

I could see that this excited his enthusiasm. My idea was that
the republics of the two continents should agree to guarantee
each other's territorial integrity and that they should also agree
to government ownership of munitions of war. I suggested that
he take a pencil and write the points to be covered.

He took a pencil and this is what he wrote:

1st. Mutual guarantees of political independence under

[1] *The Intimate Papers of Colonel House* (1926), i. 214-15. See also
pp. 246-9. In making use of this record it must be remembered that
President Wilson's letters have not yet been made available in textual
form, though Colonel House's editor was allowed to paraphrase them.

republican forms of government and mutual guarantees of territorial integrity.

2nd. Mutual agreement that the government of each of the contracting parties acquire complete control within its jurisdiction of the manufacture and sale of munitions of war.

He wished to know if there was anything else. I thought this was sufficient, taken in conjunction with the Bryan peace treaties which had already been concluded between the republics of the two continents.

He then went to his little typewriter and made a copy of what he had written, and handed it to me to use with the three South American Ambassadors with whom it was thought best to initiate negotiations.

The negotiations which followed began hopefully but soon ran into difficulties which do not concern us here. Gradually 'the Pan-American Pact was pushed to one side and with the entrance of the United States into the European War in the spring of 1917 it slipped into a forgotten grave'.

But its central idea remained immutably fixed in the President's mind. In the first article of the Revised Draft of the Pan-American Pact[1] it appears in the following form: 'The high contracting parties to this solemn Covenant and agreement hereby join one another in a common and mutual guaranty of territorial integrity and of political independence under republican forms of government'.

Thus we understand, what was a mystery to those studying the subject in London at the time,[2] how, when, early in 1918, the President outlined his idea of the League of Nations, he did so in what seemed the old-fashioned language of guarantees. 'A general association of nations', he said in his Fourteenth Point,

_____

[1] House, i. 239.   [2] See p. 186 above.

on January 8, 1918, 'must be formed under specific covenants for the purpose of affording mutual guarantees of political independence and territorial integrity to great and small states alike.'[1]

Let us pause to examine what these words imply. A guarantee of political independence and territorial integrity, as we have seen, is a form of protection afforded, under the old international system, by a strong state to a weaker state. In a world in which war is frequent and faithlessness abounds, a weak state secures additional protection—a sort of re-insurance— by having its treaty with one power countersigned by another and stronger power. The treaty is, so to speak, put into an envelope on which there are additional signatures inscribed.

Wilson takes up this old-fashioned idea and tries to bring it up to date without destroying the basis of sovereignty on which it reposes. The guarantee becomes *mutual*. It is given, and taken, by strong and weak states alike. Great and small are put under the same régime, and this is to be both *expanded* and *democratised*. There is to be a *general association* of

[1] The same form of words is used in the speech of May 27, 1916, which, according to House, 'sums up the gist of his [President Wilson's] international aims in the following years'. See House, ii. 298-9, who emphasises that the programme of self-determination there proclaimed for the peoples of Europe ('Every people has a right to choose the sovereignty under which they shall live') is simply a positive and concrete application of the principles of the Mobile address. See also Professor Rappard's account of his conversation with President Wilson on November 1, 1917. The President told him: 'What I should like to do for the world is what I unsuccessfully attempted to do for the American continent a year or two ago' (*International Relations as Viewed from Geneva* (1925), p. 103). How tenaciously Wilson held fast to this central idea is illustrated by his remarks in Paris supporting the 'Monroe Doctrine amendment' to the Covenant, where he describes it as 'nothing but a confirmation and extension of the Monroe Doctrine' (Miller, i. 444: see also his remarks on board ship, i. 42).

nations, thus making the strength of many—great and small alike—available for each one. The envelope is to be covered with a whole cluster of signatures. And, just as in the Pan-American pact it was to be a bond between peoples living 'under republican forms of government', so, in Wilson's thought, as expressed in many other speeches, the mutual guarantees would be given and taken by democracies: they would help 'to make the world safe for democracy'.

With this central idea in his mind, Wilson authorised House to take up the detailed study of the subject. He thus started off from the first on a track entirely different from that of President Taft and the League to Enforce Peace, whose proposals, says House, 'it does not appear that he studied seriously'. At the same time, whilst stimulating enthusiasm for the idea of the League of Nations, he did his best to damp down discussion of its details, on the ground that it would provoke controversy which might endanger success at a later stage. It was at his instance that the British Government agreed to resist the strong demand for the publication of the Phillimore Report.

Colonel House's reflections and consultations took shape on July 16, 1918, in the form of a draft 'Covenant of the League of Nations'. It is a curious amalgam, a strain of ethical idealism being intermixed with a number of practical suggestions somewhat loosely strung together.

The keynote is struck by the Preamble and the first four articles, which run as follows:

Preamble.—International civilisation having proved a failure because there has not been constructed a fabric of law to which nations have yielded with the same obedience and deference as individuals submit to intra-national laws, and because public opinion has sanctioned unmoral acts relating to international affairs, it is the purpose of the States signatory to this Convention to form a League of Nations having for its purpose the maintenance throughout the world of peace, security, progress, and orderly government. Therefore it is agreed as follows:

Article I.—The same standards of honour and ethics shall prevail internationally and in affairs of nations as in other matters. The agreement or promise of a Power shall be inviolate.

Article II.—No official of a Power shall, either directly or by indirection on behalf of his Government, be expected or permitted to act or communicate other than consistently with the truth, the honour and the obligation of the Power which he represents.

Article III.—Any attempt by a Power, either openly or in secret, whether by propaganda or otherwise, to influence one Power or nation against another shall be deemed dishonourable.

Article IV.—Any open or direct inquiry regarding the acts or purposes of a Power may be made by another Power as of course, and shall be regarded as an act of friendship tending to promote frankness in international relations, but any secret inquiry to such end shall be deemed dishonourable.

'The Preamble', wrote House to Wilson, 'and Articles I, II and III are the keystone of the arch. It is absolutely essential for the peoples of the world to realise that they can never have international peace and order if they permit their representatives to sanction the unmoral practices of the past.'

Here we have the first enunciation of a theme—one might call it a *leitmotiv*—which we shall find running through the thought of Wilson and his intimate. It is the appeal to the conscience of the plain people against the evil practices of their rulers, an appeal akin to that of the prophets of the Old Testament against Baal-worshipping kings. For Wilson the Presbyterian (as opposed to Wilson the Southern Democrat) was not a political thinker, still less the head of a government: he was a preacher, with a voice going out unto the ends of the earth, with an invisible Church, a congregation of believers in all countries, hanging on to his words. When this cosmic mood was on him he overleaped the boundaries of states and ignored the obligations of civic allegiance, calling on all men to obey him. It was in this spirit that, in his voyage to Europe in December 1918, he assembled his collaborators like a body of apostles and told them that they 'would be the only disinterested people at the peace conference', that the men whom they were about to deal with 'did not represent their own people', and that it was to be their business at the Conference 'to fight for a new order, agreeably if we can, disagreeably if necessary'. This explains how he came later to appeal to the people of Italy, on the Fiume question, over the heads of their rulers, and how he reconciled his conception of an 'organised opinion of mankind' with a notion of sovereignty so stiff as to rule out, immediately and unceremoniously, as 'unconstitutional' and 'impossible' the idea of an international police force to uphold 'the new order'.[1]

The opening articles of the House draft disappeared under Wilson's hand: but their spirit was preserved in the Preamble of Wilson's first draft, which was drawn up not long after he had received that of Colonel House. It is worth reproducing here, not simply because of its ethical content, but for purposes of comparison with the final state which it assumed after the incorporation of British amendments:

Preamble.—In order to secure peace, security and orderly government by the prescription of open and honourable rela-

[1] See Miller, i. 41, 43, 209.

tions between nations, by the firm establishment of the under-standings of international law as the actual rule of conduct among governments, and by the maintenance of justice and a scrupulous respect of all treaty obligations in the dealings of all organised peoples with one another, the Powers signatory to this covenant and agreement jointly and severally adopt this constitution of the League of Nations.

When we turn to the details of the House scheme we find that its central feature is taken from the Philli-more Report, which, as we saw, had been sent to Washington in the spring of 1918. It is the meeting of Ambassadors which the Phillimore Committee itself adapted from the Administrative Council of the Hague Convention.[1] The rest of the scheme is equally eclectic. There is to be 'an International Court of not more than fifteen members'. This is the Hague project of 1907 of which Mr Elihu Root, one of those whom Colonel House had consulted, was an ardent advocate. Its powers were, with one surprising exception, carefully circumscribed. It was to deal with any difference, not settled by other means, relating 'to the existence, interpretation or effect of a treaty or which may be submitted by consent or'—and here the advocate of a liberalised Monroe Doctrine takes a sudden leap into the unknown—'which relates to matters of commerce, including in such matters the validity or effect inter-nationally of a statute, regulation or practice'. The wording here is somewhat obscure, but in throwing the door of the proposed Court wide open for the reception of 'matters of commerce', hitherto almost unknown to International Law, House was adding a revolutionary appendix to what was otherwise a mildly conservative proposal.

[1] See p. 183 above.

As it turned out, however, the President deleted this entire proposal. He was ready to be audacious, but only on ground already familiar to him in thought. Moreover, as he was later to make clear in Paris, he wished to keep his plan free from any intermixture with the tradition of The Hague.[1]

For disputes other than those taken up by the Court —that is, after Wilson's editing, for disputes in general —a rather complicated system of arbitration is proposed, leading up in the final stage to a binding decision. This arrangement, which makes no reservation for questions affecting the Monroe Doctrine or any other special American interest, goes far beyond both the Phillimore Report and the plan of the League to Enforce Peace. It was not, however, for Wilson a matter of the first importance and, though he now accepted it from House, he made no difficulty at a later stage about withdrawing to the Phillimore system.[2]

The provisions for the prevention of war are also closely modelled on the Phillimore plan. This, it will be remembered, provided for penalties or, as they were there termed, 'sanctions', in three cases—when there had been resort to war (1) without inquiry, (2) without delay, and (3) against a state which had accepted an award or report arrived at according to the procedure laid down. The House plan provides for penalties, in addition, (4) against a state which, without resorting to war, has either failed to make use of the agreed procedure for disputes or 'failed or neglected to carry out' any decision arrived at by

---

[1] 'He has cut out the Court. We were in absolute disagreement about this', reports House in his diary, August 15, 1918 (House, iv. 48).

[2] See p. 185 above.

that procedure. In this fourth case, however, where the offence is one of omission rather than of commission, the penalty is proportionately milder. In this case the state is to be deprived 'of all rights of commerce and intercourse with the contracting power', presumably by means of action taken by each of them individually: in the other cases, where war is involved, this deprivation of intercourse is to be enforced by a blockade which will effectively 'close the frontiers' of the offending state 'to commerce and intercourse with the world'.

Here we have the same distinction between economic sanctions and naval or military sanctions as we found in the Phillimore Report. But the basis on which the distinction is made is different. The Phillimore Report grades its sanctions according to the capacity of the members of the League to make an effective contribution; the House plan grades them according to the degree of culpability on the part of the victim to whom they are to be applied. It is interesting to note that when Wilson edited the draft he emphasized the distinction between the two kinds of penalty by adding a specific reference to the use of 'any force that may be necessary to secure complete non-intercourse'.

But by far the most interesting points in the House draft are those which are completely independent of the Phillimore Report and of the influence of The Hague and its sponsors. There are three such points and each stands by itself, without organic connexion with the others or with the rest of the scheme.

The first is a clause in which an attempt is made to harmonise the two Wilsons—the Southern Democrat with his stern sense of the immutability of state rights, and the Congregationalist with his disposition to favour the hiving-off of groups according to their particular predilections. For a draftsman, faced with the task of embodying both in the same document, the difficulties must at first have seemed inexorable. How could the League's guarantee of territorial integrity and political independence be made compatible with the principle of self-determination? Only, it would seem, by squaring the circle. Nevertheless the intrepid Colonel House did not shrink from the effort. Here is the product of his cogitations:

> The Contracting Powers unite in several guarantees to each other of their territorial integrity and political independence subject, however, to such territorial modifications, if any, as may become necessary in the future by reason of changes in present racial conditions and aspirations, pursuant to the principle of self-determination, and as shall also be regarded by three-fourths of the Delegates as necessary and proper for the welfare of the peoples concerned; recognising also that all territorial changes involve equitable compensation and that the peace of the world is superior in importance and interest to questions of boundary.

This is not a form of wording which could pass the muster of the lawyers. What are 'racial conditions and aspirations'? How are they to be defined and, when defined, ascertained? What is the principle of self-determination? *Who* has the right of determining *what*? Here is a feast for legal wits, foreshadowing, not the conclusion of controversy but its reawakening, not the appeasement of peoples but their disintegration into warring fragments.

But, apart from this difficulty of giving legal precision to a way of thinking which belongs to the spiritual rather than to the political realm, the clause reveals a dawning consciousness that the League would have to

function in a world of real forces and that adjustment
and compromise might have to be the order of the day.
How else can we account for the introduction of the
idea of 'compensation', a notion as characteristic of
the 'old diplomacy' and its Balance of Power as it
would seem to be out of place in that New Order of
which President Wilson was the spokesman?

Perhaps it was a dim perception of this which led the
draftsman to take over from the Phillimore Report
the two paragraphs, already cited,[1] which seek to make
a formal separation between the old order and the new.

The insertion of these paragraphs suggests two brief
observations. One is that if 'the same standards of
honour and ethics' were to prevail in international
politics as in private life, as laid down in Article I of
the same draft, their addition would seem to be quite
superfluous. For, as between gentlemen, and gentle-
manly states, it is surely self-understood that a later
agreement, bearing the same signatures and covering
the same ground, supersedes all that has gone before it.
The second is that it was upon this very point that the
President later made what was one of his greatest
tactical blunders. Had he boldly asserted this principle
immediately after the European allies had accepted
his Fourteen Points on November 5, 1918, and insisted
on receiving their endorsement of it, he would have
been protected from being entangled in the discussion
of the details of the so-called 'Secret Treaties'. He
could have urged, without fear of contradiction, that,
in so far as they conflicted with the Fourteen Points,
they were no longer valid.

The next special point in the House draft is the
clause relating to armaments. We have already seen

[1] See p. 185 above.

the importance that President Wilson and Colonel
House attached to the private manufacture of arms,
to which their attention was called in the first instance
by the important part played by the arms traffic in the
relations between the United States and the Latin-
American peoples. House embodied a provision about
this in his draft: but he preceded it by a broader clause
which, little as he guessed it, was to play a prominent
and most unhappy part in the history of the post-war
period:

'The Contracting Powers recognise the principle that
permanent peace will require that national armaments
shall be reduced to the lowest point consistent with
safety, and the Delegates are directed to formulate at
once a plan by which such a reduction may be brought
about. The plan so formulated shall not be binding
until and unless unanimously approved by the Governments signatory to this Covenant.

'The Contracting Powers agree that munitions and
implements of war shall not be manufactured by
private enterprise and that publicity of all national
armaments and programmes is essential.'

It should be noted that this article follows immediately after the guarantee article. But House made no
specific reference to the duty of mutual protection and
assistance involved for each member of the League,
thus making the armaments of each available for all.
Wilson noted the omission and inserted the now
familiar reference to the 'enforcement by common
action of international obligations'. He also added the
word 'domestic' in front of 'safety'. Thus it became
clear that armaments, under the Covenant, would be
needed for two distinct purposes, firstly, the maintenance of civil order at home; secondly, the carrying-

out of the guarantee given to fellow members of the League.

The last point to be noted in the House draft, seen in retrospect, is the most important of all. It is the introduction into the scheme, side by side with provisions springing from ideas wholly inconsistent with it, of the principle of the Hue and Cry.

Tucked in between Article IV, where espionage is 'deemed dishonourable', and the arrangements for the Council of Ambassadors in Article VI, we find, as Article V, the following brief but pregnant form of words: 'Any war or threat of war is a matter of concern to the League of Nations and to the Powers, members thereof'.

What does this mean? Is it simply the introduction into the League of the idea of the Final Act of the Congress of Vienna—namely, that the occurrence of war or of a war crisis gives the Powers a right of intervention in order to safeguard their own interests? Possibly we might read it in that light did we not possess documentary evidence as to how the words came to be drawn up and taken over into the draft. They emanated from Senator Elihu Root, the leading political thinker of the Republican Party.

On April 11, 1918, Colonel House's diary records a luncheon party at which were present, amongst others, President Taft, Senator Root and the Archbishop of York (the present Archbishop of Canterbury). The conversation ranged over a wide field, but it was decided at the close that Mr Root should draw up a memorandum embodying certain points. The first of these was 'that every nation was interested in war, no matter how small or in what portion of the globe'. That in laying this down Mr Root was not simply acting as a draftsman but formulating a conception of his own is clear from a letter which he addressed to Colonel House four months later in which he set forth his view on the subject at length. It is so important for our purpose, which is to understand the different philosophies which are explicit or implicit in the Covenant, that the paragraphs in it bearing on this subject must be reproduced in their entirety:

CLINTON, NEW YORK
August 16, 1918

MY DEAR COLONEL HOUSE:

I promised to give you in writing the substance of some things I said during the luncheon at your apartment some time ago:

The first requisite for any durable concert of peaceable nations to prevent war is a fundamental change in the principle to be applied to international breaches of the peace.

The view now assumed and generally applied is that the use of force by one nation towards another is a matter in which only the two nations concerned are primarily interested, and if any other nation claims a right to be heard on the subject it must show some specific interest of its own in the controversy. That burden of proof rests upon any other nation which seeks to take part if it will relieve itself of the charge of impertinent interference and avoid the resentment which always meets impertinent interference in the affairs of an independent sovereign state. This view was illustrated by Germany in July 1914, when she insisted that the invasion of Serbia by Austria-Hungary was a matter which solely concerned those two states, and upon substantially that ground refused to agree to the conference proposed by Sir Edward Grey. The requisite change is an abandonment of this view, and a universal formal and irrevocable acceptance and declaration of the view that an international breach of the peace is a matter which concerns every member of the Community of Nations—a matter in which every nation has a direct interest, and to which every nation has a right to object.

These two views correspond to the two kinds of responsibility in municipal law which we call civil responsibility and criminal responsibility. If I make a contract with you and break it, it is no business of our neighbour. You can sue me or submit, and he has nothing to say about it. On the other hand, if I assault and batter you, every neighbour has an interest in having me arrested and punished, because his own safety requires that violence shall be restrained. At the basis of every community lies the idea of organisation to preserve the peace. Without that idea really active and controlling there can be no community of individuals or of nations. It is the gradual growth and substitution of this idea of community interest in preventing and punishing breaches of the peace which has done away with private war among civilised peoples.

The Monroe Doctrine asserted a specific interest on the part of the United States in preventing certain gross breaches of the peace on the American Continent; and when President Wilson suggested an enlargement of the Monroe Doctrine to take in the whole world, his proposal carried by necessary implications the change of doctrine which I am discussing. The change may seem so natural as to be unimportant, but it is really crucial, for the old doctrine is asserted and the broader doctrine is denied by approximately half the military power of the world, and the question between the two is one of the things about which the war is being fought. The change involves a limitation of sovereignty, making every sovereign state subject to the superior right of a community of sovereign states to have the peace preserved. The acceptance of any such principle would be fatal to the whole Prussian theory of the state and of government. When you have got this principle accepted openly, expressly, distinctly, unequivocally by the whole civilised world, you will for the first time have a Community of Nations, and the practical results which will naturally develop will be as different from those which have come from the old view of national responsibility as are the results which flow from the American Declaration of Independence compared with the results which flow from the Divine Right of Kings.[1]

[1] House, iv. 42 ff.

Here, on American lips and in words redolent of the American tradition, we have the same doctrine as had been set forth shortly before by Lord Parker in the House of Lords. Like Lord Parker, and unlike President Wilson, Mr Root cuts right under the notion of sovereignty and *assumes* the existence of a Community of Nations, the members of which have duties flowing, not from special obligations or guarantees, but from the unescapable fact of community. Once community is realised and accepted as one of the dominating facts in the modern world, then resort to war ceases to be an expedient open for adoption by sovereign states and becomes, purely and simply, a crime—that is, an anti-social act forbidden by law. Thus there is no further need for precise stipulations or guarantees. The prevention and suppression of this crime, as of all others, becomes the natural and necessary duty of all law-abiding members of the community.

There is no evidence that Mr Root had read the House of Lords debate. But, even if he had, he could not have couched his idea in language at all similar to that of Lord Parker. For, however much they may be at one in their moral attitude and social objective, British and American thinkers will always differ in their mode of approach to a political problem. Behind Lord Parker, moulding his philosophy and finding expression in his language, is age-long Custom and the venerable Common Law. Behind Mr Root, although to us they seem of yesterday, are the Declaration of Independence, the United States Constitution and the Monroe Doctrine. Thus it was inevitable that, while Lord Parker would have been satisfied for the present with a change of *usage*, Mr Root should have wished at once to see his idea embodied in *institutions*: and this

explains—what to a British mind will always remain
a paradox—how, holding the views expressed in his
letter, he should also have been an advocate of a World
Court, as projected at The Hague in 1907. For an
Englishman the Hue and Cry and a Supreme Court of
the Realm 'go ill together'. They do not seem to belong
to the same stage of social development. In fact, they
seem centuries apart: and to establish an up-to-date
Court under conditions where the fact of community,
recognised by the enlightened few, has still to be made
understood by the many, would seem to be a misuse of
language.

But Mr Root would have a ready reply, drawn from
the philosophy of pragmatism and the outlook and
habits of a forward-looking people. On our side of the
Atlantic, he would say, communities do not grow like
trees. They are constructed by the labours of pioneers.
The sense of Community will make its appearance as
quickly as you can provide a suitable environment for
its reception. The community of the American West
was largely *made* by the transcontinental railways.
The community of the world can be made likewise, by
the devising of suitable institutions with names point-
ing ahead to what they will ultimately become. Just
as the freshman in an American University dates himself by the year in which he hopes to have won his
degree, so for Mr Root there was nothing misleading
or unreal in attaching the name of 'Court' to the
project of a body which he must have known full
well would not realise that high appellation for many
years to come. The main thing, after all, he would say,
is to have a *sense of direction*. If by speaking of
'institutions', and by the names which we attach to
them, we can give mankind a sense of the direction in

which it is moving, we shall speed human progress and make regression more difficult. The world community exists. The difficulty is that men will not recognise its existence. Let us get them to recognise it in words: words will set up associations, associations will lead to habits and habits will eventually issue in acts. Thus by calling a body a Court we are taking the first steps towards making it a Court. And, by the same process of reasoning—for President Wilson was also an American—by calling a document a Covenant we are taking the first step towards making men recognise its sanctity and bow before its authority.

But we must return to the draftsman. Colonel House, replying to Senator Root on August 23, said that he had discussed his letter with the President, who had been staying with him, and that he did not anticipate much difficulty in 'bringing their minds in harmony upon some plan'. There is nothing to indicate whether he appreciated the far-reaching implications involved in the short article which he had already in July inscribed in his draft.

We have mentioned previously the principal changes made by the President in his editing of the House draft. This particular article obviously attracted him by its wording. But that he did not understand the thought behind it is plain from the way in which he reformulated it, incorporating it into his Ambassadors' Conference. Here are Colonel House's two lines in the form in which the President brought them to Paris:

'Any war or threat of war, whether immediately affecting any of the Contracting Powers or not, is hereby declared a matter of concern to the League of Nations and to all the Powers signatory hereto, and those Powers hereby reserve the right to take any

action that may be deemed wise and effectual to safeguard the peace of nations.'

Who is it that is to prevent war? Is it an associated
group of sovereign states who have pledged themselves
to do so and 'reserve the right' to determine how? Or is
it the community of civilised peoples in the enforcement of the Common Law?

At the time, this seemingly theoretical distinction
was clear to very few. The article therefore excited no
attention and passed through the Committee at Paris,
without discussion and apparently without even a word
of comment, to take its place as Article XI of the
Covenant.[1]

---

[1] Miller, i. 173. The addition of the second paragraph ('it is also declared
to be the friendly right', etc.) was made by the President at Paris. At one
time he had expanded the article into four paragraphs: see Miller, ii. 83.
The second sentence of the first paragraph, laying down ways and
means, was a French addition (Miller, ii. 347).

CHAPTER X

THE DRAFTING OF THE COVENANT

I

We can now return to the stage that we had reached at the end of Chapter VIII—the point of junction between the British and American streams that joined their waters in the Covenant. Henceforward we can quicken our pace; for we are concerned in this volume not with the precise form in which ideas were clothed, still less with the detailed applications drawn with them. Our interest is in the ideas themselves, in their interaction and in their influence upon policy. Moreover, so far as the actual drafting of the Covenant is concerned, the task has already been performed by a master hand. There is nothing of substance to be added to the work of Mr David Hunter Miller. There are only certain comments to be made and conclusions to be drawn along the line of our previous inquiry.

By the time that the League of Nations Committee of the Peace Conference met at the Hôtel Crillon on the afternoon of February 3, 1919, President Wilson had made no less than four drafts of the Covenant. The first, dating from the summer of 1918, was that referred to in the last chapter. The other three drafts were made in Paris during the weeks preceding the meeting of the Commission. They therefore bear the marks of the Peace Conference discussions, which were then in full swing. Thus the Mandates article, though drafted by President Wilson, formed no part of his original programme for the League. In the same way the article providing for the regulation of labour conditions was an afterthought, due to the efforts of trade unionists in the United States and in Europe. There was also at one stage an article on the lines of General Smuts's paper, providing that there should be 'exacted' of all states seeking admission to the League of Nations a promise of equal treatment 'to all racial or national minorities' within their jurisdiction. This was, however, later taken out of the draft Covenant and provided for in the individual treaties with the states concerned. There was, however, one new article which originated from the President and to which much history was to be attached. It provided for what may be called religious equality:

> The Contracting Parties agree that they will make no law prohibiting or interfering with the free exercise of religion, and that they will in no way discriminate, either in law or in fact, against those who practise any particular creed, religion or belief whose practices are not inconsistent with public order or public morals.

It was not, however, Wilson's latest draft which served as the basis for the Committee's discussion on February 3, though as late as the morning of that day he had intended that it should. It was the so-called Hurst-Miller draft, the result of a conference between the respective Legal Advisers of the British and American Delegations, held on February 1.[1] As a result of this sudden change, which Colonel House had

---

[1] This is to be found in Miller, ii. 231. It is also printed in Florence Wilson, *The Origins of the League Covenant: Documentary History of its Drafting* (1928), p. 173 ff.

pressed upon the President in order to conciliate Lord Robert Cecil, the Committee began its meetings on the basis of a document of which no French translation was ready. In any case few of the representatives of the ten delegations present had seen either document. Thus when it was ruled that there should be no general debate and that discussion should proceed on the single articles of the document before the Committee, the main lines of the League were almost automatically fixed; for changes could now only be made by way of amendment. Thus this initial decision made the Covenant what it is—a British-American document with here and there an addition or amendment to meet the wishes of others.

What is of interest to us in the story of the drafting of the Covenant, as recorded in Mr Miller's pages, is the conflict of ideas between the various parties. There is, firstly, the clash between the British and the Wilsonian conception of the League; then the three-cornered contest between France, Britain and President Wilson; then the issue between the Great Powers, as such, and the other states; and then the suggestions or claims put forward by the Italians and the Japanese in order to secure recognition for their particular views.

II

The clash between the British and Wilsonian conceptions took place, for the most part, during January, before the meeting of the Committee. In truth, except for one crucial point, it was not so much a clash as a convergence or adjustment. For on the British side the chief object in view was the establishment of a framework ensuring continuous co-operation between the Great Powers. President Wilson's mind, on the other hand, was concentrated on certain particular policies. He did not care so much about the framework so long as the picture inside it was to his taste. Or, to change the metaphor, he was not interested in the design of the envelope so long as he could slip his own missive inside it. He was passionately excited about political ideas but more or less indifferent about political machinery. Thus, with the exception of the vague requirement of 'open covenants', his Fourteen Points leave questions of method on one side. Instead, they take up problems of substance—disarmament, the freedom of the seas, the breaking-down of trade barriers, the European settlement, the colonial settle-ment and, above all, guarantees.

The upshot of the discussions was therefore as might have been anticipated. There emerged a *British frame-work* together with a number of *Wilsonian policies.* Wilson's meeting of Ambassadors, presided over by the Foreign Minister of X, disappears. It is replaced by the two Conferences—the larger and the smaller—of the Foreign Office memorandum, the latter body being described in the Hurst-Miller draft as 'an Executive Council representing the states more immediately con-cerned in the matters under discussion'. 'The United States of America, Great Britain, France, Italy and Japan', the draft goes on to say, 'shall be deemed to be directly affected by all matters within the sphere of action of the League.' Here is the *enlarged and organised Concert of the Great Powers* which was the heart of the British plan.

But what of the Wilsonian policies? The chief of these, as we have seen, was mutual guarantees. Was the Concert of Powers, great and small (but, in particular, the great), to be bound together by a common guarantee? And, if so, what sort of a guarantee? Here, in 1919, was the old question which had dogged Castlereagh a hundred years before.

When we look at the Hurst-Miller draft we find that, in the process of convergence, two important changes have been made from the original Wilsonian guarantee article. In the first place, the second half, providing for what has now come to be called 'peaceful change', has disappeared. It was too full of loopholes to survive close scrutiny.[1] But this, of course, left the article in a very unsatisfactory condition, both in British and American eyes: for it consecrated the *status quo* with a guarantee of perpetual duration. Hence efforts were made to provide in a separate article for the limitation of the guarantee. These after much travail eventually produced Article XIX, an expression of a pious hope or of a principle which leaves untouched the binding obligation of any guarantee provided for elsewhere.[2]

The second change is the disappearance of the actual word 'guarantee'. It is replaced by a milder term, 'undertake', which is free of all eighteenth-century associations:

> The Contracting Parties undertake to respect and preserve as against external aggression the territorial integrity and

---

[1] See p. 226 above.

[2] A suggestion for a stronger provision, ultimately rejected, is printed in Miller, ii. 118-19. It provides that if a League recommendation for the modification of 'any feature of the settlement guaranteed by this Covenant' has been 'rejected by the parties affected, the States members of the League shall, in the case of territorial questions, cease to be under the obligation to protect the territory in question from forcible aggression by other States'.

existing political independence of all States members of the League.

But even in this edulcorated form the obligation still remained distasteful to British minds. Thus when this clause came up for consideration in due course Lord Robert Cecil proposed to omit the words 'and preserve as against external aggression'. The discussion which followed is recorded in telegraphic form in Mr Miller's notes, 'written as the debate went on'. They show with naked precision the attitude of the chief parties at this first general encounter in what was to be a contest prolonged through many years.

Cecil suggests as to the extent of the obligation which means war if it means anything.

Wilson thinks the words add little to the implied obligation of the whole Covenant.

Orlando supports the article.

Larnaude thinks it imports only a principle.

Wilson thinks the obligation is central but recognises its serious character.

Smuts thinks it goes further than anything else in the document.

Wilson thinks . . . there must be a provision that we mean business and not discussion. This idea, not necessarily these words, is the key to the whole Covenant. . . .

Cecil thinks that things are being put in which cannot be carried out literally and in all respects.

The *dénouement* in this seemingly irreconcilable conflict of principles was surprising. The French delegate, M. Larnaude, a veteran jurist, allowed his taste for precision to lead him along a dangerous path. He proposed that there should be an addition to the article specifying the ways and means of its execution.

R

This idea was accepted and put into shape by the Chairman. It was adopted in the following form:

In case of any such aggression, the Executive Council shall advise the plan and the means by which this obligation shall be fulfilled.

Thus the meeting ended with a British victory. For the insertion of the new words made it clear that without them, as M. Larnaude had argued, the first part of the clause was 'only a principle'. But the fact that the Council was now empowered only to 'advise' on means of enforcement threw the whole responsibility back from the League upon the individual states, who could justly argue that, in its final form, the article was a mere expression of moral obligation and did not 'mean business'. And so those of them for whom the English text of the Covenant is binding have not failed to argue.

But M. Larnaude, no doubt, also believed himself to have been, up to a point, victorious. For the French version of the amendment, which in the official French minutes is attributed to Signor Orlando, empowers the Council, not to *advise upon* but '*aviser*', which means to *look to*, 'the dispositions and means for ensuring the execution of the engagements'. 'So far so good', M. Larnaude must have said to himself. 'The principle is accepted: the need of means for carrying it out is admitted: it remains to specify these in detail in a later article.'

Thus the 'key to the whole Covenant', so far from unlocking the riddle, became itself a cause of confusion, conveying one meaning to the French-speaking and another to the English-speaking members of the League. President Wilson, however, seems never to have realised how much ground he had yielded to his British colleague. How otherwise can we explain the battle he waged in the United States on behalf of an article which was now a mere shell without a core?[1]

Meanwhile what had happened to the 'guarantee of peace' proposed in the Foreign Office memorandum? This, it will be remembered, was designed to rule out resort to war altogether and was carefully dissociated from any special connexion with territorial integrity and the new frontiers. It would appear that this conception of the guarantee had become lost to view in the course of the discussions with the President, whose personal ideas on the subject, dating from December 1914, were so firmly fixed. Thus there is no trace in the Paris discussions of any effort to revert to what may be called the *Hue and Cry Guarantee*; and in consequence the remaining part of the original British scheme was left in the air. The only definite safeguard against war which remained was the system of the Disputes Articles, taken over from the Phillimore Report. But this only provided for Inquiry and Delay and

---

[1] On the above see Miller, i. 168-9; ii. 430 and 550. At the ninth meeting of the Committee on February 13, two further amendments were made. The 'plan' to be drawn up by the Council disappeared, thus leaving the position even vaguer than before. At the same time a reference to a 'threat or danger' of aggression was inserted. These decisions seem to have been taken, no doubt on Lord Robert Cecil's initiative, without debate. At the following meeting M. Bourgeois expressed his satisfaction at the second, but he does not seem to have felt uneasy about the first. See Miller, i. 240, line 24 (where Mr Miller's notes are incomplete), and 257, and ii. 305. As late as March 20, when he met the representatives of the neutral states, M. Bourgeois seems to have remained unaware that the Covenant left a gap open for war. He told the neutral delegates that 'although arbitration was not compulsory in the Covenant, a pacific solution *was* compulsory' (italics in original) (Miller, ii. 628, French text, p. 599). See also Mr Miller's notes (i. 174) on the drafting of Article XV ('Bourgeois raised the point of no war, Cecil opposes the idea as going too far).

laid down nothing as to the position when these expedients had been exhausted.[1] The idea had been that
in such an event disputes would remain in cold storage,
which there is ample ground for saying is sometimes
the wisest way of dealing with them. But it had certainly not been intended that a gap should thus be
opened for war. With the disappearance of the guarantee of peace, however, this was just what happened.
No doubt the gap would have been closed again if the
Wilsonian form of guarantee had been maintained in
the form intended by its author. But with the weakening of the territorial guarantee and the disappearance
of the guarantee of peace there remained a yawning
breach in the Covenant.

Moreover, by a concession made to Republican sentiment in the United States a few weeks later, this
breach was considerably widened. For a paragraph
(XV, § 8) was added to the Disputes Articles debarring
the Council and the Assembly from dealing in any
way, under those articles, with a dispute which is
'claimed by one' of the parties, 'and is found by the
Council, to arise out of a matter which by international
law is solely within the jurisdiction of that party'. This
led to the curious result that no sanction whatsoever
was provided for a war arising out of such a dispute,
since the sanctions of Article XVI apply only to
breaches of XII, XIII and XV. Thus such wars are not
even subject to the check of Inquiry and Delay. This

[1] Some of the smaller states, supported by France, wished to
strengthen the Phillimore system by introducing the principle of
'compulsory arbitration', *i.e.* compulsion to comply with the arbitrators' award, backed up by a sanction. This was opposed by the United
States in the person of Mr Miller (Miller, i. 193) and by Great Britain,
and the proposed clause was rejected. Hence the abrupt termination
of the disputes procedure in Article XV, § 6 and the vague language
on the same subject in XIII, § 4.

paragraph, in fact, if pushed to its logical limit, endangers the whole peace-preserving structure of the Covenant, since, as has been pointed out, 'the great majority of really dangerous international disputes arise out of matters which indisputably fall within the category of domestic jurisdiction and the problem of how to deal with them is the most crucial, and unfortunately also the most intractable, of all international problems'. Such issues could, of course, still be raised under Article XI: but the parties are left quite free, under that article, to accept or reject any suggestion made by members of the Council. Thus there remained a grave underlying contradiction between Article XI and Article XV, § 8 as to the League authority in this class of dispute.[1]

By the time that the Covenant had taken final shape in June 1919 the latitude left in it for war was thoroughly recognised in British circles and a new philosophy, very different from that of Lord Parker, had been evolved to explain it. It is set forth in the official British commentary[2] which, if President Wilson and M. Bourgeois ever read it, must have caused them to raise their eyebrows. For the leading idea of that document is that the League is an agency, not for the restraint of crime, but for the gradual formation of law-abiding habits. 'Private war' is still 'contemplated as possible' in default of a moral

---

[1] See Brierly, article in *British Year-book of International Law* for 1925, and Miller, *The Geneva Protocol* (1925), pp. 64-5, who entertains no doubt that 'under the Covenant, the Members of the League entered into no commitment against going to war in the case of a dispute about a domestic question'. This licence is, however, subject to the moral obligations implied by membership of the League. On this see Schücking and Wehberg, *Die Satzung des Völkerbundes* (2nd ed. i. 593).

[2] Cmd. 151 (1919).

reformation. 'If the nations of the future are in the main selfish, grasping and war-like, no instrument or machinery will restrain them.' They can no more be made virtuous by Covenants than individuals can be converted by Acts of Parliament. All that can be done is 'to establish an organisation which may make peaceful co-operation easy and hence customary and to trust in the influence of custom to mould opinion'. Excellent doctrine for islanders, who can afford to think in terms of generations and centuries! But could one be sure—indeed, was it honest to assume—that a world still addicted to Power-politics would grant the new-born League a respite whilst 'the golden stain of time' was leaving its mark on its walls and mellowing the characters of those who assembled there? The official commentary is an admirable exposition of the League as seen through English spectacles. With the necessary adjustments of detail it might serve as a commentary on the British League of Nations, whose members have neither renounced war nor agreed to the compulsory arbitration of their disputes. But to imagine that such a League could function in the wider world as it was in 1919, and remains in 1935, was to assume that the Continental and Asiatic peoples, not to mention those of the two Americas, had simply been turned into Englishmen. And that would have supposed not a change of heart, but a complete reversal of fixed habits, attitudes and temperaments. Despite the commentary, the members of the League are not yet, after fifteen years, behaving like Englishmen, though many Englishmen have not even yet given up the expectation that they are just about to do so.

By the weakening of the territorial guarantee clause President Wilson and M. Bourgeois had conceded the one vital point on which the United States and France stood together as against Great Britain. But this did not deter the French, confident in their own text of the article, from pressing on with their effort to specify the ways and means for implementing the guarantee and enforcing sanctions when necessary. Unfortunately, however, when it came down to a discussion of practical details, they found the President no longer at their side.

The French official scheme had by now been laid on the table of the Committee. It provided, it will be remembered, for the maintenance of 'Peace through Law' by a carefully worked-out system for putting Might behind Right. This, when reduced to concrete terms, involved for the French mind, as it had for Mr Taft in his day-dream, the organisation of an international force—in the first instance a military force. M. Bourgeois, however, did not insist on this. The difficulties in the way, both diplomatic and technical, were too obvious. The demand on which he concentrated and for which he fought up to the open meeting on April 28 was twofold: firstly, the establishment of an international General Staff to prepare and keep up to date the military and naval measures needed to ensure the speedy enforcement of the obligations of the Covenant; secondly, the establishment of a Permanent Commission to keep watch over armaments and armament programmes, including 'industries susceptible of being adapted for war purposes'. This latter proposal he coupled with President Wilson's own disarmament article. There must, he said, be a 'real, effective, permanent limitation of armaments'. How could this be ensured without a permanent Commission of Control? And in the last of the several cogent speeches in which

he developed this theme he made a special appeal to
British susceptibilities by trying to show how this
collaboration of high staff officers in the atmosphere
of the League would kindle feelings of mutual confidence
and esteem which would penetrate from above through
the ranks of their respective armies. At the same time
he cited numerous past utterances of President Wilson
which, if they meant anything at all, seemed to a
French mind to ensure his support of the proposed
amendments.

It was not difficult for M. Bourgeois to argue in defence of his scheme: for it was not only in the interests
of France but also along the natural line of French
thinking. It was an extension to the world-community
of Rousseau's Committee of Public Safety. The French
mind makes quick speed along a prepared road: and
the road towards World-government, or what is bar-
barously named the Super-state, had been constructed
long ago. Bodin and Rousseau, Louis XIV and
Napoleon, had all surveyed at least its early stages.
Thus, from the meetings of the Paris Committee onwards, the French have been the most consistent and
pertinacious and also, it cannot be denied, the most
loyal and whole-hearted supporters of the League *as
they have understood it*. They have been more willing
than any other government or people to surrender
national *rights* in favour of the League. But what they
have not realised, what was hidden alike from Bourgeois and from Briand, was that this League, to them
the only possible kind of League either in theory or
practice, was a French League.

President Wilson, however, was a Southern Democrat. That is to say, that, though a disciple of Rousseau,
he was a disciple at one remove. He believed in concen-

trating power into firm hands, but he did not believe in enlarging its sphere. To World-opinion he was prepared to appeal. But World-government was a conception that no Virginian could entertain.

The result of this clash between World-Sovereignty and American Sovereignty, between a Rousseau enlarged by the experience of the World War and a Jefferson who had accepted, however reluctantly, the complete Union of the United States, is given in Mr Miller's brief account of the eighth meeting of the Commission, when the French amendments were first presented. He slipped a note across to the President in these terms:

> It is not a question of joint military operations, but of an international control of our Army and Navy *in war and in peace*—these are under the President. I don't think it is good.

'The President', Mr Miller continues, 'said it was unconstitutional and also impossible. He said it was a question which required a decision.' At the tenth meeting, on the afternoon of February 13, M. Bourgeois returned to the charge. 'Nothing very new', remarks Mr Miller, 'was said during a long and tiresome and confused discussion'—not the last of its kind. President Wilson stuck to his position, boldly declaring that 'no country would accept an international General Staff which would have the right to interfere with its own naval and military plans'.[1] Finally the French amendment was rejected by twelve votes to three. But, in an

---

[1] This is from the French minutes, Miller, ii. 478. Miller's own notes read: 'Nor would any country permit an international staff to know and interfere with its own military and naval plans so long as they consist [*sic*] with the policy of the League of Nations' (i. 253). Evidently the French précis-writer regarded the last clause as meaningless, since it begs the whole question.

effort to go some way to meet the French, President
Wilson and Lord Robert Cecil proposed the insertion
of an article (Article IX) providing for a Permanent
Commission to 'advise the League on the execution of
the stipulations of Article VIII'—the disarmament
article—'and in general on military and naval questions'. 'This', explained the President, 'is neither
investigation, nor is it supervision.' With this M.
Bourgeois and M. Larnaude had to be content. The
'means and dispositions' for giving effect to the advice
of the Council had dwindled down to further 'advice'.[1]

III

The clash between the Great Powers and the smaller
states arose over the composition of the Council or
'Executive Committee', as it was still called in the
French minutes of the crucial meetings on February 4
and 5.[2] It will be remembered that the Foreign Office
memorandum had conceived of the League as an
organisation of the Concert, enlarged to include all the
Great Powers, and that General Smuts had modified
this idea by suggesting the inclusion of other states
drawn from two panels. When President Wilson
received the Smuts memorandum he was at first
attracted by it and modified his own amorphous project in that sense.[3] But when Mr Miller conferred with
Lord Robert Cecil on the various points of difference
between the Wilsonian and British drafts he found
that there were two matters only which were 'regarded
by the British as very important'. One was the repre-

---

[1] Miller, i. 209, 251, 256; ii. 460, 476-9, 706-13.
[2] Miller, ii. 425-8.   [3] Miller, ii. 67, 98, 146.

sentation of the Dominions, which does not concern us here. The other was 'the limitation of the membership of the Council to the Great Powers and those Powers, if any, which the Great Powers shall subsequently choose to add'. He therefore gave way on these points. Thus the Hurst-Miller draft, on which the Commission was working, provided for a Council consisting normally only of the Great Powers.

It was at the second meeting of the Committee that this article in the draft was reached. It was at once heavily assailed by the representatives of the five other states present: Serbia, Belgium, China, Brazil and Portugal. Indeed opportunity was taken, there and then, to move that the Committee itself should be enlarged by four more members and a motion was carried asking that Roumania, Greece, Poland and Czechoslovakia should be added. No less than three versions of the debate are recorded by Mr Miller, in addition to the official minutes.[1] From these it appears that the President had now become convinced of the superiority of the British plan on practical grounds. But he was hampered by the fact that the members of the Committee had seen his own first Paris plan and that there was therefore a chorus of voices demanding what was called 'the first American plan'. At this critical juncture French judgment was again at fault. M. Bourgeois, his mind filled with reminiscences of The Hague, felt that the moment had come for a gesture of idealism. He declared that, after hearing the representatives of the smaller powers, he was speaking 'not as a representative of a Great Power but as a member of the future Society of Nations'; and he recalled the fact that the French scheme made no

[1] Miller, i. 138-53; ii. 255 ff., 425 ff.

distinction between great and small nations. What he failed to remind the Committee, of course, was that the French scheme was quite remote from the subject under discussion. It was an arrangement for dealing with disputes, not a system for the normal conduct of international affairs—an improved Hague Tribunal, not an improved Concert. Signor Orlando showed an equal pusillanimity or lack of insight. The two Japanese delegates remained silent. General Smuts, who was present, also seems to have said nothing, but his views were already on record. The two English-speaking Great Powers thus found themselves isolated. In vain Lord Robert Cecil argued that everything discussed in the Council could go on for discussion in the larger body (later called the Assembly), and that, though there was 'much to be said for the idea of the equality of the powers', he 'did not see how a plan for it could be worked out'. He was finally forced to admit that the Committee would not accept his plan. The article was sent back to be redrafted.

The British redraft, which was ready next day, placed the number of 'representatives of the other members of the League' at two. This was again hotly criticised, General Smuts this time joining in the attack. M. Hymans wished to raise the figure to five: M. Vesnitch said he would be satisfied with four, and this was supported by M. Bourgeois. Lord Robert Cecil again tried manfully to stem the tide. He advised the Commission to 'go slow' on the proposal to raise the figure to four. The chief need, he reminded them, in order to make the League a working body, was the support of the Great Powers. Of the support of the others, frankly, they were sure in any case. He succeeded in securing the postponement of the decision.

But at a later meeting on February 13, with the four extra members present, after another debate of the same character, the number was finally fixed at four.[1]

IV

The Italian members of the Commission were Signor Orlando, who was Prime Minister of his country, and Signor Scialoja, one of the acutest minds and ablest and most sympathetic teachers of Law in his own or any other country. They brought with them their own project for a League of Nations. The minutes record that this was placed on the table at the first meeting of the Committee. This, however, says Mr Miller, is inexact and was inserted *par politesse*.[2] It seems to have been the only *politesse* which was meted out to the scheme throughout the meetings of the Committee: for it was never discussed and its authors, with remarkable self-abnegation, abstained from pressing their views upon colleagues who were proceeding upon quite different lines. Nevertheless the document, which was no doubt from the hand of Signor Scialoja, is important not only because it gives faithful expression

---

[1] Miller, i. 159-62; ii. 259-60 (third meeting), 301-2, 470-71 (minutes of ninth meeting). Mr Miller gives no other record of this discussion, which seems to have been lost. It was agreed at the outset of the proceedings, in order to preserve the atmosphere of informality, that no shorthand record should be taken.

[2] Miller, i. 132. The document seems to have been available shortly afterwards, since Signor Scialoja referred to it next day (i. 150). The text is given in ii. 246 ff. (in English), 411 ff. (in French), and 539 ff. (in Italian, undated). Mr Noel-Baker, who was in Paris at the time, says that 'it had been prepared without great care', meaning no doubt that the draftsman, who took pains enough, had a very light sketch to work on (*Les Origines et l'œuvre de La Société des Nations*, ed. Munch [Copenhagen, 1923], ii. p. 23).

to the opinions and interests of a great country but also because it represents a philosophy different from any that we have hitherto encountered in these pages.

The Italians, like the French, regarded the League as an agency for securing Justice. *Peace through Justice* was their watchword. Thus, in its general lines, their scheme was not unlike that of M. Bourgeois. An important part of it was devoted to the settlement of disputes, including the establishment of an 'International Court of Justice'. Sanctions, too, figured largely, no less than seventeen different varieties being enumerated specifically, followed by a direction for the employment of 'any other form of coercion, direct or indirect' which might 'seem appropriate to overcome the resistance of a guilty state'.

But it is where the Italian scheme deviates from the French that it becomes most interesting. The difference centres round the meaning to be attached to 'Justice'. Whilst the French scheme looks to a Judicature which will interpret the existing law, the Italian plan, starting from the notion of what it calls 'international equity', sets out boldly to change the law. It proposes what is in fact nothing less than an international legislature. This body, composed of representatives nominated by the governments, is to meet every year, and more frequently if necessary, 'in order to deal with general affairs of common interest'. It is also empowered to take up disputes not otherwise settled. The procedure provided in this respect is very bold. If this politically constituted 'Council' decides that 'the dispute ought to be settled according to the rules of international law rather than according to political considerations or reasons of equity, it sends the parties to the international Court of Justice'. But if these representatives of the governments, by a two-thirds majority, decide otherwise, and prefer to settle a dispute themselves, they are empowered to do so. They are then directed to base their decision, which again requires a two-thirds majority, on grounds[1] of equity and political expediency, with the object of securing a just and stable arrangement between the parties to the dispute. Cases of special difficulty may be referred back by the Council to a larger body, equally political in character, called 'the Conference'. In each case the decision is absolute and all the members of the League are bound to join in applying the sanctions decided on by the Council against a recalcitrant state. States refusing to join in sanctions, or doing so tardily and insufficiently, will themselves incur sanctions.

What is this international equity, or perhaps we might say international social justice, which the Italian scheme so carefully distinguishes from legal justice? Here the scheme breaks absolutely fresh ground. It lays down a number of 'fundamental principles' designed to provide every independent political community with a 'guarantee'. But it is a guarantee very different from the two varieties which we have hitherto examined. It is a guarantee, not of existence and territorial integrity nor of peace, but of *growth*. What are to be ensured for every member of the League are the 'necessary conditions of its independent and autonomous development'. We cannot here enumerate these 'fundamental principles': the most interesting amongst them declares that 'the international distribution of the foodstuffs and raw materials required to sustain

---

[1] The Italian word is '*criteri*', which the French translation stiffens into 'principles'.

healthy conditions of life and industry must be controlled in such a way as to secure to every country
what is indispensable to it in this respect'. It must be
remembered that Italians, and not Italians alone, were
at this moment experiencing the consequences of the
break-up of the war-time machinery of rationing and
control.

But the scheme went further than the mere elaboration of principles. It put forward at least a rudimentary
system for giving effect to them. On the analogy of the
Foreign Office memorandum the Council was to have
Committees working under it. Three of these are specified—an Economic Commission, a Labour Commission
and a Military Commission, the object of the first-
named being 'to procure and furnish data for the
solution of international problems of an economic and
financial character in such a way'—here follows a
beautiful piece of draftsmanship anticipating the technique of Geneva—'as to facilitate the progressive and
harmonious co-ordination of the interests of every
country in this field'. Here Adam Smith joins hands
with Karl Marx. The League of Nations is to guide the
'invisible hand' in order to minister to the growing
needs of 'proletarian' states. And to this conception of
the League, in spite of many rebuffs, Italian statesmanship continually recurred.[1]

---

[1] An example of this was the Italian proposal to the Assembly in 1931
for the co-ordination of National Economic Councils in a World Economic Council. See on this Salter, *Recovery* (1932), p. 221. At the first
meeting of the Assembly in 1920 the Italian Delegation raised the question of the distribution of raw materials and was severely rebuffed by
Canada. It had previously been brought forward in the Council by
Signor Tittoni, who provoked a characteristic rejoinder from Mr Balfour
(ninth meeting of the Council, Annexes 121 and 121a). It was also
raised, with similar lack of success, by the Italian Workers' delegate
at the first International Labour Conference, held in Washington in

V

Japan too is a proletarian in the World of States. Her problem in this respect was, and is, more severe than that of Italy. Nevertheless it was not on this aspect of the New Order that her eyes were fixed. Grave as were her economic preoccupations, something else, graver still, was on her mind. She was haunted by the problem of race relations. For four centuries the white man, by his mastery of the arts of power, had been hammering into the mind and spirit of the non-white peoples the conviction that they were his natural inferiors. The Russo-Japanese War had indeed demonstrated that this supremacy could be challenged in the field of battle. But the stigma still remained. Habits and attitudes were slow to change. Now the moment seemed to have come, at the turning of a new page in the world's history, for lifting this question on to a higher plane and setting race relations, once and for all, on a basis of equality. This was to be the Japanese contribution to the Covenant.

But the occasion would lose more than half of its grace if the initiative were publicly taken by those whose status was to be vindicated. Thus the task of the Japanese delegates, Baron Makino and Viscount Chinda, was a delicate one. They came with a national demand which they hoped that they would find others to voice. It was in this mood that, on February 4, they sought out Colonel House. 'On July 8', they told him, 'you expressed to Viscount Ishii sentiments which pleased the Japanese Government: therefore we look

November 1920. Later on, the subject was deliberately eliminated from the agenda of the World Economic Conference of 1927.

S

upon you as a friend and we have come to ask for your advice.[1]

Then followed a drafting and redrafting of resolutions. At one moment the Japanese stood out for a clause on immigration. This seems, however, to have been quickly abandoned in the face of determined opposition both from the American and the British side. It remained to find a formula which would satisfy Japanese *amour propre*.

At this point Colonel House and the Japanese found that the British Empire Delegation blocked their path. It was not Great Britain which stood in the way but principally Australia: or rather it was a single Australian, Mr William Morris Hughes, then Premier of the Commonwealth, who constituted himself champion of the cause of White Supremacy. On February 9, Colonel House records: 'Every solution which the Japanese and I have proposed, Mr Hughes of the British Delegation objects to'; and the British Delegation apparently were unwilling to override his objections.[2] By February 12 Viscount Chinda had decided in disgust to present a resolution himself. He would not secure its adoption but at least he would show his people in Japan that he had done his best.

[1] House, iv. 320-21.

[2] See House, iv. 325, under date February 13, 1919: 'Makino agreed upon a form the other day which the President accepted and which was as mild and inoffensive as possible, but even that the British refused. I understand that all the British Delegation were willing to accept the form the President, Makino and Chinda agreed on, except Hughes of Australia. He was the stumbling-block.' Mr Noel-Baker, *op. cit.* ii. p. 25, says that General Smuts 'played a leading part' in these unsuccessful negotiations. It is worth noting that the attitude of President Wilson, as a Southern Democrat, on this matter is a testimony to his courage and loyalty to principle. In Japan, however, where the full facts were not known, President Wilson was held up to obloquy when the negotiations broke down (House, iv. 466).

The resolution which he had drafted was for the insertion of a new clause, ingeniously conceived as a pendant to President Wilson's clause on religious equality which we have already noted. Its text was as follows:

The equality of nations being a basic principle of the League of Nations, the High Contracting Parties agree to accord, as soon as possible, to all alien nationals of States members of the League, equal and just treatment in every respect, making no distinction, either in law or fact, on account of their race and nationality.

The moment for its discussion came at the tenth meeting of the Committee, on February 13, from which President Wilson happened to be absent, Lord Robert Cecil being in the chair. It was moved by Baron Makino as an additional paragraph to the religious equality article, to which Colonel House had just said that the President attached special importance. Baron Makino's speech, which was read, is given in full in the minutes.[1] It is an earnest, dignified, courteous and moderate statement of his case. He pointed out that the Covenant was creating a system of mutual obligations between states 'comprising all kinds of races' and asked that 'the principle at least of equality among men should be admitted and be made the basis of

---

[1] Miller, ii. 323-5. See also i. 268-9. Whilst thus endangering Japanese membership of the League of Nations, Mr Hughes was simultaneously engaged in an attempt to ensure the *inclusion* of Japan in the proposed International Labour Organisation, in order that her industrial competition might be less dangerous for Australia. This led him to favour complete separation between the two organisations. (See *The Origins of the International Labour Organisation*, ed. Shotwell: New York, 1934, i. 200.) At the same time Australia, Canada and the United States opposed the insertion into the 'Labour Charter' of the principle of 'equality of status and working conditions of foreign workers' (*op. cit.* i. 213.)

future intercourse'. At the same time he admitted that deep-lying prejudices were involved and therefore he did not expect an immediate practical realisation of the principle that he was putting forward. He would be content to 'leave the working out of it in the hands of the responsible leaders of the States members of the League, who will not neglect the state of public opinion'.

When he had finished, Lord Robert Cecil said that this was 'a matter of a highly controversial character' and 'raised extremely serious problems within the British Empire'. 'In spite of the nobility of thought which inspired Baron Makino, he thought that it would be wiser for the moment to postpone its discussion.' Mr Venizelos and other members of the Commission concurred. The matter then dropped and with it the article on religious equality. 'That subject', says Mr Miller, ' was never again considered.'

The postponed discussion on racial equality took place at the fifteenth and last meeting of the Committee, on the evening of April 11. It came on towards the close of a long sitting directed mainly to the discussion of the Monroe Doctrine. The Japanese now no longer pleaded for a special article. All they asked for was the insertion of a sentence in the Preamble, the relevant part of which would then read as follows:

By the prescription of open, just and honourable relations between nations.

By the endorsement of the principle of equality of nations and just treatment of their nationals.

By the firm establishment of the principles of international law, etc.

Baron Makino was again studiously moderate in his presentation. His amendment, he claimed, did no more than lay down a general principle. (This was indeed clear from the fact that it would have taken its place in the preamble, with no substantive article to follow it up.) The work of carrying out this principle came 'within the indisputable competence of the proper authorities'. But his speech contained an ominous note of warning. 'Pride', he said, 'is one of the most forceful and sometimes uncontrollable causes of human action. I state in all seriousness that, although at this particular centre of international life the practical bearing of such a dangerous development of the question may not at this moment be properly realised, I, for one, entertain much anxiety about the possible future outcome of this question.'[1]

He was followed by Viscount Chinda, and when the two Japanese speakers had concluded their argument, 'it seemed', says Mr Miller, 'that they were supported by the feelings of almost everyone present. Lord Robert Cecil refused to accept the amendment and stood on his refusal, acting, as he said, under instructions from his government. It seemed to me at the time that Cecil felt that he was performing a difficult and disagreeable duty. After making his statement Cecil sat with his eyes fixed on the table, and took no part in the subsequent debate.' This was continued by Signor Orlando, M. Bourgeois, M. Larnaude, Mr Venizelos, Mr Kramař of Czechoslovakia, Mr Dmowski of Poland and Mr Koo, the representative of China. All of them supported the amendment, some on theoretical grounds, others on practical grounds also. Then President Wilson spoke, and his words on this occasion were taken down by a stenographer. By this time both he and Colonel House had shifted their ground, no doubt

---

[1] Miller, i. 461. The minutes are in ii. 387 ff.

as a result of the discussion of the matter in the United States. Delay had worked havoc. During the debate House, who always sat next to the President, had passed him a note in these words: 'The trouble is that if this Commission should pass it, it would surely raise the race issue throughout the world'. This gave the President his cue. He said that already discussion of this matter had 'set burning flames of prejudice' and pleaded with the Commission to do its best to damp them down. 'How can you treat on its merits in this quiet room a question which will not be treated on its merits when it gets out of this room?' It was a dangerous and indeed sophistical argument: for it ignored the fact that, now that the issue was raised, attention would attach to the vote and deductions would be drawn from it, whichever way it went.

When the President had finished, the Japanese pressed for a vote. Eleven of the nineteen members of the Commission voted in favour of the amendment. Two (one of whom was General Smuts) were absent. No negative vote was taken. President Wilson then ruled that, in view of the 'serious objections on the part of some of us' the amendment was not carried. His reason for doing so was that the practice of the Committee had been to require unanimity, and that since in this case the objectors were unwilling to meet the majority by framing their objection in the form of a reservation to the majority view, he had no alternative but to declare the amendment defeated. The question at issue was, however, far too great to be decided on a technicality. As Mr Miller remarks, 'regardless of any question of procedure, it was clear that the objection of the British Delegation was of such a character that, notwithstanding the views of the United States or of any other Delegation, the Japanese proposal could not become part of the Covenant'.[1]

Baron Makino once more raised the matter at the plenary meeting of the Peace Conference on April 28. This time he reverted to the terms of his original proposal. He ended his speech with the following words:

In closing, I feel it my duty to declare clearly on this occasion that the Japanese Government and people feel poignant regret at the failure of the Commission to approve of their just demand for laying down a principle aiming at the adjustment of this long-standing grievance, a demand that is based on a deep-rooted national conviction. They will continue in their insistence for the adoption of this principle by the League in future.

On the same day, April 28, Mr Balfour wrote to Baron Makino conceding the demand, on which the Japanese were now 'adamant', for the handing over by Germany to them, rather than direct to China, of the Shantung Peninsula. The 'New Order' had not yet been inaugurated in the Far East.[2]

---

[1] Miller, ii. 702. The Japanese view of the President's action is no doubt correctly stated by Viscount Ishii in his article in *The Foreign Policy of the Powers* (New York, 1935), pp. 106-7. He there enumerates the countries which supported Baron Makino's proposal and describes the President's ruling as 'somewhat sophistical, for the rule of unanimity was not then a *chose jugée*'. This article, written fifteen years after the incident, is a clear indication that the matter is still a very living issue in Japan.

[2] House, iv. 465 ff.

CHAPTER XI

THE FINISHED COVENANT AND ITS PREAMBLE

WE have concluded our examination of how the Covenant came to be framed. We have watched the play of contending principles that went to its formation. We are in a position to realise that the League of Nations, in which so many diverse elements meet and mingle, could not be expected to run a smooth and uneventful course. We have now, in the third part of our inquiry, to see how these various influences acted and reacted upon one another under the impact of experience, when, through the ratification of the instrument to which it was attached, the Covenant became part of the Treaty Law of the world and the League of Nations part of its governmental machinery.

I

But let us first sum up the result of our analysis and try to make it clearer by illustrating it in certain particular cases.

Five strands are intertwined in the Covenant. Four of them we encountered in our survey of the pre-war system: the fifth was a product of war-time thinking. Thus the Covenant embodies five different systems, each with its appropriate method. These systems and methods, if we may recapitulate them, are:

1. *An improved and enlarged Concert of the Powers, using the method of regular Conference.*

2. *A reformed and universalised Monroe Doctrine, using the method of all-round mutual guarantees of territorial integrity and independence.*

3. *An improved Hague Conference system of Mediation, Conciliation and Inquiry, using the political organ of the Conference for this purpose.*

4. *An improvement and co-ordination of the Universal Postal Union and other similar arrangements for the carrying on of world services and the administration of world public utilities, by the establishment of a Secretariat of Secretariats.*

5. *An agency for the mobilisation of the Hue and Cry against war as a matter of universal concern and a crime against the world community, the political Conference being employed for that purpose.*

It is the interaction of these five elements which gives the Covenant the very special and indeed unique quality which has proved at once so attractive and so baffling to students of political science and to the world at large. Unlike most other great declarations and constitutions, it is not the expression of a single political doctrine. It does not emanate from a body of men animated by a common thought or purpose. On the contrary, it represents a dovetailing of doctrines and the adjustment of widely differing and, in some cases, contending wills. Thus the final work is not, like the usual treaty or constitution, a neat and orderly arrangement of chapters, sections and clauses,[1] but a

---

[1] Such an arrangement was at one time considered and even provisionally worked out: but it was rejected by President Wilson, on the advice of Mr Miller (Miller, i. 219-20).

succession of single articles, arranged in some cases almost at haphazard, with no clear idea running through them and no clues provided as to their mutual bearings. The whole that thus results is not a solid construction resting upon an assured foundation but a delicate equipoise between separate elements each resting on a basis of its own. No-one understood this better than Lord Balfour, who, though not one of the original draftsmen, was, as leader of the British Empire Delegation in the First Assembly, amongst the earliest of those called upon to supervise the functioning of the new arrangements. In the historic paper in which in 1925 he set forth the reasons for which the British Government could not accept the Geneva Protocol he does not attempt to argue that the Protocol is *contrary* to the Covenant. He says that it would 'destroy its balance and alter its spirit'—that spirit being, if we may presume to interpret his thought, a spirit of neighbourly accommodation between separate theories and principles juxtaposed in a single document.[1]

Broadly speaking and leaving out of account niceties of drafting and adjustment, we may divide the twenty-six articles of the Covenant between the different systems as follows:

1. *Concert System:*
Articles I (general scheme), II (the substance but

---

[1] Cmd. 2368 (1925), p. 6. The same note runs through the report which he presented to the First Committee of the First Assembly on the relations between the Council and the Assembly. He refers there to 'the undoubted vagueness which—probably intentionally—has been introduced into the Covenant' and pleads for the application of 'tact and commonsense' and 'mutual toleration' in order to avoid 'legal wrangles which would be utterly destructive of the League's utility' (*Records of the First Assembly: Meetings of the Committees*, p. 94).

not the names), III, IV (§ 1 modified by Smuts), V, VI, VII, XVIII, XIX,[1] XX, XXVI.

2. *Monroe Doctrine System:*
X (clause 1), XIX (in capacity of relic of second part of original X),[2] VIII (consequential on X).

3. *Hague Conference System:*
XII, XIII, XIV, XV (except § 8), XVI, XVII (as enlargement of system of preceding articles).

4. *System of World-Services:*
XXII, XXIII, XXIV, XXV (together with III, IV and VI).

5. *System of Hue and Cry:*
XI, XVII (in case of war between two non-members).

Two articles are missing in this enumeration, namely IX and XXI. Both are excrescences on the composite design. IX, as we have seen, was introduced as a concession to M. Bourgeois. It can therefore be considered as belonging to the Hague system—a sort of appendix to XVI. XXI was inserted as a concession to Republican sentiment in the United States. It represents a more conventional conception of the Monroe Doctrine than that sponsored by President Wilson. It does not therefore fit into System 2 and had better stand by itself. The same is true of I, § 3, another concession to the Republicans in the United States.

A word must be said about I, § 2. Its ancestry is complicated, though mainly British. The reader can trace it for himself in Mr Miller's book, with the aid of

---

[1] In this setting XIX is nothing more than an application of an accepted nineteenth-century principle. See p. 75 above.

[2] See p. 226 above.

his invaluable index. But it is worth while making clear that the last clause, relating to the armaments of states claiming admission to the League, has nothing to do with VIII. It is not part of the Wilsonian system whereby Mutual Guarantees render possible Reduction of Armaments. It is a relic of General Smuts's system of League control over the new states in Central and Eastern Europe. The insertion of the word 'guarantee' —the only place in which it is found in the English text of the Covenant—was due to a French amendment of the Smuts formula which President Wilson had incorporated in his Paris draft.[1]

II

But the mixing of the various elements can be best observed in the Preamble, which, both in its English and its French dress, invites close attention.

We have already had before us the original Wilsonian draft. Here is the finished product of the Commission, which the reader can compare with the version on page 222. The phrases are numbered for convenience of reference.

THE HIGH CONTRACTING PARTIES—In order

(1) to promote international co-operation and
(2) to achieve international peace and security
(3) by the acceptance of obligations not to resort to war,
(4) by the prescription of open, just and honourable relations between nations,
(5) by the firm establishment of the understandings

---

[1] Miller, ii. 90, 105, 461, 472-3 (French minutes); 303 and 305 (English minutes).

of international law as the actual rule of conduct
among Governments,

(6) and by the maintenance of justice and

(7) a scrupulous regard for all treaty obligations in
the dealings of

(8) organised peoples with one another,

(9) agree to this Covenant of the League of Nations.

Here the first phrase, the promotion of international
co-operation, belongs to Systems I and IV—the Concert and the World Services. That it was inserted into
the Wilsonian draft and then placed in the forefront of
the Preamble was due to British action.[1]

The second phrase, with its association of *Peace* with
Security, is Wilsonian in origin and belongs to the
Guarantee or reformed Monroe Doctrine system.

The third phrase, which is not Wilsonian and was
interpolated into his text in Paris, belongs to the Hague
Conference system. It conceals an ambiguity, as we
shall see in a moment.

The fourth phrase is Wilsonian, the product not
of the Southern Democrat but of the Presbyterian
preacher. The same may be said of the fifth, where
the use of the word 'understandings' indicates very
clearly President Wilson's intellectual position in the
controversy between International Law and State
Sovereignty.

The sixth phrase lays the stress on justice, but in an
Old Testament rather than a Hague Conference sense.
All these three phrases are really attached to no *political*
system. Their content is ethical rather than political.

With the seventh phrase we return to the Southern
Democrat. It belongs, one may say, to the Guarantee
system.

[1] Miller, ii. 256.

The eighth, still from Wilson's original draft, is again Jeffersonian. It indicates that the League is to be a League of peoples—that is to say, a democratic League—but of peoples who have organised for themselves effective systems of government. We cannot pause to go into the complicated question of the admission of states into the League, either as original members or later: but it is clear that, *in principle*, President Wilson was close to the position which we saw was taken by the League to Enforce Peace during the war.[1] He thought of the League as an association of organised peoples enjoying what his first draft of the preamble called 'orderly government', rather than as a universal body.

Finally, the ninth phrase—'agree to this Covenant' —indicates that the League is composed of sovereign states who of their own free will sign what is before all things a moral—one might almost say a religious— engagement. By so doing they do not form a new state, a new sovereign body. They merely dedicate themselves in their individual activities to a new political way of life.

Let us now turn to the other equally authoritative text and see what the French draftsman has made of the Wilsonian language. The reader will have the original at his elbow. Here is a literal English translation, with the points of difference slightly overstressed, rather than the reverse, where an exact rendering was impossible.

THE HIGH CONTRACTING PARTIES—Considering that, in order to develop co-operation between states[2] and to

---

[1] See pp. 164-5 above.
[2] Quite literally this should be rendered 'between nations [in the English sense of the word] organised as states' or 'between nation-states'.

guarantee to them peace and security, it behoves them
to accept certain obligations not to resort to war;
to carry on openly international relations based upon justice
and honour;
strictly to observe the rules of international law, to be recognised henceforward as an actual code of conduct among
Governments;
to promote the reign of justice and scrupulously to respect
all treaty obligations in the mutual relations of the
organised peoples;
adopt the present Pact, which establishes the Society of
Nations.

The first impression that this makes on the mind is
—as in almost all translations—one of flatness. The
sharp edges of the Wilsonian phrases are worn down;
in their conventional respectability they seem half
meaningless. For the translation fails to bring out,
what a Frenchman will wrongly read into the French
text, the traditional *French* meaning of the two key-
words *Justice* (which occurs twice in the French text
as against once in the English) and *Honour*. 'Justice',
for the Frenchman, bears a juridical rather than an
ethical content, calling to the mind, not the Old
Testament but Roman Law. And 'Honour' suggests,
not 'fair play', with its spacious tolerance and com-
fortable associations with the world of sport, but the
rigorous punctilio of the tournament and the duel.

A number of particular points also call for notice.

The first phrase is turned round in order to take
away what must have seemed to the French draftsman
the too easy-going approach to the subject. The insertion of 'it behoves' (*il importe*) introduces an element
of dignity, one might almost say of seriousness, in
contrast with the looser phraseology of the English.

There is a similar stiffening in the words chosen

throughout the preamble. *Achieve* becomes *guarantee*: the *understandings* of international law become *rules* (*prescriptions*), and these are not simply to be '*firmly established*', as in the English text, but *strictly* (*rigoureusement*) *observed*, not as a '*rule of conduct*' (which has a moral flavour) but as a legal regulation or *code*. Again justice is not to be '*maintained*' but to be '*made to reign*', and the parties do not simply '*agree*' to the Covenant of the League of Nations but '*adopt*' it, and by so doing '*establish*' or 'inaugurate' a new régime in the world, that of the Society of Nations.

We have left one point to the last. In the French text the parties do not 'accept obligations not to resort to war': they accept '*certain*' obligations. The English text glosses over the fact that the door to war is still left half ajar. The French draftsman could not reconcile it with his intellectual conscience to allow so important a point to be left in deliberate obscurity. The resulting phrase undoubtedly lowers the dignity of the composition. A system the members of which are only half committed, committed in certain particular ways, to join in the prevention of war is far from being the new world-order of the prophet's dream. But that, in truth, is all that the Covenant does: and, for the scrupulous French mind, a preamble is dishonest unless it accurately indicates the contents of the document to which it is attached.

III

This leads on to our last illustration, which is chosen as a typical example of a 'legal wrangle' arising out of the desire, natural to the legal mind, to weave into a harmonious whole the loose ends of the Guarantee and Hague Conference systems.

Article XV allows private war; Article X guarantees the 'territorial integrity and existing political independence' of all members of the League. How are these two articles to be reconciled?

At least six (possibly more) answers have been given to this question. We will enumerate them without comment, for the reader's edification:

1. *Article X forbids any and every attack upon a member-state.* This follows, it is argued, from the prohibition of the violation of territorial integrity, since attack of any kind can hardly fail to lead to *some* violation of the territorial integrity of the state attacked.

2. *Article X* does not forbid all attacks but only *aggressive attacks*—that is to say, attacks made in the course of a war waged in contravention of the Covenant. This follows, it is argued, from the use of the word 'aggression' in the article.

3. *Article X abolishes the right of conquest*—even after a legitimate war. This follows, it is argued, from the use of the word 'integrity' in the article.

4. The fourth view is an attenuation of the third. If, it is argued, a state may be invaded and otherwise punished, in conformity with the Covenant, for recognised misdeeds, why should it be protected from the particular form of punishment or correction involved in the alteration of its frontiers? This is the view put forward by Lord Balfour in 1925 and by the British Government in an official communication to the League of Nations in 1928. 'His Majesty's Government', it is there stated, 'regard the Article, whilst of great sanctity, as the enunciation of a general principle the details for the execution of which are contained in

T

other articles of the Covenant.' This, it is needless to say, is only to push the difficulty a stage further back. It amounts to saying that the Article does not forbid violation of territorial integrity in all cases but that the exceptional cases in which it is legitimate cannot be laid down in a general rule.

5. *Article X allows annexation under certain definite conditions*: viz. when one state invades and seizes the territory of another in the execution of an arbitral award or a judgment of the Permanent Court of International Justice. In such a case, it is argued, there is no question of a *violent* change but merely of the securing of a legal right.

6. *Article X allows annexation or conquest in a private war waged legitimately under the Covenant.* This is a variant on (2) above, laying more stress on what is permitted than on what is forbidden.

Perhaps we may most fitly close this brief excursion into the dialectics of the Covenant by a quotation from the British official commentary, with the addition of a single adjective: 'If the nations of the future are in the main selfish, grasping, *litigious* and war-like, no instrument or machinery will restrain them.'[1]

---

[1] On the above see Spaight, *Pseudo-Security* (1928), esp. p. 35 ff.; Komarnicki, *La Question de l'intégrité territoriale dans le Pacte de la Société des Nations* (Paris, 1923), *passim*; *League Official Journal* (May 1928), p. 694 ff., esp. p. 702; Cmd. 2368 (1925), pp. 5-6. See also the discussion on this subject in the First Commission of the Assembly in 1921, especially the speech of Signor Scialoja; Ray, *Commentaire du Pacte* (Paris, 1930), p. 343 ff.; and Struycken, *La Société des Nations et l'intégrité territoriale*, in Bibliotheca Visseriana (Leiden, 1923), where material relating to the Canadian motions regarding Article X at the first three sessions of the Assembly is conveniently collected.

PART III

THE WORKING OF THE LEAGUE

CHAPTER I

WHAT IS THE LEAGUE OF NATIONS?

THE final provision of the Treaty of Versailles, following on its four hundred and fortieth article, laid it down that the treaty would enter into force so soon as it had been ratified 'by Germany on the one hand and by three of the Principal Allied and Associated Powers on the other hand'. This condition was fulfilled on January 10, 1920. This, then, was the birthday of the League.

What was it exactly that was born on that day? There were many godfathers round the cradle; but none was ready with the appropriate name. It was then, and it still is, much easier to define what the League is *not* than to sum up in a word or a formula just what it is.

It is not a 'Super-state': on that all are agreed, both the politicians who have to quiet the apprehensions of sovereign parliaments and peoples and the political scientists who seek vainly in the Covenant for the attributes of government.

Since it is not a 'Super-state', it follows that it is not a Federation. Whether it is a Confederation depends upon the meaning given by the inquiring political scientist to that elusive word. Certainly it is not a Confederation at all resembling the specimen which is most familiar to us, the Helvetic Confederation of the twenty-five Swiss cantons of which the sovereign republic of Geneva is one.

But in fact the attempt to find old-fashioned political labels to fit new and unprecedented political entities is as futile in the case of the League of Nations as in the parallel instance of the British 'Commonwealth' or 'Empire'. In both cases the familiar categories no longer apply and the new material does not yet lend itself to scientific classification. Perhaps even the very notion 'state' is obsolete or obsolescent. Are the 'states members of the League' states in the same sense as the states of 1914? To ask the question is to realise how impossible it is as yet to give a satisfactory answer to it. We are in fact living through an interregnum in political science. The old books are out of date and the new cannot yet be written.

If the League corresponds to no particular kind of state, it corresponds as little to any recognised form of relationship between states. In the first place it is not, what it was designed to be in the Phillimore Report, an Alliance. This is clear both from its composition and from the terms of the Covenant.

An alliance is an exclusive relationship between two or more parties. As such, whatever its precise terms, it carries with it a private and intimate character which is, if not strictly incompatible at least not easy to reconcile with the public, formal and, so to speak, anonymous obligations of an inclusive system such as that of the Covenant. To be everybody's ally is to be nobody's ally. To undertake the same duty towards X as towards an old-time associate is to weaken an existing attachment. To go further, as in the Covenant, and to engage oneself, in a particular eventuality, to support X in opposition to an old associate is to transform an alliance into something wholly different, an impersonal relationship in which cold general principles have taken the place of particular interests and affections. A collective system and special alliances belong to different worlds. That does not mean that, in a period of transition, bridges cannot be constructed between them. But with this we are not concerned at this point of our inquiry.

The Covenant was indeed drawn up by a group—though a somewhat extensive group—of 'Allies and Associates'. But its framers disclaimed from the first any intention of confining it within their own circle. The consultation of representatives of the neutral European states while the Covenant was still being drafted showed that the League was not being established as an Alliance of Victors, and this was confirmed by the invitation addressed, in the Covenant itself,[1] to thirteen neutral states in Europe, Asia, and Central and South America.

At the same time the Peace Conference itself was taking action in a similar sense by bestowing upon the League duties of various kinds extending far beyond the scope of an exclusive association. Some of these duties were immediate, such as the taking of a decision as to the results of the 'public expression of opinion' by the inhabitants of Eupen and Malmédy: others were temporary, such as the 'trusteeship' of the Saar Territory: others were of a more or less permanent character, such as the responsibility for the 'protection' of Danzig, and of racial, religious and linguistic 'minorities' in certain states: others again involved political liabilities of a far-reaching character, such as the control over German commercial policy, over the

---

[1] Annex II.

union between Germany and Austria and over the armaments of Germany, Austria, Hungary and Bulgaria.[1]

But the strongest evidence that the League is not an Alliance is to be found, as M. Larnaude pointed out within a few weeks of the League's birth, in the Hue and Cry articles. What has an Alliance between two or even twenty powers to do with a 'war or threat of war whether immediately affecting any of the members of the "Alliance" or not'? For a mind trained in Roman Law, Article XI was decisive on this point. Allies are not concerned with the mutual relations of outside parties. The members of the League are therefore, so logic would have it, not Allies. The League is not an Alliance.[2]

If the League is neither a Super-state nor an Alliance, is it then something *less* than an Alliance? Is it perhaps nothing more than an unusually elaborate *Multilateral Treaty*, of the type familiar from nineteenth-century practice? Does not the Covenant, like the Postal Union Convention, provide for common action by its signatories *for certain defined purposes*? And is it not terminable, like any other multilateral

---

[1] The relevant articles of the Treaty of Versailles are 34 (Eupen and Malmédy), 49 (the Saar), 102 (Danzig), 280 (commercial policy), 80 (Austria), 213 (armaments). A complete list of the points at which the League and the Peace Treaties interpenetrate is given in Schücking and Wehberg, *Die Satzung des Völkerbundes* (2nd ed., p. 35 ff.; 3rd ed., i. 40 ff.).

[2] Larnaude, *La Société des Nations: Conférences faites à Messieurs les Officiers du Centre des Hautes Études Militaires et de l'École supérieure de Guerre et de l'École supérieure de Marine le 20, 28 février et 12 mars 1920*, Paris, Imprimerie Nationale and Sirey, 1920. (A further lecture, entitled *La Société des Nations depuis 1920*, was given in March 1921 and published in the same form.) After citing the terms of Articles XI and XVII ('in the event of a dispute . . . between States not members of the League'), M. Larnaude contrasts them with the Roman Law rule, '*Res inter alios acta aliis nec nocere nec prodesse potest*', and points out that the Covenant thus *assumes* an 'international solidarity' before which 'certain traditional principles must bow'.

treaty, by any or all of the parties after a specified period of notice? On that hypothesis, the League might be described as a glorified Postal Union, comprising indeed a somewhat smaller membership than its nineteenth-century prototype but entrusted by the participant governments and peoples with business of considerably greater importance. But this definition in its turn reveals itself as insufficient—if only because the purposes for which the League exists, unlike those for which the Postal Union exists, are nowhere exactly defined and, in fact, have since been found to defy exact definition.[1] By Articles III and IV of the Covenant the Assembly and the Council are empowered by the states which have signed that document to 'deal with any matter within the sphere of action of the League or affecting the peace of the world'. And by Article XI, § 2, a narrow interpretation of this latter clause is ruled out by the formal recognition of the 'friendly right of each Member of the League to bring to the attention of the Assembly or of the Council *any circumstance whatever* which threatens' — not simply 'to disturb international peace' but to disturb 'the good relations between peoples on which peace depends'.

Evidently a treaty containing such articles as these is not simply an ordinary, or even a glorified, multilateral convention. It is a Multilateral Treaty and

---

[1] During the Assembly of 1926 a proposal was put forward by the British Delegation to circumscribe the activity of the League on the ground that it was spreading its net too wide. But the difficulty of finding a satisfactory definition of its legitimate field proved so great that the proposal was eventually withdrawn. The debate on this subject in the Committee and in the Assembly is noteworthy for having mustered the French and Italian jurists in defence of the principle of flexibility and 'deciding each case on its merits' as against the British appeal to considerations of logic and orderliness.

something more. Yet that 'something more' makes the League less than a super-state. The League, in fact, lies in an intermediate zone between these two extremes. Or, to use a more fitting image, it *swings* between these two poles, drawing nearer sometimes to the one, sometimes to the other, but never remaining fixed. And the direction and force of these oscillations are due, not to anything inherent in the League itself, not to its constitution or (except in a wholly minor degree) to its so-called 'Civil Service', but to the attitude and policies of its component states, particularly of the Great Powers. What the League *is*, at any given moment, is determined in fact by the degree of willingness on the part of the powers to co-operate with one another. It was because, after wrestling with his British colleagues, M. Larnaude had come to recognise this that he abandoned the attempt to describe the League in juridical or, as he would have said, in political terms, and looked elsewhere, if not for a definition at least for an analogy. And he found it in those voluntary, non-governmental organisations which were anathema to Rousseau and to his disciples of the Revolution. 'All this', he declares, after discussing certain points in the Covenant, 'is not Government or Politics. It is Voluntaryism (*Tout cela c'est de l'Association, ce n'est pas de l'État*). These are the principles out of which free Associations and Trade Unions are constructed and not political principles (*principes de l'État*) at all.' What, then, is the League of Nations? It is 'not a super-state' but 'akin rather to an Association or Trade Union or Co-operative Society of States (*une Co-opérative d'États*)'.

It is an apt French formula crystallising a British conception. A Co-operative Society is maintained by

the contributions of its members, who expect in return
to draw from it regular benefits. But every Co-operator
knows that he cannot expect to draw out from the pool
more than he and his fellows have put into it. Whether
the pool consists of financial resources or of security
from attack or of general confidence, every member of
the 'Co-operative Society of States' must recognise
that his own interest is bound up with the interest of
the whole enterprise and that he cannot expect an
assured dividend unless the society in its turn is assured
of the loyal support and contributions of its individual
members.

The League of Nations is, in fact, *an instrument of
co-operation*. It is a standing agency facilitating common
action by states animated by the co-operative spirit.
In so far as they are desirous of co-operation the
League is available for their use. When this temper of
sociability, this sense of solidarity, this team-spirit,
are present in full measure, the League organisation
functions with a minimum of friction and the League
itself becomes almost—but never quite—a Confederation. But whenever this spirit wanes and competition
and jealousy resume their sway, the League's activity
dies down until it is reduced to routine tasks such as
the Postal Union continued to carry on throughout the
World War. At such times the true League has ceased
to exist. The machinery remains, but the spirit has
departed from it. There is a condition of suspended
animation which may, if the crisis is sufficiently prolonged, end in complete inanition.

Thus 'the League', from which some have expected
wonders, is, in and by itself, politically impotent. It
cannot function by its own effort nor survive indefinitely by its own momentum—a momentum originally

supplied from outside. It is inextricably bound up with
the larger life of the world—not simply with this or
that set of technical activities but with international
politics taken as a whole. By itself it is nothing. Yet
the peoples persistently regard it as Something. That
impalpable Something is not a legend or a myth. It
exists. It has even exercised authority, controlled the
rulers of states and prevented war. But that Something
does not reside in a tabernacle at Geneva. It is communicated to Geneva by the peoples of the Member
States. It is their will and their will alone which can
make the League a living reality.

This is what M. Larnaude tried to convey when,
summing up his analysis, he declared that 'the League
of Nations (*La Société des Nations*) is neither more nor
less than *a new form of international political life*'.
Another Continental scholar, who had not had the
advantage of sitting on the League drafting Committee
but who approached the whole subject from a standpoint unusual amongst the legal confraternity, attempted at this time to reduce the same thought to
more precise terms. Writing at the end of 1919, Dr.
Max Huber thus sums up the characteristics of what
he calls, looking backwards to Sully, Penn, Cruce, the
Abbé St. Pierre and Kant, and perhaps prophetically
forwards also, 'the first League of Nations to become
a political fact'. In its form and method, he says, 'it
is neither contractual (*vertraglich*) nor constitutional
(*staatsrechtlich*). It is something different from either of
these, something quite unique, the product of the conditions of our time. Its method can be described as
that of the codification of practical politics. It is a
systematic dovetailing (*Zusammenfassung*) of all the
elements in the politics of the last hundred years which

are either themselves safeguards of peace or which, having originally formed part of the system of Power-politics, can now be made to serve the cause of general peace.'[1] Here the finger is laid on what is the real and, indeed, details apart, the one and only problem of the League. The process of dovetailing or codification or synthesis carried through in the letter of the Covenant *assumes* a new spirit in the whole field of international politics. It presupposes a transformation of Power-politics into Responsibility-politics, or, at the very least, a sincere and consistent effort on the part of the Great Powers to begin to face the innumerable tasks of adjustment which such a transformation would carry with it. It involves the inauguration of a real Society of States in place of the anti-social traditions and policies of the pre-war era. And it tacitly admits that, failing the adoption of such a new attitude, the new machinery not only cannot by itself bring about the passing of Power-politics, but may even provide a new and more sensational and even dangerous arena for its exercise.[2]

[1] Article on 'Die konstructiven Grundlagen des Völkerbundvertrages' in *Zeitschrift für Völkerrecht*, xii. 1-2.

[2] For a rather different treatment of the question dealt with in this chapter see the chapter entitled 'The Status of the League of Nations in International Law' in Sir John Fischer Williams, *Chapters on Current International Law and the League of Nations* (1929), with references there given, and the article on 'What is the League of Nations?' by P. E. Corbett, in the *British Year-book of International Law* for 1924, who regards the League as a Confederation, although a 'looser species of the genus'.

CHAPTER II

THE HISTORY OF THE LEAGUE OF NATIONS

INTRODUCTORY

SINCE the life of the League is so closely bound up with international politics as a whole, its true history cannot yet be written. For this could not be done without drawing on a large part of the history of international politics from 1920 onwards. The materials for much of this lie in the archives of the League and of Foreign Offices and Cabinets which have issued instructions to League delegates and received their confidential reports in return. None of this, however, is as yet available. Some of it will perhaps never see the light and will thus elude the future historian, like the conversations face to face and over the telephone which have done so much in recent years to take the life out of written records. Diplomacy by Conference may be an improvement in technique, but it adds immensely to the difficulties of the scientific inquirer. Against this must be set the advantage derived from the publicity which has been extended to most of the Geneva meetings. But this gain is more apparent than real, since what is said before the curtain does not always correspond with what is said behind it, and may even on occasion serve to set the student off the track.[1]

---

[1] The above caution applies to all the books, whether official or unofficial, which have hitherto appeared on the League. Thus the official

With these reservations an attempt may be made to trace the course of the League during the first fifteen years of its existence. It is a record full of vicissitudes, such as none of the framers of the Covenant, least of all President Wilson, could have predicted; and their end is not yet. Nevertheless, for the historian certain general lines are already discernible.

The First Phase: 1919–20

The history of the League during these years falls into four distinct phases.

The first period may be described as embryonic. It begins with the process of gestation described in the Second Part of this book and it closes with the official birth of the League in January 1920. In spite of the fact that the League was not then as yet, properly

volume, *Ten Years of World Co-operation*, issued in 1930 for the tenth birthday of the League, was necessarily composed from published sources alone. On the whole, it is the American writers who have done most to pierce through the official veil. Mr Felix Morley, author of *The Society of Nations: its Organization and Constitutional Development* (London, 1932), spent nearly three years studying the League on the spot and the result of much close observation is reflected in his pages. He even refers (p. 314) to the weekly meetings of the Directors of Section in the Secretariat under the chairmanship of the Secretary-General, in terms which suggest that he has had access to some at least of their minutes. But this glimpse of the forbidden fruit only serves to whet the reader's appetite. The same may be said of the memoranda published by Sir Arthur Salter after his retirement from the Directorship of the Financial and Economic Section (see his *United States of Europe*, 1933). What would one not give for similar material from the pens of his quondam colleagues! Finally, in studying League publications and League proceedings generally, the reader should always keep in mind the dictum: 'You can generally achieve a success, if you are prepared to forgo a victory'. Much has been achieved at Geneva by public-spirited individuals and countries through transferring the prestige and glory of an initiative or a decision to others who have a greater taste for them. For an instance of this see Salter, *op. cit.* p. 32.

speaking, in existence, these months were nevertheless the most determining period in its life—at least so far as can be judged in 1935. For it was during this period that the assumptions upon which the Covenant was drafted were undermined and indeed very largely destroyed. This was due to the operation of three new and unexpected factors.

I

The first of these, which perhaps should not strictly be included in this period, has already been referred to. It is the admission of a group of lesser states, side by side with the Great Powers, on to the interstate Conference or what we must henceforward call by its official title of the Council of the League. This made it impossible for that body to become, what it had been designed to be, the organ of an improved and enlarged Concert of the Powers.

This modification of the original plan was due, in the first instance, as we have seen, to General Smuts. Whether without his initiative the smaller powers would have pressed their claims as they did must always remain a matter for conjecture. At any rate the upshot was that they secured four places in 1919, and that since the Covenant interposed no bar, these were increased to six in 1923, to nine in 1926, and to ten in 1933. Once the other states had secured a footing, such a development was, practically speaking, inevitable: for the position of the Great Powers, who thus became 'Permanent Members' side by side with 'Temporary' colleagues, was too invidious for them to resist it, and an extension of the number of elected places was the only means of soothing the susceptibilities of the numerous and importunate claimants. In vain did the

Dutch Delegation in 1923, through the mouth of Mr Struycken, point out that the change was not being made in the interests of the League as a whole but to meet the self-regarding claims of particular states. The opposing current, composed of many separate rivulets, was too vehement and Holland found herself alone in the minority.[1]

The result of this development was that the Council became something new and strange, a hybrid and, as time went on, a more and more unwieldy body, unrelated to anything in the nineteenth century. With the characteristics that it thus developed and the place that it has occupied in the League system and in international politics generally we must deal in a later chapter. Here it is sufficient to say that the admission of other powers on to the Council made it virtually impossible for that body to become the natural and habitual organ of Conference between the Great Powers. This did not necessarily mean, as we shall see, that the Great Powers could not or would not resort to Geneva for their discussions. But it did mean that, whether these took place at Geneva or elsewhere, they would not take place as part of the regular work of the Council, with a train of lesser powers, animated by varying degrees of responsibility, listening and joining in.

[1] M. Motta spoke in the same sense as Mr Struycken in the debate, but Switzerland did not press her objections and voted with the majority. Unanimity was not required as it was a question of procedure. One result of the increase in the number of Council members was a distortion of the arrangement made for the election of the Judges of the Permanent Court of International Justice. The difficulty of reconciling the claims of the great and smaller Powers, which had proved insuperable in 1907, was overcome in 1920 by arranging for a simultaneous vote by the members of the Council and of the Assembly. At the second election of Judges in 1930, the small states were predominant in both bodies, Guatemala, for instance, having two votes.

U

Thus the Great Powers were placed on the horns of a dilemma. They could deliberate wholly outside the League, through an Ambassadors' Conference (as in the early years after the war) or at special meetings at Locarno, Stresa or elsewhere. In that case they were open to the accusation of being unfaithful to the League or of 'putting Geneva in the framework of Locarno'[1] or of Stresa, as the case might be. Or they might meet in Geneva but outside the Council room. In that case they would be criticised for being disrespectful to the League and for preferring 'hotel diplomacy' to constitutional methods of discussion. The broad fact remains that the Council, whatever its usefulness in other respects, is unserviceable as a means for maintaining regular contact between the Great Powers. Yet that such means are needed, even more than in the pre-war period, must be apparent to every attentive observer of international politics.

II

The second new factor that emerged was the discovery that post-war international politics would be carried on under conditions very different from those with which pre-war statesmanship had had to deal. Cabinets and Foreign Offices found themselves working in a different climate. This was due to the combined effect of the democratic movement and of the interest —to use no stronger word—everywhere engendered by the war. In 1919 the peoples were awakened. They had learned, many of them through bitter experience, that

[1] 'It is . . . Locarno which must be brought within the framework of the League of Nations and not the League which should be brought within the political framework of Locarno': M. de Mello-Franco, Delegate of Brazil, in the Assembly, March 17, 1926.

international affairs were not a bundle of remote and mysterious topics better left in the hands of experts, but something of immediate concern to themselves and to their lives and fortunes. Thus there was now a wind of public opinion constantly astir around the subject. Its nature and force varied greatly from country to country. Moreover, its operation was incalculable, being largely dependent on local, rather than on general, conditions. It was difficult even for the most experienced political meteorologist to foresee how soon the weather would change and from what quarter of the sky the breeze would blow next. But, whatever its idiosyncrasies, this new element of public opinion had now constantly to be reckoned with. Diplomacy would need henceforward to be kept in line with democracy.

The first effect of this was not at all as President Wilson—the preacher, not the Southern Democrat—anticipated. The concern of the peoples with the affairs of the Chancelleries did not make for tranquillity or for brotherly understanding. On the contrary, it introduced into international affairs elements which were, and must for long remain, profoundly disturbing. No doubt the peoples as a whole desire peace and an improved world order. No doubt the number of individuals in any country who wish for disturbance or would profit by disturbance is relatively small. But unfortunately each of the peoples, in its ignorance, generally desires peace on its own terms and along the lines of its own habitual thinking and feeling. Thus the intrusion (as the nineteenth-century diplomats would have called it) of public opinion and popular feeling into the field of international affairs has had the immediate effect of intensifying existing differences and of creating new areas of friction. What had previously been matters of routine or questions tacitly allowed to remain dormant have too often been magnified into issues of principle in which considerations of prestige and national sensibility are deeply involved. Journals read by the million dispatch special correspondents to League or other meetings with instructions to send back a daily quota of words palatable to their *clientèle*.

The result of all this in the long run is no doubt to educate the public, if only through a prolonged series of disillusionments. But the effect in the short run is to render fruitful and business-like discussion between the governments very much more difficult. For a negotiation, from the nature of the case, can never, even when it is a hundred per cent success, result in a hundred per cent victory. And few are the publics which, when they have been keyed up by dramatic expectations, are satisfied with a mere fifty per cent.

Thus, by the force of circumstances which were not foreseen and could not in any case have been arrested, the League, in so far as it was destined to be a centre of international politics at all, was bound to develop, not into the quiet and efficient Secretariat of a group of co-operating governments, with a Whitehall Gardens atmosphere, but into something between a market-place, a public meeting and a revivalist place of worship. Since nationalism is the prevalent religion or superstition of the age, it was inevitable that, when allowed to run riot in foreign affairs, it should produce creeds and dogmas admitting of ready application in that field. Thus once the idea of the League was invested by its partisans in this or that country with an emotional or semi-religious significance and presented, in the current French phrase, as *une mystique*, nothing could prevent Geneva from becoming, not the central Church of the New Order with a single doctrine and a common spirit, as President Wilson had dreamed, but a congeries of national churches with a babel of discordant and hence contending worshippers. For the student of national characteristics or of psychology—particularly abnormal psychology—the result has been fascinating. It has made Geneva one of the most interesting sociological laboratories in the world. But it has not made it a place such as a Castlereagh or a Bismarck or a Salisbury or any other experienced pre-war Minister would have chosen in which to try out a new experiment in the conduct of international business.

These considerations have taken us beyond the embryonic period; but they are referred to here because it was during these months that the new influences first became apparent. One instance of their practical working must suffice.

One of the first issues which the post-war Concert of the Powers, or, as they called themselves, the Allied and Associated Powers, had to face was that of their policy towards Soviet Russia. Here was a new 'Eastern Question' for which a common policy was obviously desirable, both on urgent practical grounds and as a demonstration of the technique of the 'new order'. But the elements of the problem were such that not only agreement on a common policy but even a harmonisation of differing policies proved quite impossible of attainment. Stubborn popular forces were in the way. We cannot here analyse them in detail. It is enough to recall that French policy was necessarily influenced by the opinions of holders of Russian bonds, both great

and small, Japanese policy by proximity to the Far
Eastern province, British policy by domestic differences in the appreciation of the Soviet régime, and
United States policy by somewhat similar preoccupations at home, coupled with suspicions of Japanese
designs in the Far East. The result was that, after
pursuing a zigzag course for several months, under the
continuous fire of their various public opinions and their
organs, the powers assembled at Paris abandoned all
attempt at co-ordinating their Russian policies and
fell back on the line of least effort, which was to pass
the problem on to their respective Foreign Offices to be
dealt with on strictly self-regarding lines.

This brief and summary description of the first post-
war effort to arrive at a Concert of Policy is sufficient
to illustrate how, in the psychological conditions of our
time, foreign and domestic issues have become inextricably intertwined. Thus the pursuit of a common
policy by the Great Powers for the solution of particular
political problems, such as the nineteenth century was
able, at fortunate moments, to achieve, has been
rendered immensely more difficult under present-day
conditions.[1] It could be carried through in the earlier
period because the statesmen of the Great Powers had
plenty of elbow-room for manœuvre. There were relatively few pieces on the international chessboard of
which account needed to be taken and the game was
carried on in an atmosphere of relative calm. To-day,
not only have most of the pawns come alive and
acquired a capacity for manœuvring by themselves or
in lesser groups, but a crowd of bystanders is watching

---

[1] This is said without reference to the special relations between the
Great Powers resulting from the war and the peace treaties. The influences analysed in the text are due to deeper and more permanent causes.

the play and is even able to interrupt its course by its manifestations.

Thus we are driven to a conclusion which, because it seems to be paradoxical, many who have set their hope in the League of Nations have stubbornly refused to accept. The overwhelming majority of the states of the world have become members of the League of Nations. Yet, in spite of their regular meetings, they have not been able to work out a common policy. There is no such thing as a *League of Nations policy*. Or to express the same thought in more old-fashioned language, the post-war world has not seen, and is not likely to see, a Concert of Policy between the Great Powers. If such a concerted programme were practicable it would naturally be worked out under the auspices of the League, assured, as it would be, of the support of the lesser states. But it is not practicable: and its impracticability is due, not to mistakes in statesmanship— though these have not been lacking— nor to the bad will of particular powers, nor to temporarily abnormal conditions resulting from the war or the peace treaties, but to more deep-lying tendencies such as were first revealed during the course of the Peace Conference.

It is as well to state the position in blunt language, since difficulty after difficulty has arisen in detail through misconception on this point. No means exist by which the peoples of the modern world can be compelled to walk abreast. The Covenant does not demand it of them: and, if it did, it would soon have become a dead letter. It is not that the peoples are too unruly or that they are bent on mischief. It is simply that they are too much alive. And, being alive and glorying in their freedom, they claim what is surely

one of its most innocent prerogatives—the right to
'gang their ain gait', to see and judge things for
themselves and, if necessary, to take their own time
over coming to a decision on them. This may often
cause them to miss valuable opportunities and even to
embark on disastrous adventures. But how else are
they to acquire the wisdom of experience? How else
have the older and wiser powers—if such there be—
acquired such mastery of the art of government as they
possess? To imagine that a peace made on the basis
of 'self-determination' could inaugurate a system in
which national policies would be kept in a perpetual
strait-waistcoat was to ignore elementary facts not in
the life of Europe alone but of the whole world, not
least of the British Dominions.

If then, it will be asked, the task of co-ordinating
national policies has proved to be beyond the League's
power, if we must abandon the idea of what may be
called, in the language of diplomacy, a 'Geneva Front',
what usefulness remains for the League?

Some, who have never become reconciled to the
inevitable, are inclined to despair of an answer. For
them the League is 'all or nothing': and if it cannot be
the instrument of a World Policy, of a programme of
what is called 'World Unity', it seems to be cheated
of its destiny. But in truth there remain for it two
functions, separable in thought but interrelated in
practice, which we shall have opportunity to observe
more closely in other connexions. They may be briefly
outlined here, as a guide to more detailed later
discussion.

One of these functions is that of acting as a *permanent limiting factor* in the policies of individual
states or groups of states.

It is not for the League to take the place of the Foreign Offices, the cabinets, the parliaments and the electorates of its members. That issue, as we have seen,[1] was settled well before the drafting of the Covenant. It was one of the decisive results of the war. Policies have therefore continued, and will continue, to be worked out in London, Paris, Berlin, Rome and Moscow, as in Warsaw and Madrid, Prague, Belgrade and Bucharest, Brussels, Stockholm and The Hague, Ottawa and Buenos Aires and—last but not least—in Washington. In this respect the principle of the 'free hand', practised by Great Britain throughout the nineteenth century, has been widely, if tacitly, adopted by other states in recent years—though out of a mistaken loyalty to the League of Nations some of them are apt to cry out when this right is exercised by others. It would be interesting but invidious, and indeed irrelevant, to make a list of these so-called infractions against an imaginary 'League policy'.

But the provision of a framework within which policies, national and international (the two cannot be differentiated in this connexion), can alone be carried out is a wholly different matter. Here is the League's appropriate sphere of *authority*. Here it can, or should, say to its members, not 'Thou shalt' but 'Thou shalt not', or, in more measured language: 'Thus far and no farther'. If this degree of authority is not embodied in the League none of its other activities can be expected to bear fruit: for they presuppose the existence, at least in embryo, of a *constitutional system*. For this reason it is necessary to make this point very clear before we deal with the working of the League in detail.

[1] See p. 149 above.

The second function of the League is to discover, through conference and discussion, the matters on which common policies or standards are attainable, whether for the world as a whole or between a larger or smaller number of League members.

Here the League must necessarily start, as the wartime organisers started, with a frank acceptance of the principle of self-government. We live in a democratic age and democracy, whether parliamentary or plebiscitary, is inseparable from decentralisation, both in domestic and in foreign affairs. The ordinary citizen of a modern state understands his own immediate interests and those of his country or region or professional group better than he understands, or can ever be expected to understand, their interaction with the interests of other countries and of the world as a whole. He will therefore refuse to take his policies from Geneva unless or until he or those who speak in his name have been persuaded that the proposed uniformity is in his own interest. Why should he consent to walk in step with the rest of the world until it has been made clear to him that both the discipline and the objective of the march are worth his while? If he was a disciple of Rousseau he might perhaps be ready to accept what was claimed to be in the interests of all. But where the interests of *all* and *each*—a particular each—do not seem to coincide, common sense, which is often another name for small-scale thinking, is apt, at the very least, to dictate prudence and delay.

In some cases, such as postal arrangements, the interests of all are obviously the interests of each: and for this reason it was found possible to establish a world system, on an almost[1] uniform basis, already in

---

[1] For the exception made in favour of Persia see p. 45 above.

the nineteenth century. There are numerous matters, such as the allocation of wave-lengths, on which it has not proved difficult since the war to convince the peoples of the desirability and urgency of uniformity. But there are other matters of great importance— financial and economic policy, for instance—on which uniformity was more easily attained, or even taken for granted, in the pre-war period. Advance in these regions must necessarily be slow, for there is a far greater volume of opinion to be carried forward than before the war. No doubt as a set-off to this, better means have been devised for carrying it. To this we shall return in a later section.

Thus it is not the function of the League to impose Geneva standards upon reluctant or refractory peoples. So far as policies are concerned, the League is not a seat of government but merely a centre of influence. It can promote ideas, organise discussion, initiate projects, set up standards. But the further and decisive stage of passing these into law rests—and, humanly speaking, will always rest—with the governments and peoples of the member states.[1]

---

[1] It is for this reason that the Secretary-General and the other officials of the League have never regarded it as part of their duty to be active in promoting the signature or ratification of treaties negotiated at League conferences or even by the Assembly itself—*e.g.* the Geneva Protocol of 1924 or the 'General Act' of 1928. (The practice of the International Labour Office has always been quite different in this respect.) The duty of Secretariat officials is not to promote or advocate any particular programme on issues discussed at Geneva but the more general one of ensuring the observance of the Covenant and of other obligations assumed by the League. Normally speaking, this should involve the provision of facilities for the negotiation of collective treaties but no direct concern with their contents. The Covenant is careful to lay down broad general principles, not policies and programmes, in this respect. Note the language of Articles XXIII, XXIV and XXV. Unfortunately, however, development on these lines has been interfered with, and the true position obscured, by Article VIII, or rather, by the interpretation

We have spoken of these two functions of the League
—as a limiting factor and as a centre of influence—as
interrelated in practice. How, it may well be asked,
can they be kept distinct? *At what point* is a member
state to find itself faced with the 'No Farther' notice?
Where and how is the frontier to be drawn between
the policy of the free hand and the obligations of the
Covenant, between voluntary initiative and anti-social
behaviour, between self-determination and lawlessness?
This is precisely the issue round which difficulty

placed upon this article by the League Assembly from 1920 onwards.
The League found itself in this way committed to a *programme of
action* on what is probably the most complicated and contentious of all
international problems, that of armaments. It is tempting to speculate
on how the League would have developed if it had been less directly
identified with the effort to draw up a collective treaty on this subject,
with its far-reaching political reactions, and had confined itself to
carrying out the letter of Article VIII, § 2. There is one clear instance in
the Covenant of a policy or programme directly imposed upon the
League, the Mandate Article (XXII). Here again one is inclined to speculate as to what would have happened if the Covenant had gone no
farther into this problem than the statement of principle laid down in
XXIII, § 2. Doubtless the ex-German colonies would have been less well
governed—of the ex-Turkish territories one cannot be so sure—but there
might well have been greater progress in regard to colonial problems as
a whole, since the defensive reaction set up by the system imposed under
XXII would have been absent. Conversely, let the reader ask himself
how the general financial and economic work of the League in its early
years would have been affected if the Treaty of Versailles had made the
Reparations Commission a League organ, or if the Financial Section of
the League had been concerned with inter-Allied debts. (On the modest
and 'harmless' rôle designed by President Wilson for the Financial
Section of the League see Miller, i. 292.) The fact remains that *the
League cannot govern.* Therefore it can no more administer mandated
areas or provide fair treatment for minorities or effectively control
national armaments than it could have collected reparations. And nothing
is so irritating to a trustworthy or so easily evaded by an untrustworthy
government as a general right of haphazard interference in its work by
an outside authority. The best justification of the Minorities Treaties is
that they serve to protect states which are honestly grappling with this
problem from other and less impartial and more vexatious forms of
outside interference. See on this point the Foreign Office memorandum,
pp. 199-200 above.

after difficulty has centred in practice—not least in the field of economic policy. We cannot attempt a summary answer at this stage. It is enough for the present to remark that this was the very problem for which the framers of the Kellogg Pact attempted to find a solution. But this belongs to a later phase of League history.

III

The third new and unexpected factor during this phase of the League's life was the discovery that the United States would not for the present become a member of the League. The refusal of the United States to join in the League system, with which it had become so closely associated in the eyes of the world through the activities of its President, was a crushing blow.[1] It changed the entire international situation and, in particular, transformed the prospects of the League. Its effect in this connexion was threefold.

In the first place, it meant that the League would now not include all the Great Powers. It is true that it had already been decided in Paris that invitations should not be extended at this stage to Germany and Russia. But the Covenant had been so framed as to leave room for them and, as regards Germany at any rate, entry into the League was generally regarded as

[1] With the reasons which led to this decision we are not here concerned. It may, however, be remarked that much of the controversy on the subject centred round the guarantee in Article X and that President Wilson never seems to have realised the extent to which the original sense and scope of that article had been modified by the addition of the second clause (see pp. 242-3 above). It is tempting to ask how events would have developed had this point been clearly put to the people of the United States. Had the United States joined the League it would no doubt have given powerful support to the Canadian proposal, debated in the Assembly of 1923, for an authoritative interpretation of the article in a restrictive sense.

only a question of time. The absence of the United
States was quite another matter, both because of the
preponderant power of that country and of the volume
and intensity of anti-League feeling revealed by the
prolonged controversy carried on there. It became
clear that, for the present at any rate, the claim of
the League to be a world authority, the point of convergence between Power and Law, would need to be
considerably modified. There was even talk at this
time in the United States of the summoning of a third
Hague Conference. Many Americans, who could not
conceive that a League without the United States
could carry on at all, dismissed the subject from their
thoughts. They would have none of the League: therefore it had ceased to exist or had never come to life.

A second consequence was the abandonment, or at
least the suspension for the time being, of the Guarantee
function of the League. Great Britain, it will be remembered, had never favoured this feature of the Covenant.
After the defection of the United States it became, in
British eyes, unworkable. Henceforward Great Britain
made the most of the loophole provided by the second
clause of Article X and used every opportunity to
weaken the interpretation both of Article X and
of Article XVI. Thus, of the two leading sea-powers,
who together could have provided a Police-power for
civilisation, one was out of action and the other determined at all costs to deny or ignore the responsibility.

This is not said in criticism of British policy. It is
important to understand the position in which the
British Government found itself placed. Great Britain
had joined the League in 1919, after two days' debate
in the House of Commons not on the League alone but
on the whole Treaty of Versailles. She had accepted the

obligations of the Covenant in the assured belief that the United States would be by her side in the new co-operative enterprise. Suddenly she discovered that the League to which she was now committed was not the League that she had joined and that, so far from promoting close and constant association with the American government and people, it cut her off from them, throwing her together with a host of other governments and peoples to none of whom, not even her European neighbours and ex-allies, she felt herself attached by an equal bond of common sentiment. Worse than that, the revival of American isolationism, coupled with the determination of the American people to become a sea-power second to none, involved real possibilities of a clash between the two navies over the old question of neutral rights. For if Great Britain should take it upon herself to use her sea-power to vindicate a decision of the League, whose authority and very existence Americans refused to recognise, she might find herself involved from one day to the next in a second but far more disastrous War of 1812.[1]

[1] On this see Mr Balfour's remarks at the eighth meeting of the Council, August 2, 1920 (*Minutes*, p. 26): 'When the Covenant was drafted it was believed that the United States, Russia and eventually Germany would be members of the League. He inquired how the League was in practice to compel these States to break off relations.' As a result of this discussion an 'International Blockade Committee' was set up to study ways and means for carrying out Article XVI in case of need. Its report, which weakened the article in important respects, especially as regards the immediacy and the universality of its enforcement by member-states, came before the Second Assembly in 1921 and formed the basis of a series of Resolutions adopted on October 4 of that year. These were at the time only adopted provisionally, for the guidance of the Council and of member-states, pending the coming into force of certain proposed amendments. But since the amendments were never ratified the 1921 Resolution remained the only authoritative pronouncement as to the carrying out of Article XVI. The Resolutions are conveniently reprinted, with other relevant official matter, in a League document of 1927

Under such circumstances, Great Britain and the British Dominions might well have given notice of withdrawal from the League. They did not do so and there is no evidence that they ever contemplated such a course. Certainly there was no public discussion on the subject. It was decided—and no doubt rightly decided—to make the best of what was not merely a bad situation but essentially also a false situation. But that this decision was not taken lightly or in disregard of the grave considerations involved is clear, not simply from the whole course of British policy at Geneva thenceforward, but also from the frank statement made to the Council on the subject in 1925. 'The League of Nations in its present shape', said Lord Balfour in that document, 'is not the League designed by the framers of the Covenant. They no doubt contemplated and, so far as they could, provided against, the difficulties which might arise from the non-inclusion of a certain number of States within the circle of League membership. But they never supposed that among these states would be found so many of the most powerful nations of the world, least of all did they foresee that one of them would be the United States of America.' And on this he bases an argument which may be broadly summarised as an admission that the League could, for the present, be neither a World Concert of Great Powers nor a guarantee of security for its members against an upheaval such as that of the Great War. With 'ordinary misunder-

(*Reports and Resolutions on the subject of Article XVI of the Covenant:* A.14, 1927). See also Ray, *Commentaire*, p. 504 ff., where the Resolutions are also reprinted. On the International Blockade Committee and the problems which it left unsolved see Bertram, 'The Economic Weapon as a form of Peaceful Pressure', in *Grotius Society Transactions*, vol. xvii., 1931, p. 139 ff.

standings' the League was indeed 'admirably fitted to deal': but to prevent wars arising from 'deep-lying causes of hostility' between 'great and powerful states' was, he declared, beyond its strength. For such 'extreme cases' other means must be sought. In reasoning thus Lord Balfour was only putting into words a conclusion at which most Englishmen had long since arrived, however reluctantly, as a consequence of the absence of the United States from the League system.

Thus the League was prevented at the outset from exercising three of the five functions which were conferred upon it by the Covenant. The Concert, the territorial guarantee and the Hue and Cry were all removed from its purview. What remained? The Hague system for dealing with disputes, but shorn of its new sanction, and the system of World-services, to which additions had been made in the treaties. But disputes were not an everyday matter: this then was something for to-morrow. For to-day there remained only what we called on an earlier page 'gas and water internationalism'.

But here too the defection of the United States brought a bitter disappointment. For the system for the co-ordination of World-services through the League was based on the willingness of the signatories to the various treaties concerned to accept such supervision. 'There shall be placed under the direction of the League', so runs Article XXIV, 'all international bureaux already established if the parties to such treaties consent.' Therefore the whole plan for this side of the League's work fell to the ground. The Postal Union, the Telegraph Union and the other pre-war international bureaux remained outside the League. If

x

contact was to be established with them, as was necessary in some cases, where the Covenant provided for
new activities overlapping with those of existing bodies,
it could only be on the basis of negotiation between
equal and independent parties.[1]

As a result, Article XXIV has remained practically
a dead letter. And when, in 1928, the Council and the
Assembly eventually took it in hand and drew up
rules for its operation, the original idea of the framers
of the Covenant was abandoned and replaced by a
system of mild and friendly co-operation.[2]

The Second Phase: 1920–1924

I

This then was the situation when the League's
official existence began on January 10, 1920. President
Wilson had insisted that it should be linked with the

[1] Thus three years of negotiation were required in order to bring
together the new Health Organisation of the League (under Article
XXIII (f) of the Covenant) with the Office International d'Hygiène
Publique, established in Paris under a Convention dating from 1907.
The delay was due to the negative attitude of the United States Government. (See Schücking and Wehberg, 2nd ed., p. 751.) No similar coordination has been established between the League Organisation for
Transit and Communication (under Article XXIII (e) of the Covenant)
and previously existing bodies in this field. (See on this the chapter in
Ten Years of World Co-operation, esp. pp. 214-15.)—One far-reaching
consequence of the non-co-operative attitude of the United States was
the failure to deal with the problem of the traffic in arms at the time
when an immense quantity of surplus arms was available. The history
of post-war China—to take only one instance—might have been very
different if the Treaty of St. Germain, drawn up at the Peace Conference
on this subject, had been ratified by the United States.

[2] It amounts to little more than an obligation to supply regular information and to admit a League representative to meetings of the organisation. Only six international bureaux have so far availed themselves of
the article.

treaties. Nothing therefore could prevent it from becoming an accomplished fact. But its own author could no longer watch over its destinies. So it lay like a foundling at the door of the European Great Powers. Behind the sonorous phrases with which M. Bourgeois presided over the first meeting of the Council, doing his best to magnify the importance of the miscellaneous tasks on its agenda, one detects a note of surprise, almost of bewilderment, that the much-discussed Covenant should actually have descended from the realm of theory and taken shape in the workaday world.

And how different a world from that envisaged in President Wilson's war-time speeches! The wave of cosmic sentiment, on which he had relied as the ultimate sanction of the League's authority, was fast receding in all countries. In Europe the new states were building up their administrations and making sure of their boundaries, whilst the old were preoccupied with their budgets and with a host of long-neglected domestic problems. In the Near East a state of war still continued and Mustapha Kemal was consolidating his authority with the intention of restoring Turkish rule over Asia Minor by force of arms. In Russia civil war was raging, intensified by surplus arms and other assistance from outside powers. Denikin's effort had lately come to naught but Wrangel was still in the field. A true Far Eastern settlement had also been delayed. China had refused to sign the Treaty of Versailles and thereby to acquiesce in Japanese rights in Shantung, and the situation as between Japan and the United States was causing serious anxiety. Moreover, what was even more alarming, relations between Great Britain and the United States at this time and during the first two years of the League's life were

being subjected to a severe strain, as British public
opinion gradually realised that the United States Navy
had come to stay and that the era of unchallenged
British maritime supremacy had passed away for good.

It is, no doubt, highly probable that, even if there
had been no such increase in the United States Navy,
the days of British sea-power, in its nineteenth-
century form, would have been numbered. For the
war had revealed what had hitherto been latent and
perhaps hardly even suspected—the overwhelming
strategic importance of sea-power in a world in which
wars were no longer fought out between armies but
between entire industrial systems, mobilised for com-
bat. Every Chancellery now knew, however some of
them might disguise it, for reasons of prestige, from the
ordinary citizen, that it was the 'industrial potential'
which would count for most in a future struggle, and
that therefore to command the high road between the
mine and the plantation on the one hand and the
factory on the other was to possess a decisive strangle-
hold over the development of military operations.
In these circumstances it is at least very doubtful
whether the world would have acquiesced in the continuance of a hegemony the full dimensions of which
had been masked, in pre-war days, by the prudence
that had generally been observed in its exercise.
Indeed the wonder is that it was enabled to continue
for so long as it did without provoking the formation
of a hostile coalition. That it successfully avoided this
standing danger is perhaps, for the historian, the most
striking feature in its whole record.[1]

---

[1] It remained, and still remains, a fixed point in British policy to
maintain naval supremacy, against all conceivable combinations, in
European waters and along the two sea routes to India. Thus Mr Baldwin

II

In these circumstances, what could be made of the League? This was the question which the group of able and enterprising officials, whom the Secretary-General had by now gathered round him, must have put to

told the House of Commons on June 2, 1930, that British requirements as to naval defence were based 'on European standards, and what might be necessary for our defence in any conceivable circumstances so far as our narrow seas and certain naval communications were concerned'. At no time and by no post-war British Government has the League of Nations been regarded as a guarantee of protection for Great Britain or the British Empire at sea or even as affording the smallest contribution towards such protection. And at no time did it ever occur to the British public that the notion of 'equality' or 'parity' had any relevance for British naval armaments in European and Near and Middle Eastern waters. A ratio of from 30 to 35 per cent of the British forces has been considered quite reasonable. This did not, however, prevent influential British spokesmen from exhorting other peoples, exposed to greater immediate dangers, to trust in the League of Nations, rather than in their own land armaments, for their protection, or from sponsoring programmes based on a so-called principle of equality of which there is no trace to be found in the Covenant.—On British-American relations between 1919 and 1921—a subject deserving of closer study than it has received—there are interesting glimpses in the House Papers. Thus during the Peace Conference the British Premier told Colonel House that 'Great Britain would spend her last guinea to keep a Navy superior to that of the United States or any other Power and that no Cabinet official [sic] could continue in Government in England who took a different position' (House, iv. 186). For the attitude of Lord Robert Cecil (as he was then) at this time see his letter to President Wilson, reproduced in House, iv. 433-5, where the underlying assumption is that British naval supremacy and the League of Nations are mutually inter-dependent and that the only conceivable alternative to the former is competition in naval armaments. A co-operative attitude towards American sea-power, based upon co-operation in general policy and on common political ideas, was at that time still inconceivable. This makes it possible to measure the distance traversed, under the impact of hard facts, between 1919 and the summer of 1921, when what was euphemis-tically called the 'One-Power Standard' was adopted vis-à-vis the United States.—The evidence as to British naval policy during this period and after is conveniently collected, with full use of the available sources, in Chaput, *Disarmament in British Policy*, 1935.

themselves. And short of a policy of despair the conclusion at which they arrived was the only possible one
under the circumstances. 'The League is dead. Long
live the League!' The League, in other words, must be
built up, at least in its early years, on other lines from
those projected by the framers of the Covenant. And
to the making of this new League, to the discovery of
new activities to set within the now almost empty
framework, they devoted all the energy and experience
that they had brought with them from war-time tasks.

Once the problem was approached in this spirit it
was not difficult to devise a programme. Europe—
not to speak of the wider world—was in a state of
unsettlement and public opinion everywhere was
demanding the establishment of what were vaguely
described as 'normal' conditions. Why should not the
League take the initiative in a co-operative effort to
bring the world back to stability and good government?
And how could this be better done than by employing
the method, worked out during the war, of co-operation between government departments other than the
Foreign Offices—that is to say, between the departments concerned with the various fields of public
administration?

Thus originated what is often comprehensively
called the 'technical' work of the League. It would be
better described as a system of world-services functioning through League secretariats. These secretariats
form an integral part of the League organism, subject
to the authority of the Secretary-General and through
him to the Council and to the Assembly. The League
thus arrived, though by a somewhat different route
from that which had been mapped out for it by
the framers of the Covenant, at one of its projected

destinations. It became a Secretariat of Secretariats. It was the successes achieved in this field and the driving force of which men soon became conscious behind them which constituted the outstanding feature of the League's history during this early period. The League lived because of the *élan vital* infused into it by the freshly recruited Secretariat, conscious of a debt to the fallen to be paid in daily duty. Thus was developed 'the Geneva spirit' of those years, that compound of pioneering initiative, administrative resourcefulness and loyal and unselfish team-work which first revealed to the world the possibilities of peace-time international co-operation.

Work along these lines was set on foot well before the first meeting of the Council in January 1920. The Secretariat was indeed in action earlier than its masters. Already in the spring of 1919 Sir Arthur Salter had worked out a tentative plan. 'It will be necessary', he urged, in a paper circulated to the embryonic Secretariat on May 10, 1919, 'to have a very elastic machinery for effecting *direct contact between the main national Governments in the world under the direct auspices of the League.*[1] The relevant ministers of the several cabinets will have to be encouraged to meet frequently . . . and discuss their national policies, so far as they are international in their effect, in direct contact with each other. . . . Beyond these arrangements for occasional meetings of the Allied Ministers, there should be some form of permanent association and co-operation of officials who would, as in the case of the Transport Executive,[2] endeavour to adjust the development of national policy within their respective spheres so as to facilitate agreement on policy when the

[1] The italics are in the original.   [2] See p. 147 above.

Ministers actually met.'[1] It was in pursuance of the
ideas thus outlined that there came into existence, very
early in the League's life, the three so-called 'Technical
Organisations'—the Communications and Transit Organisation, the Health Organisation and the Financial
and Economic Organisation.

Each of these had a different history. The Transit
Organisation took its rise from a Peace Conference
Committee—the Committee on Ports, Waterways and
Railways. This body had been responsible for Part XII
of the Treaty of Versailles, which contained certain
provisions of a general character and actually provided,
in Article 338, for the drawing up of a General Convention to be 'approved by the League of Nations'. Indeed
it was only lack of time and the complexity of the
material which prevented the insertion of a comprehensive section on this subject in the treaty itself, on the
lines of the International Labour Charter of Part XIII.
Thus already in October 1919, on the initiative of the
French Government, the work was taken up afresh.
Representatives of certain neutral states, amongst
whom the Argentine was the only extra-European
power, were added to the Committee and it was provided with a League official as its Secretary. Later, by
a resolution of the League Council in February 1920,
it was definitely empowered to work out a plan for a
permanent organisation. The first Conference on Communications and Transit assembled in Barcelona in
March 1921 and arranged to meet henceforward, like
the Postal Union, at intervals of four years.[2]

[1] Salter, *The United States of Europe* (1933), pp. 27-8. Some further
details are given by Krabbe in *L'Origine et l'œuvre de la Société des
Nations* (Copenhagen, 1924), ii. 264 f.

[2] Schücking and Wehberg (ed. 1924), pp. 734-6; *Ten Years of International Co-operation*, pp. 207-8.

The Health Organisation originated in a decision of the Council at its second session in February 1920, when preliminary steps were taken to form a permanent body under the League in this field. But while this complicated task was being undertaken events occurred which presented the League with a challenge that it could not ignore. Epidemics of typhus and cholera had spread from Russia to the countries of Eastern Europe and were threatening to move westward. In May 1920 therefore the Council set up a temporary Epidemics Commission and asked the governments to raise contributions up to a total of £2,000,000 for the carrying out of its work. In spite of the fact that, after repeated appeals, only just over a tenth of this amount was forthcoming, the help given by the League to the national authorities in Poland, Russia and the Baltic States held the danger at bay and, though there was later renewed anxiety due to the consequences of the Russo-Polish War and the return westward of hundreds of thousands of refugees from Central Russia and Siberia, Central Europe was saved from infection. Similar work also fell to the Epidemics Commission in the autumn of 1922 when 750,000 refugees from Asia Minor were driven into Greece, bringing with them smallpox, cholera and typhus.

For reasons already stated, however, it was not till May 1923 that the scheme for a permanent organisation was drawn up. It was passed by the fourth meeting of the Assembly, in the September of that year.

International co-operation in financial and economic policy was one of the subjects most neglected at the Peace Conference. The financial scene was dominated by the spectre of reparations and economic policy

involved issues of so controversial a character that—
wisely or unwisely—it was felt that it would be better
not to face them just yet. Thus, though both the
United States and the British delegations had prepared
plans on this subject, on the basis of President Wilson's
Third Point—'the removal of all economic barriers and
the establishment of an equality of trade conditions'—
nothing whatever was done. Instead, the President's
formula was whittled down by the substitution in the
Covenant of the word 'equitable' for 'equal'. Even
this, however, still left the door open for a large programme, whenever the governments might feel inclined
to consider the problem.[1] Thus the whole subject
needed to be taken up afresh after the Peace Conference.

The new starting-point is to be found in a decision of
the Council at its third meeting, which took place in
London under the chairmanship of Mr Balfour (as he
then was) on February 13, 1920. At the end of a long
sitting he made a brief statement introducing 'one
item which does not appear upon our programme, an
item, however, of considerable importance'. It was
nothing less than a proposal for the summoning of an
international Financial Conference, to deal with the
'world-wide financial and exchange crisis'. A resolution
was there and then passed empowering the President
of the Council to arrange for the sending of invitations
'to the states chiefly concerned' and to convene the
Conference 'at the earliest possible date'.

The Brussels Conference, which met in September

[1] On the programmes of economic policy prepared for the Peace Conference and the reasons why they were put on one side see the article by
Allyn Young in *The History of the Peace Conference of Paris*, ed. Temper-
ley (1921), vol. v.; on the British plans see p. 72, on those of the U.S.,
p. 67, and *Senate Hearings* (1919, Doc. No. 106), p. 1209 ff. The Board
of Trade material on this subject is, of course, not yet available.

1920 and sat for a fortnight, has a very special place in the history of the League. It was the first important Conference held under its auspices and its organisation and methods of work turned out to be an invaluable dress rehearsal for the first meeting of the Assembly which followed immediately after. It was in Brussels, for instance, that the Committee system in the form later adopted at the Assembly was first tried out. Another fruitful innovation related to the character of the delegates. Though the Conference was official in the sense that its delegates were nominated by the governments, they nevertheless attended without instructions. They were appointed 'as experts and not as spokesmen of official policy'. In this way not only was a freer discussion secured but the Conference was able to arrive at resolutions which, if they were not 'practical politics' for all governments at the moment, nevertheless mapped out an agreed line for further advance.

Such a Conference in fact is not summoned to legislate but to explore. Its function is that of a pioneer or a pace-maker for the more slow-moving governments. That there is a place for such a type of assemblage has been amply proved during the last fifteen years, in spite of all their setbacks. It may indeed be described as a notable post-war invention in the technique of international politics.

It is worth mentioning also that the eighty-six delegates at the Brussels Conference hailed from thirty-nine countries, including Germany and the United States. The American representative, Mr Roland W. Boyden, was, however, an 'observer', not a full delegate, and did not owe his place to the United States Government. From this tentative beginning there gradually developed the present system under which the United States voluntarily participates in all the regular 'technical' work of the League and also in some of its major political activities, without accepting the obligations of the Covenant.

The resolutions of the Brussels Conference, which have been described as 'a compendium of financial orthodoxy', provided ample material for League activity in this field. Thus the first meeting of the Assembly authorised the creation of a regular Economic and Financial Committee, to replace the provisional body which had organised the Brussels Conference. It was divided into two sections, one financial, the other economic, composed of ten members each. Thus by the end of 1920 the new organisation was launched.[1]

Side by side with these three officially designated Technical Organisations must be set the so-called Permanent Advisory Committees, which began to be formed early in this period. Thus in January 1922, in pursuance of its duty under Article XXIII (c) of the Covenant, the Council decided to set up an Advisory Committee on the Traffic in Women and Children. In 1924 this was enlarged in scope to include the protection of children generally, being divided into two sections, one specifically devoted to Child Welfare. Another duty resulting from Article XXIII (c), the supervision of the traffic in opium and other dangerous drugs, was dealt with already at the first meeting of the Assembly, when the creation of an Advisory Committee on that subject was decided upon.

One other activity initiated in this period must be mentioned. At the first meeting of the Assembly Senator La Fontaine of Belgium proposed that the

[1] In the above paragraphs use has been made of the chapter on the subject in *Ten Years of World Co-operation*.

League should concern itself with 'international intellectual relations', a subject which M. Hymans, the Belgian member of the League Committee at the Peace Conference, had unsuccessfully attempted to include in the Covenant. This led the Council to propose to the second meeting of the Assembly in 1921 the appointment of a Committee 'to deal with questions of intellectual co-operation and education'. On objection being raised by a Canadian delegate, the reference to education was dropped. The Council then proceeded to nominate a Committee on Intellectual Co-operation, to be presided over by M. Bergson. A working instrument was provided for it by the generosity of the French Government, which in 1924 offered to provide facilities in Paris for this purpose. Thus in 1925 the International Institute of Intellectual Co-operation, housed in the Palais Royal, opened its doors. The actual Secretariat of the League Committee remained, however, at Geneva and the work was thus divided between the two centres. Stimulated by the example of France, the Italian Government proceeded to offer two similar benefactions—an International Institute for the Unification of Private Law and an International Institute of Educational Cinematography. These were accepted by the League, and provided with Governing Bodies somewhat on the lines of that of the Paris Institute. In 1928, however, it was thought wise to put a check to what might otherwise have become a dangerously centrifugal tendency. The Council therefore adopted a set of rules determining the conditions to which Institutes offered in this way must conform in the future.[1]

[1] The initiative in this rather delicate matter was taken at the Assembly of 1927 in a motion brought forward by Dame Edith Lyttelton.

III

It is beyond the scope of these pages to describe, and still more to appraise, this 'technical' work of the League. It is doubtful indeed whether there is any single person living who is competent to do so.[1] Each of the different fields of activity demands a separate study, in which account would need to be taken not only of the organisation at the centre but of the influence exerted and the results achieved in the various countries to which the work has extended. In these circumstances any attempt at a summary account could only be misleading. But something must be said of the theory of the League to which these early achievements gave rise.

One of the discoveries of this period, as has already been noted in connexion with the Brussels Conference, was the use that could be made of 'experts' in international affairs. It was found that the League was able to draw upon a reservoir of knowledge and public spirit which few, if any, national governments had hitherto systematically employed. Thus the League Technical Organisations and Advisory Committees and their numerous Sub-Committees began to number an array of names of a quality unknown to public life before the war. 'Practical men', averse from the tumult of 'politics' and masters of theoretical knowledge,

---

[1] In June 1935 a Committee, appointed by the Council, sat for a week in Geneva 'to study the Constitution, Procedure and Practice' of League Committees. It numbered in its ranks two of the original members of the Secretariat and some other close observers of the League. Its brief report contains some unexceptionable statements of principle but makes no attempt to survey, still less to pass judgment on, the work of individual Committees.

averse alike from politics and practical affairs, came to Geneva to sit together on Committees under the skilful marshalling of the Secretariat. From this period dates the story of the banker—whether in the City of London or in Wall Street we need not inquire—who, when requested to allow his name to be used as a supporter of the League of Nations, declared that he had no time to consider the matter as he was just now so fully occupied with the Austrian Loan. So accustomed was he to the pre-war watertight separation between 'business' and 'politics' that his practical mind had not grasped the fact that the arrangements for this loan were being negotiated under the auspices of the Financial Committee of the League. Equally remote from politics in the pre-war sense were the high medical authorities—to take only one instance— invoked by the Health Organisation for such tasks as the Standardisation of Sera.

Thus the League was becoming, in a sense and to a degree of which this could be said of no national centre of government, *a point of convergence between Knowledge and Power*. 'If youth but knew, if age but had the strength'—this old French adage had been in the minds of the very few, such as Lord Haldane, who had pleaded already in pre-war days for closer association between Science and Government. 'If only the governments *Knew*: if only the experts *Could!*' Now, on the international plane, this hoped-for contact was unexpectedly being established. And it was discovered that, by a natural but unanticipated psychological process, it was actually less difficult to create an *esprit de corps* and to promote efficient team-work amongst a group gathered from numerous countries than in a purely national Committee. For the change of atmosphere, affecting everyone alike, tends to eliminate inhibitions and to shake off minor encumbrances. The familiar difficulties incidental to professional collaboration—the undue emphasis on petty issues, the routine habits, the repugnance to new ideas—disappear almost by magic in the atmosphere of an international gathering. There was nothing of the close spirit of the guild in the round-table groups which now became a familiar feature of Geneva life. Men who, faced with a similar problem in their home surroundings, might be sticklers for habit and precedent, were led by a natural combination of motives—personal emulation, national pride and genuine international feeling—to vie with one another in dealing with the problems set before them according to the best lights of their professional craft. Sometimes such bodies, inspired by the atmosphere of mutual collaboration and under the pressure of urgent need, ventured on practical policies which might well have been dismissed as Utopian by any single one of their members at his own fireside. What student of government would have predicted in 1914 that a body of business men, picked as individuals from as many countries and set to work at a table together, would have been able to rescue a European state from bankruptcy and chaos? Who again would have imagined that the same body would have had the courage to make itself responsible for a reconstruction scheme following upon the greatest migration in history and involving the care of some one and a half million human beings? [1]

[1] Use has been made in the above of the writer's article on 'Democracy and the Expert' in the *Political Quarterly*, January 1930. See also his *Learning and Leadership*, written in 1926 for the Committee on Intellectual Co-operation, where a programme is sketched in this spirit. For details as to the work of the Financial Committee in Austria, the Near

By the adoption of this method the particular international problems selected for treatment were dealt
with scientifically and on their own merits. This
involved a radical change—indeed a revolution—in
the conduct of international affairs. For to deal with
an international problem on its own merits is to detach
it from entanglement with Power-politics and to bring
it within the orbit of a new co-operative system in
which Power-politics play no part. The doctors, the
bankers, the child welfare experts and the 'intellectual
co-operators' were all of them concerned with finding
the best solution for their own particular problem
along the lines of their *expertise*. They were fellow professionals animated by a common spirit. And this
applied, as a general rule, even when they were not
private individuals or representatives of professional
bodies but civil servants from departments other than
the Foreign Offices. Thus, to take an instance familiar
to Geneva, attached though they were to the administrative system of a Great Power, the Home
Office experts concerned respectively with Dangerous
Drugs and Child Welfare would have found it difficult even to conceive of their tasks in power-political
terms.

If this method worked so satisfactorily and led to
results both more rapid and substantial than was
expected in 1920, why, it was natural to ask, should it
not be extended indefinitely throughout the field of
public affairs? Why should not one problem after
another be detached from the complex of 'high politics'

East and elsewhere see the chapter in *Ten Years of International Co-
operation* where, however, important aspects of this curious post-war
association between the League and the agencies of capitalism are
necessarily left on one side.

Y

and subjected to scientific treatment in the new atmosphere of international co-operation? And why should not this lead, in the long run, to the elimination of the causes of war? What, after all, were those causes? Did they not consist in an intricate and tangled web of issues round which bitter poisons had been allowed to gather because they had never been scientifically surveyed and analysed, and then explained, in reasonable terms, to the peoples concerned? No doubt it would be a more prolonged and complicated task to disentangle the issues that had become coagulated, so to speak, round tariffs or colonial policy or migration or the movement of capital—not to speak of 'self-determination'—than to co-ordinate the statistical methods of governments or the terminology employed in their customs duties. But 'every mickle makes a muckle'. The thin end of the wedge had been successfully inserted. All that was needed was to persevere.

Thus there emerged, in League circles, what may be described as a new form of the old Fabian or gradualist doctrine, based upon the assimilative power of the Geneva spirit and of the institutions which it was creating. Little by little, so it began to be believed, the morass of 'high politics' would dry up along its edges, as one issue after another was drained off to Geneva. Thus eventually there would be a world-wide co-operative system held together by a network of contacts between government departments (other than Foreign Offices), professional organisations and individual experts. It was, indeed, a curious combination of Fabianism and Cobdenism. The Fabians had looked forward to a co-operative system resulting from public ownership or control. The Cobdenites had expected to arrive at it through the multiplication of individual commercial contacts guided by Adam Smith's 'invisible hand'. Under the League, private and public agencies were to work together with the same object in view. The expectation, or at least the confident hope, that such an advance would prove practicable was based upon the belief that the world had learnt the lesson of 1914, that the problems left by the war and the peace treaties were steadily yielding to treatment and that there would, at the very least, be a considerable respite from the more dangerous manifestations of Power-politics, during which the League and its new methods and institutions would be able to gather strength and stability. If these calculations proved to be unfounded, who can regret that they were entertained? For, if much of the work that was done during these years has proved abortive, the method and the record of achievement remain.[1]

Whilst this was the current of thought amongst those in close touch with the League, outside opinion was reacting very differently to these developments. On the Continent the principal concern was, as we shall see, the failure of the League to provide adequate safeguards for peace. In Great Britain, on the other hand, the recital of the League's technical achievements led the public, which had become determined to ignore the security problem, to regard the League as a philanthropic and humanitarian agency, differing only in the scope and dignity of its work from the voluntary agencies of beneficence which are so familiar a feature

---

[1] For the above see especially Part V. of Sir Arthur Salter's *Allied Shipping Control*, written during this period (where, however, there is no such definite formulation of theory). See also Greaves, *League Committees and the World-Order* (1931), esp. p. vii.

of British life. It was in these days that the League became a 'cause' for which personal support, in the shape of good wishes and even a subscription, was due from the well-meaning. Even to-day, in very much altered circumstances, it is not uncommon to meet private individuals who claim with pride that they 'belong to the League', in virtue of their membership of an unofficial association formed to promote a knowledge of its work and to further its fundamental objects. Thus, by an unhappy concatenation of circumstances, due, at bottom, to deep-lying differences of outlook and temperament, the results achieved at Geneva during this period had the effect of widening the gulf, large enough already since the withdrawal of the United States, between the British and the Continental attitude towards the League. The promotion of co-operation upon one plane was serving to make co-operation more difficult upon another.

IV

Meanwhile, side by side with the development of these new 'technical' activities, the League was also a scene of political history. For, in spite of the absence of the United States, the Covenant remained, with its obligations as to security, armaments and the peaceful settlement of disputes. These formed the main staple of public discussion at the Assembly and in the press, whilst the 'Fabian' efforts described above necessarily attracted much less general attention. What could the League, in its weakened condition, do to carry out these major tasks? And how much, under the circumstances, ought it to attempt to do or even to pretend to do? Round these underlying questions, seldom so openly formulated (for the idea that the League had a 'prestige' to be maintained was early in the air), ranged the principal debates in the Assembly and the Council during these years.

The lines were already clearly drawn at the first session of the Assembly in November 1920. Three sections of opinion—one might almost call them parties —emerged. There was first the group which was later wittily described by a Canadian speaker[1] as that of the 'consumers of security'. These were the states who wished that everything possible should be done to enable the League—imperfect though it was—to fulfil the purpose designed for it by President Wilson, that of a society for mutual assistance against aggression. The leadership in this group fell naturally to France, both because the French, since the failure of the alternative system of guarantees provided for them at the Peace Conference,[2] were urgently preoccupied with this problem and also because, as we have already seen, their whole bent of mind impelled them to try to fill in the vague outlines of the Covenant and convert it into a precise and formal system of Peace through Law. Together with France stood Belgium, most of the new or enlarged states of Central and Eastern Europe, with several of whom France contracted alliances during this period, and also a number of other

[1] Senator Dandurand in the Assembly, September 12, 1927. He ascribed his *bon mot* to 'a well-known Oxford Professor'. Senor de Madariaga occupied a Chair at Oxford at that time.

[2] The unratified treaties of 1919 between Great Britain and France and the United States and France both stipulated that their obligations should remain in force until 'the Council, acting if need be by a majority, agrees that the League itself afford sufficient protection'. That the French should have consented to a form of words under which they might have been outvoted on a decision as to their own security is a testimony to their fidelity to the 'Super-state' philosophy.

states, such as Persia, China, Haiti and Panama, which had special reasons for feeling anxious about their security.

The second group was composed of those League members who were eager to establish what the Scandinavian states had called, in a joint scheme drawn up already in December 1918, 'an international juridical order'. They were, in fact, disciples of President Taft—with this difference, that they refused, at least in the existing conditions of the world, to face the problem of how to ensure that these juridical decisions should be enforced. This, they no doubt felt, might involve them, individually, in dangerous political complications. They therefore took up a negative attitude towards French and other schemes for the better organisation of sanctions and concentrated on the task of filling up what was in their eyes the principal gap in the Covenant, its failure to provide for a binding or compulsory system for the settlement of disputes. But, above all, they favoured disarmament, which they regarded as the surest means for bringing about the supremacy of Law over Force and therefore as a direct contribution to the problem of sanctions. By disarmament they meant, in the last analysis, the reduction of the armed forces of the members of the League, and especially of the Great Powers, to the scale needed for the maintenance of domestic order. As this was the scale to which the armed forces of the defeated powers —above all of Germany—had been reduced, it was inevitable that this line of policy should seem to associate them, however undesignedly, with the policies of the vanquished rather than of the victor states. The leadership in this group fell to the Northern peoples, with whom Holland, Switzerland and, at a later stage, Spain were in general agreement.[1]

Somewhere between these two groups, which may be described as the Security Party and the Arbitration and Disarmament Party, Great Britain took up her position or, it would be more accurate to say, moved uneasily to and fro. Her equivocal attitude during this period was indeed bewildering, not to say exasperating, to her fellow members in the League. This was due partly to the fact that, as we have seen, she had drifted into a false situation, so that she never felt at ease in her relations with the League. But an even more potent cause of her vacillations was the influence of a romantic and sentimental strain in public opinion, blankly unintelligible to the Continental mind. To a section of the British people the League had now become a symbol, the one visible gain resulting from the war, a consolation for many disappointments at home and abroad. It became almost a religious duty to 'believe in' it and to 'support' it and declarations in this sense, necessarily quite non-political in character, were made by the highest in the land. But this was not at all the same thing as to pay serious attention to

---

[1] The memorandum of the Northern states, which was the basis of their proposals at the meeting of the League of Nations Committee with the representatives of the neutral states, is printed among the early documents of the Court (reference in Miller, i. 305), and, more conveniently, in Florence Wilson, *The Origins of the League Covenant* (1928), p. 211 ff. There were, of course, differences of detail and of emphasis between the policies of the various states in this group. On Swedish policy see Bellhouse, *Some Aspects of the Recent Foreign Policy of Sweden* (University of California Press, 1929), on Danish, Munch, *La Politique du Danemark dans la Société des Nations* (Geneva, 1931). For a Swiss approach see the scheme drawn up by Max Huber (printed in *La Conférence de la Paix et la Société des Nations* (Paris, Les Éditions Internationales, 1929), p. 252 ff., which takes for its basis a Federal Pact (analogous to the original Swiss Federal Pact) between mature and trustworthy peoples, the nucleus of a future more widespread international community.

the obligations embodied in the Covenant. When it came to the actual formulation of policy these clouds of aspiration were blown away and a very different atmosphere prevailed. For the bewildered foreigner, the climax was reached when the glaring discrepancy thus revealed between their professions and their practice seemed to cause no qualms whatsoever to these illogical islanders. The League of theory and the League of fact were simply in separate worlds. What was good for Sunday 'did not work' on Monday. So a sensible people postponed the major programme to the Greek Calends—but without summoning up the moral courage to say so openly. To nations schooled to regard intellectual honesty as one of the cardinal values this seemed, not simply a mistake of political judgment, but a lapse from the recognised moral standard.

Yet, viewed in relation to the general scheme of British foreign policy, the British attitude at Geneva— with an exception to be presently mentioned—was intelligible enough. It was quite natural that Great Britain, together with the Dominions, should offer a firm resistance to any reinforcement of the security provisions of the Covenant. How could she do otherwise when she was essentially a 'producer' rather than a 'consumer' of security, and indeed, if not the sole, at least, as the principal sea-power in the League, the pre-eminent producer? Moreover, for the reasons explained on an earlier page, she also viewed unkindly the principle of compulsory arbitration. The Cabinet and the Foreign Office were no more willing now than before the war[1] to promise beforehand to submit any dispute falling under a given classification to be decided by an international body of uncertain character

[1] See p. 122 above.

and composition. No doubt, as a British Cabinet Minister remarked at the time, 'the principle of compulsion' was agreeable 'to the equalitarian sense that pervaded the Assembly', which had visions of 'a tiny state, with half the population of Sheffield, hauling a big Empire before an international Court of Justice'. But for Englishmen, under these circumstances, as he went on to say, 'there was obvious force in the argument that the plant' of international justice 'was most likely to flourish in a soil of freedom'.[1]

On the other hand, British opinion, both official and popular, strongly favoured the reduction and limitation of armaments.

Official circles arrived at this conclusion through reasoning on strictly common-sense lines. Although at the Peace Conference the Admiralty had maintained the objections tenaciously held since 1899, it had by now become apparent that the state of the national finances rendered some form of naval limitation advisable. Moreover, the abolition of the submarine by international agreement was greatly to be desired. These considerations, however, had little to do with the League, where at this time the United States took no part in disarmament discussions. It was in Washington, as part of a general Far Eastern settlement, that they found practical application, in the winter of 1921–2, not in the form of a multilateral treaty negotiated between fifty or more powers but in a limited agreement between the five powers principally concerned.[2]

[1] See Rt. Hon. H. A. L. Fisher, *An International Experiment*, p. 16 (Earl Grey Memorial Lecture, 1921).

[2] The Washington Naval Treaty was renewed, this time between the three principal sea-powers alone, in London in 1930. Events since that date have made it clear that, in the Far East, as in Europe, the arma-

Since the naval question could not be dealt with at Geneva, the question arises as to why the British peoples, in these years, took so active a part in sponsoring disarmament, which in practice at that time meant land disarmament, thus impelling the League along a course which it later became impossible to abandon.

It is not very easy to answer this question. To any careful political observer it would have seemed to be, to say the least, unwise to press forward an issue that could not fail to evoke proposals for further commitments in the domain of security which the people of Great Britain (not to speak of the Dominions) were then in no mood even to consider. The explanation no doubt is that this eventuality, however obvious it may seem in retrospect, was overlooked in the enthusiasm for what had become, for a certain type of British opinion, a moral crusade rather than a realistic political programme. Wherever the responsibility is to be assigned, whether to the spokesmen of the churches or to the leadership of influential voluntary organisations in this field or, in more general terms, to a missionary temper in foreign affairs dating back to pre-war times, the fact remains that it was due, if not to British initiative, at least to British support and persistence, that disarmament was taken up by the Assembly as one of its principal tasks and, as time

ments question cannot be dissociated from the general political situation. —The Admiralty memorandum on disarmament at the time of the Peace Conference, given in Miller, *The Drafting of the Covenant*, i. 286-7, is worth quotation in the light of after events. It pointed out that 'the introduction at the present stage of proposals for the limitation of armaments, before the League of Nations has established its power to afford security to its members, may delay rather than advance the reduction of armaments, since many intricable and delicate questions, the solution of which should preferably await an atmosphere of security, will be involved'.

went on, became more and more the centre of League activity during this period.

The adoption of this policy involved a change in the interpretation of Article VIII which amounted almost to a reversal of the original intention of its framers and, particularly, of President Wilson, to whom its actual formulation was due. For Article VIII calls on the members of the League to reduce their armaments 'to the lowest point consistent with . . . the enforcement by common action of international obligations'. In other words, it was inserted into the Covenant, and into the League system, on the assumption that (apart from their use in aid of the police for the maintenance of domestic order) armaments would henceforward be the instruments of a co-operative international policy on the part of the powers. When the basis which had been thus designed for a League disarmament policy disappeared through the withdrawal of the United States, the whole situation was transformed and the discussion of the subject was bound to take place in a spirit not of co-operation but of competition. The dominant consideration in the mind of the governments and their advisers then became, not what is the minimum force *which we need to maintain* in order to contribute our rightful share to the common effort—a question much debated in Denmark, but in Denmark alone—but what is the maximum *on which we must insist* in order to have at least an 'equal', that is to say a fifty per cent, chance of victory in the next 'private war'. To expect to arrive at an agreed Disarmament Treaty between fifty states, or between the Great Powers alone, upon a competitive basis of this kind was to expect to succeed in squaring the circle. Disarmament, in fact, has never at Geneva been a subject in and for itself. It has always been a function or aspect of the general international situation.

For reasons with which we are not concerned in these pages, post-war statesmanship did not succeed in establishing relations of confidence, still less of co-operation, between the Great Powers, either in the wider world or even in Europe. Under these conditions the result of the effort to force on a system of dis-armament was, as Castlereagh would have predicted, that 'difficulties were rather brought into view than made to disappear', for as a recent Continental Foreign Minister has remarked, when the political sky is overcast 'difficulties do not contract at Geneva: they expand'.[1] Thus what eventually emerged from this prolonged imbroglio was not the replacement by Con-tinental governments of their accustomed method of conscription, embodying the democratic tradition of the French Revolution, by small professional armies on our island model, but the adoption by both France and Germany of a new and more formidable and burdensome military system, under which the pro-fessional army, Britain's gift to the defeated peoples, forms the nucleus of the old organisation of 'the nation in arms'.[2]

---

[1] Signor Grandi in his essay in *The Foreign Policy of the Powers* (New York, 1935), p. 87.

[2] The competitive spirit in which the disarmament discussions at Geneva were conducted throughout comes out most clearly in the reports of the technical Committees. See especially the report of the military experts on the so-called Sub-Committee A (really the Permanent Advisory Committee disguised under another name to spare American susceptibilities) which is filled with instructive information and argu-ments, each set of experts naturally attempting to minimise the value of their country's armaments. Thus, for instance, in order to depreciate the importance of the 'industrial potential' of the United States it is recalled (p. 20) that 'only four guns of all those manufactured by the United States during the war for their own needs reached the front before the

end of hostilities, nineteen months after the declaration of war'.—
For the British responsibility for imposing a professional army upon
Germany see Chaput, p. 254 ff. Foch was throughout opposed to the
idea. As he put it: 'We can no more limit the number of men trained
to arms in Germany than the Germans could limit the output of
coal in England'. According to Sir Henry Wilson's diary, President
Wilson too was opposed to the imposition of voluntary service on
Germany and only consented when the British Premier threatened
to oppose his project of the League of Nations, whereupon 'Wilson
collapsed'. The British Premier's stand was due to his election pledge
to secure the abolition of conscription in all countries. He therefore
declared that 'no General's opinion would shake his decision'. On
this see Chaput, p. 258; Callwell, *Field-Marshal Sir Henry Wilson*
(1927), ii. 174; and Miller, *My Diary at the Peace Conference*, xv.
246. On Foch's attitude see Miller, *Diary*, xiv. 249. The abolition
of compulsory service in Germany left a gap in German life that was
soon filled by non-official organisations which developed into private
armies—with results that are familiar.—Some may be inclined to argue,
in this connexion, that the one-sided disarmament imposed upon Germany and the other ex-enemy states in the peace treaties made it
imperative for the League to deal with the disarmament problem. There
was, of course, no *legal* obligation in this connexion. The opening words
of Part V of the Treaty of Versailles (which were formulated on the same
hypothesis as Article VIII, viz. that there would henceforward be a
co-operative international system) are a statement of intention, not a
binding pledge. Nor can a legal obligation be derived from the fact that
by Article 213 of the Treaty the League of Nations is empowered to
exercise a supervision over German armaments—a clause which has
remained a dead letter. Was there, however, a moral obligation? This
raises issues which transcend the scope of this volume. This much, however, can be said. Granting that the Peace Conference left the Continent
in a condition of instability which was bound to end, sooner or later, in
an alteration of the conditions imposed on Germany in Part V of the
Treaty of Versailles, it was nevertheless a political and psychological
mistake to bring this problem into connexion with Article VIII of the
Covenant and to attempt to solve it through the League. The best evidence of this is the fact that at no time after this issue had been brought
to Geneva were German demands for 'equality' based, by the German
Government and people, on the desire to make an 'equal' contribution,
worthy of Germany as a Great Power, to 'the enforcement by common
action of international obligations'. On the contrary, Herr Stresemann
did not regard it as practical politics for Germany to join the League in
1926 until her obligations in this respect under Articles XVI and VIII
had been whittled down. (See on this *Stresemann: Vermächtnis*, vol. ii.
passim, e.g. pp. 148 and 182.) Thus Germany's entry into the League
and participation in its disarmament work only increased the prevailing confusion of motives. That what may be called the problem of

V

With this guiding thread we can quickly find our way through the political history of the League during these years.

When the Assembly first met, in November 1920, it found the Permanent Advisory Committee provided for under Article IX of the Covenant already in being. It had been set up by the Council and consisted of a naval, military and air expert from each of the states represented on that body.

This arrangement was modelled, naturally enough, on that adopted in 1917, when the Supreme War Council was provided with a body of military advisers. The duties assigned to the Committee recalled the same precedent. On the one hand, it was to prepare schemes for the Council so as to enable it to perform its duty under the Covenant; on the other, its members were to constitute a standing liaison with their own services in order to facilitate the carrying-out, in their respective countries, of any decisions taken by the Council. Thus the Committee, like its war-time predecessor, was in close touch with the standing Conference of the powers. If the powers desired to take common action, as in 1918, its advice and the information at its command would facilitate the process. But if they were not so disposed, there would be little for it to do, as the British Commentary on the Covenant had

political equilibrium, arising out of the unwise provisions of Part V of the Treaty of Versailles, would have yielded to treatment if it had been dealt with quite apart from the Covenant (*e.g.* on 'Locarno' lines) cannot, of course, be positively asserted. But the recent successful negotiation of an Anglo-German naval agreement is, at least, suggestive.

already foreshadowed, beyond the collection of 'non-confidential information of military value'.[1]

As if to emphasise the close relations between the members of the Commission and their respective governments, their salaries and allowances were not a charge upon the League but upon the individual states, to whose armed forces, of course, they continued to belong. The Commission was provided with a Secretariat of its own at Geneva. It too was constituted on the war-time model, consisting of a British, a French and an Italian member, to the exclusion of representatives of the elected members of the Council. Each of these three officers had his own clerical staff and their files were not sent to the general registry of the Secretariat.

Thus the Commission has never been a League body of the ordinary type, but has remained, both in temper and organisation, somewhat apart from the other 'technical' activities at Geneva. It may be compared rather with the Geneva 'National Secretaries', responsible to their own governments whilst working for the League, whose appointment was recommended by Sir Arthur Salter in his Paris memorandum.[2]

The reason why the work of the Commission was organised so differently from the rest of the activities of the Secretariat will be clear to anyone who recalls the history of international co-operation in the nine-

[1] Cmd. 151 (1918), p. 17.

[2] On the above see especially Madariaga, *Disarmament* (1929), chap. iv., and Salter, *The United States of Europe*, p. 25, but compare the note on p. 13.—In 1921, on the demand of the Assembly, as if to emphasise the contrast between these 'national' servants and the international Secretariat to which they were attached, a regular 'Disarmament Section of the League' was set up with a civilian head, who, after some difficulty, was eventually given administrative authority over the Permanent Advisory Committee Secretariat.

teenth century.[1] Of all the departments of national policy defence is the most vital and its secrets therefore the most jealously guarded. International cooperation in defence was therefore bound to develop far more slowly than in matters where an unwise or premature bestowal of confidence would entail less serious risks. Between the Defence departments of the members of the British Commonwealth confidence exists in full measure and co-operation is therefore maintained, even without any special organisation for that purpose. But to expect a similar spirit to be manifested between the members of the League of Nations, with their wide differences in outlook and standards, or even between the Great Powers on the Council, was to be blind to political realities. Much sarcasm has been expended upon the members of the 'Permanent Advisory Commission'. They have been reproached for their consistently negative attitude towards the suggestions put before them by civilians. But these criticisms should have been addressed rather against those who destroyed the original guarantee scheme on which the disarmament policy of the Covenant was founded.

A body so reminiscent of Power-politics as the Permanent Advisory Committee was naturally not likely to find favour with the Assembly, particularly at its first meeting where, as one of the British delegates remarked, a 'romantic and sentimental' attitude was much in evidence.[2] The Northern states, who regarded armaments in themselves as a cause of war, called for a programme of disarmament pure and simple. Seeing no hope of securing an advance along this line from the

[1] See p. 45 above.
[2] H. A. L. Fisher, *An International Experiment* (1921), p. 24.

Permanent Advisory Committee, the Norwegian delegation, urged on by Lord Robert Cecil,[1] put forward a
proposal for the appointment, side by side with it, of a
civilian Commission to study the problem of disarmament. In spite of the opposition of a Dutch delegate,
who suggested that it would be more practical to attach
the civilians as experts to the Permanent Advisory
Committee of professional soldiers, the Assembly
accepted the Norwegian proposal, the Great Powers
not venturing to restrain its ardour. Thus there came
into existence what was known as the Temporary
Mixed Commission, composed of persons 'with the
requisite competence for the study of the political,
economic, social, historical and geographical aspects'
of the armaments problem, with instructions to prepare for the Council 'a report and proposals for the
reduction of armaments under Article VIII of the
Covenant'.

One of the experts thus appointed was Lord Robert
Cecil, who had sat in the Assembly, on the nomination
of General Smuts, as a delegate of South Africa.
Another was Lord Esher. The latter proceeded to take
the bull by the horns. He prepared a detailed project
for European land-armaments based upon units of
30,000, exclusive of colonial troops. France was to have
six (*i.e.* 180,000 men); Italy and Poland four each;
Great Britain, Czechoslovakia, Greece, Yugoslavia,
Holland, Roumania and Spain three each; Belgium,
the Scandinavian states and Switzerland two each;
and Portugal one. The result was what might have
been expected. There was a general outcry. The
plan received a first-class funeral—not the last of such
ceremonies at Geneva. Lord Esher retired from the

[1] Madariaga, p. 80.

Z

Commission. And no comparative scale of figures was seen again at Geneva in an official project until Mr Ramsay MacDonald's heroic effort to save the Disarmament Conference by his draft Convention of March 1933.

The direct road to disarmament being thus barred, Lord Robert Cecil began to consider the alternative route by way of security. Hence originated the long and complicated negotiations which for so many years occupied the forefront of the League stage. In effect, what was aimed at was a bargain between Great Britain and France, in which Great Britain should make concessions on Security whilst France made concessions on Armaments. But if the main idea was simple, the details were extremely complicated. To begin with, there was the problem which Castlereagh had already expounded to the Tsar.[1] How could a British government make a binding commitment in advance of the decision of the House of Commons on a particular issue? If this difficulty could be overcome (as it had been, in the nineteenth century, in the case of Belgium), the question arose as to *how much disarmament* should be given in return for *how much security*. Britain desired a substantial measure of French and general disarmament. France in return asked for precise guarantees, involving an 'automatic' system for the definition of the aggressor, which would exclude a dilatory or even negative response on the British side. Failing that, or even in addition to that, the French wished that the Council should be enabled to take a decision on this issue by a majority vote, or, at the very least, that unanimity should not be required. To this the British reply was that any defini-

---

[1] See pp. 69-70 above.

tion of aggression was likely to be more dangerous than helpful, since an unscrupulous aggressor would be able to make use of it in order to put himself legally in the right. As for doing away with the requirement of unanimity, this would be to introduce the super-state principle by the backdoor. No British government conscious of its responsibility to the House of Commons and to the country could surrender its right to judge each situation as it arose. To which the French, distrustful, as ever, of the mental processes of their island neighbours, retorted that on these lines there was no real security in prospect at all, since the proposed contract was as full of loopholes as the Covenant itself. In addition to all this wrangling on principles there was the extremely awkward question as to the moment at which the goods should be delivered. At what stage in the proceedings should disarmament begin and at what pace should it be carried through?

At bottom, of course, what were at issue in the controversy were the two rival conceptions of the League. For Britain it remained a co-operative association of independent states. For the French it was an incomplete project of a super-state. As this intellectual trench warfare went on year after year, each side became more strongly fortified in its convictions. It was no wonder that no agreement was arrived at, for at no moment was there a common basis of principle on which agreement could be founded. Moreover, the agencies of public opinion which might have been educating the two peoples so as to promote mutual understanding were busily engaged in popularising their own particular notions of the League.

The external sequence of events can be rapidly recorded.

In July 1922 Lord Robert Cecil laid before the
Temporary Mixed Commission a proposal for disarmament through a system of mutual guarantees. The
Commission accepted it and passed it on to the Assembly, where Lord Robert Cecil still sat as a delegate
of South Africa. (It may be mentioned in passing that
the meetings of the Assembly coincided in that year
with the Turkish victory in Asia Minor, followed by the
rout of the Greek army and the burning of Smyrna.)
Lord Robert Cecil and the French delegate, M. de
Jouvenel, then together sponsored a Resolution, known
as Resolution XIV, which declared that 'no scheme
for the reduction of armaments, within the meaning of
Article VIII of the Covenant, can be successful unless
it is general', and that 'in the present state of the
world, many governments would be unable to accept
the responsibility for a serious reduction of armaments
unless they receive in exchange a satisfactory guarantee
for the safety of their country'. 'This guarantee', the
resolution went on to say, 'can be found in a defensive
agreement which should be open to all countries,
binding them to provide immediate and effective assistance in accordance with a prearranged plan'. What
was envisaged, it will be observed, was a new treaty
filling in the gaps of the guarantee system of the
Covenant. M. Bourgeois' amendments were to be dis-
interred and embodied in what may be described as a
Super-Covenant.

Armed with this mandate from the Assembly, Lord
Robert Cecil set to work and in February 1923 laid
before the Temporary Mixed Commission the draft of
what may be described as a Security and Disarmament
Treaty. To discuss its details would carry us too far.
Its main proposal was that, in addition to the strength-

ening of the general guarantees of the League, the Council should take it upon itself to draw up certain special guarantee treaties for the benefit of particularly exposed states. In the event of an outbreak of war the Council was, within the space of four days, to determine which state was the aggressor, whereupon the defence organisation was to be set in motion, the command of the common force being assumed either by the attacked party or by a state designated by the Council. Thus, it will be seen, the scheme took it for granted that the Council was, if not an organic body, at least a body animated by a strong sense of common responsibility. The draft is also noteworthy because it brought into the light for the first time the problem of regional agreements. Recognising that a system of military guarantees could not be worked out for the world as a whole, it proposed that the obligations of assistance should, in principle, only apply in the continent in which the aggression occurred.

Lord Robert Cecil's draft treaty was then submitted to the Permanent Advisory Commission. Thus stimulated, its French military member, Colonel Requin, set to work to prepare an alternative draft. He rejected the idea that the Council should itself draw up the special treaties of guarantee but proposed to knit together a series of separately negotiated treaties of mutual assistance into a League guarantee system on Lord Robert Cecil's lines. The Temporary Mixed Commission thereupon proceeded to amalgamate these two drafts into a single document. In September 1923 this was laid before the Assembly, in which Lord Robert Cecil now sat as a delegate of Great Britain.

In the debates of that Assembly—the Assembly of the Corfu incident and of the admission of Abyssinia—

the British and French theses were for the first time
publicly observable at close grips over the details of a
text. From their efforts there emerged an agreed
Treaty of Mutual Assistance, which was sent to the
governments for their observations. Twenty-nine replies
were received, of which eighteen were favourable 'in
principle'. What would have been the reply of Mr
Baldwin's government must remain a matter for
speculation. For in the winter of 1923–4 it was succeeded by the administration of Mr Ramsay Mac-
Donald, which proceeded to reject the treaty outright.
What particularly provoked the criticism of the Labour
Government were Colonel Requin's special treaties,
superimposed upon the League system. It saw in them
a return to the system of alliances which had characterised the decade before the war.

This destruction of the main work of the 1923
Assembly confronted the British Government with the
responsibility of putting forward a scheme of its own.
It happened that, just at this moment, a change of
government took place in France, bringing to power in
M. Herriot a statesman of markedly idealistic temper.
To sanguine minds therefore, there seemed more than
a possibility that Britain and France might be able to
agree on a common scheme. Mr MacDonald and M.
Herriot came together to Geneva, attracting thither
a train of Prime Ministers and Foreign Secretaries,
and in a mood of high enthusiasm, during the longest
Assembly session on record, the 'Geneva Protocol' was
put into shape.

Before we examine this document it is necessary to
retrace our steps in order to follow another stream of
League history, that of arbitration.

Once more, the starting-point is in the North. We

have already seen that the Northern states looked forward, like Mr Taft, to the institution of 'an international juridical order'. In their detached position, above the *mêlée* of European Power-politics, one of their principal concerns was to keep this ideal 'unspotted from the world'—in other words, removed from all connexion with the ordinary workings of politics. They desired a League which should be, if one may so express it, as non-political as it was possible to make it. Hence they were much surprised and displeased when they discovered that the League of Nations Committee at Paris had placed the machinery of mediation and conciliation, hitherto secluded at The Hague, under what seemed to them a dangerously political body, the Council. In their own scheme they had reverted to the system of the Bryan treaties and had proposed the setting up, within a broad juridical framework, of conciliation commissions between individual states, a plan which diminished even the amount of centralisation involved in the multilateral Hague Conventions of 1899 and 1907.

Having failed to secure satisfaction for their ideas in their meeting with the League Committee in Paris, they returned to the charge at the first meeting of the Assembly. Norway and Sweden there proposed that Article XV should be amended to provide for establishment between every pair of League members of Conciliation Commissions of the Bryan type, recourse to which should be obligatory. Their object was, quite frankly, to deprive the Council of its functions of conciliation, owing to their suspicion of it as a political body.[1]

[1] On this see Schücking and Wehberg (ed. 1924), pp. 581-4, and the references there given. The authors sympathise with the Scandinavian point of view. They regard even The Hague arrangements as having been

The project was referred to a Council Committee, then back to the second meeting of the Assembly, thence to another Council Committee. It finally emerged from the third meeting of the Assembly in September 1922 in the form of an agreed resolution. In carefully worded terms, the Assembly, 'in order to promote the development of the procedure of the conciliation of international differences in a spirit in conformity with the League', recommended League members to conclude treaties between one another providing for the establishment of bilateral conciliation Commissions. At the same time a set of model rules was adopted and it was laid down that the Council, acting under Article XV, could itself, in case of need, make use of the services of such Commissions.

Thus the Northern states, if they had not succeeded in inserting the principle of compulsory arbitration into the Covenant, had at least gained an authoritative pronouncement from the Assembly in favour of their particular type of conciliation procedure. But at this stage there was a brusque change of tactics. The Assembly of 1923 brought a new factor into the situation. The Treaty of Mutual Assistance was under discussion, and Norway saw in it an opportunity for making an advance in arbitration, even if not on the previous lines. With this object Dr. Lange moved a series of amendments the object of which was to confine the benefits of the proposed guarantee of mutual assistance to states which had accepted compulsory arbitration, according to one of the procedures provided by the Covenant. These amendments were debated at length but found no favour either with

unduly political and suggest that this led to the Central Powers' refusal to make use of them in 1914. 'Depoliticise conciliation' is their watchword.

Lord Robert Cecil or with the principal French dele-
gate in the Committee, Senator (now President)
Lebrun. 'Compulsory arbitration', remarked Lord
Robert Cecil, 'will come in its own time.'

Very soon it appeared as if this time would come
sooner than anyone anticipated in 1923. For in the
following year, when Mr Ramsay MacDonald and
M. Herriot laid down the principles of the Geneva
Protocol, the despised Norwegian amendments of 1923
became one of the corner-stones of their edifice. The
Protocol, in fact, was an attempt to embody in a single
document the application of the three hitherto dis-
connected principles — Security, Disarmament and
what was described at the time as Arbitration but
would be perhaps better (though even then not accurately) described as Equity Jurisdiction.

The disarmament provisions of the Protocol were
short and simple. They merely laid it down that a
Disarmament Conference should be summoned for
June 15, 1925. The Protocol was not to come into force
until this Conference had 'adopted' a disarmament
plan. This was to be prepared by the Council and communicated to the governments 'at the earliest possible
date, and at the latest three months before the Conference meets'. So short and easy still seemed at that time
the task of arriving at an agreed solution of the
armaments problem!

The security articles were carefully drafted so as
to fill in the familiar gaps in Articles X and XVI of
the Covenant. They contained a definition, or rather
several alternative definitions, of aggression, the effect
of which was to withdraw from the individual members
of the Council a large measure of their discretion in
judging an emergency situation as a whole and left

them with little more than the duty of registering a
formal verdict. They also provided in certain cases for
the Council to be enabled to take a decision by a two-
thirds majority. When the Council had given its
verdict, each of the signatory states was obliged 'to co-
operate loyally and effectively . . . in the degree which
its geographical position and its particular situation as
regards its armaments allow'. This skilful formula was
designed at once to prevent a state from slipping out of
its obligations by refusing to act on the 'recommendations' of the Council under Article XVI and to make
allowance for the particular conditions in which individual members might find themselves placed. For
those who held the 'strong' view of the Covenant, it
introduced a new element of flexibility. But for those
who, like Britain, had hitherto taken this flexibility
for granted, it involved of course a new commitment.

As for the 'arbitration' provisions, they were the
most elaborate of all. The object to be attained was
no easy one. It would have been simple, on paper, to
provide 'an international juridical order' on 'non-
political' lines. The gap in Article XV could have been
closed by sending all disputes for binding settlement to
arbitral tribunals. But the difficulty was that the arbitral procedure had to be kept in connexion with a
political body, the League Council, and this involved
a change in the meaning of the term arbitration. For
hitherto, as we have seen, arbitration had been conceived of as a judicial process—'the settlement of disputes between states by *judges* of their own choice and
on the basis of respect for *law*'.[1] What was required

---

[1] Article 37 of The Hague Convention of 1907, quoted by M. Politis in
the Introduction to his report on the Protocol. See Hunter Miller, *The
Geneva Protocol* (1925), p. 165 and p. 110 above.

now was to discover a *binding non-juridical* method
for settling disputes which yielded to no other form of
treatment—that is to say, the disputes out of which
war was most likely to arise.

By this time the Permanent Court of International
Justice, provided for in Article XIV of the Covenant,
had been set up at The Hague. But its jurisdiction had
not been made obligatory. The devotees of compulsory
arbitration had had to content themselves with the
so-called 'optional clause', under which states might
voluntarily accept the jurisdiction of the Court for
disputes of a legal character, with any reservations
which they might wish to attach to their signature. So
far as legal disputes were concerned therefore, the
framers of the Protocol experienced no difficulty. They
had only to provide that the 'optional clause' system
should become the general rule. It was the non-legal
and 'reserved' disputes, which fell within the domain
of the Council, for which it was difficult to provide.

The system by which the gap in Article XV was filled
in and a binding decision of political disputes arrived
at was somewhat complicated. If one of the parties
requested it, the dispute was to go to a 'Committee of
Arbitrators', formed, in the first instance, by agreement between the parties. If, however, the parties
failed to agree upon the members, names, powers or
procedure of the 'arbitrators' the Council was to step
in and 'settle the points remaining in suspense'. It was,
with the utmost dispatch to set up what was in effect
rather a Tribunal of Equity than a judicial body: for
the report expressly lays it down that the 'arbitrators need not necessarily be jurists'. Indeed, it goes
further and declares that, even when they have submitted a point of law to the Permanent Court of Inter-

national Justice for an 'advisory opinion', this advice
is not to be 'legally binding upon them, although its
scientific authority'—a revealing phrase—'must, in all
cases, exercise a strong influence upon their judgment'.
They were to have the law at their elbow: but it was to
be their instrument. They were not to be its servants,
or even its wise interpreters.

If neither party asked for 'arbitration', the Council
was to deal with the dispute itself and if it reached a
unanimous decision, this was to be binding. But if it
failed to agree, then again recourse would be had to a
Committee of Arbitrators, with the setting up of which
the Council would, in this event, be solely concerned.

This final tribunal would consist of 'persons who by
their nationality, their personal character and their
experience' appeared 'to furnish the highest guarantees
of competence and impartiality'. To these Elder Statesmen, these latter-day Solomons, was assigned authority
to settle issues which had baffled the chancelleries, the
cabinets and the parliaments of contending peoples.
An effective sanction was, of course, attached to their
award.

Thus the circle appeared to be complete. Security,
Disarmament and Equity were drawn together into a
logical whole, an indissoluble trinity. Nevertheless
there was one minor blemish, or perhaps one should
call it a beauty spot, in this otherwise so perfectly
proportioned offspring of the Continental mind. For
there was 'one class of disputes', so remarked M.
Politis, almost by the way[1] in the course of his report,
to which it was impossible to apply the proposed new
system. These he defined as 'disputes which aim at

[1] Apropos of Article iv. .7. See text in Miller, *The Geneva Protocol*,
p. 181.

revising treaties or international acts in force or which seek to jeopardise the existing territorial integrity of signatory states'. From the legal point of view M. Politis was undoubtedly right. Such disputes called, not for arbitration or any other kind of judicial process but for fresh *legislation*. But when he went on to argue that it was equally impossible 'from the political point of view' to deal with such disputes under the Protocol system he was on more dangerous ground. It was 'obvious', said the report, that 'compulsory arbitration' could not be applied to such cases. Even Solomon, in other words, could not deprive states, against their will, of their existing rights. The argument is perfectly valid. But does it not prove too much? Why should it apply only to one class of rights? Is it not in reality an argument against compulsory arbitration in general? Is it not, in fact, the familiar argument of the Foreign Offices against outside interference, the argument which led them to draw up the old pre-war reservations about 'honour and vital interests'?

This reservation of a particular class of disputes from the operation of the Protocol system reveals indeed the weakness of the whole scheme. It is a legal system with no constitutional system on which to repose. In the last analysis therefore it can only ensure the observance of the law and not its change, still less its growth. And what is that except to say that the Protocol system is a dead system? Changes in the law, or, to use the language of the lawyer, surrenders of rights cannot be imposed upon states by Solomon from above, or by the wisest or most imposing Board of Solomons. For the days of Papal authority in inter-national affairs are gone past recall and the Solomon of to-day can speak neither in the name of the Law nor of the Prophets. He represents nobody but himself. And, in this democratic age, the peoples prefer, and will continue to prefer, methods of settlement, controlled, if not always actually employed, by their own representatives, to the decrees of non-representative personalities, however eminent. They will prefer, in other words, to negotiate freely about their rights, in a spirit of mutual confidence and respect. That, however, implies the existence of a *system of co-operation*. But that is the system of the Covenant rather than that of the Super-Covenant which we have been engaged in analysing.

Taken all in all, however, the Protocol was a brave and consistent attempt to bring down to earth the ideal of Peace through Law. As the *rapporteurs* told the Assembly, it was the culmination of 'five years' hard work', years of painful effort to recover, inch by inch, ground lost during the drafting of the Covenant. Its adoption by the plenary Assembly in October 1924 was the high-water mark of the first period of the League's life. No-one who listened to the speech of M. Paul Boncour, that latter-day representative of the orators of the French Revolution, will ever forget how he thundered against the crime of war and pointed a long accusing finger at the 'anonymous aggressor' who would expose himself to swift and certain punishment by the sword of Justice. The principle of the Hue and Cry seemed at that moment to have found entrance into the consciousness of the assembled peoples, driving out, once and for all, the forces of violence and disintegration.

Few had noticed that, as a result of a request made in Committee by Sir James Allen on behalf of New Zealand, the delegations did not there and then commit their governments to approval of the Protocol but merely recommended it to them for their 'serious consideration'.

THE THIRD PHASE: 1924–1929

I

The next phase in the history of the League of Nations opens with the determination of Mr Austen Chamberlain (as he then was), who had succeeded Mr Ramsay MacDonald at the Foreign Office in November 7, 1924, to attend in person the December meeting of the Council. Thereafter he became a regular participant in the quarterly[1] meetings of the Council, and in the annual meetings of the Assembly. His example was followed by the Foreign Ministers of most of the other powers, particularly those within fairly easy reach of Geneva.[2] In this way the League

[1] During the previous period the Council had gradually fallen into the habit of meeting at quarterly intervals, *i.e.* in December, March, June and just before and during the Assembly meeting in September. In 1929 the interval was extended to four months, with meetings in January, May and September.

[2] The figures for the attendance of Prime Ministers and Foreign Ministers at League Council meetings are given in Rappard, *Uniting Europe* (New Haven, 1930). They show that *none* attended in 1921, 1922 or 1923: the percentage to the number of Council members rises to 18 in 1924, 36 in 1925, reaching a peak figure of 48·6 in 1927. Taking European members only, we get a figure of 25·7 for 1924, 51·4 for 1925 and 79·1 for 1927. Similar figures for the Assembly, including the year 1930, are given in the same author's *The Geneva Experiment* (1931), p. 56. They show that the proportion of European Prime Ministers and Foreign Secretaries to other delegates in the period 1920-1923 never rose above 36 per cent, while in and after 1924 (the Protocol year) it never sank below 69 per cent and on one occasion, the Assembly of 1929, reached 100 per cent. The corresponding figures for all League members are 18 (maximum before 1924), 36 (minimum after 1924), 55 (maximum after 1924). Neither Signor Mussolini nor the Japanese Foreign Minister have ever found their way to Geneva. But Moscow and Ankara have not been

began at last to fulfil the principal regular function designed for it in the British scheme. It became a centre for a standing Conference between the powers, particularly the Great Powers. As soon as this began to be understood, non-members also became interested in what was happening: for in diplomacy, as in other matters, the absent are always at a disadvantage. It was during this period therefore that relations of regular collaboration in the *political* tasks of the League were established both with the United States (which collaborated with the Preparatory Committee for the Disarmament Conference from 1926 onwards) and with the U.S.S.R. (which was represented at the World Economic Conference of 1927 and on the Preparatory Committee from the same year). Thus the Secretariat ceased to be simply a bundle of technical activities with a central co-ordinating department and became actively engaged also in issues of high policy—with consequences that call for separate discussion. There was a Concert with a permanent organisation, as originally designed. But it turned out to be a Concert so greatly changed in composition, in the character and possibilities of its work and in its general outlook as to be unrecognisable under the old discredited title. It is better to think of the League henceforward as a *standing political Conference* with an organisation ready to be set in motion whenever there is sufficient agreement between the principal parties to make a meeting worth while.[1]

Sir Austen Chamberlain has lately borne testimony

---

found too distant. Nor has Ottawa, where the Prime Minister is also the Minister for External Affairs. Mr Mackenzie King attended the Assembly of 1928. At the Assembly of 1935, 23 European Foreign Ministers attended out of an effective European League membership of 27.

[1] The classical example of a Conference which failed for lack of previous agreement between the parties concerned was the special

to the fact that it was the experience of these regular
meetings of the Council and the Assembly, gained
during his five years' tenure of office, which dissipated
for him the idea that the League was a 'beautiful
dream' and convinced him of its practical value.[1] These
five years were the most successful period—let us be
bold and say the most normal period—which the
League has yet passed through. They were marked by
a spirit of co-operation between the European Great
Powers, particularly between Great Britain, France
and Germany, cemented by a happy personal relationship, regularly renewed at the Geneva meetings,
between Sir Austen Chamberlain, M. Briand and Herr
Stresemann, each of whom, as it happened, enjoyed an
unusually long spell of office.[2]

Assembly of March 1926, summoned for the admission of Germany into
the League. The negotiations which should have *preceded* the calling of
the meeting took place, mostly in the Secretary-General's private room,
whilst the Assembly was nominally in session and the journalists waited
downstairs. Held under such circumstances they broke down and the
Assembly could only register the failure and disperse. This is an example
on a small scale of what has frequently happened on a larger, with an
extended period of agony. The post-war public has been compelled to
learn by bitter experience what was a commonplace for the 'old diplomacy'—that the purpose of a Conference is not to negotiate but to
gather up the results of previous negotiation.

[1] German political circles were taught the same lesson more roughly
in March 1926. Lord D'Abernon records this in his diary as follows,
under the date of March 22, 1926 : 'The recent negotiations at Geneva
have produced this paradoxical result—the bargaining, the intrigues
and the compromises of the last fortnight have convinced the partisans
of *Realpolitik* that they cannot afford not to be there. Hitherto they
had regarded Geneva as an assembly of ideologues—now they take
the opposite view' (*An Ambassador of Peace*, 1930, iii. 238).—Sir Austen
Chamberlain's testimony was given in his speech at the opening meeting
of the International Studies Conference in London on June 3, 1935.

[2] There is, however, an obvious danger in basing co-operation too
exclusively upon a personal relationship. This was exemplified at the
Assembly of 1928. On that occasion the principal German delegate was
the Chancellor, the Socialist leader Hermann Müller, Herr Stresemann
being absent through illness, and he met with a markedly cold reception

2 A

In this atmosphere and with these facilities much was accomplished which could hardly have been brought about by the ordinary processes of diplomacy. It is true that, as has already been remarked, most of this was necessarily done outside the actual meetings of the Council. It was in the hotels of the delegations or in secluded resorts in the neighbourhood, such as Thoiry[1] and Versoix, that the really important discussions took place. But, though the lesser powers grumbled behind the scenes at the waste of time imposed upon them by these methods, and occasionally, as at the Assembly of 1927, even complained in public, on the whole they accepted with good grace a procedure which, however unflattering to themselves, they at bottom quite well understood. Nevertheless there was a continual strain involved in bringing the real situation into a correct relationship with the formal requirements of the Covenant, particularly as regards the powers which, though not, technically speaking, 'great', were certainly not 'small' and were therefore all the more susceptible.[2]

from M. Briand, himself an old Socialist.—Whether M. Briand was wise to continue in office after the rejection by the French Cabinet of the policy which he outlined to Herr Stresemann at Thoiry raises an issue which cannot be pursued here. It is only mentioned as an instance of the interpenetration between foreign and 'domestic' affairs which is, and will remain, a permanently complicating factor for those engaged in the work of international co-operation at Geneva.

[1] Stresemann's notes on the Thoiry conversation have been published. (Stresemann, *Vermächtnis* (1933), vol. iii.). The brief reference to British domestic affairs (p. 23) invites serious reflection. It shows what completely false judgments may be formed about Britain by experienced Continental Foreign Ministers even when they have the best possible means of information. In spite of their constant contacts with British statesmen, extending in M. Briand's case over a great many years, both he and Herr Stresemann were fundamentally ignorant about Great Britain and the British Commonwealth.

[2] In the case of Brazil there is complete failure to be recorded in this connexion, though she had been a Council member since 1920.

The actual results achieved by means of this co-operation lie outside the scope of these pages. It is sufficient to say that the object aimed at by Sir Austen Chamberlain and M. Briand was to appease the feelings of bitterness and humiliation aroused in Germany by the dictatorial methods of the Peace Conference and thus to draw Germany into friendly partnership on the basis of the new world order, which was also, for better or for worse, a new European order. It was with this object that such efforts were expended to ensure that Germany should occupy the 'permanent seat' on the Council envisaged for her by the framers of the Covenant, and that important concessions—one might even describe them as revisions—were made in the Treaty of Versailles. Thus the League control over German armaments was allowed to become a dead letter, the one-sided economic clauses were tacitly per-mitted to expire, and arrangements were made for the ending of the Rhineland occupation five years before the appointed date and for the replacement of the Dawes plan by what was expected to prove both a less humiliating and less burdensome scheme for the pay-ment of reparations. With these immediate problems out of the way, the road would be open for fruitful co-operation in the regular tasks of the post-war world. Chief among these was the reshaping of international economic relations, or, in other words, the substitution of an international economic policy based on agreed principles for the 'invisible hand' of Adam Smith and the 'automatic' working of the pre-war system. How seriously Herr Stresemann, in particular, viewed the responsibilities and opportunities of the League in this field is shown by his choice of economic questions as the subject on which Germany should be the regular *rapporteur* in the Council. It was no accident, therefore, that, early in this period, already in 1925, conditions should have seemed sufficiently normal for the League to embark upon the project of summoning a World Economic Conference. The emergency tasks in the economic and financial field had been successfully disposed of and the general political weather was 'set fair'.[1]

II

Meanwhile what of the Protocol and of the problem of security which its framers had so bravely attempted to solve?

Within a few days of the close of the 1924 Assembly Great Britain was plunged into a General Election, in which the echoes of M. Paul Boncour's eloquence, which had been but faintly heard across the Channel, were drowned in the clamour aroused by the 'Red Letter'. Thus it will never be known whether the Labour government, whose delegation had helped to draw up the Protocol, would actually have ratified it. All that can be said is that one of its most influential members, the Lord Chancellor, Lord Haldane, was opposed to this course.[2]

A Conservative government came into power and Mr Austen Chamberlain found the Protocol on his doorstep as his predecessor had found the Treaty of Mutual Assistance. He at once took it under discussion,

---

[1] See Salter, *The United States of Europe*, p. 32 ff.

[2] See his speech in the House of Lords on November 16, 1927, and the extracts from his memorandum setting out the reasons against the signature of the 'optional clause' of the Statute of the Permanent Court of International Justice, quoted by Sir Austen Chamberlain in the House of Commons a week later (November 24), reprinted in *Peace in our Time* (1935), pp. 202-3.

drawing the Dominions into consultation. There was much in the document which was clearly unacceptable. Its form alone would have made it unpalatable to any British House of Commons. The almost Byzantine subtlety which characterised its definitions and dispositions made it as un-English a composition as could well have been conceived. Nevertheless, the natural course would have been, not to repeat the gesture of rejection, thus for the second time throwing the work of a whole Assembly of some fifty delegations on to the scrap-heap, but to draw up a reasoned series of objections, accompanied by corresponding amendments. Had this been done, the real underlying differences between the British and the Continental view of the League would have been threshed out in a favourable atmosphere, rather than as an embittering by-product of a Disarmament Conference. There is some evidence that this course was under discussion as late as February 1925. If so, however, it was abandoned as too difficult and, so far as the text of the Protocol was concerned, it was a blank negation which was embodied in the famous Balfour memorandum that Mr Austen Chamberlain read to the Council of the League on March 12, 1925.[1]

Lord Balfour's main argument we have already expounded. It was that, in the absence of the United States, the League was crippled and that it was therefore impossible for the British peoples, either at home

[1] In his memorandum on 'The Problem of Security', dated February 1925, the Historical Adviser to the Foreign Office speaks incidentally of the 'revision of the Protocol' (Headlam Morley, *Diplomatic Studies*, p. 187). Sir Austen Chamberlain has several times in recent years publicly acknowledged the real authorship of the memorandum that he fathered at Geneva. The correspondence with the Dominions on this subject will be found in Cmd. 2458 (1925) and the memorandum itself in Cmd. 2368.

or overseas, to take the 'strong' view of the Covenant
and its obligations. The League could prevent small
wars—such wars as the Concert of Europe, when
acting together, had been able to prevent in the
nineteenth century. These had their root in what he
delightfully described as 'ordinary misunderstandings
inseparable from international (as from social) life'—as
though the ill-temper of a small people were something
different in kind from that of a powerful people. But
with the 'extreme cases', 'springing from deep-lying
causes of hostility, which for historic or other reasons
divide great and powerful States', the League was
powerless to deal. Under these circumstances the wisest
course for the League was not to dwell upon dangers
which it could do nothing to avert. They belonged 'to
the pathology of international life, not to its normal
condition. It is not wholesome for the ordinary man to
be always brooding over the possibility of some severe
surgical operation: nor is it wise for societies to pursue
a similar course. It is more likely to hasten the dreaded
consummation than to hinder it.' With this cheerful
recommendation to adopt a policy of Couéism—it
might almost be described as the policy of the ostrich
—Lord Balfour dismissed the Sanctions provisions of
the Protocol.

With its policy of compulsory arbitration he made
even shorter shrift. He simply pointed out that the
framers of the Covenant must have known what they
were doing when they 'provided no specific remedy for
certain international differences' and that presumably
they felt 'that the objections to universal and compulsory arbitration might easily outweigh its theoretical
advantages'. He added, rather maliciously, that this
was illustrated by the reservation which the Labour

government had made when, in the enthusiasm of 1924, it had adopted the 'optional clause' of the Hague Statute.[1]

But in spite of this persiflage, Lord Balfour and the Cabinet of which he was the mouthpiece took too serious a view of the European situation to be content with a policy of negation. In the last paragraph of the memorandum therefore a positive policy is suddenly brought out. But it is not, in the full sense of the words, a League policy. 'His Majesty's Government conclude', so run these memorable words, 'that the best way of dealing with the situation is, with the co-operation of the League, to supplement the Covenant by making special arrangements in order to meet special needs. That these arrangements should be purely defensive in character, that they should be framed in the spirit of the Covenant, working in close harmony with the League and under its guidance, is manifest. And . . . these objects can best be attained by knitting together the nations most immediately concerned and whose differences might lead to a renewal of strife, by means of treaties framed with the sole object of maintaining, as between themselves, an unbroken peace.'

This new policy was open to various interpretations. On a superficial view it might seem to reintroduce the

[1] It must not be thought that Lord Balfour's objections to compulsory arbitration were at that time shared only by Conservatives. They were supported by many Liberals, in some cases with great vehemence. Thus the *Nation and Athenaeum*, in an editorial article in its issue of October 11, 1924, described compulsory arbitration as 'a grotesquely inappropriate, an inherently fantastic method for settling non-justiciable disputes' and declared that 'only harm can result from basing international agreements on principles that are absurd'. And the writer goes on to claim authority for his views from 'the famous Bryce Committee, the League to Enforce Peace, the League of Nations Society and the other bodies which during the war-years did the hard constructive thinking which made the League of Nations possible'.

'regional' system of Mutual Assistance embodied in Colonel Requin's plan and, less obtrusively, in the 1923 Treaty, in contrast with the 'universalism' of the Protocol. Others discerned in it a desire to retain the method of the Protocol and regarded it as simply proposing a pocket edition of the larger scheme. It is unlikely, however, that Lord Balfour drew his inspiration from Geneva models, either of the 1923 or the 1924 season. His own recent experience had been at Washington. There he had succeeded, in the winter of 1921-2, after the most delicate negotiations, in 'knitting together' in a new kind of international arrangement 'the nations most immediately concerned' with the problems of the Far East and of the Pacific.

The Washington treaties were wholly independent of the League of Nations. Nevertheless they belonged to the new era. In three respects they mark a considerable advance on the pre-war system. In the first place they were inclusive rather than exclusive. Unlike the pre-war alliances, they were not combinations *against* some other party or group. They were designed for the purpose of discussing and settling future differences within the bosom, as it were, of a single family. This conception led naturally to the second innovation. This was the principle of obligatory consultation or, as it is described in the Washington treaties, 'full and frank communication'. The Concert of Europe had afforded its members the *right* to be consulted or, in the language of Mr Lloyd George's speech during the Agadir crisis of 1911, the right not to be 'treated as of no account' in the 'Cabinet of Nations'. The Washington treaties turned what had been a self-regarding right into a social duty; the parties are under an *obligation* to keep in touch, with all that this implies of civility,

CH. II THE HISTORY OF THE LEAGUE OF NATIONS 361

consideration and neighbourly feeling. Thus the Agreements were, in the fullest sense of the words, *Consultative Pacts*. There was no obligation as regards action. The American people were no more prepared for this in 1922 than they were when John Hay was sounded previous to the Anglo-Japanese alliance, at the turn of the century. But the theory was that if two or more powers, well disposed towards one another and desirous of the maintenance of peace, kept closely in touch, they would find no difficulty in an emergency in deciding upon a common course of action. It is the theory which is exemplified in practice in the working of the British Commonwealth.

Thus the principle implicit in the Washington treaties closely resembles that of the British framers of the Covenant. Both repose upon confidence in the *method of regular conference*. The difference is that the Washington treaties provided no organ for that purpose. The need for such an organ, for what may be called a Far Eastern Geneva, was never so clearly demonstrated as in the history of the decade between 1921 and 1931. It was because there was no regular occasion for their meeting that the signatories to the Washington treaties lost touch with one another, so that, when the test came, the Nine-Power Treaty became 'a scrap of paper'.[1]

---

[1] The consultative provision of the Nine-Power Treaty 'relating to principles and policies to be followed concerning China' is contained in Article VII, which runs as follows: 'The Contracting Powers agree that whenever a situation arises which, in the opinion of any one of them involves the application of the stipulations of the present Treaty and renders desirable discussion of such application there shall be full and frank communication between the Contracting Powers concerned'. The Four-Power Treaty deals with controversies between the parties by means of 'a joint conference' and reserves 'full and frank communication' for occasions when their rights are threatened by 'the aggressive action'

The third advance embodied in the Washington treaties was that they included a measure of disarmament. This was not the first disarmament treaty concluded by the United States: the Rush-Bagot agreement had kept the Canadian frontier unfortified for over a hundred years. But what was attempted at Washington was a far more difficult enterprise, affecting as it did the five principal naval powers of the world. That such substantial results were achieved proves that, when the ground has been carefully cleared of political obstacles, disarmament, in spite of its technical complexities, is a perfectly practicable policy. The mistake made at Geneva, from 1920 onwards, was to treat it as a primary objective. So long as the political sky remained clear in the Far East the disarmament provisions of the treaty caused no difficulty. But the moment that the political arrangements broke down the United States Government was the first to declare that, since the Agreements formed an indivisible whole, the disarmament obligations must also be subject to revision.

The policy of the British Government then was to apply the technique of what may be called *Inclusive Association and Regular Conference* to the principal danger-spots in international politics, taking them one by one. The Far Eastern problem had been satisfactorily disposed of, at least for the time being, though the absence of the United States from the League and the American people's distrust of permanent international machinery left the settlement

of any outside power. For the importance attached to this provision by the Government of Great Britain see the mention of it in the communication made to the League of Nations in 1928 (*Official Journal*, May 1928, p. 701).

without an adequate safeguard. The next step was to attack the European problem at its most crucial point. This, of course, was the relationship between France and Germany. How could these two countries be 'knit together by means of treaties framed with the sole object of maintaining, as between themselves, an unbroken peace'?

It could not be done by means of a purely Franco-German arrangement, a small-scale Protocol between those two countries. This was politically and psychologically inconceivable. Britain must, in some shape or other, be a party to the arrangement. France and Belgium both regarded this as indispensable and it was also something of a moral obligation for Britain, after the non-ratification of the Franco-British alliance which had been, for the French, one of the cornerstones of the Versailles Settlement. Negotiations for its replacement had indeed been taken up by the Lloyd George government in 1921, leading to the abortive conversations at Cannes, and had been continued, though in desultory fashion, under the succeeding government by Lord Curzon. Thus, when the Protocol failed, there was a thread ready to be taken up.[1]

There was also a British interest at stake, since, following the breakdown in 1914 of the Belgian neutrality Treaty of 1839, there was a gap in the British defence system which must somehow be filled in—at least until the League of Nations was strong enough to be regarded as a sole defence for the British Isles.[2]

---

[1] The record of these negotiations can be traced in Cmd. 2169 (France, No. 1, 1924): see especially p. 112 ff.

[2] 'Our island is so close to the Continent that we cannot afford to ignore what goes on there, and so there follows the fundamental requirement, that the opposite shores of the Channel and North Sea should

On the other hand a small-scale Protocol between Great Britain, France, Germany and Belgium was equally out of the question, because, as the Balfour memorandum had made clear, Great Britain could not accept, even on a regional basis, the rigid Protocol system of sanctions and arbitration. As between France, Belgium and Germany the system could be made as rigid as those countries, with their continental outlook, would accept; but, if Great Britain was to be a party, a more flexible arrangement must be devised.

One point seemed clear. Since the new scheme was to be 'framed in the spirit of the Covenant, working in close harmony with the League and under its guidance', the arrangements for regular Conference must obviously be centred at Geneva. This would involve Germany's entry into the League, for which French opinion was now ripe.

When the Balfour memorandum was read to the League Council on March 12, 1934, both the British and French governments were already in possession of a German proposal, dated February 9. This was a suggestion for a Security Pact, supplemented by 'a comprehensive arbitration treaty', between Great

---

never be brought under the control of a single great military and naval Power. It is to prevent this that nearly every great war in which we have been engaged from the time of Edward I has been fought' (Headlam-Morley, p. 176, from a memorandum dated February 1925). In addition to this, it is a standing British interest that the coast and immediate *hinterland* of the Low Countries should not fall under the control of a strong inland power. But the same strategic consideration has for a long time past not been felt to apply as regards France. It has been replaced, in the words of Lord D'Abernon, by 'a peculiar reciprocal trust hardly to be explained on logical grounds.' Hence 'while England has always considered that the occupation of the Low Countries by a Great Power would constitute a menace to our island security, we view without alarm the presence of France on the much nearer coast of Calais and Boulogne' (*An Ambassador of Peace* (1929), ii. 11).

Britain, France, Italy and Germany—in other words a small-scale Protocol between these four countries: by what was perhaps a Freudian lapse Belgium was omitted from the combination. But the principal feature in the arrangement was that, although it was to 'prepare the way for a world convention to include all States along the lines of the Protocol drawn up by the League of Nations', the German Government did not follow out the Wilsonian plan of making the League as a whole the guarantor of the settlement. On the contrary, it looked round for a 'powerful sovereign' outside the League to act as guarantor. And it found him in the United States of America. The German proposal was that 'the Powers interested in the Rhine —above all, England, France, Italy and Germany— should enter into a solemn obligation for a lengthy period . . . vis-à-vis the Government of the United States of America as trustee[1] not to wage war against a contracting state'.

Needless to say, this interesting proposition fell upon deaf ears. Nevertheless it provided the main outline of the arrangement ultimately arrived at. As the German Government had suggested, the scheme agreed to at Locarno was a combination of a Security Pact and arbitration treaties, with an outside guarantee attached, on old-fashioned eighteenth-century lines. But the guarantee was not given by the United States but by two of the European members originally designated as equal parties to the Security Pact—Great Britain and Italy. By this device Great Britain was relieved from the obligation of subscribing to a system of compulsory

---

[1] This is the English translation of the German 'zu treuen Händen'. The memorandum is given in German and English in Cmd. 2435 (Miscellaneous No. 7, 1925).

arbitration. It is true that, in return, she received no
pledge of security: but at that time the slow-moving
British mind had as yet no idea that Britain could be
a 'consumer of security'.[1]

We cannot here enter into all the details of the
Locarno agreements. They are complicated by the need
for safeguarding the demilitarised zone in the Rhineland: by the requirements of France's Eastern allies,
who were all the more in need of protection through
the frank limitation of British commitments: by the
gap left open for war in the Covenant, which was
difficult to combine with a system of perpetual peace
in the Rhineland: and by the difficulty of enlisting as a
guarantor a power like Great Britain whose executive
was so dependent on parliament and public opinion.
Moreover, there were the further difficulties involved in
Germany's entry into the League and her attitude
towards the general obligations of the Covenant.[2]
All this necessitated close and laborious negotiation,
issuing in a series of agreements which, as Signor
Scialoja remarked when they were deposited at Geneva,
might 'at first sight appear complicated'. Their main
lines, however, were relatively simple. There is what is
called 'a treaty of Mutual Guarantee' between five
powers—France, Germany, Belgium, Great Britain
and Italy. The guarantee, however, although 'mutual',
only concerns the territory of three of them, since it is

---

[1] M. Poincaré had reminded the British Prime Minister in 1922 that
'although her insular position and naval power afford Great Britain a
sense of security . . . the evolution of armaments . . . might rob her of the
advantages derived from her natural defences': he therefore proposed to
insert a 'reciprocity clause' in the draft Anglo-French Treaty (Cmd. 2169,
p. 145). The suggestion was coldly received. A proposal on similar lines
made by Lord D'Abernon in 1925 was equally ignored. See *An Ambassador
of Peace* (1930), iii. 178-9.

[2] See p. 333 above.

limited to the Rhineland. These Rhineland parties 'mutually' (that is, Germany and Belgium vis-à-vis one another and Germany and France vis-à-vis one another) 'undertake that they will in no case attack or invade each other or resort to war against each other'. In the event of the breach of this engagement all the other signatories are severally bound each to 'come immediately' to the help of the attacked party. Normally, it is the Council of the League which is to decide as to whether and by whom the engagement has been broken: it is then to 'notify its finding without delay' to the signatories, who will then lend their aid. In cases of 'flagrant violation' of the treaty there is obligation to take action before the meeting of the League Council. But in that event each power must have 'been able to satisfy itself that this violation constitutes an unprovoked act of aggression and that, by reason either of the crossing of the frontier or of the outbreak of hostilities or of the assembly of armed forces in the demilitarised zone, immediate action is necessary'.[1]

As for the arbitration treaties, a leaf was taken out of the Scandinavian book. Conciliation Committees were to be set up as between the various pairs involved,

[1] The drafting was complicated by the position of Belgium. No obligation was included between France and Belgium, corresponding to those between France and Germany and Belgium and Germany, because this had already been provided for by the Franco-Belgian Treaty of 1920. At the same time, France is equally bound with Great Britain and Italy to defend Belgium, if attacked, and Belgium to defend France. Similarly, if France were to attack Belgium, or Belgium France, Germany would be bound to come to the help of the attacked party. Thus the inclusion of Belgium makes each of the Rhineland powers also a guarantor. Hence the title 'Treaty of Mutual Guarantee', although, realistically speaking, the guarantee is not mutual at all, but a guarantee given by the two non-Rhineland parties to the three Rhineland parties. Italy took no part in the negotiation (see Cmd. 2435) and only decided at the last moment to participate in the guarantee system.

France and Germany, Belgium and Germany, Poland
and Germany, Czechoslovakia and Germany. But this
Scandinavian system was linked up with the League,
somewhat in the way proposed by the Northern states
in the 1920 Assembly. If the Commissions failed to
reach agreement, the dispute would then pass to the
Council under Article XV, thus lengthening the 'cooling-
off period'. But, as regards the Rhineland powers, the
gap left open for war under that Article is closed, as
we have already seen. It is, however, still left open as
regards Germany's relations with her two Eastern
neighbours and provision is therefore made for the
Franco-Polish and Franco-Czechoslovak alliances to
come into play in that event.

Thus by a masterpiece of drafting, worthy of the
authors of the Protocol itself, Great Britain succeeded
in providing for the Rhineland powers, who were intel-
lectually prepared to accept it, a system considerably
more rigid than she retained for herself.[1]

III

The Assembly met in September 1925 in a mood of
chastened resignation. Its ambitious achievement of
the previous year had been ignominiously destroyed

[1] The complexities of the Locarno system have been forcibly illustrated by the controversies to which the Franco-Russian Treaty of 1935
has given rise. It raises the question as to what the situation under the
Locarno agreements would be if war broke out in the Rhineland in consequence of hostilities elsewhere. Is the word 'unprovoked' to be understood in a general or in a local sense? There is also the further question
as to how far the agreements remain valid if one or more of the signatories cease to be members of the League. On this latter point and indeed
on the general British interpretation of the treaties see the speech of
Sir John Simon in the House of Commons on November 7, 1933, with
which compare the speech of Sir Austen Chamberlain to the Assembly on
September 10, 1927 (reprinted in *Peace in our Time*, p. 172 ff.).

and it was now not even at liberty to make a fresh attempt on the problem: for the principal powers had been negotiating amongst themselves and were shortly to meet at another Swiss lake-side resort. Nevertheless it was understood that disarmament formed no part of these outside discussions. This then remained on the League's agenda. If the Disarmament Conference had not met, as proposed in the Protocol, on June 15, 1925, at least plans could be made for it to meet later on. A resolution was therefore adopted inviting the Council to engage in preparatory studies so that the Conference might be summoned 'as soon as satisfactory conditions had been assured from the point of view of general security as provided for in resolution XIV of the Third Assembly'—the Cecil-Jouvenel Resolution of 1922.[1]

Thus it was that in December 1925 the Council set up the 'Preparatory Committee for the Disarmament Conference', handing on to it the unsolved problem of Security, which the Preparatory Committee, after years of arduous labour, handed on in its turn to the Disarmament Conference in 1932. The decision taken by the Council in December 1925 was thus of crucial importance. For it meant that the Council was abandoning the procedure laid down in the Covenant, under which it was itself to formulate a scheme and submit it to the governments for 'consideration and action', and had decided to adopt the indirect method of working through an international conference. From that moment onwards no retreat was possible. Sooner or later, whether the security problem had been solved or not, the Disarmament Conference would have to be convened. Once set in motion, the Geneva procedure is inexorable. It works like a steam-roller. By the Assembly

[1] See p. 340 above.

2 B

of 1930 it had become morally impossible to refuse to
fix a date. The Germans wished to have it fixed in the
autumn of 1931: the French preferred a date some six
months later. Eventually, as a compromise, February
2, 1932, was chosen. So, on that long-awaited day,
with cannon-music in the Far East as an unrehearsed
accompaniment, the Conference was duly inaugurated.

But this is to anticipate. We need not here follow
the work of the Preparatory Commission, one Sub-
Committee of which alone we are told, used 3,750,000
sheets of typescript, 'enough to enable the Polish or
the Swedish delegation to walk home on a path made
of League paper'.[1] But one aspect of the work of the
League during these years calls for particular attention. It is the rediscovery of Article XI—Mr Root's
article—and its employment as a convenient instrument for the standing Conference of the powers.[2]

The great value of Article XI lay in its flexibility. It
did not bind the League down to a particular procedure
but enabled it to 'take any action that may be deemed'
—in other words, which the Great Powers in consultation deemed—'wise and effectual to safeguard the
peace of nations'. It thus gave them the authority of
the Covenant for developing to the full the Hague
procedures of Conciliation and Mediation which had
been transferred to Geneva, including the whole technique of Inquiry. 'The great strength of the Covenant',
according to this view, which was that conveyed by the
British Government to the League at this time, 'lies in

[1] Madariaga, p. 167.
[2] It had been already used on several occasions, *e.g.* in the Aaland
Islands dispute between Finland and Sweden (the settlement of which
in 1921, due to the public spirit of Sweden, was the first considerable
achievement of the League), in the Mosul dispute between Great Britain
and Turkey and in the Upper Silesian question.

the measure of discretion which it allows to the Council and the Assembly in dealing with future contingencies which may have no parallel in history and which therefore cannot, all of them, be foreseen in advance. The elaboration and multiplication of rules must tend, not only to turn the Council into an automaton but to weaken its power of initiative in any contingency not wholly provided for in such rules.'[1] The possibilities open to the League under Article XI were most opportunely and vividly illustrated by the Graeco-Bulgarian dispute of October 1925, which happened to break out at a time when the chances of alphabetical rotation had brought round the Presidency of the Council to France, in the person of M. Briand.

Greek forces had crossed the Bulgarian border and the Bulgarian Government appealed to the League. Within an hour of his receipt of the appeal M. Briand telegraphed 'exhorting' the two governments to cease from further military movements and to withdraw their troops behind their respective frontiers. Three days later the Council met in Paris. Having received no satisfactory reply from the Greek Government, it repeated its exhortation, this time in the form of a 'request', asking to be informed within twenty-four hours that unconditional orders for withdrawal had been given. It also 'requested' France, Great Britain and Italy to send officers of their own, who were within reach, to the scene of the conflict and to report direct to the Council as to the withdrawal of the troops. The two governments were asked to provide all necessary facilities for these officers.

This vigorous action was taken just in time. The order from Athens to suspend hostilities reached the

[1] *Official Journal* of the League, May 1928, p. 703.

scene of action two and a half hours before an offen-
sive was to be launched. The Council followed up the
matter by appointing a second body, this time of a
diplomatic character, charged with the duty of inquiring into the responsibilities for the conflict and for
fixing the compensation due. Within a few months this
body's report was received, adopted by the Council
and accepted and carried out by the parties. The
incident was closed.

The Graeco-Bulgarian dispute was the culminating
moment of this phase of the history of the League. It
might almost have been staged for the purpose of
illustrating the potentialities of this new international
instrument, of which M. Briand, no mean performer,
knew how to make such superb use. No one who was
present at the meetings during this episode is likely to
forget the scene. M. Briand had before him the representatives of the invading and invaded countries,
sitting as equal members of the Council, each armed,
according to the Covenant, with his right of veto on
any resolution proposed. But his personal mastery was
such that all considerations of procedure were over-
whelmed by the moral ascendancy of the League, of
which he, as the Chairman of the Executive Committee, was the impersonation. He did not sit there as
a judge, with all the majesty of the Law at his back.
Nor did he sit as an Elder Statesman, bringing the
experience of a lifetime to bear on a problem that
admitted of no strictly legal solution. Still less was he
a conciliator, attempting to assuage ruffled tempers
and to promote an atmosphere in which a compromise
could eventually be arrived at. He was simply the
living embodiment of the Covenant, giving to its letter,
which one of the governments represented on the

Council had violated, the living touch which it needed if it was to be a power in international politics. At that moment the League was more than a multilateral treaty, more than a piece of machinery for the convenience of governments. It was the Charter of a new World Order.

During these days M. Briand wore the mantle of President Wilson. He felt himself to be the interpreter of the inarticulate hopes and desires of the great peace-loving mass of ordinary men and women, for whom the League had become a symbol. It was this that inspired the authority which characterised his voice and bearing—indeed his whole personality—on this occasion and brought to the historic room in the Quai d'Orsay the Something which distinguishes a meeting of the Council of the League of Nations from an ordinary gathering of the powers. No doubt it can be said that the League, in preventing a war between two Balkan states, did no more than the powers would have accomplished in a similar emergency in the nineteenth century, had they been equally united and determined. France and Britain were still France and Britain, even though the one was President of the League Council and the other, in the person of Sir Austen Chamberlain, its *rapporteur*. There is a measure of truth in this. Certainly, the Council of the League can only function if the old Concert is embedded inside it. But the Council is the old Concert *with a difference*. And it is this difference which is crucial. It is this which enabled M. Briand to enunciate on this occasion certain general principles which were to be available as a precedent for future action. They were in fact evoked by Lord Cecil at the first of the many meetings at which the Council discussed the Japanese action in Manchuria in the autumn of 1931. But on that occasion M. Briand, though he was still Foreign Minister of France, was not in his place. There was no Concert inside the Council. Therefore there was, for all practical purposes, no Council and no League. There was only a miscellaneous group of delegates representing their respective Foreign Offices and governments. The extra Something had mysteriously vanished.

IV

The Graeco-Bulgarian episode provided the Council with a stimulus for further action. It now proceeded to appoint a Committee to gather up the experience just gained by undertaking a study of Article XI with special reference to its application in cases of emergency. This body, which consisted of Lord Cecil, Senator de Brouckère and M. Titulesco, produced a report[1] which was regarded for the next few years as a sort of authorised guide for League practice. It distinguished between the occasions 'when there is no threat of war or it is not acute' and those 'where there is an imminent threat of war' and it enumerated a number of suitable expedients to be adopted or selected in each case. Amongst those recommended in the latter eventuality was the sending of 'representatives' to the locality of the dispute and it was suggested that the Secretary-General should 'keep lists of experts—political, economic, military, etc., on the basis of lists supplied by the states members of the League and of applications for employment submitted direct to him'—a modest beginning for a sort of outdoor service of the League. Should the situation become still more serious the Council might 'manifest its

[1] Cmd. 2889 (Miscellaneous No. 5, 1927).

formal disapproval' and take the further step of
recommending 'its members' (apparently not all the
the members of the League) 'to withdraw all their
diplomatic representatives accredited to the State in
question, or certain categories of them'. If the 'recalcitrant State' should still persist 'in its hostile preparations or action, further warning measures' might
be taken, 'such as a naval demonstration. Naval
demonstrations,' it is remarked, 'have been employed
for such a purpose in the past.'

The report concludes by remarking that if, 'in spite
of all steps here recommended, a "resort to war" takes
place, it is probable that events will have made it
possible to say which State is the aggressor, and in
consequence it will be possible to enforce more rapidly
and effectively the provisions of Article XVI'. This
indicates the new technique which the standing Conference had now adopted for solving the problem of
security. Article XVI is no longer to be treated as a
dead letter. It is simply to be kept in the background,
the brunt of the work falling on Article XI with its
greater flexibility. It became recognised in Geneva
during these years that Article XI was the emergency
article *par excellence*, resort to XV (which is the gate-
way to XVI) being discouraged. Meanwhile various
practical steps, such as the improvement of wireless
communications with Geneva, were undertaken to
facilitate League action in a crisis.[1]

This new basis for security having been discovered,
it was inevitable that resourceful minds should plan to
build up something upon it. It was the German delegation which took the initiative at this point. At a meet-

---

[1] Conwell-Evans, *The League Council in Action* (1929), dates from
this period. Its title reveals its underlying assumption.

ing of the Arbitration and Security Committee of the
Preparatory Committee for the Disarmament Conference—this was the particular form which the association of the Geneva trinity assumed in 1927—Herr von
Simson suggested that parties might undertake *in
advance* to accept certain recommendations of the
Council in a crisis. Here was a new and more flexible
form of Super-Covenant. The idea was taken up and
led to the framing of a 'Model Treaty for Strengthening
the Means to Prevent War'. During the 1930 Assembly,
on the proposal of Great Britain, this 'model' was
transformed into an actual draft Convention. In this
form it was put on the agenda for the 1931 Assembly,
which eventually approved it and opened it for signature on September 26, 1931, a week after the Japanese
occupation of Mukden.[1]

If such progress was being made in the sphere of
security it was not likely that the advocates of 'arbitration' would lag behind. They were indeed more
active than ever during these years. At the 1927
Assembly, Norway, through the mouth of Dr. Nansen,
whose name will live in League history in connexion
with more practical and life-giving tasks,[2] put for-

---

[1] Japan took up a negative attitude to the project throughout and
never at any stage held out any hopes that she would sign it. Of the ten
ratifications needed for the treaty to enter into force only four (from
Holland, Nicaragua, Norway and Peru) had been received by the end
of August 1935.

[2] Dr. Nansen was one of the great figures of the first decade of the
League. His work for the refugees should have won him assured sympathy
and support, carried on, as it was, with complete self-devotion in the
name of the League. Instead, the Assembly and the governments
treated his last enterprise, on behalf of the Armenians, with the same
cruel want of consideration as had been meted out to the Armenians
from 1919 onwards. See his speech, the last he made in Geneva, of
September 21, 1929, when he described the scene as 'the last act in a
great tragedy'. He spoke 'with a bleeding heart' to empty benches, for
it was a Saturday afternoon.

ward an ingenious plan. He suggested the drawing-up
of an international convention for compulsory arbitration with an Optional Clause attached to it. In other
words, he proposed to do for non-legal disputes what
the Hague Court statute had already done for legal
disputes—to provide a general framework which
would serve as a standing invitation to states which
were slow to commit themselves to the whole document. In this way a system of compulsory arbitration
for all disputes—'all-in arbitration', as it was now
called—would be built up, as he said 'piece by piece'.
But it is important to make clear already at this stage
that these 'pieces' would not consist of the individual
states, some 60 in number, but of the relations of each
of these states with every other state, that is, not 60
but 60×59. For in the world of real politics, as in the
world of real people, detailed engagements are not
entered into blindly or according to a cut and dried
scheme. They are entered into with particular states
for particular reasons, the chief of which is mutual
confidence. Therefore it is but common sense to recognise that 'in contracting an obligation towards another
State a country must take into account the nature of
its relations with that State. Obligations which it may
be willing to accept towards one State it may not be
willing to accept towards another.' It follows from this
that 'more progress is likely to be achieved through bilateral agreements than through general treaties open
to signature by any State which so wishes'. In other
words, the acceptance of compulsory arbitration in
disputes with *all* countries involves undertaking the
same obligations towards the less trustworthy as
towards the more trustworthy. This inevitably leads
to the framing of 'all-in' reservations as a pendant to

'all-in arbitration'. The pace of advance has to be adjusted to the most backward of the parties.[1]

It was at this Assembly that it was decided to establish a 'Committee of Arbitration and Security' as part of the work of preparation for the Disarmament Conference. This Committee, amongst other tasks, was to 'promote', 'generalise' and 'co-ordinate' arbitration agreements. There was certainly a considerable need for such co-ordination, for since the failure of the Protocol bilateral arbitration and conciliation treaties had once more come into fashion, on the lines of the original Scandinavian policy of 1920. In fact, no less than 130 such treaties were concluded between 1918 and 1928, 94 of them subsequently to 1924, embodying no less than eleven different methods of procedure.[2]

With all this material, including Dr. Nansen's project before it, the Committee drew up a series of 'model treaties' for the peaceful settlement of disputes, which were laid before the Assembly in 1928. The object of the 'models' was to show states who wished to conclude engagements with other states how best to do it, in accordance with their various wishes. Three 'models' were presented. One consisted of conciliation procedure

[1] The quotations in the above are from the closely reasoned communication addressed to the Committee on Arbitration and Security by the Government of Great Britain. They are to be found in the *Official Journal* of the League for May 1928, pp. 694-704. It is to be regretted that they were not made more conveniently available in a White Paper.

[2] See Habicht, *Post-War Treaties for the Pacific Settlement of International Disputes* (Harvard University Press, 1931), where the facts on this subject from November 1918 to November 1928 are set out and the texts of the 130 treaties in question reprinted. See especially the spider's web of bilateral arrangements on p. xxv and the diagram on p. 985 showing the eleven different systems of pacific settlement to be found in the treaties.

and nothing more. The second provided, in addition to conciliation, for the compulsory jurisdiction of the Hague Court in legal disputes or 'conflicts of rights'. The third embodied a system of 'all-in arbitration', providing for a special 'Arbitral Tribunal' for the final determination of non-legal disputes.

In its admiration for these 'models', the Assembly, or rather its First and Third Committees, decided, somewhat late in the session, to knit the three texts together into a single document. A *liaison* Committee was formed and the work was rapidly taken in hand, the concluding stage of the drafting being carried through on the morning of Monday, September 24, at a joint meeting of the two Committees, containing over a hundred persons in all. Thus, in spite of the criticism of Sir William Harrison Moore and others, who thought the procedure rather precipitate, the plenary meeting had before it, just before the session closed, a document entitled the 'General' (that is, inclusive or comprehensive) 'Act for the Peaceful Settlement of International Disputes'.

The General Act is noteworthy as the most systematic presentation of the doctrine of international juridical organisation. One speaker in the debate even went so far as to use the expression 'International Juridical Union'. Although framed by a League Committee and adopted by the League Assembly, it completely eliminates the League Council from any part in the settlement of disputes. The work is divided instead between three types of body, all strictly 'non-political'. There is the Permanent Court of International Justice, which is to have the last word as regards legal disputes. There are Conciliation Commissions, which are to deal, in the first instance, with

non-legal disputes. And, finally, there are Arbitral
Tribunals, which are to have the final determination of
non-legal disputes.

Once more recourse is had to a Board of Solomons,
but this time they are not to be nominated, as in the
Geneva Protocol, by the League Council but wholly
apart from it. Of the five members of the Tribunal, 'the
parties shall each nominate one member, who may be
chosen from among their respective nationals. The two
other arbitrators and the Chairman shall be chosen by
common agreement from among the nationals of third
Powers. They must be of different nationalities and
must not be habitually resident in the territory nor be
in the service of the parties.' In case of disagreement
'the necessary appointments shall be made by the
President of the Permanent Court of International
Justice'.

On what principle are these Solomons to 'arbitrate'?
The answer to this question, no doubt due to hasty
drafting, is a little confusing. 'If nothing is laid down
in the special agreement or no special agreement has
been made, the Tribunal shall apply the rules in regard
to the substance of the dispute enumerated in Article
38 of the Statute of the Permanent Court of International Justice. In so far as there exists no such rule
applicable to the dispute, the Tribunal shall decide *ex
aequo et bono*.' This is a roundabout way of saying that
the Tribunal is not an arbitral body at all, in the strict
sense of the term, but a Tribunal of Equity, or something roughly equivalent to it. For if there existed a
'rule applicable to the dispute' it would have been
taken to the Court rather than to the 'Arbitral
Tribunal'. But perhaps it was felt that something had
to be inserted, however misleading, to justify the use

of the term 'Arbitral' in this section of the Act.[1]

Before leaving this subject it may be remarked that the history of the working of Conciliation Commissions is still to be written—or rather, to be made. The Locarno Commissions, for instance, have not only never met but their existence has at no time since 1925 been a factor of any importance in the relations between the countries concerned. When the rulers of Germany and Poland determined to improve their mutual relations they did so through direct negotiations and the difficulties and pinpricks of fifteen years disappeared as by magic. The two Conciliation Commissions were in no way concerned. The existence of a treaty providing for a Conciliation Commission may even be a source of added difficulty and complication in a serious situation. Thus the Italian-Ethiopian Treaty of 1928, which is a product of this phase of League history, proved little more than a cover behind which

[1] It is worth noting that the British Labour Party was as precipitate in endorsing the General Act as the Assembly was in drafting it. The annual Conference opened on October 1, within less than a week of the close of the Assembly. It proceeded to draw up, or rather to approve, an election programme into which was pitchforked a pledge to sign the General Act. How many Labour 'supporters of the League of Nations' knew that the Act was an embodiment of the Scandinavian view of the League as against that of the framers of the Covenant? The new Labour government, after letting some time go by, eventually acceded to the Act with careful reservations. These will be found in Annex 2 of Cmd. 3803 (Miscellaneous No. 8, 1931) together with a statement by Mr Arthur Henderson, dated February 23, 1931. They are on the same lines as the reservations to the same government's signature of the 'Optional Clause', which are set out in Cmd. 3452 (Miscellaneous No. 12, 1929). The most important of these, from the point of view of this study, is the right to refer disputes to the Council of the League before they are dealt with either by the Permanent Court or the Arbitral Tribunal of the General Act.—For a more detailed account of the General Act and its 2450 conciliation commissions see the article in *International Affairs* for May 1931 by Sir John Fischer Williams, and Professor Brierly's article in the *British Yearbook of International Law* for 1930.

one party was able to accumulate military forces
whilst the other appealed vainly to the Council to deal
with the whole issue. The moral is simple. There is no
short cut to the confidence which alone can make
Conciliation Commissions and other such devices effective. The success of the United States-Canadian Joint
High Commission is not due to the *device*, but to the
spirit of the two peoples, which is naturally reflected in
that of their agents.

V

The interest now shifts from the European progeny
of Mr Bryan to the country of their origin.

We have seen how, in the spring of 1918, the principle of the Hue and Cry was enunciated almost
simultaneously by Lord Parker in Great Britain and
by Mr Root in the United States and how it was laid
aside at the Peace Conference in favour of President
Wilson's more limited form of guarantee. Then came
the bitter political fight over the treaty and the League,
which left a lasting mark on the American public mind.
The path towards membership of the League was
barred by a powerful obstacle, due in part, perhaps, to
deeper causes, but in which the fear of entanglement
was the most prominent feature. Thus American public
opinion remained ill at ease. Far from experiencing a
sense of liberation at having cut themselves loose from
the affairs of Europe, Americans were haunted by a
sense of duty somehow neglected or evaded. For the
people of the United States are at heart idealists: the
word indeed applies to them more completely than to
any other people in the modern world. Moreover, their
idealism had been accustomed to find a vent in international affairs. Had they not been the pioneers of

Arbitration, bound up as this was with the very fixing of their national frontiers? Had they not originated the movement which brought about the Universal Postal Union, the most uniformly successful of all international bodies? Had they not rescued the Hague Conference system from its torpor and provoked the holding of the Second Conference in 1907? And if, in his campaign for the League of Nations, President Wilson had failed to carry the American people with him, should this signify that the United States was abandoning what had become one of her principal traditions? [1]

This condition of what may be described as 'balked idealism' left the American people in a mood of peculiar readiness to respond to an international call, provided only that it had nothing to do with the League of Nations. Indeed, such a call had all the more chance of evoking a powerful movement if it visibly outran the League of Nations, which embodied so much of European subtlety, compromise and reaction. Let America show what she could do. Then Europe might turn from her old ways and follow the pioneers. Thus the United States would fulfil, and more than fulfil, any duty that Europe could claim from her.

It was against this background that there was launched,[2] in the Middle West of the United States, the movement for the Outlawry of War. Its originator

---

[1] See on the above Pitman B. Potter, *The Myth of American Isolation* (World Peace Foundation, 1921), where the main facts on this subject are compactly set forth.

[2] Mr Levinson's first public statement was made in an article in the *New Republic* on March 9, 1918, but Mr Levinson did not develop a movement of his own till it had become clear that the League of Nations Covenant had not closed the door to war. The Outlawry movement, as such, is a product of the years following the defeat of the League in the Senate.

was a Chicago lawyer, Mr S. O. Levinson. He was powerfully aided by a Christian minister, the Rev. Charles Clayton Morrison, editor of a Chicago weekly journal, *The Christian Century*.

What does the Outlawry of War mean? Outlaws are, strictly speaking, persons. How can a practice or an institution be outlawed? What sense would there be in campaigning on behalf of the 'outlawry' of murder, or of kidnapping or of the practice of capital punishment? Why not use a simpler term such as 'abolition' or 'repression' or 'prevention'? Such were the questions asked by meticulous Europeans when echoes of the movement first crossed the Atlantic. But these criticisms failed to reckon with the psychological basis of the new campaign. The essence of its appeal was that war was not just an ordinary social abuse or crime to be repressed or prevented; it was *the* abuse, *the* crime, *the* evil *par excellence*. It was *the* great canker in modern civilisation which must be eradicated at all costs. War and modern civilised life had become incompatible. It was a fight to the death between the two. War must be banned for ever, driven into the wilderness, cut off once and for all from the ordinary life of mankind—in a word, *outlawed*. Thus, as Mr Morrison expressed it, 'the term "Outlaw War" sits like a tongue of flame upon many diverse groups, whose understanding of its technical meaning may not be identical, but for whom the term expresses a higher and a more uncompromising purpose than any previous proposal offered on behalf of world peace'.[1] Ever since 1923, when it had first attempted to close the gap in Article XV, the League of Nations Assembly had been playing with the notion that war was a crime. For Mr Levinson and

[1] Morrison, *The Outlawry of War* (Chicago, 1927), p. 29.

Mr Morrison war was more than a crime. It was a *sin*.

But it was not enough to denounce sin. Practical measures must be taken to extirpate it. For the leaders of the movement were not only prophets but pragmatists, and Professor John Dewey, the philosopher of pragmatism, had lent them his support from the first. What form should such measures take? What other form than a treaty? True, the Covenant of the League of Nations was a treaty. But it was a treaty drawn up in Europe and abounding in 'ingenious and highly technical and subtle devices of diplomatic craftsmanship'. What was needed in order to give precision to the 'luminous concept' of Outlawry was something simpler and saner, 'which can be grasped by a sage or a child'.

Here is the document which Mr Levinson drew up in order to crystallise his idea in set terms:

'Draft Treaty to Outlaw War

'We the undersigned nations of the world hereby condemn and abandon for ever the use of war as an instrument for the settlement of international disputes and for the enforcement of decisions and awards of international tribunals, and hereby outlaw the immemorial institution of war by making its use a public crime against the fundamental law of nations. Subtle and fatal distinctions between permissible and nonpermissible kinds of war are blotted out; the institution of war is thus outlawed, as the institution of duelling has been outlawed; but the question of genuine self-defense, with nations as with individuals, is not involved in or affected by this treaty. In order to provide a complete and

2 c

pacific substitute for the arbitrament of war, we hereby agree to take immediate action for the equipment of an international court of justice with a code of the laws of peace, based upon equality and justice between all nations. With war outlawed and the code approved and ratified, the court shall be given jurisdiction over all purely international disputes as defined and enumerated in the code or arising under treaties, with power to summon in a defendant nation at the petition of a complaining nation and to hear and decide the matters in controversy. We hereby agree to abide by and in full good faith to carry out the decisions of such international tribunal. The judicial system thus established, being a complete substitute for the outworn and destructive war system, will enable the nations to adopt far-reaching and economically vital programs of disarmament.'

'This Levinson treaty', remarks Mr Morrison, 'reads more like Lincoln's emancipation proclamation, or our fourteenth amendment abolishing slavery, than the usual document put forward in the name of peace.' Nevertheless it contemplates the attainment of its end by means of machinery; and the machinery chosen was that of Mr Taft—a World Court. But the working of this Court was not to be left to chance or to the processes of growth. It was to administer justice from a ready-made code. The first practical step to be taken then was to construct such a code.

How was this to be accomplished? This was not quite clear. But there was one thing, at any rate, that could be done. A Resolution could be passed by the Congress of the United States. Thus in February 1923 Senator Borah of Idaho introduced a resolution into the Senate. It is too long to be given here, extending, as it does to nearly a thousand words. But its most important clause demands quotation:

'Resolve further, that a code of international law of peace based on the outlawing of war and on the principle of equality and justice between all nations, amplified and expanded and adapted and brought down to date, should be created and adopted.'

How and by whom was this task of creation, adoption, amplification, expansion, adaptation and bringing down to date to be performed? The question remained unanswered.

The scene now moves back to Europe, where in the meantime idealistic forces had also been mustering again after the set-back of 1920.

Amongst the 'annexes' to the Proceedings of the Third Committee of the League of Nations Assembly of 1924, which drew up the Geneva Protocol, there will be found one bearing the heading 'Proposals of the American Group' and opening with the words 'Declaration Outlawing Aggressive War'. The American group in question was small in numbers but great in spirit, as well as in experience. It consisted of General Bliss, one of the five full United States delegates to the Peace Conference, Mr David Hunter Miller and Professor James T. Shotwell of Columbia University. They had already in the previous June circulated a 'Draft Treaty of Disarmament and Security' to the members of the Council of the League. The paper submitted to the Assembly was on identical lines.[1]

Its principal features were three. First, 'the outlawry of War' which is formulated in the following terms:

'Article 1.—The High Contracting Parties solemnly

[1] It is also printed in Miller, *The Geneva Protocol* (1925), p. 253 ff.

declare that aggressive war is an international crime. They severally undertake not to be guilty of its commission.

Article 4.—The High Contracting Parties solemnly declare that acts of aggression, even when not amounting to a state of war, and preparations for such acts of aggression, are hereafter to be deemed forbidden by international law.

Secondly, the Permanent Court of International Justice (and not, as in the Covenant and the Protocol, the Council of the League) is the body which is to determine the aggressor and "to make a judgment to the effect that the international crime described in Article 1 has or has not in any given case been committed".

Thirdly, the sanctions are not to be military but economic. The article in question runs as follows:

Article 8.—In the event of any H.C.P. having been adjudged an aggressor pursuant to this Declaration, all commercial, trade, financial and property interests of the aggressor shall cease to be entitled, either in the territory of the other signatories or on the high seas, to any privileges, protection, rights or immunities accorded by either international law, national law or treaty.

Any H.C.P. may in such case take such steps towards the severance of trade, financial, commercial and personal intercourse with the aggressor and its nationals as it may deem proper and the H.C.P. may also consult together in this regard.

The period during which any such economic sanction may be continued shall be fixed at any time by the Court at the request of any signatory.

In the matter of measures of force to be taken,

each signatory shall consult its own interests and obligations.'

It will be observed that this scheme is drafted with American opinion very much in view. Those who framed it believed indeed at the time that, whilst the American people would continue to refuse to join the League, it might be possible to induce them to go *beyond the League*. In other words, it might, psychologically speaking, be easier for the United States to accept the Protocol than to accept the Covenant. But it must be a Protocol not too rigid in structure and capable of being explained to the American people as embodying ideals and principles which were not simply European but also their own.

Once again an opportunity for adjustment and understanding was let slip. In spite of a conversation between Professor Shotwell and M. Herriot at Lyons, a few days before the Assembly opened, no real effort was made at Geneva to bridge the Atlantic and the scheme never reached the stage of being threshed out in Committee.

The American group returned home disappointed but not disheartened. For they knew that there was a movement under way in the United States which must 'sooner or later rank' the United States 'side by side with the nations who' were 'the chief supporters of the Covenant and the Protocol'. The sanctions clauses of the latter and the stiffening of Articles X and XVI of the Covenant, which were just the articles most obnoxious to American opinion, would doubtless provoke much criticism that might have been avoided. But a way through would ultimately be found.[1]

---

[1] The quotation is from an article by Professor Shotwell in *Europäische Gespräche* for November–December 1924.

The scene now passes to Paris in April 1927. The tenth anniversary of the United States entry into the war was approaching. Why should not the occasion be used to launch the Outlawry Movement in Europe? This was the idea which Professor Shotwell lodged in the receptive mind of M. Briand. Thus on April 6, 1927, M. Briand addressed a message to the people of the United States saying that 'France would be willing to subscribe publicly with the United States to any mutual engagement to outlaw war, to use an American expression, as between these two countries. The renunciation of war as an instrument of national policy', he added (the phrase runs less clumsily in English than in French), 'is a conception already familiar to the signatories of the Covenant of the League of Nations and of the Treaties of Locarno.'

The response to this remarkable proposal will rank as one of the curiosities of journalism. Its importance 'escaped notice both in America and in Europe'. It was awarded neither a front page position, nor headlines, nor editorials. The subject remained dormant for nearly three weeks, until on April 25 the *New York Times* published a letter from Dr. Nicholas Murray Butler which proved the starting point of a movement for a world-wide treaty on the lines of the Briand message.[1]

On June 20 the United States Ambassador in Paris handed to M. Briand a draft treaty in two articles:

Article 1.—The High Contracting Parties solemnly declare, in the name of the French people and the people of the United States, that they condemn recourse to war and renounce it respectively as an instrument of their national policy towards each other.

[1] Shotwell, *War as an Instrument of National Policy* (1929), pp. 39-40.

Article 4.—The settlement or the solution of all disputes or conflicts, of whatever nature or of whatever origin they may be, which may arise between France and the United States of America, shall never be sought by either side except by peaceful means.'

This document was not published at the time. Its presentation was followed by an interval of several months, during the course of which the Three-Power Naval Conference initiated by President Coolidge met at Geneva, though not under League auspices, and broke down. Eventually on December 28, 1927, Mr Kellogg, the United States Secretary of State, replied to M. Briand accepting his suggestion and proposing further that France and the United States should join 'in an effort to obtain the adherence of the principal Powers of the World to a declaration renouncing war as an instrument of national policy'. This led to a long and complicated exchange of views, in which all the Principal Powers and a number of others took part. Finally it was agreed that the Pact should be signed in Paris on August 27, 1928, the original signatories, fifteen in number, being the United States, Great Britain, France, Germany, Italy and Japan (the Great Powers), Belgium, Czechoslovakia and Poland (as 'Locarno Powers'), and the British Dominions and India. Other states were invited to 'adhere' later and the great majority hastened to do so. The Pact came into force on July 24, 1929, the date of the deposit of the Japanese ratification at Washington. By 1933 no less than 65 states were bound by the Pact, a larger number than that of the signatories of the Covenant. Certain Latin-American states, who had susceptibilities about the Monroe Doctrine, failed to sign, amongst them being the Argentine, Brazil and Bolivia, but not

Paraguay. Brazil is the only state of any importance which remains outside both systems.[1]

This new multilateral Treaty or Pact or Covenant is the most far-reaching engagement so far entered into by the sovereign states of the world. In the first place, it is, practically speaking, irrevocable. The parties are not at liberty, as under the Covenant, to give individual notice of withdrawal. They are bound, in Mr Miller's words, 'for ever and for ever'. They have renounced war: they are not free to *unrenounce* it. This could only be done by means of a request for release made to all the signatories. Since this is not to be thought of, the pact is in force for each and all of the parties 'as long as grass grows and water runs'.[2] It is part of the regular order of the world.

In the second place, the Kellogg Pact undermines the traditional doctrine of sovereignty by taking its stand on the social principle enunciated by Senator Root to Colonel House.[3] Like Article XI of the Covenant, it *assumes* the existence, however embryonic, of some kind of world society whose members, however much they may differ in other respects, are at least all agreed that war is an anti-social practice which should not be permitted to continue.

On the other hand, the Pact does not take the further step and lay down in set terms the principle of the Hue and Cry. Its guarantee is negative,[4] not positive. The

[1] See *Treaty for the Renunciation of War* (Government Printing Office, Washington, 1928, reprinted 1933), which contains all the relevant material about the treaty and its negotiation: also Hunter Miller, *The Peace Pact of Paris* (1928), which gives a full analysis of the negotiations.

[2] Miller, *The Peace Pact of Paris*, pp. 146-9.

[3] See p. 230 above.

[4] Mr Lansing had proposed in January 1919 at Paris to formulate President Wilson's territorial guarantee in this form. See Hunter Miller, i. 29.

citizen pledges his own good behaviour but not his neighbourly services. Did this mean that he acknowledged the obligations of neighbourliness but preferred not to be bound by a rigid formula? Or was the new Pact simply an expression of opinion or intention, subject to all the changes and chances of the popular mood? This was the all-important question. It has not yet been answered definitely either one way or the other.

One thing must, however, be made quite clear. The Pact, as signed on August 27, 1928, contained no reservations. Various statements were made in the course of the negotiations which might have led to the framing of reservations. Thus the British Foreign Minister referred, in a dispatch of May 19, 1928, to 'certain regions of the world the welfare and integrity of which constitute a special and vital interest for our peace and safety', and went on to say that, since 'their protection from attack is to the British Empire a measure of self-defence', His Majesty's Government in Great Britain 'accept the new treaty upon the distinct understanding that it does not prejudice their freedom of action in this respect'. But this was not a reservation or even a suggestion for one. It did not claim for the British Government the right to use war as an instrument of national policy in the region of the Suez Canal. It merely claimed for Great Britain the right to associate herself in any measures of self-defence, legitimate under the Pact, adopted by the governments and peoples in these 'regions'.[1] Nor did the insistence of the

---

[1] On this point see the statement by Mr Beckett, the delegate of Great Britain on the Legal Committee of the Assembly in 1931, on September 18, 1931. He makes it clear that the letter of May 19, 1928, so far from being a reservation, was simply a contribution to the preparatory work for an international agreement which, unlike most such agreements, was

United States Senate that the Pact left the Monroe Doctrine untouched involve a claim that the United States had a right to use war as an instrument of national policy where the Monroe Doctrine was concerned. British policy in 'certain regions' and United States policy in Central and South America are both based on the maintenance of the *Status Quo*, to be modified only by means of 'peaceful change'. No doubt, the *principle* behind the letter of the Pact—the replacement of the use of force by a system of equal and neighbourly co-operation—involves the adoption of a new attitude and new habits by all the Great Powers. This, however, must inevitably be a question of time and growth. The essential first step is the abolition of the recourse to war, in the traditional sense of the word. Till this has been achieved, it is idle to discuss consequential issues, such as 'economic aggression' or financial pressure.

Thus the Kellogg Pact and the Covenant became complementary parts of a single structure. The Kellogg Pact ruled out recourse to war. The Covenant provided the machinery of Inquiry and Delay for disputants

not negotiated in a conference but by means of correspondence between governments. Moreover, when the despatch was written the project for the Pact was still confined to a limited circle of states: it was therefore necessary to safeguard the right of Great Britain to resort to war against a state which had accepted the Pact in its relations with Great Britain should it commit an aggression against an outside state as to whose protection Great Britain had special obligations. By the later adhesion of states such as Egypt, Iraq and the Kingdom of Saudi Arabia to the Pact the need for this safeguard fell to the ground. During the Italo-Abyssinian controversy the Italian representative at Geneva publicly stated that Italy had signed the Briand-Kellogg Pact with the same reservations as Great Britain, these reservations applying 'to Africa and certain parts of the Empire'. (*Journal des Nations*, September 5, 1935, p. 1.) This is incorrect as regards both countries. The Italian note of acceptance, signed by Signor Mussolini, is given in the United States official volume, already cited, p. 70.

and, in practice, under Article XI, enabled means to be taken to deal with an emergency situation. Could not the two systems be knit into one? It was a natural question to ask and there was an equally natural answer. Since the Kellogg Pact was a return to the principle underlying Article XI, its proper place in the Covenant was under that Article. Thus, as was suggested at the time, Article XI could have been amplified by two new opening paragraphs, as follows:

§ 1. The Members of the League condemn recourse to war for the solution of international controversies and renounce it as an instrument of national policy in their relations with one another.

§ 2. The Members of the League agree that the settlement or solution of all disputes or conflicts of whatever nature or of whatever origin they may be, which may arise between them, shall never be sought except by pacific means.

§ 3. Any war or threat of war, whether immediately affecting any of the members of the League or not, is hereby declared a matter of concern to the whole League, and the League shall take any action that may be deemed wise and effectual to safeguard the peace of nations. In case any such emergency should arise the Secretary-General shall on the request of any member of the League forthwith summon a meeting of the Council.

§ 4. It is also declared to be the friendly right of each member of the League to bring to the attention of the Assembly or of the Council any circumstance whatever affecting international relations which threatens to disturb international peace or the good understanding between nations upon which peace depends.

There was, however, one objection to this procedure. It was illogical or rather, unsymmetrical.[1] For it would not formally have closed the gap in Article XV and consequently it would not have brought in the sanctions of Article XVI against a state which embarked on a hitherto legitimate kind of war. Symmetry could only be secured by remodelling the dispute articles. This would obviously be a hazardous undertaking, for it involved stirring the embers of the old controversy on the subject of sanctions. Unfortunately, however, this was the course adopted, with British support, at the Assemblies of 1929 and 1930. The result was to provoke a combined opposition from the Northern states and Japan.[2] The entanglement eventually became such that the whole project was allowed to drop. Once more, to use the language of Mr Morrison, 'the windings and indirections of diplomatic' or rather of juridical 'thinking', allowed a great opportunity to slip by. For the knitting together of the Covenant and the Kellogg Pact would have been a powerful influence for the closing of the breach of 1920. And never, as it turned out, was the ending of that Great Schism more needed.

---

[1] The Covenant is, of course, by no means a symmetrical document as it stands. It contains plenty of 'dead wood' (such as Article XV, §§ 6 and 7, and Article XIII, § 4, would have become under the arrangement suggested), for instance, Articles 1 § 1, 4 § 1, 5 § 3, 6 § 2, 14 clause 1.

[2] See the speeches in the First Committee of the Assembly in 1930 by Messrs Ito (Japan), Unden (Sweden) and Raestad (Norway) in *Records of the Eleventh Assembly*, pp. 54-7 and 60-61.

THE FOURTH PHASE: 1929-1935

I

When the year 1929 opened it seemed as though, after a long series of vicissitudes, a solution had finally been found for the problem which had haunted the League since the withdrawal of the United States in 1920. There was at last a new international system, to replace the discarded system of pre-war days: and if, like its nineteenth-century predecessor, it was neither simple in design nor automatic in its working, there was nevertheless no technical reason why it should not ensure harmonious relations between the powers for many years to come.

Let us briefly survey the elements of the new system as they appeared at that time. It is all the more necessary to do since, partly out of deference for the susceptibilities of the American people, they were never explicitly set forth by responsible statesmen on either side of the Atlantic and the memory of these years has become faded through the rapid movement of later events.

As in the nineteenth century, the structure of international politics rested on a double foundation. But, in contrast with the pre-war period, when Britannia and the European Concert each occupied a separate dwelling, the double foundation was wholly international and virtually homogeneous. It consisted of two multilateral treaties of peculiar solemnity to which the honoured title of 'charter' could not unfitly be applied.

These twin charters, the Covenant of the League of

Nations and the Kellogg Pact or, to give it its official title, the 'Treaty for the Renunciation of War', formed a sort of constitutional framework within which the public affairs of the world were henceforward to be conducted. They had been freely accepted by practically all the governments and peoples of the globe. The great majority were bound by them both: and the reasons which prevented two Great Powers—the United States and Russia—from signing the Covenant, like the reasons which prevented certain Latin-American states from signing the Kellogg Pact, sprang from considerations of a domestic order and were in no way due to any lack of sympathy with the aims and objects of those documents.

Both the Covenant and the Kellogg Pact were indeed lacking in precision. The one revealed fissures at numerous points in its structure, openings purposely left there in order to allow the fresh air of everyday politics to circulate freely through the building.[1] The other was not a building at all, but simply the basis for a building. Its designers had contented themselves for the present with laying good and true foundations. In the existing embryonic condition of the world community, when 'the sense of mutual obligation which lies at the root of every legal system'—to recall Lord Parker's words—was still undeveloped or at least untested, they had not ventured to go beyond the very first stage in the practical application of the principle of international solidarity.

But it was part of the same composite design that this ramshackle structure for the general protection of mankind against the crime of violence should be re-

---

[1] The metaphor is taken from Sir Austen Chamberlain's speech at the Assembly in 1927.

inforced by buttresses at points exposed to particular strain. These were constituted by regional agreements between states 'whose differences'—in Lord Balfour's words—'might lead to a renewal of strife', and these agreements, like the Covenant itself, laid an obligation on the parties to consult together in case of difficulty. Thus all danger of misunderstanding appeared to be removed and the structure of peace was strengthened just where it would otherwise have been weakest.

Two such regional arrangements had been made in the course of the preceding decade. One had relieved the strain between the United States, Great Britain, Japan and China. It consisted of a series of treaties the object of which was to promote normal and peaceful development on the Far Eastern mainland and throughout the Pacific. It set up no regular machinery and its signatories exchanged no mutual guarantees or other pledges of action in the event of the occurrence of a breach of faith. The obligations were deliberately placed upon a basis of mutual trust such as seemed better to befit the honourable traditions of the peoples concerned. No sanction was provided except the opprobrium to which the treaty-breaker would be exposed. But this was considered sufficient. 'If any nation hereafter deliberately separates itself from the collective action that we have taken in Washington in this year of grace', said Mr Balfour on February 4, 1922, at the session when the treaties came up for adoption, 'it will stand condemned before the world.'[1]

[1] This is the text of the passage in Mr Balfour's speech at the sixth plenary meeting of the Conference as it appears in the official record of the Conference, with parallel English and French versions of the proceedings. In another official record, however, *Senate Document No. 126, 1922*, instead of 'it will stand condemned before the world' the sentence

The other regional agreement was that entered into at Locarno. Its object was to promote normal and peaceful relations between Germany and her neighbours to the West and to the East and to help to wipe out memories of defeat and subsequent humiliation. It set up no regular machinery outside the system of conference provided by the League of Nations: in deference, however, to the fears of two invaded countries, France and Belgium, it included solemn mutual guarantees of assistance against aggression, given and taken by five of its seven parties. But, for the British negotiators at any rate, the guarantees were not the centre of the Locarno settlement but a mere incidental part of a broad policy of reconciliation.[1] It was not for having pledged the word of Britain to intervene in a Franco-German conflict or for having pushed back the strategic frontier of his country from the cliffs of Dover to fifty kilometres east of the Rhine, that the British Foreign Secretary, on his return from Locarno, was honoured by his sovereign and applauded by his fellow-citizens. It was because he seemed to have been successful in the delicate task of promoting a true and durable understanding between the French and German peoples—an understanding cemented by the entry of Germany into the League of Nations with a permanent seat in the standing Conference of the powers.

ends as follows: 'that nation will not be able to plead ignorance, it will not be able to discuss private arrangements that it may have made with that or that Chinese government'. It may be conjectured that all the words quoted fell from the speaker's lips and were taken down differently by different official reporters. But such a discrepancy in the record of so important an occasion is certainly surprising.

[1] See Sir Austen Chamberlain's speech in the House of Commons on November 18, 1925 (reprinted in *Peace in our Time*, 1928).

Within the next few years this new system, so ingenious in its design, so imposing in its façade, was unexpectedly put to the test, first at one point, then at another. It failed to withstand the strain and by the middle of 1935 little of the ambitious structure remained intact. How did this sudden *débâcle* take place? And why was it permitted to take place by the governments and peoples concerned?

The answer to these questions fills a large part of the record of the League during the fourth phase of its history. Since the actual events are familiar and, in particular, since no new constructive idea emerged during these years, we can move forward more rapidly than in the preceding sections.

II

The third phase of League history—what may be called the period of the Tripartite Understanding —ended abruptly with the sudden death of Herr Stresemann on October 1929—a tragedy undoubtedly hastened by his recent labours at Geneva. His partnership with Sir Austen Chamberlain had already been broken by the latter's retirement from office in the previous May. Thus the Assembly session of 1929, the first attended by Mr Arthur Henderson as British Foreign Secretary, appears in retrospect as something of an interlude.

Within a few weeks of Herr Stresemann's death there occurred the panic on the New York Stock Exchange which proved to be the prelude of an economic depression unparalleled in modern times. Throughout the following years this exerted upon the League a continuous and demoralising influence which sapped the vitality of the whole system of international co-operation as it had been developed since 1920.

It might have been expected that the economic crisis, extending as it did, though in varying degrees of intensity, to every country in the world, would have reinforced the dawning sense of the social solidarity of mankind and would thus have strengthened the authority of the League for collective remedial action. But this was not at all the manner in which the situation presented itself to the small-scale minds of the afflicted peoples. Not only did they shrink from the adoption of common measures for dealing with this belated aftermath of the World War, but they allowed their economic plight to become the occasion, if not the pretext, for the recrudescence of types of national policy of which, in the preceding years, men had too confidently expected that the world had seen the last. These crude manifestations of pent-up feeling were, no doubt, in part a reaction against the equally immature 'internationalism' that had recently enjoyed a rather sensational vogue. We have not here to follow the workings of this reaction in individual countries. It is enough to say that this new spirit, being in essence *non-co-operative*, undermined the very foundations of the League. When the governments are individually determined to concentrate their attention on their own most immediate interests, regardless of the effects of such a policy upon their relations with other peoples, the League, which is 'the maximum of co-operation between governments at any given moment', is perforce reduced, if not to inaction, at least to a mechanical routine. Thus the Geneva spirit of these years, though it was clothed in the same forms and inhabited the same buildings, was hardly recognisable by those who were familiar with it in the years immediately following 1920.[1]

One result of the depression was to complicate and ultimately to bring to naught the application through the League of the principles of economic orthodoxy laid down in the World Economic Conference of 1927. These had at first won the formal acceptance of the leading governments and for a time the upward movement of tariffs and other obstacles to trade was definitely checked. In 1927 a full-dress diplomatic Conference on Import and Export Prohibitions met in Geneva and, strange as it may seem to-day, drew up a Convention providing, although with some reserves, for their abolition. In the Assembly of 1929 a more ambitious effort was made under the sponsorship of Mr William Graham, as President of the Board of Trade, for the reduction of economic barriers. He advocated a Tariff Truce, agreed to over a period of years, as a first step towards a gradual but general process of tariff reduction, warning the Assembly at the same time that, if this proposal proved abortive,

---

[1] A striking example of this is the diminution in the League's activity for the protection of minorities. At the Assembly in 1934 Poland, who had always resented having been forced to assume obligations from which the Great Powers were exempt, announced her intention of refusing to co-operate further with the Council in the matter. In practice this meant that all League communications on this subject henceforward remained unanswered—the method of the 'stay-in strike'. The Great Powers protested: but this had no effect on Poland, and the blow to the authority of the League took the life out of this whole side of its work. The sincerity of the Great Powers' concern over the matter is illustrated by the careful way in which, in order to secure Polish support, the Council resolution of April 1935, protesting against the *German* breach of treaty obligations, was so phrased as to cast no blame on Poland. The Assembly could, of course, manifest its concern by failing to re-elect Poland to the Council. But no advantage was taken of the opportunity thus offered in 1935. Poland was re-elected with a good deal more than the necessary two-thirds majority.

Great Britain would probably be obliged to give up her traditional policy of Free Trade.

Long and laborious effort was devoted to this scheme before it was abandoned as incapable of realisation under League auspices. Soon afterwards Sir Arthur Salter, who had been the Director of the Financial and Economic Section of the League from the beginning, resigned his post, his work being divided between two successors. Thus there was now no single initiating or directing mind for this side of the League's activity.

Later on indeed, when the situation had undergone further deterioration, a World Economic Conference of governments, the first ever held, was summoned under League auspices and met in London in 1933. It had been preceded by a preparatory Committee of Experts, including two members from the United States, who provided it with 'Annotated Agenda' of unimpeachable objectivity. But by this time the Great Powers were ranged in different and virtually competitive financial camps. The negotiations between them—particularly between Great Britain, the United States and France—which alone could have transformed the scientific analysis of the experts into practical common policies, were not pushed sufficiently far: or, if they were, they were rendered abortive at the last moment by unforeseen developments in the United States. Be that as it may,[1] the Conference registered failure on almost every count

[1] The paucity of official information available to the public on the conduct of this new branch of foreign affairs makes possibilities of its 'democratic control' somewhat remote. It is to be hoped that the material is in a shape in which it can some day be made use of by historians. Meanwhile it is inevitable that Rumour should take the place of Blue-books and White Papers, and that ability which might otherwise have gone to the writing of detective stories should be spent upon the doings of Treasuries, Central Banks and private agencies in this field.

and almost all that can be said to its credit is that, unlike some other League activities, it did not 'take an unconscionable time in dying'.

Thus the problems which it had been hoped would be settled in a series of general Conventions have remained unsolved, such small progress as has been made having been achieved through bilateral negotiations.

The League's activity in the economic field has therefore since 1933 been more and more concentrated upon economic intelligence work. In this it has happily been left relatively free from intrusion or control by high politics, and the information at its command, so much more abundant than that available to any private institution, has been utilised with a skill and a detachment worthy of the best academic traditions.[1]

III

But we must hark back from this excursion into the later years to the events which broke up the standing conference of the powers and with it what we have called the Locarno buttress.

The final evacuation of the Rhineland five years before the date set in the treaty had been agreed upon in principle between Lord Cushendun (on behalf of Sir Austen Chamberlain, who was ill at the time), M. Briand and Herr Müller at the Hotel Beau Rivage during the Assembly of 1928. The practical details were settled at the Assembly of 1929 with Herr Stresemann,

---

[1] The Assembly of 1929, following on a resolution passed by the International Studies Conference in London in March 1929, authorised the preparation of a 'comprehensive annual survey of economic developments'. These annual volumes have appeared since 1932. A short account of the earlier work of the Economic Intelligence Service is given in *Ten Years of International Co-operation*, pp. 205-6.

just before his death. During the spring of 1929 the new arrangement for reparation payments, which was the concession made to France in exchange for the evacuation, was negotiated in Paris, the eminent authorities concerned with drawing up the 'Young Plan' making insufficient allowance for the artificial character of the economic conditions of the time. The one lasting result of their deliberations was the establishment, in the Bank of International Settlements at Bâle, of a permanent liaison between the Central Banks of the leading countries, thus filling what had hitherto been a serious gap in the machinery of international co-operation. Henceforward regular means existed for organic co-ordination in financial policy, if the governments concerned desired to make use of them.[1]

The departure of the French troops from the Coblenz sector had been expected in some quarters, particularly in Great Britain, to lead to a lasting improvement in Franco-German relations. The effect, however, was exactly the contrary. Manifestations in the very first days of July showed that a new spirit was abroad in

[1] See p. 314 above. On the Bank of International Settlements see the Annual Reports of that institution, which are interesting not only for what they describe but also from the standpoint of doctrine. See also the evidence given on this subject by Mr Montagu Norman on February 18, 1931, before the Macmillan Committee (conveniently reprinted in Einzig, *Montagu Norman*, 1932, p. 241 ff.), and especially the confession (on p. 246) showing that the inexorable limits of the 'Fabian' method of advance have revealed themselves as clearly at Bâle as at Geneva. An abortive attempt was made in the Assembly session of 1929 to place the Bank under some kind of League control. One reason, no doubt, why it failed and the Bank was kept independent of the League in any shape or form was the desire not to endanger participation in its activities by representative bankers in the United States. In those days bankers were still considered in the United States as too respectable to be exposed, however indirectly, to the contamination of European politics.

Germany and the elections held two months later brought over a hundred National Socialist deputies into the Reichstag.

This news reached Geneva while the Assembly was in session, with M. Briand's scheme for European Union as the principal object of its deliberations. It caused consternation among the delegates, both among the minority who had taken M. Briand's idea seriously and among the greater number who looked forward to the continued development of international co-operation on world-wide lines. Well might the delegates be anxious: for the German elections portended, not merely the abandonment of all hope of the ambitious superstructure which M. Briand had proposed to build on a basis of Franco-German reconciliation, but the break up of that basis itself and of the standing conference which had been its symbol. The world, and especially the Geneva world, had indeed become so much accustomed to the working of the conference system that it was hard to realise that the days of the co-operative policy of which it was the expression must now be regarded as numbered. For the rising temper in Germany, combined with her economic plight, now made it impossible, even for a statesman as well-intentioned as Herr Brüning, to continue collaboration with the Western powers in the spirit and rhythm of the preceding years. From this time onward Franco-German relations were again overhung with menace. It was no longer a question of adopting common measures for the welfare of Europe and of the world, but of placating an outraged national sentiment by timely concessions—or of firmly resisting its pretensions. Since its principal members could not agree amongst themselves as to which of these policies should be adopted, no 'League policy' on the subject was possible. In the deepening economic depression the situation was allowed to drift.

It was in this atmosphere that, in accordance with the programme drawn up in September 1930, the Disarmament Conference eventually assembled in February 1932. Thus it was never at any moment of its eventful history a League Conference in the true sense of the word. It was not conducted under the sign of international co-operation. It was a political Conference centring round the problem of the balance of power in Europe. That balance, as it had existed from 1871 to 1914, had been disturbed by the defeat of Germany and the restrictions consequently placed upon her armed strength. This created an abnormal situation, for Germany was potentially the most powerful state on the Continent. Was this problem to be solved by the voluntary abdication by the victorious Continental powers, great and small, of their predominance? Or, if this was too much to ask, would the end be that Germany took the law into her own hands and reasserted her strength? The third solution, that of the Covenant, a régime of co-operative armament within the framework of a common law and common obligations for the use of force, had, as we have seen, been ruled out already in 1920.

What was involved, however, was far more than a mere Franco-German contest. France had in the early years of the League consolidated her position by alliances with Belgium, Poland and the three states of the Little Entente. This combination had sufficed to maintain an uneasy peace for a decade. But in the period after 1930, when rapid manœuvre became the order of the day, the Little Entente, already something of a

Great Power, became reinforced by a 'Balkan Entente', which brought Greece and Turkey into the same combination. Poland, on the other hand, profiting by the breakdown in 1933 of the close relationship which had existed since 1922 between Germany and Russia—one of the fixed points in Stresemann's policy—drew closer to Germany, at the expense of her relations with France. France at once parried the stroke by making overtures to Russia, which resulted in Russia's entry into the League in 1934, followed in 1935 by a Franco-Russian treaty which was a masterpiece of drafting in its respect for the letter of the Covenant. It provided, in fact, for common action in any private war, directly affecting either of the parties, which might arise through the failure of the Council—the name itself seems strangely inappropriate in the conditions of this period—to arrive at a unanimous report under Article XV. Meanwhile Italy, who, true to the principle of balance, had throughout the first fourteen years of the League been on bad terms with France and had favoured the claims of Germany, began, like Poland, to move from her fixed alignment.

Thus the period from 1930 onwards was characterised by a play of power in the course of which Europe rapidly slipped back from the 'new order', not into the nineteenth century but into the eighteenth. Geneva became an immense chessboard on which not only the Great Powers but knights and bishops and multitudinous pawns practised the art of manœuvre. In its twentieth-century setting in the austere city of Calvin the game called for all the more skill and ingenuity because it had to be carried on according to the forms and rules of the Covenant. In this way there crept into League procedure and League methods in general a quality of peculiar subtlety and *finesse*, the working of which was mostly hidden from the world at large. Apart from the general intricacy of international machinery, there were particular reasons why this rapidly growing evil was left unrebuked. Few of those who understood what was going on were in a position to open their mouths. Moreover, to speak frankly on the subject was to offend tender consciences and to admit defeat beforehand when there might yet be faint possibilities of success. Thus there was a steadily widening gulf between Geneva as it really was and the Geneva which had become a symbol and an ideal for millions of honest and peaceful folk in all parts of the world. It was a tragic example of the operation of the time-lag.

It is a compatriot of Machiavelli who, writing from recent experience, has given the clearest description of the spider's web at Geneva during this period. This is indeed natural enough: for the conditions were better suited to the touch of students of the great Florentine than to the heavier hand of the disciples of Bismarck. 'We are faced at Geneva', writes Signor Grandi,[1] 'with the following reality: that the Powers—large and small—carry their difficulties and their conflicts of interest to the League of Nations. These conflicts do not shrink at Geneva: they expand. The Great Powers, in conflict with another, seek for allies among the lesser Powers and form hostile groups which complicate and aggravate the situation; the small states court the support of the Great Powers, who, in order to maintain their diplomatic combinations, at once take sides. Thus all the disputes brought to Geneva finish sooner or later, either directly or indirectly, as conflicts between

[1] *The Foreign Policy of the Powers* (New York, 1935), pp. 86-7.

the Great Powers. During my stay in Geneva I never saw a dispute of any importance settled otherwise than by an agreement between the Great Powers. They alone are responsible for the situations that arise. A few states that remain outside of fixed diplomatic combinations, and are therefore able to maintain an independent attitude, have from time to time exercised a conciliatory influence at Geneva. But this only happens in the case of secondary disputes, and, moreover, these lesser Powers, not having at their disposal the forces that might become necessary to back their action, are themselves compelled to have recourse to the Great Powers.

'The whole of the Geneva procedure is, in fact, a system of detours, all of which lead to one or other of these two issues: agreement or disagreement between Great Britain, Italy, France and Germany.'

Such being the atmosphere at Geneva it was natural to suggest that better progress may be made if the four principal European powers, upon whose agreement or disagreement the fate of Europe depended, should come together by themselves for the peaceful solution of the now hopelessly entangled European problem. This was the idea behind the Four-Power Pact sponsored by Signor Mussolini when Mr Ramsay MacDonald and Sir John Simon, then British Foreign Secretary, visited Rome in March 1933. It was an attempt to set on foot a system of regular consultation independent of the Council and Assembly of the League, such as had grown up already between several groups of lesser European powers. But the promoters of the idea had underestimated the strength of the states outside the circle of the Great Powers. Vehement protests were at once aroused against the project and, though it was

accepted in its main outlines by the French government
of the day, it was never given practical application.
Quite apart from the complications introduced by
other powers, the unresolved issues between the
members of the Great Four themselves were too great
an obstacle to their regular co-operation.

The Four-Power Pact project of 1933 will be remembered as a clear-sighted attempt to rescue European
politics from the eighteenth-century morass in which
they had become embogged and to carry them forward
at least into the nineteenth century. It must be admitted, however, that, in the prevailing political and
economic disorder, accentuated over parts of the Continent by the open abandonment of the traditional
standards of civilised life, the Great Four would have
left an evil trail behind them wherever they had
assembled. The promoters of the Pact were, however,
hampered by an obstacle unknown to Castlereagh. They
dared not openly admit to a democratic electorate
that, on its political side, the Geneva system was
proving unworkable. Still less could they publicly set
forth the causes of its breakdown. No democratic
European statesmen could at this time afford to run
the risk of being branded as an 'enemy of the League
of Nations'. He would have been driven from office by
the victims of the time-lag. There was no way out of
this dilemma except through some testing shock that
would awaken public opinion to the realities of the
situation.

IV

We have seen how the Locarno system fell into
disintegration in the years following 1929. We have
now to turn our attention to the Washington system.

It too was exposed to the strain produced by the world-wide economic depression. This was the underlying cause that set in motion a train of events which transformed the political situation throughout the Far East and the Pacific.

For over five years after the rejection of their amendment to the draft Covenant the Japanese gave no sign of resentment, or even of impatience, at the proceedings of the League. They took part diligently in its work, both in the Assembly and in the Council, where their status as a permanent member often brought their services into request for purely European business, such as minority questions. During the Assembly meeting of 1923 there occurred the earthquake which destroyed a large part of their capital. The stoicism of the members of the Japanese Delegation on this occasion, when the extent of the national disaster and of their own personal losses was still in doubt, will not be forgotten by those who witnessed it.

At the Assembly session of 1924, during the protracted discussions on the text of the Geneva Protocol, an incident occurred which showed that there was a hot fire concealed beneath the surface of grey embers. It will be remembered that, by Article XV, § 8, of the Covenant, disputes on matters of domestic jurisdiction had been removed from the purview of the Council under that article and that therefore there was no bar against a war which arose out of such a dispute. The Council could indeed take action under Article XI: but for such action unanimity, including the votes of the two disputants, was required. The Protocol, however, closed the gap which rendered war permissible under the Covenant: and, in closing it for disputes submitted to the Council procedure of Inquiry and Delay, it closed it also for disputes arising out of matters of domestic jurisdiction. Thus, while a war arising out of a dispute over immigration restrictions had previously been as legitimate under the Covenant as it had been before 1914, it was now suddenly to be made illegal. But nothing was proposed in compensation so as to facilitate the discussion by the League of grievances caused through the domestic policies of states. It was as though, while the door were being more securely barred and bolted, a window which had hitherto been left open was being tightly closed. There is no cause for wonder that informed Japanese opinion should feel strongly on the subject.

The text embodying this important new principle was passing quietly through the Legal Committee of the Assembly when, quite unexpectedly, the Japanese delegate, Mr Adatci, a well-known jurist who later became President of the Permanent Court of International Justice, raised his voice in protest. This was a text which Japan could under no circumstances accept. Although he spoke with an emphasis and in accents which Geneva had never yet heard on the lips of a Japanese delegate, the first inclination was to treat the objection as purely verbal. But when the discussion was resumed in private it was found that Mr Adatci was in dead earnest and for four or five days a state of extreme tension prevailed at Geneva. Not only did the draft Protocol seem to be endangered but a vista of unexplored problems, economic, social and racial, loomed up before the delegates. Suddenly and without warning the Goddess of War, as one journalist expressed it, cast her shadow on the walls of the Geneva temple.

As it turned out, the crisis proved as short as it was sharp. A compromise formula was adopted under which the test of aggression was not to apply to wars arising out of domestic questions unless such disputes had not been previously submitted to the Council under Article XI. In effect, the result was a Japanese defeat: for the road to war on such issues was now barred. But if the object of the Japanese was to provide their fellow-members in the League with serious cause for reflection, they were certainly successful for the time being. Unhappily, however, preoccupation with more ephemeral issues soon caused the effect of the warning to wear off. Japanese statesmen, meanwhile, were no doubt devoting closer study to Article XI.

Another note of warning was sounded in 1931, when M. Briand's plan for European Union was under consideration by the Second Committee of the Assembly. The Japanese representative pointed out with all due politeness that the maintenance of the collaboration of non-European members in the economic activities of the League was highly desirable.

The attitude of Japan towards the Treaty for the Means of Preventing War, mentioned on a previous page,[1] also belongs to this period.[2]

On Saturday September 19, 1931, the Assembly was busy with the details of an Italian motion for an Armaments Truce, as an appropriate prelude to the Dis-

---

[1] See p. 376 above.

[2] When Japan is reproached for not having brought the Manchurian problem before the League, the psychological effect of M. Briand's scheme for European Union must not be overlooked. That scheme in itself belongs to the general diplomatic history of the period rather than to that of the League. The hard kernel concealed within its soft and shapeless exterior was a Franco-German Entente. But the conditions for this had never been properly thought out. Nor had the reactions of the scheme upon the lesser states been sufficiently considered. See their replies, conveniently reprinted in Mirkine-Guetzevitch and Georges Scelle, *L'Union européenne*, Paris, 1931.

armament Conference summoned for the following
February, when the news of another Japanese incident
spread through the corridors—not in Geneva this time
but at Mukden. At first, as in 1924, there was an inclination to make light of it. Few realised that the Far
Eastern buttress of the new international system was
endangered, and with it the stability of the main
structure. But the circumstances in which the incident
occurred were sufficient to cause anxiety to those who
could see the situation as a whole.

During the four preceding months Europe had been
passing through a financial crisis which, beginning in
Austria on May 11, with the failure of the Credit-
Anstalt, had led in July and August to a drain of gold
from London and, on August 24, to the fall of the
British Government. A new government had been
formed on a broader basis and had started upon a policy
of retrenchment in the armed forces and elsewhere.
At this juncture, on September 16, through a mistake
in the transmission of an administrative regulation,
insubordination broke out at Invergordon, an important naval centre, its proportions being naturally
exaggerated in the press of other countries. Britain
was visibly out of action. One great restraining influence against violent policies was removed. Within
forty-eight hours of the Invergordon incident a prearranged plan was set in motion by the Japanese
military authorities in Manchuria. Two days later the
financial repercussions of the trouble at Invergordon
compelled Great Britain to abandon the Gold Standard.
The interdependence which is the characteristic
feature of twentieth-century politics could not have
been more vividly illustrated. Political and economic
issues, foreign and domestic, European and Far

Eastern, were inextricably intermingled. This time, however, they were not to be disentangled by statesmanship. In the Far East, at any rate, they were to be cut by the sword.

On September 29, 1931, the League Assembly adjourned after its President had recalled to the delegates 'the affirmation by the Japanese Government and by its Representative that it never had or will have any intention of occupying Manchuria militarily'. From October onwards Japanese military operations were steadily extended. By March 9, 1932, the Japanese hold on the country was sufficient to justify the setting up of a new 'independent' state. On September 15, 1932, just twelve months short of the original 'incident', this 'state' was formally recognised by Japan. Shortly afterwards, the belated report of the League Commission of Inquiry was published. Its recommendations were eventually adopted by the Assembly and in February 1933 Japan gave notice of withdrawal from the League.

This is not the place in which to describe the vicissitudes of the Sino-Japanese dispute at Geneva.[1] We are only concerned with its repercussion upon the new international system and in particular upon the League. In both domains, the dispute and the war that followed it were a crucial test: and the result was to prove the inner weakness both of the larger composite structure and of each of its component parts. Neither the League-

[1] The best detailed account of the Sino-Japanese dispute, as seen from the Geneva angle, is contained in the series of papers on *The League and Manchuria* published by the Geneva Research Information Committee. Use is there made of information from the United States not included in League publications or easily available in Europe. The briefer account in Morley, *The Society of Nations*, is also instructive from this point of view.

Kellogg Pact combination nor the League and the Kellogg Pact individually proved equal to the strain.

When we examine the reasons for this failure we shall find them to be both general and technical.

The general cause for the breakdown of the new international system was the absence of any real sense of social solidarity between the leading peoples of the world. That there is no world-society was clear already in 1931 to anyone who knew the meaning of words. But what was not so certain, what called for a test, was whether the sense of a common obligation for the prevention of war was still as embryonic as in 1914. The League of Nations had been in existence for over a decade. Public opinion in the United States had been actively exercised over the issue of peace and war during the same period—all the more actively because the United States was not a member of the League. What did all this preoccupation with international affairs amount to in an emergency? Would it issue in a clear call for common action? Or would twin Charters of the New Order prove to be no more than pious wishes on pieces of paper?

Everyone knows the answer. The principle of the Hue and Cry was tacitly abandoned. None of the Great Powers was willing to take the lead in taking action against the aggressor. None was even willing publicly to promise co-operation if and when others took action. Each, like the wedding guests in the parable, pleaded other preoccupations. The 'anonymous' aggressor of the Geneva Protocol orations turned out to be an abstract and purely theoretical personage, with no connexion in real politics with the power which on September 18, 1931, violated the Covenant, the Kellogg Pact and the Nine-Power Washington Treaty. Never was it so forcibly demonstrated that 'there is safety in numbers'. The Japanese had against them a coalition of pacts. Their tactics were simple. They had only to sow discord between three groups of signatories, the most prominent members of each of which were anxious to shuffle their responsibilities off elsewhere. The ramshackle peace structure with its Far Eastern extension turned out not to be a convenient, if informal, resort for concerting policies of co-operation, but a series of sealed chambers in which the prudent representatives of unready, if well-meaning, peoples shut themselves in and composed elaborate make-believes for action, or equally elaborate excuses for inertia.[1]

From the technical point of view, however, one or two particular points call for mention. One is the nature of the attempted co-operation between the Covenant and the Kellogg Pact or, to be more specific, between Geneva and Washington. Here a good beginning was made. At the first meeting of the Council at which the matter was gone into in detail, on September 22, it was decided that all the material on the case should be submitted to the United States Government. But within a few days the effort to co-operate across the Atlantic, even with the aid of the telephone, led to a serious difficulty. The natural course for the League would

---

[1] 'The truth is that when public opinion, world opinion, is sufficiently strong and unanimous to pronounce a firm moral condemnation, sanctions are not needed. Yet that is the class of case in which sanctions would be most likely to be applied. While, therefore, Britain will stand most firmly by its obligations under every Article under the Covenant—and nothing that I have said in the least degree suggests the opposite—I suggest to all who study this subject that it is best to keep the coercive and the mediatory functions of the League distinct and that this has been proved to be a case in which the effective action of the League is best applied by mediatory and conciliatory action' (the British Foreign Secretary in the House of Commons, March 22, 1932).

have been to follow the Graeco-Bulgarian precedent
and at once to dispatch a Commission of Inquiry to the
scene of the trouble. But when the League Council
sounded Washington on this proposal it met with a
discouraging reply. Thus the project was abandoned,
to be taken up later in very different circumstances,
when the area of the military operations had been
immeasurably extended.[1]

This proved the first of a series of confusions and
misunderstandings the details of which cannot be
known and assessed until the archives of the period
have seen the light of day.[2] All that can be said with
certainty is that the attempt to harmonise the Covenant
and the Kellogg Pact in their actual working, without
a common organ,[3] ended in producing an atmosphere

[1] On this point see Morley, p. 442 ('On this sign of a divergence
between the League and the American attitude the Japanese position
immediately hardened'), and *Geneva Special Studies*, October 1931, p. 29.
The first week was undoubtedly the crucial period, and the Council
meeting on Friday September 25, in which Great Britain, represented by
Lord Cecil, retreated from the Graeco-Bulgarian precedent of the previous week, was the crucial *moment*. (See *Geneva Studies*, pp. 23-4.) It was
at this meeting that the British member referred to the Japanese
member, who was sitting beside him, as 'my Japanese colleague', whilst
he spoke of the other party to the dispute, seated at the extreme end of
the horse-shoe table, as 'the representative of China'.

[2] For the refusal of the U.S. Government to appoint a representative
on the 'Consular Committee' formed by the League at Shanghai after
the bombardment of January 30, 1932, see Morley, p. 487.

[3] Such a common organ existed for a short time in October 1931 when
the United States Consul-General at Geneva sat at the same table as the
members of the League Council. Unfortunately, however, the understanding thus established was not sufficient to ensure the support of the
United States for the resolution setting a time-limit for the evacuation
of the Japanese troops. After this *contretemps*, which seems to have been
due to the unwillingness of certain members of the Council to ascertain
the mind of a colleague who was instructed to act under the Kellogg
Pact, there was an increasing divergence between the policies of the
League Council and of the United States. At the Council meeting in
Paris during November and December Ambassador Dawes, who, as

of mutual recrimination. Public opinion in the United States, from official circles downwards, became convinced that Great Britain had been deliberately remiss in her task of co-operation and had thereby made herself responsible for bringing discredit on the League and on the whole peace system. Emphasis is laid in particular on the negative response of the Foreign Office to Mr Stimson's dispatch of January 7, 1932. In this, it will be remembered, he informed the Chinese and Japanese governments and the other signatories of the Nine-Power Treaty that the United States 'does not intend to recognise any situation, treaty or agreement which may be brought about by means contrary to the covenants and obligations of the Pact of Paris of August 27, 1928'. British opinion, on the other hand, is equally convinced that the government and people of the United States, from Mr Hoover downwards, were never, at any moment during the long-drawn controversy, prepared to join in any form of collective action involving a real, as contrasted with a paper, conflict with Japan.[1]

Senior ranking Ambassador had been instructed to follow the proceedings, reduced co-operation with the Council to a minimum. 'He kept away from its meeting-place, in his hotel, and only saw some of its members personally and separately. This change in principle, if not in method, chilled the League representatives' (Malcolm W. Davis, *Councils against War*, Geneva Special Studies, vol. iii. No. 11, p. 15).

[1] Evidence of this is provided by the failure of the sporadic attempts to organise an unofficial boycott of Japanese imports and by the vigorous official statements, as, for example, by the Under-Secretary of State, Mr Castle, deprecating any idea of an official boycott as liable to lead to war. That general opinion in Great Britain was no more prepared for a boycott is best illustrated by one simple fact. In the week between June 29 and July 6, 1932 (*i.e.* just five months after the bombardment of Chapei), Japanese 6 per cent Government Bonds rose 15 points in consequence of the conversion of a portion of the British National Debt. No other foreign government stock was equally favoured.

At bottom what was at issue in this play of cross-purposes was a difference of temperament that could easily have been smoothed out round a common table. Great Britain, traditionally cautious, all the more so as she had great interests at stake in the Far East, refused to take a single step along a new road without measuring the possible consequences. The United States, on the other hand, at once more legally minded and less afraid of adventurous courses, naturally inclined to a forward policy—at least for a certain distance. In such a situation, where both parties are animated by a common purpose but differ in their practical judgment, there is no way out except through Conference. But Conference was exactly what this new composite peace system did not provide.

This raises the question as to whether the Chinese Government did not make a mistake of judgment in appealing to the League of Nations at all. Would China not have been better advised in seeking help in such a way as to bring Great Britain and the United States round a common table? Such a means existed in the Nine-Power Treaty, to the signatories of which, as we have just seen, Mr Stimson himself made appeal in his 'non-recognition' dispatch. It was no doubt too much to expect China, who, only a few days before, had been elected once more on to the League Council, to look into the future. Even the closest students of the League failed to realise at that time how little security there was behind the imposing League façade and how sadly the spirit of co-operation, which is Geneva's all-in-all, had diminished since the days of the Graeco-Bulgarian dispute. But that this is the moral to be drawn from the whole episode seems clear in the light of after-events.

Finally it must be pointed out that the Sino-Japanese dispute destroyed the whole elaborate machinery that had been built up at Geneva on the basis of Article XI. That article, as we have seen, had been used as a convenient and flexible instrument for the standing Conference and an attempt had even been made to secure the consent of the members of the League beforehand to abide by Council recommendations made in this way. But the assumption behind all this was that the Council was a Council and not a Conference—in other words, that it was an organic body with a *morale* and a sense of responsibility of its own. This proved to be the case, for the time being, during the Graeco-Bulgarian dispute, when the Greek representative was either too loyal to the Covenant or too much embarrassed to make use of his voting power. But in the Sino-Japanese dispute the psychological situation was very different. From the very first moment the Japanese were conscious that they possessed a veto on all that was proposed, outside the region of procedure, under Article XI, and they used this means of pressure to the full. The result was that the article became quite unworkable as a means for preventing or repressing aggression: for nothing could be done under it except with the consent of the aggressor. Moreover, the admission that the parties to the dispute had the right of veto under Article XI actually led to the claim that a similar right existed under Article X. Thus juridical reasoning arrived at the absurd conclusion that the League could take no action to 'preserve the territorial integrity' of any of its members except with the agreement of the member who was engaged in violating it. Such doctrines, of course, brought the League to a condition of complete impotence: for they reduced the pace of its movement not to that of the slowest—already a sufficiently serious difficulty—but to that of the worst intentioned. In these circumstances the term 'collective system' ceased to have a meaning. The Concert of Europe, with all its defects, was a far superior body to a League of Nations bound hand and foot in red tape by the attorneys of unscrupulous governments. What had been devised as a firm union between Force and Law had become a shifty alliance between Force and Casuistry.[1]

V

After Asia, America. In 1932 hostilities broke out between Bolivia and Paraguay, both of them original members of the League. The cause of the conflict was a disputed frontier in the Chaco region, the evidence in regard to which went back to the early part of the sixteenth century. With the particular causes which now blew these smouldering embers into flame we are not concerned. What interests us here is the part

[1] On this see Lauterpacht, *The Development of International Law by the Permanent Court of International Justice* (1934), who argues, from the precedent set by the Permanent Court of International Justice in the Mosul case, that the disputants are not entitled to a vote under Article XI. See also the report of the legal Sub-Committee of the 'Sanctions Committee' set up in April 1935 where the two alternative views on this question are clearly set forth. The report concludes by merely stating the two opinions. 'One opinion, based on the consideration that the Council has a duty to perform and on grounds of common sense, would refuse to count the vote of the State which has endangered peace by repudiating its international obligations; the other view, which flows from the language of Article V (of the Covenant), does not permit that State's view not to be counted.' The Sub-Committee consisted of representatives of the United Kingdom, France, Italy, Holland, Poland, Turkey, U.S.S.R. and Yugoslavia, but no clue is given as to the views held by individual members. On Article X see Morley, pp. 482-3 and footnote.

played by the League in the ensuing war and the influence of these happenings upon its technique and *morale*.

A previous conflict over the same issue had arisen in December 1928. On that occasion the Council happened to be in session under the Presidency of M. Briand when the news arrived, and the Secretary-General took it upon himself to bring the matter to its notice. M. Briand got into touch with the parties as well as with representatives of the United States and of the Argentine and explained that, unless the two governments within the next few days agreed to accept some form of procedure for pacific settlement, the Council would hardly be able to avoid holding an extraordinary session. Within eight days of the Secretary-General's first action, M. Briand was able to inform his colleagues that no extraordinary session would be needed.

In 1932 the parties proved less tractable. The war which began, as was not known till a year later, with a Bolivian attack on a Paraguayan outpost on June 15, 1932, dragged on for three years before the Cease Fire sounded on June 12, 1935. And its close was not due to any outside efforts but simply to weariness and financial exhaustion. Two members of the League, in fact, had waged a war of attrition.

This was not due to any lack of attempts to intervene between the parties. Indeed the would-be mediators were so numerous and so much at variance amongst themselves that their behaviour—or at least that of some of them—probably contributed not a little to the prolongation of the war. In the Sino-Japanese conflict the aggressor achieved his end because he was confronted with a coalition of pacts. In the Chaco War both belligerents profited by this advantage, which enabled them and their respective backers to pursue operations without any effective restraint on the part of the League and thus to produce what a United States writer has described as 'the first serious break in the American tradition of peace since 1879'.[1]

Four separate agencies were engaged in these efforts at mediation—the Pan-American Commission of Inquiry and Conciliation at Washington, the Washington Commission of Neutrals, the so-called A.B.C.P. *bloc* composed of the neighbouring powers, Argentine, Brazil, Chile and Peru, and, lastly, the League of Nations. Apart from the machinery thus provided, it should be mentioned that both belligerent governments were parties to the Protocol of the Permanent Court of International Justice, the appropriate body to pass judgment on the voluminous material relating to the disputed frontier. At the outbreak of the conflict neither had adhered to the Optional Clause. Paraguay, however, did so unconditionally on May 11, 1933, the day after she had declared that a state of war existed between herself and Bolivia. Paraguay had also adhered to the Kellogg Pact,[2] but, since Bolivia had not done so, this did not tie her hands.

Nevertheless the fact remained that Bolivia and Paraguay were both members of the League. Moreover, the Covenant was the only engagement which definitely bound them both to settle their dispute by peaceful means. Thus the League could not refrain from intervention; but its attempts encountered one difficulty after another. Already in May 1933 the Spanish repre-

---

[1] R. S. Kain in the *Political Science Quarterly* for September 1935.

[2] Kain, *loc. cit.* p. 326, is at variance with the State Department publication on this point.

sentative on the Council complained that its action had been 'paralysed and thrown out of gear' on nine separate occasions within a space of five months. When, following this, the Council decided to send out a League Commission, not to affix the responsibility for the conflict but to attempt to bring it to an end, its departure was postponed for many weeks at the request of both parties, whose agreement on this point certainly gave cause for surprise. When it eventually reached South America, in the winter of 1933, the war took a favourable turn for Paraguay and, in spite of a temporary truce, a settlement proved unattainable. An attempt was then made, through the League, on the initiative of the British Government, to stop the supply of arms to both belligerents, the United States being the first Great Power to put this embargo into effect. This measure, however fair in appearance, was distinctly inequitable, since not only was Paraguay in suspiciously close relations with the Argentine, with whom she had a long common frontier, but the Argentine declared herself legally unable to prevent arms from being shipped to Paraguay by the international waterway of the Paraná. Chile on her part declared that a treaty dating from 1904 prevented her from cutting off the transit of arms through her ports to landlocked Bolivia.

The embargo, together with the steady advance of the Paraguayan forces, had the effect of inducing Bolivia to throw herself, for the first time, whole-heartedly upon the League. On May 31, 1934, nearly two years after the outbreak of hostilities, she invoked the application of Article XV of the Covenant, which is designed to apply to disputes 'likely to lead to a rupture'. The problem thus raised came before the

Assembly in September. It was referred to the Legal Committee, which decided that, in spite of the peculiar circumstances, Bolivia's request was in order. A Committee was then appointed under Article XV and the somewhat cumbrous procedure of this article set in motion.

The Committee first made an effort, under paragraph 3 of the article, to arrive at a settlement by conciliation between the parties. When this failed it moved on to paragraph 4 and proceeded to draw up 'a report containing the facts of the dispute and the recommendations which are deemed just and proper in regard thereto'. This report, with certain amendments, was adopted unanimously by the Assembly at an extraordinary session held from November 20 to 24. It included a provision for the setting up of an Advisory Committee which was to meet within the next four weeks. The United States and Brazil were invited to be represented on this: both invitations, however, were declined.

Bolivia at once accepted the Assembly recommendations. On January 11, 1935, the delegate of Paraguay informed the League that his government could not agree to them. Thereupon the Committee, ingeniously dovetailing the provisions of Article XII and Article XV, § 6, informed the members of the League that the moratorium on war within three months of the adoption of a report by the Assembly would expire on February 24. After that date, therefore, Paraguay must refrain from continuing the war with Bolivia, who had accepted the report. Thus, by starting upon the procedure of Article XV in the midst of the conflict, the League arrived at the peculiar position of legitimising the resort to war by one of the parties, who, as it happened, was the original aggressor. It is not surprising that under these circumstances Paraguay should have notified the League on February 24 of her decision to withdraw from it.

Following this decision the Advisory Committee met again on March 11. This time they were faced with a new diplomatic situation: Argentine and Chile were acting in concert and had intimated that they had reason to believe that a plan 'based upon' the November recommendations might prove acceptable to the parties. The Committee therefore decided to summon the Assembly again on May 20. During the intervening period many members of the League withdrew their embargo upon the supply of arms to Bolivia. The Assembly, when it eventually met in May, had before it a joint declaration submitted by the governments of Argentine and Chile recording that the Foreign Ministers of the two belligerents had both agreed to come to Buenos Aires to meet a 'mediatory group' consisting of the Argentine, Brazil, Chile, Peru, Uruguay and the United States. It therefore contented itself with conveying its best wishes to this group and placing the 'dispute'—still so called—on the agenda of its ordinary session of September 1935. At that stage, presumably, the time would have come for placing on record the violation by Paraguay of Articles XII and XV of the Covenant and of applying against her the sanctions or, as one speaker preferred to call them, the 'admonitions' of Article XVI.

Justice, however, is proverbially slow-footed. By the time that the Assembly met, all thoughts of Article XVI belonged to the past. The Argentine delegate was able proudly to inform his colleagues that 'the hopes of the League of Nations, which had been

several times expressed by the various League bodies
and other mediating nations', had 'not been in vain',
that hostilities had ceased on June 14, and that the
demobilisation stipulated to take place within three
months was now practically complete.

Such, in brief outline, is the story of the latest, and
not the least horrible, war waged on American soil.
Those who ask how it could take place 'within the
framework of the League'—to use a familiar expression—are referred to the proceedings of the Advisory
Committee and of the two extraordinary sessions of
the Assembly. They will not fail to admire the talent
there exhibited in finding flowers of speech with which
to characterise the deviations of League members from
the letter and spirit of the Covenant.[1]

VI

After America, Africa. During the course of the
summer of 1935 the world gradually became aware
that a crisis was approaching in the relations between
Italy and Abyssinia and, as a consequence, between
Italy and the League of Nations, of which Abyssinia
was a member.

Abyssinia occupies a peculiar position on the political
map of the world. She is 'somewhere east', or rather
south, 'of Suez' and therefore beyond the confines of
Europe. The concern of the Concert, which was devoted, during a large part of the nineteenth century,
to Egypt and the lower valley of the Nile, had never

---

[1] This does not, of course, refer to all the participants in these discussions. A special exception must be made for the interventions of the
delegates of the U.S.S.R. and Czechoslovakia in the Advisory Committee debates.

been extended to the Soudan and beyond: the tentative effort made in certain European Chancelleries to direct its attention to that region at the time of the Fashoda crisis never even reached the stage of diplomatic conversations.[1] Thus for old-fashioned Europeans —and there are many such in the post-war world— Abyssinia is classed as a colonial area and any conflict occurring there falls under the rubric of a 'colonial war'.

On the other hand, Abyssinia does not belong, either geographically, politically or culturally, to Tropical Africa. Historically the relations of her people have been with Arabia and Palestine, whence she drew her religion: and strategically she lies close to the main sea-route that passes through the Suez Canal and the Red Sea into the Indian Ocean and beyond. She is thus more closely linked with North Africa and the Near and Middle East, regions within the sphere of the old Concert, than with that overseas world where British sea-power enjoyed undisputed sway during the nineteenth century.

Under post-war conditions too, as resulting from the change in the balance of sea-power and the Washington and London Treaties, the position of Abyssinia is exceptional. Supremacy in the oceans of the world has come to be divided between the United States, Japan and the British Empire, the United States controlling the Western Atlantic and the Eastern Pacific, Japan the Western Pacific and Great Britain the Eastern Atlantic and the Indian Ocean.[2] Supremacy in the waterways that connect these two oceans naturally

---

[1] See p. 86 above.
[2] On this see the frank remarks of an Australian writer, Colonel J. D. Laverack, in the *Army Quarterly* for Jan. 1933, p. 211.

forms part of this scheme. Thus Abyssinia lies within a region where the police-power of the League would, in the event of trouble, naturally fall to be exercised mainly by Great Britain. In accordance with the spirit of the collective system she would not wish to exercise it alone; but it could not be exercised at all without her active co-operation.

Thus the strategic position of Abyssinia bears some resemblance to that of Belgium. It is a point of junction between pre-war Europe—the Europe of the Concert—and the overseas world. A conflict arising there would put to the test whether, after the defection of the Far East and of the Americas, the authority of the League could be made effective in any part of the overseas world. Three possibilities would be open. Either Europe and Africa would prove to be a homogeneous political area, in which the principles of the Covenant would be applied without partiality or discrimination. Or the old 'colonial' doctrine would prevail and, whilst the whole region would remain within the orbit of the League, there would, as in pre-war times, be two sets of weights and measures, one for the inhabitants of the metropolitan area and the other for 'colonials'. Or, lastly, the predominance among influential League members of an exclusively European outlook would cause British public opinion to feel that the two regions could not be maintained any longer together under the League without a flagrant violation of the letter and spirit of the Covenant. In that event the League would lose its last claim to universality and the value of its survival as a political organ for the old area of the Concert would be open to serious question. The Italian 'break-through' of 1935, so reminiscent of the German 'break-through' of 1895 and the following years, would reopen for Great Britain the whole question of the orientation of her foreign policy.

So large were the issues raised by the Head of the Italian Government when, at a 'certain moment',[1] long foreseen, in the interval between the end of the French hegemony in Europe and the completion of the German military reorganisation, he slipped in, as Italian diplomacy had so often slipped in before, in order to seize what fruits he could. With one eye on France and another on Germany, he had overlooked, or underrated, Great Britain.

Abyssinia had been admitted into the League in 1923. This step was undertaken in pursuance of the general policy of seeking to make the membership of the League as large as possible, in contrast to the more exclusive membership originally favoured by President Wilson, who was in accordance on this point with the various projects put forward in Great Britain and the United States.[2] This latter conception was still adhered to in the choice of the neutral states to be invited to become original members of the League, when Mexico, Costa Rica and San Domingo were excluded from the list.[3] The incorporation of the Covenant into the peace treaties had, however, automatically brought into the League, without any inquiry into their qualifications, a number of states, such as Liberia and Siam, whose claims to be 'self-

[1] See the speech of May 26, 1927, the crucial passage in which is quoted in Toynbee, *Survey of International Affairs for 1927*, p. 120. But this determination to have recourse to force followed upon successive failures to secure consideration by the League of the problems arising out of Italy's unfavourable economic position. See p. 256 above.

[2] See pp. 165, 169, 180 above.

[3] Miller, i. 467.

2 F

governing' certainly involved a distortion of the usual meaning of that word.[1]

Moreover, the working of the League had made it clear that it was difficult, if not impossible, to set up exacting standards of domestic government for the admission of new members, if only because there was no practical means available for testing the eligibility of existing members for continuance in the League. Thus year by year the credentials of Assembly delegates were accepted without question if they emanated from a *de facto* government, irrespective of its character or of the method, constitutional or other, by which it had ensconced itself in power. There was therefore nothing revolutionary in the proposal that admission should be accorded to the proud and ancient, if primitive, kingdom of Ethiopia, however surprising this would have appeared to President Taft, Lord Bryce and other old-time exponents of the League idea.

Nevertheless the privilege of equal membership in the League was not granted to Abyssinia without misgivings.[2] The Sub-Committee of the Political Com-

---

[1] The French term for 'self-governing' in Article I of the Covenant is 'qui se governe librement'. To interpret this in the sense of 'independence', without any reference to the form and spirit of the government in question, involves a similar distortion as in the case of 'self-governing'. For what Frenchman, trained in the tradition of 1789, would admit that the France of Louis XIV enjoyed *Liberté*?

[2] Nothing was said in the debate about the obligation that the members of the League would be assuming towards Abyssinia under Article X. Great Britain, as has been explained, has generally tended to favour a 'weak' interpretation of that article: but a different view has sometimes been expressed when the admission of a relatively defenceless state has been under discussion. Thus at the First Assembly in reply to Lord Cecil, who had argued (in connexion with an application from Georgia) that the obligations of Article X, 'like all obligations, must be construed reasonably', and that South Africa (which he was representing at the time) would not be prepared to send a force to protect Bulgaria

mittee of the Assembly, to which the application was referred, found itself faced with the question whether Abyssinia was 'fully self-governing'. It reported that although it found itself 'unable to determine exactly the extent of the effective control of the central authority over the provinces remote from the capital', it was of opinion that 'Abyssinia was fully self-governed'. At the same time, however, it considered that some doubt existed as to Abyssinia's ability to fulfil her international engagements, including, of course, the maintenance of 'fair and humane conditions of labour' as provided for in Article XXIII of the Covenant. 'In order therefore to assist Abyssinia to overcome the difficulties', which might 'in the past have been the obstacles to such fulfilment', the Sub-Committee recommended that the Assembly, before giving its opinion on her application for admission, should ask Abyssinia to sign a declaration of her intention to conform to the obligations she had assumed in existing treaties for the suppression of the slave trade and the regulation of the traffic in arms. By one clause in that document Abyssinia was to declare herself 'ready now or hereafter to furnish the Council with any information which it may require, and to take into consideration any recommendations which

or Luxemburg or Costa Rica, the delegate of Great Britain, Mr H. A. L. Fisher, replied in language to which the exponents of the strongest interpretation could take no exception: 'We must either treat the League of Nations seriously or not. If we treat the League seriously we must treat the Covenant seriously, and if we treat the Covenant seriously we must treat our obligations under the tenth article of the Covenant seriously. It is because I do treat the Covenant seriously that I earnestly ask the Delegates in this Assembly to consider when they are voting on the admission of a new State whether they are prepared to take the responsibility of advising their respective governments to come to the assistance of that state in the hour of need' (*Records of the First Assembly*, p. 635).

the Council may make with regard to the fulfilment of these obligations, in which she recognises that the League of Nations is concerned'.

Abyssinia signed this declaration and was thereupon duly admitted into the League by unanimous vote—not, however, until after a debate in the Political Committee in which her claims were espoused by France and Italy against the doubts and hesitations of Great Britain, Norway, Switzerland and Australia. Sir Joseph Cook, the representative of the last-named country, true to the tradition of Mr Hughes, expressed dissatisfaction and even disdain at the notion that Abyssinia should in future be entitled to supervise and pass judgment on the administration by Australians and others of territories such as New Guinea, whose inhabitants were at somewhat the same stage of social development as those under the sway of the proposed new member of the League.[1]

Thus Abyssinia took her place in the Assembly, where she played a modest and unobtrusive but dignified part. And until the matter was referred to by the Italian Government at the height of the crisis, no proposal was ever submitted to the Council for an inquiry into the manner or degree in which she was carrying out the obligations to which she had pledged herself.

The immediate occasion of the conflict was a serious frontier incident between Abyssinian and Italian native troops at the wells of Walwal, in the region of the undelimited boundary between Italian Somaliland

---

[1] In the Political Committee of the Assembly in 1929 the Abyssinian representative, 'speaking in the name of the Christian Power in Africa and in the name of the direct descendants of Solomon', did in fact make some observations on the British administration of the Palestine Mandate.

and Abyssinia. This took place on December 5, 1934. On December 14 the Abyssinian Government reported the matter to the League. In the weeks that followed the League received numerous communications from both parties, and when the Council met in January 1935 it found a request from the Abyssinian Government that the matter should be taken up under Article XI, § 2.

The Italian Government, which, as was later learnt, regarded intervention by the Council in this matter as derogatory to its dignity as a Great Power or, perhaps, as a European Power, proposed that it should be dealt with under the Treaty of Arbitration and Conciliation concluded by the two governments in 1928. The Abyssinian Government thereupon agreed to postpone its application under the Covenant till the next session of the Council. When the Council came together in April, on the occasion of the extraordinary session called by the French Government in connexion with German rearmament, the situation had grown more serious. The shipment of troops and war material by Italy to her colonies, which had been proceeding since December, if not before, was steadily increasing and a hitch had occurred in the application of the procedure of arbitration and conciliation. The Abyssinian representative therefore urged that the dispute should be taken up by the Council. Again, however, the matter was postponed, this time until the ordinary Council session in May, the hope being expressed by the British representative, Sir John Simon, that by that time the arbitrators would be appointed and the terms of reference fixed. In May the Council found it necessary, under the impulsion of Great Britain, now represented by Mr Eden, to take measures to speed up the arbitration and conciliation procedure. A time-limit of three months was laid down on May 25, and it was also decided that the Council should meet again after two months, on July 25, if this should be necessary in order to secure a decision from the arbitrators. By this time it was generally known that the military operations, for which alone the continual dispatch of troops to Italian East Africa must be intended, could not be undertaken until after the end of the rainy season, towards the close of September.

The farther meeting projected for July was held, the arbitration procedure was at length put in motion and it was arranged that a tripartite Conference between Great Britain, France and Italy should take place simultaneously in Paris. The basis for this was a treaty dating from 1906, or rather that portion of it which, not being inconsistent with the Covenant, had not automatically become invalid under Article XX of the Covenant. It proved, however, to be abortive, the Italian Government refusing to enter into discussion on the suggestions put forward by the other two. The arbitration procedure, on the other hand, was carried through and an award rendered on September 3 which exonerated both sides from responsibility for the 'incident' of December 5, 1934.

On the following day the Council met at Geneva. The Walwal issue having been satisfactorily cleared out of the way, it might have been expected that the tension between the two member-states would subside. But it now appeared that there was a larger issue of long standing concealed behind the original 'incident'. The Italian representative handed in a memorandum on the general situation in Abyssinia, designed to prove that that state had failed to fulfil its obligations under the Covenant, and he declared that 'Italy's dignity as a civilised nation would be deeply wounded were she to continue a discussion in the League on a footing of equality with Ethiopia'. The Head of the Italian Government had for some time past been employing similar language in addresses to his own people and interviews with foreign press representatives and defiantly proclaimed that Italy would pursue her African designs 'with Geneva, without Geneva or against Geneva'.

In the face of this challenge, the Council acceded to the Abyssinian request for the application of Article XV to the Italo-Ethiopian dispute as 'likely to lead to a rupture'. It appointed a Committee of Five, under Spanish chairmanship, to seek a settlement by conciliation, under paragraph 3 of Article XV. Its suggestions were accepted by Abyssinia as a basis for negotiation but rejected by Italy. On September 26 therefore the Council was faced with the task of drawing up, under paragraph 4, a report for which it could itself accept responsibility as a 'right and proper' settlement of the dispute. It proceeded to do this, its recommendations taking the form of a scheme of assistance for Abyssinia, under League auspices, in order to raise 'the economic, financial and political level' of that country. This was accepted, in principle, by the Abyssinian Government but rejected by the Italian Government on the ground that it did not provide a 'minimum basis' for the constructive realisation of the 'rights and vital interests of Italy'. A few days later, on October 3, the Italian Government informed the League that it had authorised the High Command in Eritrea, in view of the general mobilisation in Abyssinia, 'to take the necessary measures of defence'. Early next morning a general advance of the Italian forces in the northern colony was in progress.

Thus a dispute that had been within the cognisance of the League for nearly ten months, a lapse of time which should, on the theory of Mr Bryan and the Phillimore Committee, have been a sufficient 'cooling-off period', resulted in a war of aggression undertaken at the opening of the campaigning season by forces conveyed to the scene with the full knowledge of the members of the League and indeed of the whole world: for their passage through the Suez Canal enabled their numbers to be controlled by an external authority. Once more the League's machinery for prevention had been inoperative. And this time there was far less excuse for the failure to set it in motion: for whereas in the Far East and in the Chaco the exercise of the League's police-power was obstructed, or rendered very difficult, by the non-membership of the United States, war was now taking place in a region where the members of the League could, if they wished, make their authority felt instantly and decisively. Indeed, so audacious, not to say foolhardy, were the strategic dispositions of the aggressor that it is doubtful whether, had the League not been in existence, he would have risked an expedition which placed his communications at the mercy of British sea-power. It would almost seem indeed as if the Italian Government had counted on Geneva, with its divided counsels and consequent paralysis, as one of its assets in its enterprise.

Why was no effort made to set preventive agencies in motion, either under Article XI or under Article X, which authorises action by the Council in the event of 'aggression' or 'any threat or danger' of aggression? Why was the Memorandum of 1927, with its provision for a naval demonstration against a 'recalcitrant State' which 'persists in its hostile preparations', completely ignored, not only by members of the Council but even by members of the Assembly, which was in session until within five days of the opening of hostilities?

It may be answered—and this indeed was the Secretariat's answer to such questioning—that action under Articles XI or X required the assent of the prospective aggressor state. But to argue thus is to bury one's head in the sands of procedure. Had the members of the League had the will to take concerted measures of prevention they would have found the way, or rather their lawyers would have found it for them. The real reason why no preventive measures were taken was that Italy was a Great Power, and that to expose her prestige to the indignity that such measures would have involved would have been to destroy the last chances of a negotiated settlement and to precipitate a major crisis on what was, or might easily have been represented as being, a secondary matter. In other words, the League was here confronted with the major issue that had been underlying its activities for the last fifteen years. Could a Great Power be brought under the Rule of Law or was the writ of the League only to run for the lesser states? In the latter event, what claim would it have to the authority or the dignity of Law? The issue in fact lay between the League as a union of Force and Law and the League as a consortium of Great Powers, with principles as elastic and rules as variable as those of the pre-war Concert.

But the developments at Geneva proceeded so

rapidly—at least for those engaged in dealing with them—that there was little time for such reflections. The breakdown of conciliation—the ascertained proof of aggression—the vote on the basis of this proof— the consequent passage from Article XV to Article XVI of the Covenant—the discussion as to the nature of the Sanctions to be applied—the establishment of an organisation to co-ordinate and supervise them— the working out of the plans to be laid before this new body—Geneva passed through these successive phases in what, for those who had sat for fifteen years at the side of an immobile and seemingly rusty machine, seemed breathless and even breakneck speed. In Abyssinia, no doubt, where men whom the League had undertaken to protect were exposed to modern methods of mass-destruction, the pace did not seem so furious.

The formal steps must be briefly recorded. On October 7, on the report of a Committee which had before it the proclamations of the Italian High Command, the Council of the League agreed by roll-call, against the dissenting vote of the Italian representative, that Italy had 'resorted to war in violation of Article XII of the Covenant'. On October 11 fifty members of the Assembly, which had stood adjourned at the end of its ordinary session, having had the minutes of the Council meeting transmitted to them, expressed themselves in the same sense: Austria, Hungary and Albania, though not contesting the facts set out in the Council Committee's report, dissociated themselves from this collective decision. Article XVI of the Covenant having thus automatically come into play, a diplomatic Conference was constituted in order to co-ordinate the action that must now be taken by individual states under that article.

The reason for the adoption of this procedure was that it was not desired, for the present at any rate, to expel Italy from the League and that, if action were proposed to be taken under the Council or the Assembly, she could still block it by her veto. Thus, by a strange irony, on the Great Day to which President Wilson and the framers of the Phillimore Report had looked forward, the day when the 'Allies', individually and collectively, would impose the 'weightiest possible' sanction, when the enlarged Monroe Doctrine would afford instant protection 'to great and small alike' through the implementing of that general guarantee of mutual aid which was to have made the reduction of armaments by individual members possible, the machinery of the League failed to function and new arrangements of a more flexible but less immediate and formidable character had hastily to be improvised. So impossible is it in international affairs to foretell the working of human wills and the consequent constellation of circumstances that will have to be faced in an emergency.

The same element of paradox pervaded the League on the political side of the crisis. Everything seemed to fall out exactly contrary to the predictions and preparations of fifteen years. The first power to recognise that Italy and Abyssinia were at war was the United States, the power whose indifference to the affairs of the Old World had caused so much heart-searching throughout the previous years. True, this recognition was not the prelude to positive co-operation under the League or under the Kellogg Pact. But thanks to a recent Act of Congress, it led to the adoption of a policy of neutrality in which *duties* bulked larger than rights and the intercourse between United States nationals and the belligerents was greatly reduced. Thus the haunting fear of a conflict over 'the Freedom of the Seas' in the event of a League blockade was, for the time at least, removed.

In Great Britain, who naturally assumed the leadership in the collective action at Geneva, two strains of opinion, or rather of feeling, predominated—sympathy with a weak and relatively defenceless people and an intense desire, nourished on the memory of war-time hopes and pledges, that the League should not fail in this third and, as it seemed, final effort to fulfil its peace-preserving mission.

In a speech before the Assembly on September 11, Sir Samuel Hoare, who had become Foreign Secretary in June, gave expression to this new mood of resolution in a speech in which, transforming the uncertainties and negations of fifteen years into direct and powerful positives, he accepted for his own countrymen the full responsibilities and obligations of the Covenant and called upon his colleagues to follow him: if they should fail to do so, he hinted, in a concluding sentence which was stunning in the sureness of its aim, the 'main bridge' between Britain and the Continent would be broken down.

Where, one may ask, is that bridge to be found? It is the bridge across the English Channel, the bridge that unites the people of Great Britain with the people of France. And in what does it consist? Its materials are formed out of the Covenant of the League of Nations. They are hewn from the quarry of Geneva. The two great democracies of Western Europe, if they are to remain side by side to face the vicissitudes of the post-war world, must be united, and prove to the

world that they are united, by a bond nobler and more
enduring than that of individual self-interest. They are
not Allies, in the old sense of the term. Nor are they
partners in a vague and ambiguous private 'entente'.
They are the representatives and for the time being, at
any rate, the most powerful and prominent representatives of the collective opinion and conscience of mankind in its struggle for the restraint of violence. Are
the French people, whose statesmen have so often and
so eloquently proclaimed the ideal of Peace Through
Law, ready to take action against the aggressor, their
own 'anonymous aggressor', of the Geneva Protocol?
Has their public spirit, their social consciousness, their
sense, not of the Rights but of the Duties of Man,
reached the point of spontaneous willingness to co-
operate with their neighbours against the common
disturber of the world's peace? Are they prepared to
join in the Hue and Cry? If so, the concordance of wills
among two strong free peoples will have created a
precedent which will assuredly ripen into Law and
through Law into appropriate institutions. If not, then
the sense of community, in reliance on which the
League was established, has been tried and found
wanting and, so far as the world as a whole is concerned, Force still reigns supreme. Finding no mansion
ready for her in Geneva, Law can but retire to those
individual realms where her authority is undisputed
and men pay her spontaneous homage. There, amid
the free and constitutional peoples of Western and
Northern Europe, of North America, of Switzerland
and Czechoslovakia and of the British overseas
Dominions, she must abide her time until the larger
company of the peoples, having bowed the knee to
brute Force and received her blows upon their backs,

are ready to face the full responsibilities of social life under modern conditions. Then, and only then, shall we be able to say of Law that 'her seat is the bosom of God, her voice the harmony of the world'.[1]

Have the post-war years, with which we have been concerned in these pages, even served to *tune the instruments* from which, as we would fain believe, that harmony will some day proceed?

[1] Hooker, *The Laws of Ecclesiastical Polity*, end of Book I.

CHAPTER III

WE have seen how the League came into existence and what a variety and indeed confusion of ideas and projects contributed to its making. We have attempted to trace its course amid the vicissitudes of international politics over a period of fifteen years. It remains to examine how the various parts of the machine have reacted to the strain that has been put upon them. How have the Council, the Assembly and the Secretariat, as designed in the Covenant, emerged from the test of experience?

THE COUNCIL

The Council of 1920 was, as has been made clear, already very different, in its composition and potentialities, from the 'inter-state Conference' of the Foreign Office Memorandum. The inclusion of four lesser states elected by the Assembly made it impossible for it ever to serve as a regular organ of conference for the Great Powers. In 1935 the number of lesser states in its membership stands at ten, and the point has already been reached at which the absence of any prospect of election to the Council is regarded as a distinct grievance. Of these ten seats two, those occupied by Poland and Spain, have come to be regarded as 'semi-permanent', and after each re-election the affront that would be involved in discontinuing the arrangement at any future time becomes potentially more serious. Seven of the others are filled, by a tacit understanding, in accordance with a system of rotation within certain recognised groups. Three are allotted to the Latin American states, who meet to decide, by a majority vote, communicated to the press, how they and the other League members are to cast their ballots at the Assembly. One is assigned to the Little Entente, another to the Northern States and another to the British Dominions.[1] The seventh was for some time considered earmarked for Asia, but with the election in 1934 of Turkey, who is a member of the 'Balkan Entente', it seemed to revert, at least partly, to Europe. A 'temporary seat' was established in 1933 for a three-years period for Portugal, who had felt particularly sensitive at her exclusion from any of the other groups. The special claims of China, who was refused re-election in 1934, are under consideration at the present time.

There is thus every indication that enlargement rather than contraction will be the steady tendency of the future. Perhaps, under the circumstances, this is all to the good. No longer available for its original purpose, the Council provides a useful school of experience for the representatives of the lesser states and ensures that, at any given moment, the Assembly should number in its ranks a fair sprinkling of delegates who have been through the more thorough training involved in Council membership.

So far as the Great Powers are concerned, the Council

---

[1] On the circumstances under which the Dominions' seat was first secured see Morley, *The Society of Nations*, p. 347.

reached its high-water mark in the few months that intervened between the election of the U.S.S.R. and the final departure of Japan. At that time there were six chairs set for Great Powers at the inner end of the horse-shoe table. All the seven Great Powers must, of course, be counted as potential members. Thus, if all goes well, the Council is likely to stabilise its membership, for the present, at seventeen or eighteen. What its numbers will be when, in the process of time, the Assembly membership is swollen by the admission of new sovereign states or dominions from the non-Western world it is too early to venture a prediction.[1]

[1] It is idle to go back upon the past. Nevertheless it would not be right to leave this subject without recording that the system of electing states to the Council is both vicious in principle and unwholesome in practice. The states thus elected are in no sense *representatives* of the states who had promised them their votes or of the Assembly as a whole. Their statesmen would be false to their own peoples, of whose interests they are trustees, if they represented anything but their own countries. It is true that when Canada stood for election to the Council in 1927 her principal delegate was able to claim with justice that he was (i) French by race and culture, (ii) specially interested in the question of minorities, (iii) completely detached and independent in his attitude towards European questions, (iv) a native of the American Continent and (v) a representative of a British Dominion. But the possession of this unusual panoply of qualifications did not alter the fact that, after his election, he and those who followed him in the same place remained responsible solely to the government, parliament and people of Canada. No observer of the Assembly will be disposed to deny that the desire not to sacrifice votes exercises a distinct, if subtle, influence—seldom for the good—upon the policy of the candidate-states during the pre-election period. After election day, which is the Monday in the second week of the Assembly, there is a perceptible improvement in the atmosphere. Since this is unhappily so, and is likely to remain so, the best way out would seem to be to make the elections as automatic as possible. It is perhaps worth while adding that the use of the terms 'democratic' and 'aristocratic' in this connexion is wholly misleading. There is nothing necessarily 'democratic' about a small state or 'aristocratic' about a Great Power. If Great Britain, the United States and France, the three democratic Great Powers, elected half the judges of the Hague Court and a dozen or more smaller non-democratic states elected the other half, to which of the two elections would the term 'democratic' better apply?

2 G

How does this curiously constituted body carry on its work?

It was intended by its framers, as we have seen, to be the pivot of the League, a sort of Executive Committee acting on behalf of the whole body of its members between the infrequent meetings of the larger body. Hence when the Covenant has occasion to mention any organ of the League for any particular duty, it is nearly always the Council which is named. It is only the more formal or more solemn duties which are reserved for the Assembly. Thus the Council has tasks to perform arising out of each of the five systems of which the Covenant is compounded.

Under the *Concert system*, which is the cause for its meeting more frequently than the Assembly and is indeed its *raison d'être*, it is called upon to deal with numerous questions such as would have fallen to the Great Powers alone before 1914. These are for the most part questions referred to it by the treaties of the immediate post-war period when its future composition had not yet been foreseen. The most conspicuous amongst them is the Minorities problem, which, in one form or another, has figured very frequently on the agenda of the Council.[1]

Under the *Monroe Doctrine system* it is called upon to implement the guarantee of territorial integrity and independence. In this capacity its duty is to 'advise

---

[1] When the 'Minorities Treaties' were drawn up in 1919 and their obligations 'placed under the guarantee' of the League, acting through the Council, it was certainly not contemplated that Poland and a Little Entente state would enjoy what is virtually permanent representation on that body. Where, as notably in the case of Czechoslovakia, this has had the effect of promoting closer co-operation and thus of clearing up difficulties at an earlier stage than would otherwise have been the case, this has been all to the good. It has not, however, always worked out in this way.

upon the means by which this obligation shall be fulfilled'. In the same way, it is the Council which has
the task, under Article VIII, of formulating plans for
the reduction of armaments.

Under *The Hague Conference system* it is the Council
which, normally, and always in the first instance, deals
with disputes submitted to the League.[1] It is also
charged, under Article XVI, § 2, with the application
of military sanctions to a Covenant-breaking state.

Under the *system of World Services*, it is to the
Council that the various agencies report. The technical
organisations of the League have no direct relationship
with the Assembly. They are Advisory Bodies to the
Council.

Finally, under the *system of the Hue and Cry*, it is
the Council which is called together when there is 'any
war or threat of war', even though this is 'a matter of
concern to the whole League'.

Some of the duties thus laid down are emergency
tasks. But, even when these are left out of consideration, enough is left to make the ordinary work of the
Council strangely variegated. The body of men assembled round the horse-shoe table are apt to change
their quality not only from meeting to meeting but as
they pass from one item to another of the same agenda.
Thus at one moment the Council will resemble a
Cabinet receiving a report as to the working of a
government department. At another it will be a sort

---

[1] Attempts have even been made by pertinacious litigants to induce
the Council to deal with disputes in no sense 'likely to lead to a rupture',
in other words, to act as a general international tribunal or 'a kind of
court of appeal' reviewing the decisions of national courts in cases in
which foreign governments have been involved. See on this the Council
proceedings in 1935 in connexion with the claims made against Great
Britain by the Finnish and Swiss governments respectively.

of Conciliation Board, attempting to arrive at a *modus vivendi* between two disputants. At another it will be a Diplomatic Conference dealing with some issue of high policy such as would have been handled in pre-war days by the Concert of the Powers. And finally, on rare and solemn occasions, it will put these every-day concerns aside and will become the embodiment of the higher morality and the conscience of mankind.

It is obvious, of course, that in practice the distinc-tion between these different rôles is blurred and that it is the same human beings who attempt to shoulder these multifarious responsibilities. It is equally clear to every close student of the League that, while every activity of the Council reacts upon the rest, its total activities at any given moment are intimately affected by the general condition of international politics. Like the League as a whole, the Council represents 'the maximum of co-operation at any given moment'. The general climate of the Council-room influences the proceedings at every turn and may have unexpected bearings on the handling of problems in which no out-sider could detect the least speck of controversy.

Nevertheless, for the conduct of its work, it has been necessary to assume that the Council, as its name implies, is an organic body—that is to say, a body expressing a common consciousness and a common purpose—in other words, something resembling a Cabinet. Cabinets often do their work through Com-mittees. The Council of the League has adopted an analogous system—that of appointing a single *rap-porteur*.[1] A *rapporteur* may be described, for those un-familiar with Continental practice, as a personage who

---

[1] For certain purposes, both general and occasional, the Committee system is also employed.

combines secretarial duties with the dignity of full Committee membership. Thus his 'report' carries with it a considerably larger measure of authority than that of a servant of the Committee. At the beginning of every session the various standing items as the agenda are divided up amongst the different members.[1]

The duty of the *rapporteur* is to draw up a statement for the information of his colleagues and to formulate his conclusions, which generally take the form of a Resolution. The public meetings of the Council usually include some half a dozen reports of this kind. When they are of a routine character they are taken as read, copies being simultaneously distributed to the press. When the matter at issue is of more immediate interest the prepared statement is read in full, followed by a translation into English or French, as the case may be. Comments, generally brief in character, are sometimes made by other Council members. But there

---

[1] The list adopted for the Council, as reconstituted after the elections at the 1935 Assembly, was as follows:

Financial Questions . . .	Australia
Economic Questions . . .	Poland
Transit Questions	U.S.S.R.
Health Questions	Denmark
Legal Questions	Italy
Budgetary and Administrative Questions	Turkey
Mandates	Roumania
Minorities	Spain
Disarmament	Argentine
Danzig	United Kingdom
Intellectual Co-operation . . .	France
Opium	Portugal
Traffic in Women and Children . .	Chile
Child Welfare and Social Questions .	Chile
Refugees	Ecuador
Assyrians	Spain
Irak-Iran	Italy

The last three questions are of a temporary nature. The others constitute the standing items.

is seldom anything in the nature of a debate. For one thing, it is not easy to debate whilst *sitting*: the tone of an ordinary Council meeting, however large the audience, inevitably remains that of a Committee. Thus the public proceedings of this peculiar body, which is not a parliament but a sort of Cabinet meeting in public, convey an impression of artificiality, unavoidable under the circumstances. In point of fact the real deliberation is done at earlier stages.[1]

What are those stages? Let us trace them backwards from the public session.

Before the Council meets in public it meets in private. These so-called 'private sessions' are private only in name. Their proceedings are published in due course in the *Official Journal* and those present include a miscellaneous assemblage of delegates, experts and Secretariat officials. No difficulty is experienced by journalists in obtaining an account—not necessarily an official or objective account—of what has taken place.[2] Behind the 'private meeting' lies the 'secret meeting'. When this is of an official character it takes place in the Secretary-General's room, with only the Secretary-General, the Director of the Political Section,

---

[1] There have been occasions when public meetings of the Council have been really animated, but these have generally been in connexion with a dispute. Encounters of this kind took place between the representatives of China and Japan in the autumn of 1931, and between the representatives of Hungary and Roumania in the 'Optants' dispute in 1923 and the following years. Herr Stresemann on one or two occasions deliberately used a public Council meeting as a sounding-board.

[2] The 'private meeting' at Geneva remains a problem, owing to the inevitable differences in the habits and standards of those participating in them, particularly as regards discretion and objectivity. Wireless listeners can, in fact, on occasion hear detailed reports, or so-called reports, of their proceedings within a few hours of the close of the meeting. Thus the less communicative parties are liable to be penalised for their virtue. Some change in these arrangements is certainly called for.

the Council members and a very few of their closest advisers present. But there are, of course, many other kinds of secret meetings, particularly between the representatives of the Great Powers on the Council.

But behind these meetings during the Council sessions there are the steps involved in the drawing-up of the reports.

How are Council reports drawn up? Here we enter the realm of conjecture. But it is clear that we are touching the heart of the difficulty involved in the fact that the Council combines a number of separate functions.

In so far as it is a body supervising the working of a number of World Services, we may surmise that its reports are drawn up in close collaboration (to say the least) with the corresponding section of the Secretariat. What special competence has the Roumanian Government on the subject of Mandates? Or the Chilean Government on the subject of Child Welfare? Or the Portuguese Government on the subject of Opium? No doubt it is right and proper that no mandatory power should report on mandates and no poppy-growing power on opium. But it is hardly to be supposed that the governments just mentioned, even if they had the desire, would possess the experience or the staff required in order to make their reports an independent contribution to the subjects assigned to them. Thus, in point of fact, the supervision by the Council over the World Services carried on through the League almost inevitably falls back into the hands of the secretariats of those services themselves. If there is effective supervision, as in some cases there undoubtedly is, it is exercised by other and less formal means. It is both too difficult and too delicate to exercise it through a political body, such as the Council is and must be.

When, however, the task assigned to the *rapporteur* is political in character and thus belongs to the 'Concert' functions of the Council, the situation is evidently more complicated. The matter cannot simply be turned over to the Secretariat in the reliance that an adequate document will be ready at the appointed time. Before the document can be drafted there must be an agreement between the powers concerned: and, in order to arrive at such an agreement, there must be negotiation. But *who* is to conduct the negotiation, or at least to gather up its threads and to put the material into shape for the Council meeting? If the technical reports pass through the hands of the technical sections of the Secretariat, is there no secretariat personnel available for this other and more difficult kind of 'reporting'? It is here that we begin to understand the importance attached by the governments, particularly the governments of the Great Powers, to the higher posts of the Secretariat. For the small group of men occupying these posts is necessarily in a pivotal position as regards the handling of political issues within the scope of the League. They are, so to speak, the natural *liaison* officers between Geneva and the Foreign Offices—not the Foreign Offices in general but the particular Ministry of Foreign Affairs of the state of which each is a national. Thus shortly before the opening of the Council session it has become usual for visits to be paid by Secretariat officials to their respective national capitals. What transpires at these visits is neither known to the public at the time nor recorded in the published documents of the League. But that such visits are a necessary part of the preparation for the work of the Council, or, let us say it boldly, of the standing Conference of the Great Powers, is clear from the whole development of the last ten years.

This, however, raises an issue which carries us beyond the Council and must be left aside till we consider the Secretariat.

THE ASSEMBLY

When the delegates to the first Assembly came together on November 15, 1920, they had no previous experience to guide them in their deliberations. The Council had behind it the Supreme Council of the Allies, and behind that the shadowy outlines of the Concert of Europe. But a standing Conference of the majority of the states of the world, great and small alike, was something entirely new. At the Peace Conference, as at the Congress of Vienna, the smaller states had been deliberately kept in the shade. The system of the Concert had discouraged the lesser European powers from any active assertion of their interest in issues of general policy, whilst the Monroe Doctrine had certainly not promoted a lively sense of international political interdependence amongst the Chancelleries of the Americas. Moreover, there was no available guide to aid the members in organising their proceedings. The pre-war diplomatic Congress was of too specialised a type to serve as a model, and the unofficial gatherings which had concerned themselves before the war with larger questions hardly lent themselves to imitation.[1] Thus it might well have seemed doubtful whether the standing Congress which Presi-

---

[1] Compare the remarks on this subject in the Foreign Office Memorandum on page 207 above.

dent Wilson had named 'the Assembly' would discover
any real sense of unity in its ranks at all, and further,
even in that event, whether it would turn its new-found
esprit de corps to any useful purpose.

That these doubts were swiftly and triumphantly
dispelled was due, apart from more general causes, in
the main to the energy, the public spirit and the
statesmanlike equipment of the leading delegates of
some of the smaller European states. M. Hymans of
Belgium, who was elected to the Presidency, had at
his side Mr Branting of Sweden, Dr. Nansen of Norway, Mr Motta of Switzerland, Dr. Benes of Czechoslovakia, to mention only the most outstanding figures
in a group on which citizens of Great Powers have not
seldom had occasion to look with envy. They and their
fellows (amongst whom Lord Robert Cecil, as delegate
of South Africa, must not be forgotten) were determined to make the Assembly a reality. And they were
aided in their efforts by the Secretariat, which not only
provided them, in its 'technical' activities, with ample
material for discussion but had also recently, at the
Brussels Financial Conference, made a valuable experiment in the working of congress procedure.

Thus the first meeting proved decisive in fixing the
place of the Assembly in the scheme of the League.
The Foreign Office Memorandum had contemplated a
meeting every four years, on the analogy of the British
Imperial Conference. The Covenant merely laid it
down that it should 'meet at stated intervals'. But
after the First Assembly it became recognised that the
'stated' interval should be annual, that the date should
be September and that the session should cover a
period of some three weeks, including both plenary
sessions and meetings of Committees.

The procedure which was thus established has altered very little from year to year. The first week is devoted, after the opening formalities, to a general debate, the material for which is, formally speaking, provided by the Secretary-General's report on the work of the League during the past year.[1] The second week is devoted to Committees, the Assembly being divided up for this purpose into six bodies, on each of which every delegation is represented. During the third week the Committees conclude their labours and their reports are presented in plenary sessions, generally with a minimum of discussion.

A few words must be said about these Assembly Committees. To begin with, their proceedings are public.[2] Thus for the first time onlookers and newspaper readers throughout the world have been enabled to gain an insight into some of the inner workings of international politics. For the Committee discussions are necessarily both more detailed and more realistic in tone than the speeches made in plenary session. It is here that high-sounding professions of faith and vaguely idealistic declarations of policy are brought sharply up against the test of reality. It is here too that the defenders of 'things as they are', which sometimes include disreputable vested interests, find themselves exposed to cross-examination by reformers who have fortified their intentions by a close study of

[1] At the Second Assembly in 1921 the President, after consultation with the Secretary-General, made proposals which would have resulted in the abandonment of this general debate. Thanks to the prompt interposition of M. Hymans and Lord Robert Cecil these proposals were not adopted. A similar attempt was made by the President of the Third Assembly and was again successfully resisted by Lord Robert Cecil. Since then the practice has never been challenged.

[2] Recourse, is, of course, occasionally had to Sub-Committees sitting in private.

the relevant facts. Thus pertinacious defenders of good causes, with the public opinion of the world at their back, can succeed on occasion in provoking that 'mobilisation of shame' which is the real sanction of the League, whether in regard to peace or war or to less dramatic issues, such as the welfare of young people or the traffic in drugs.[1]

Both these instances are drawn from the work of one particular Committee, the Fifth. Since each Committee has developed its own technique and its own *esprit de corps*, it will be best to specify them individually. The First Committee deals with Legal Questions. It was long presided over by Signor Scialoja, under the influence of whose wisdom and wit it combined the learning and *camaraderie* of an academic seminar with the gravity of an official meeting for the discussion of living issues of policy. The Second Committee is concerned with the 'technical' work of the League, in particular with financial and economic questions. The Third Committee, which has been in abeyance since 1931, concentrates its attention on disarmament. The Fourth Committee supervises League finance and has

---

[1] One reference may be permitted. See *Records of the* 1923 *Assembly, Proceedings of the Fifth Committee*, p. 50. In this connexion regret may be expressed that the Committee proceedings of the Assembly are so inadequately preserved: a full record would have been much more enlightening for students of the League and of international affairs than that of the Plenary Sessions. The reader can judge this for himself if he will consult the proceedings for 1930, when for once the details were taken down and reproduced verbatim. See especially the 255 pages there devoted to the Fourth Committee. Official summaries of international meetings are bound, from the nature of the case, to err on the side of discretion. The same is true of the *Monthly Summary* and other similar League publications.—It is worth noting that representatives of non-member states are readily admitted to take part in the proceedings of Assembly Committees, as of other League Committees. The United States Government has participated in their work on more than one occasion.

developed a very special personality of its own. The Fifth devotes itself to social and humanitarian questions and the Sixth to 'political questions', such as mandates, minorities and the admission of non-members.

This brief account of the Assembly's procedure should be sufficient to explain the nature and scope of its activities as they have developed over the fifteen-years period. Its work can be conveniently grouped under four heads.

In the first place, it exercises a general supervision over all the work of the League. This control extends even over matters, such as minorities and mandates, explicitly entrusted to the Council either by the Covenant or by other treaties. The procedure for this is simple but ingenious. The Assembly, on a motion by one or more states, has only to decide that a particular matter mentioned in the Secretary-General's report should be referred to the appropriate Committee for closer examination. Norway proposed this as regards mandates in 1920 and the practice has been regularly continued. In this way League activities which particularly concern the Great Powers can be brought up for scrutiny and criticism at the Assembly. In theory, this might seem to involve possibilities of conflict between the Assembly and the Council. In practice, however, any overt collision has been avoided by careful handling on both sides. There can, however, be no doubt that, as regards certain spheres of League activity, the Assembly exercises a greater controlling influence than the Council. But its vigilance in this respect is considerably hampered by the shortness of the time available for the discussion of each particular activity, by the very unequal degrees of knowledge and public spirit among the delegates, and by the fact that, in practice, the Assembly Committees generally have little influence over the choice either of their chairman or of the *rapporteur* who introduces the subject into the Committee and thus largely determines the main lines of the discussion.[1]

The second sphere of the Assembly's activity is its control over the finances of the League. In this department it has successfully encroached on what was originally expected to be a prerogative of the Council.

The budget of the League for the coming calendar year (or, in other words, the Estimates) is drawn up by the Secretary-General early in the year after consultation with the various heads of departments. It is then passed on to a committee of five, known as the Supervisory Committee, which scrutinises it item by item in the light of the explanations of the Secretary-General. In its amended form the budget is then forwarded to the governments for their examination before being laid before their delegates in the Fourth Committee in September.[2]

It will be seen that the pivotal position in this complicated process is occupied by the Supervisory Com-

[1] For an instance of this see Morley, p. 528.

[2] Previous to 1930 the budget was submitted to the Council at its June meeting. When the Council decided to meet every four, instead of every three, months it was found to be administratively impossible to have the budget ready for it by May, and the Council, in the words of the Secretary-General, thus abandoned 'the opportunity of presenting observations on the budget'. It had not, in practice, availed itself of this opportunity, since this would have involved doing the work twice over, the governments represented on the Council being also represented on the Fourth Committee of the Assembly. In the case of the International Labour Office budget a double examination actually takes place, since this is discussed by the Governing Body of the Office before being submitted to the Assembly.

mittee, which stands between the Secretary-General
on the one hand and the Council and the Assembly
on the other. Thus the constitutional position of the
Supervisory Committee is the key to the control of
League finance. Under the original arrangement, made
in 1920, the Supervisory Committee was appointed
by the Council. In 1928, however, Mr Hambro, the
Norwegian delegate in the Fourth Committee, succeeded in carrying a motion transferring the right of
appointment to the Assembly and this was subsequently confirmed by the necessary unanimous vote in
the plenary meeting. Since that date the 'power of the
purse' has been fully in the possession of the Assembly,
or rather of the Fourth Committee, which jealously
controls all fresh expenditure and keeps a specially
watchful eye on salaries. The Chairman of the Supervisory Committee and the Secretary-General [1] are both
present at its meetings, the former taking the more
prominent part in the discussion.[2]

There is, however, one shadow in this picture which
cannot be passed over. This is the tendency of the
members of the Assembly to fall into arrears in their
contributions and the reluctance of their colleagues to
take strong measures to bring them into line. There is
perhaps no other department of League activity which
is so sensitive to the general international atmosphere
as that of the Treasurer. Thus on March 31, 1934, no
less than twenty-six members of the League were in

[1] The Director of the International Labour Office and the Registrar
of the Permanent Court of International Justice are also present when
their respective budgets are under consideration.

[2] The chairmanship of the Supervisory Committee has been held since
1926 by Mr Osusky, who has regularly attended the Assembly as the
second delegate of Czechoslovakia. But he does not sit in the Fourth
Committee in that capacity. Mr Hambro has been a member of the
Supervisory Committee since 1931.

arrears in their subscriptions for 1933.[1]

The Assembly has also, on occasion, essayed a more ambitious task. It has attempted to act as a law-making body—in other words, to assume the part of a diplomatic conference and to draft international treaties or conventions. It has done this, so far, on four occasions. In 1923 the Third Committee spent the bulk of its time in drawing up the terms of the Treaty of Mutual Guarantees. In 1924 the First and Third Committees collaborated in putting together the Geneva Protocol. The conditions under which the Assembly of 1928 framed the 'General Act for the Peaceful Settlement of Disputes' have already been described.[2] Finally, in 1925 the Sixth Committee, working on a draft laid before it by the British Delegation, drew up a Convention on Slavery.

Three of these documents have not had a very happy history, and this is undoubtedly due, in part, to the conditions under which they were drawn up. The Assembly is not, in all respects, a suitable body for work of this character, which properly belongs to a Conference of delegates specially convened for the particular purpose in hand. When, as in the case of the Protocol, the task is of a general character such as properly belongs to the Assembly, it would be better to spread the discussion over two sessions, according to the system in operation at the International Labour Conference. In this way the resulting document would

---

[1] An appreciable improvement, however, was reported to the Fourth Committee in 1935. The details as to arrears were given in a reply by Mr Eden to a parliamentary question on April 24, 1934. Of the twenty-six states in question, fifteen were in Latin America, one in North America, seven in Europe, two in Africa and one in Asia. The two Latin-American member-states *not* included in the list were Haiti and Mexico. (Ecuador was not yet a member.)

[2] See p. 379 above.

not only be improved in detail but would embody the mature reflection of the governments and peoples. The notion that shock-tactics can ever succeed in matters of this kind is as dangerous as it is mistaken. There is indeed no surer way of undermining confidence than to adopt methods which lead the peoples to suspect that their representatives are being exposed to the danger of giving far-reaching pledges at unguarded moments.

The last and by far the most important function of the Assembly is to provide a forum for the discussion of world affairs. The general debate which takes place during the first week provides a unique occasion, such as was nowhere available under the pre-war system, for the expression of the opinions and conscience of the peoples represented there. During that week in September Geneva is the best sounding-board in the world, and long and honourable is the list of Premiers, Foreign Ministers and statesmen otherwise distinguished (such as Mr Balfour) who have made use of it.[1] The cumulative effect of the speeches in such a debate is to provide a sort of bird's-eye view of the condition of the world, both political and psychological, at that particular moment. No doubt there is always necessarily something unreal about the general sentiments which it is mostly thought proper to enunciate on such occasions. Banality and hypocrisy are apt to rub shoulders on the Geneva platform. Nevertheless, when all allowances have been made, the net result of the Assembly debate is always both instructive and inspiring: the proportion between the two ingredients

---

[1] It is significant that none of the so-called 'dictators' has ever made use of the opportunity, available to most of them, of speaking from the Assembly platform. Marshal Pilsudski is indeed the only one of the major figures amongst them who ever found his way to Geneva. But his visit was not during the Assembly session.

varies, of course, very considerably from year to year.

But even when, as in the period following 1931, the stream of inspiration runs low, the opportunity afforded to the lesser states for meeting and taking counsel together has a value which is not to be despised. It is thanks to these potentialities of inspiration inherent in its universal character rather than to its formal quality as the 'sovereign body' in the League that the Assembly has steadily gained in influence within the circle of the League as the years have gone on. Not only has it tended—not always wisely—to impose its will on the Council, but its authority has even been invoked in spheres which in the early years of the League were considered to be entirely reserved for the Council. Thus paragraph 9 of Article XV, under which disputes could be transferred from the Council to the Assembly, remained a dead letter for twelve years until the Chinese Government made use of it in February 1932. This did not indeed result in any effective action against the aggression of Japan, but at least it secured that the discussion of the report of the Commission of Inquiry took place before the Assembly and that the vote endorsing its conclusions was taken by that body. A similar procedure was adopted in the dispute between Bolivia and Paraguay, which led to the summoning of another 'Extraordinary Assembly' in November 1934. Thus when the Assembly of 1935 found itself faced with a situation when a breach of the Covenant seemed imminent it was under no temptation to leave the whole matter to the Council, as contemplated in Article XVI. On the contrary, fortified by the general debate and by the mobilisation of world opinion to which it had given rise, it was ready to face its responsibilities.

Large and diverse though it is, changeable in its moods and unwieldy in its motions, the Assembly has now developed a continuing life of its own. If the Council has remained a Conference, the Assembly is no longer a Congress. There is no word adequate to describe what it has become. It is not a parliament or any other organ of a system of world-government. It is simply the first outward and visible manifestation of the authority of the Rule of Law in the world.

THE SECRETARIAT

The Assembly and the Council are intermittent in their activity. Their members are in Geneva to-day and gone to-morrow. When they have retired from the scene, carrying away with them the crowd of journalists and the miscellaneous throng which is attracted to League meetings on great days to see and listen to the 'stars', the Secretariat remains to put into shape the result of their deliberations.

What are its functions? And what judgment, in the light of fifteen years' experience, are we to pass upon the manner in which they are discharged?

The simplest way of setting out to answer these questions will be to concentrate first on the position of the Secretary-General and to examine it in the light of the fivefold functions of the League.

The Secretary-General is, *firstly*, the Secretary to the standing Concert of the powers. The nearest British analogy for his position, though by no means exact, is that of the Secretary of the Cabinet. He might also be described as the Permanent Secretary of an international Dominions Office.

In the second place, he is in a pivotal position for the exercise of the Guarantee function of the League. He is the Secretary of the Council when it meets to 'advise upon the means by which this obligation shall be fulfilled'.

Thirdly, he controls the levers of the machinery which sets in motion the Hue and Cry. In this connexion he is specifically mentioned in Article XI.

Fourthly, he is the Secretary for the standing machinery of conciliation set up under Article XV, resembling in this respect the Registrar of the Permanent Court of International Justice.

Lastly, he is a kind of super-secretary—the term 'Secretary-General' is particularly appropriate in this connexion—of the secretariats of the World Services operating under the League. In this he corresponds to the Permanent Secretary of the British Treasury in his capacity as Head of the Civil Service.

When we analyse more closely the nature of his activity in these various spheres we find that, in essence, his work is really twofold. On the one hand, he is a diplomat dealing with the most delicate and confidential issues of international politics. On the other hand, he is an administrator, responsible for the conduct of an office containing between six and seven hundred employees.[1] In each of these capacities the Secretary-General is in a position to wield a very considerable measure of power. It is indeed because the Secretariat is a centre of power, a place where decisions involving grave responsibilities are necessarily taken, and taken frequently, that it has come to fill such an important place in the scheme of international politics. So important indeed did it become that at a certain

---

[1] The figure in the 1936 budget is 646. In 1931 it was 699.

stage in the development of the League it could be described, by a writer who had closely watched it at work, as having 'executive functions' and as 'approaching' the position of 'an international cabinet'.[1] Since those words were written the tide of power has somewhat receded from Geneva, partly no doubt because of the attention drawn to its existence.[2] Nevertheless the Secretary-General continues to occupy a key-position in international politics.

In the League as originally designed, functioning as a co-operative association under the harmonious leadership of the Great Powers, this duality in the work of the Secretary-General, though it must always have rendered it difficult, would not have been an insuperable obstacle to its successful accomplishment. But the development of the League and of international politics has been very different from what was contemplated in 1919. The League does not include all the Great Powers: and those that it does include have proved to be competitive rather than co-operative in a large part of their mutual relations. As a result, the Secretary-General has been placed in an almost impossible position. On the one hand he is a diplomat constantly engaged in handling issues arising out of the rivalries between the Great Powers—not to speak of the others—whilst on the other hand he is at the

[1] Morley, p. 307, in a revealing chapter entitled 'The Executive Function in the Secretariat'.

[2] The controversy centring round the political activities of the high officials in the Secretariat, which culminated in the Fourth Committee debates at the 1930 Assembly, undoubtedly made the Foreign Offices more circumspect and thus interrupted the flow of power to Geneva. Moreover, whether as a result of accident or design, what may be described as the second generation of the holders of the key posts in the Secretariat has, as a whole, distinctly less driving force than its predecessors. But personal idiosyncrasies are not a safe guide for a judgment on constitutional tendencies.

head of an international Civil Service established on
the assumption that these rivalries would cease, or at
least that they would be kept within strict limits so
far as the League was concerned. Under these circumstances it has been inevitable that one part of his work
should have reacted upon the other, and also, the
world being what it is, that, in this entanglement
between the 'political' and the 'technical', the latter
should have come off second best.

Experience has in fact decisively refuted those who
believed that there was some innate virtue in 'international institutions' which would preserve them unspotted from the corruption of 'high politics'. The
contrary has proved to be the case. Except for the
relatively small group of subjects where neither the
material interests nor the prestige of member-states
or their representatives can be brought into play, the
technical sections of the Secretariat have not been able
to ignore political, not to speak of personal, considerations. This does not mean that, in the departments
so affected, useful work has not been done or that
the officials immediately concerned have not devoted
themselves to their task in the spirit of the original
Covenant. There has been a great deal of unflagging
zeal and entirely disinterested enthusiasm in all ranks
of the staff of the Secretariat throughout the course
of its vicissitudes down to the present day. There
have even been martyrs who, in their dedication to
the cause of peace, overtaxed the frail resources of
their strength. Nevertheless, all things considered, it
cannot to-day be maintained that the failure of the
original scheme [1] for the co-ordination of all World
Services at Geneva has been an unmitigated mis-

_____
[1] See pp. 193 and 204 above.

fortune. The International Labour Organisation has
certainly gained in morale as well as in independence
through its detachment from the political activities
of the League. And perhaps it is just as well that the
Universal Postal Union should have remained un-
disturbed in its seclusion and that no organic link
should have been established between its Congress and
the Council of the League.

The power of the Secretary-General and of his immediate advisers arises principally from two simple
facts—first, that he is the servant not of one master
but of many, and secondly, that these masters are
absentees for the greater part of the year.

As a servant of the Council the Secretary-General
has fourteen superiors, and as a servant of the Assembly
over fifty. Neither of these bodies, as we have seen, is
truly organic. Neither has a common consciousness or
a common will. Thus the Secretary-General and the
so-called 'international Civil Service' which is under
his orders are, so to speak, suspended in mid-air. They
are permanent officials without a Minister to supervise
their activities or to cover their blunders or to defend
them from unjust attacks,[1] and without a House of
Commons with its daily sheaf of questions bearing on
the details of their work. Such energy as they put into

---

[1] In 1924, towards the close of the first phase of the League's life, it
seemed as though the Council was becoming an organic body. This is
best brought out by the speech delivered in the Assembly on September
10, 1924, by M. Hymans, who was President of the Council at the time.
He rose to reply to certain criticisms made in the discussion on the working of the League and spoke very much in the spirit of a Minister replying
at the end of a House of Commons debate. He unhesitatingly made use
of the first person plural when speaking of the Council and even mentioned by name the Secretariat official, Mr Colban, the conduct of whose
work had been criticised. But with the change in the character of the
Council this sense of common responsibility diminished and the Secretariat was left with no official defender.

it must be generated from within. They can benefit neither by the continuing momentum which carries forward the public services, whether civil or military, of an organised modern state nor by the more intimate *esprit de corps* which animates a like-minded group of men dedicated to a common task. Their superiors indeed, so far from inspiring or supporting or even excusing them, are more apt to regard them as a legitimate target for criticism—criticism which very often, in its ignorance and small-mindedness, reveals complete lack of familiarity not only with the details but with the very nature of their work. Under these conditions, confronted with superiors who are, for the most part, neither internationally minded nor well informed, nor—it may be added—conspicuously industrious, it has been almost inevitable that the Secretariat, in sheer self-defence, should have been tempted to turn these deficiencies to its own account. The natural way of doing this was to make itself useful to those who had a will of their own and indispensable to those who had not.

What this has meant in practice can be made clear when we look more closely into the details of its work.

The Secretariat may be described as the residuary legatee of the power which flows into Geneva from the various centres of government. When this power is not used by those to whom it constitutionally belongs, it automatically reverts to the Secretariat. The elements of this power are of four different kinds.

There is, first, the power which comes from the work of *negotiation*. This arises, as we have seen, from the fact that all decisions of the Council and the Assembly require unanimity. In order to secure unanimity there must be negotiation. If there is no one else ready to

undertake the task in the time available—and the
time-factor is an all-important element in the Geneva
system with its stated meetings at recurring periods—
it falls to the Secretariat. It is all the more likely to be
remitted to it because, apart from their wide personal
acquaintance derived from their central situation,
Secretariat officials are familiar with the Geneva
machine and have acquired a mastery of the niceties of
drafting that are needed on such occasions. Thus it is
easy and natural for individual governments to make
use of their services as intermediaries. If it be asked
on behalf of whom these services are undertaken, the
question is hard to answer. The conventional reply, 'On
behalf of the League', only carries the difficulty a stage
farther back: for what, in this connexion, *is* the League?
Clearly this usurpation of the work of diplomacy by
the high officials of the League opens the door to much
casuistry in respect of motives and to considerable
possibilities of abuse in practice.[1]

The second source of the Secretariat's power is in
the domain of procedure. Procedure is always the
stronghold of a secretary, whether he be the clerk of a
parish council or of the House of Commons. But this
everyday knowledge of 'the tricks of the trade' is
particularly formidable in the international sphere
where the members of the Committee or larger body
concerned are none of them doing their work according
to familiar rules and are for the most part labouring
under a certain sense of helplessness. Moreover there
is always a proportion of new-comers who are particularly susceptible to the spell of the *habitué*. Thus the

---

[1] For an instance of such casuistry see the anonymous remarks
reported by Professor Rappard in *Proceedings of the Fourth Committee*,
1930, p. 73.

Secretariat can usually exercise a silent domination over the meeting in regard to all those apparently secondary matters on which the results of a Conference so greatly depend—the fixing of the order of the agenda, the decision as to how long the meeting shall last, the selection of the Chairman and *rapporteur*, the drafting of the resolutions and of the report and, last but not least, the decision as to the agenda for the next meeting. Under the old diplomacy, as we saw on an earlier page, all this was left to the improvisation of the moment. To-day it is in the custodianship of a body of Conference experts. But who is keeping custody over the custodians?

The third way in which the Secretariat exercises power is through being on the spot to deal with emergencies. Normally speaking, the Assembly is annually in session for three weeks out of the fifty-two, and the Council, apart from its September session, for two or three. Thus during some forty-six weeks of the year the Secretariat is left to its own resources. It is a body of working officials with no chief to consult. Now, as everyone knows, moments arise in every office, as in life generally, when an immediate decision is required and when the postponement of such a decision is itself a decision. In these conditions an official endowed with driving power will assume his responsibilities and take an initiative, while others, more circumspect or perhaps more indifferent, will seek refuge in procrastination. It is through the cumulative effect of such emergency decisions, whether positive or negative, that the tradition and morale of an international office are built up.[1]

[1] On this, and on the general issue discussed in the above paragraphs, see the article by the Director of the International Labour Office, Mr

One further element in the power of the Secretariat must be mentioned. This is its knowledge of the League as a whole and its possibilities of controlling what the world outside shall know of its working. Individual delegates, whether to the Council or the Assembly or to 'technical' Committees, are apt to know only the subjects assigned to them. They are usually presented —often at the last moment—with a substantial *dossier* sufficient to keep them busy till the end of their visit to Geneva. The number of persons who have a thorough knowledge of the League, who can see its particular activities in relation to the whole, is limited. It includes certain officials of Foreign Offices, the resident government delegates and 'Consuls-General', if they have the necessary curiosity and public spirit, and the resident journalists. Contact with the latter is maintained by the League through what is known as the Information Section, which was at one time the largest section in the Secretariat.[1] The vigilant control necessarily exercised by the Secretariat over all League publications is another factor which is not to be disregarded.[2]

We have analysed the constitutional conditions which have prevented the Secretariat from developing into a Civil Service of the ordinary national type. If we now glance briefly at its composition and method of appointment, we shall be in a better position to understand the peculiarities of its working.

H. B. Butler, in *The Journal of Public Administration*, October 1932, esp. p. 381 ff. See also the article by Sir Eric Drummond, the first Secretary-General of the League, in the same journal for April 1931.

[1] See the figures for 1932 given in Morley, p. 282.

[2] Compare the previous remarks on this subject on p. 286 (publications) and p. 460 (verbatim reports). Another difficulty in the way of students of the League is that its publications are often allowed to remain out of print. Complete sets of the *Monthly Summary*, for instance, are unobtainable.

There is no system of examinations for appointments to the Secretariat. The qualifications required vary so much, according to the section in which there is a vacancy, that no standard test could have been devised. The first officials were recruited from amongst those who had had special experience of international co-operation during the war and the system of individual selection thus adopted was adhered to later. But there was another reason why it was difficult to contemplate a competitive entrance system. The Secretariat is international and therefore open to nationals of all members of the League, and indeed to nationals of non-member states also.[1] It would have been impossible to devise an examination which would have been a fair and equal test for all potential candidates. On what principle, then, should appointments be made?

Had the object been to build up an efficient service with the maximum of homogeneity and *esprit de corps* attainable under the circumstances, there was only one possible method. This was to limit appointments *in principle*[2] to nationals of states which themselves had a Civil Service affording the necessary guarantees of competence and integrity and to assess the claims of candidates in the light of this standard. Public Administration is now recognised both as a science and an art and it would have been appropriate to give it international recognition in the building-up of the League service. Incidentally, this would have given a

---

[1] There have been a few United States members on the League staff throughout.

[2] Sufficient latitude would of course be allowed under such a system to permit of the occasional appointment of suitable persons from other states. But the persons so appointed would then have been selected strictly on their merits and without reference to their governments.

lively stimulus to the cause of Civil Service Reform in numerous countries. Needless to say, this was not the policy put forward, or even dreamt of, by the Secretary-General's superiors. They did indeed proclaim the principle of an international Civil Service, but they then proceeded to prescribe methods which rendered its practical application virtually impossible. For they emphasised the desirability of making the Secretariat as widely representative of the League membership as possible: and this demand for representation has been carried year by year to such a length that delegates have almost come to claim the presence of a certain proportion of their nationals in the Secretariat as one of the prerogatives of membership.

From this it is but one step for the governments to exercise an influence over the appointments themselves. In fact, though not in form, this is what has happened for a considerable proportion of the higher posts. It has come to be regarded as axiomatic that a member of the Secretariat occupying a responsible position should be *persona grata* to the government of the state of which he is a national. How else, it is asked, could he be expected to be a serviceable agency of *liaison*? In this way there has been a subtle distortion of the meaning of the relevant article of the Covenant. This lays it down that 'the secretaries and the staff of the secretariat shall be appointed by the Secretary-General *with the approval of the Council*'.[1] In fact what now generally happens, in the case of the higher posts, is that the appointment is made with the approval of *the member of the Council concerned*. In other words, the Secretary-General, under pressure from individual governments, has abdicated his right

---

[1] Article VI, § 3: italics inserted.

of free choice and has permitted himself to enter into discussion with the governments as to the choice of his personnel. The evils in which this has resulted are evident. The official is bound by a double loyalty from the beginning—all the more so if, as may easily be the case, he has a short-term appointment at the conclusion of which he is dependent on the favour of his government. Such officials are, for all practical purposes, seconded from their national service for a period of work at Geneva. It is idle to expect that a loyal and united staff can be built up in this way. The root of the evil, of course, is that the Council is not an organic body and that the Secretary-General could not therefore have relied on its support if he had laid the question of principle before it. The conditions which have thus resulted clearly call for reform.

The need for a change in the present system arises, however, not only from the administrative problem which has just been analysed but also from more deeply-lying psychological considerations into which this is not the place to enter. It is sufficient to say that the experience of fifteen years has shown that on the political side, at any rate, where no international professional bond has been formed,[1] prolonged activity at Geneva tends to exercise what can only be described as a mechanising influence. The cosmopolitan *milieu* is the reverse of life-giving. Perpetual adaptation to external standards and stimuli, unrefreshed by contact with the moral forces inherent in genuine community life, ends by confusing the intelligence, paralysing the will and dulling the faculties of the soul. This, rather than any inherent defect in the individual human beings concerned, explains the torpor which has come

[1] See p. 19 above.

over Geneva during the successive violations of the Covenant in recent years. Experience has shown that those who live under such conditions for a period of years often reach a saturation point after which their work declines in quality. At this stage they develop an instinctive mechanism of self-protection which leads them to cultivate deliberate insensibility, or what is often called in Geneva *sang-froid*. Such officials become automata without realising it themselves. They lose the capacity, which is the great strength of ordinary public opinion, for spontaneous moral reaction to political events. Everything, great and small, tragic and commonplace, is put on the same uniform level of routine procedure. The hunt for a formula goes on without interruption during an earthquake. How else could human nature be expected to stand the tension of living in an earthquake area?

CHAPTER IV

THE LEAGUE AND THE OLD DIPLOMACY

WHAT place does the League fill in the post-war system for the conduct of international affairs? What are the possibilities and limits of its usefulness as revealed by the experience of the last fifteen years?

In 1919 there were many who felt that the League of Nations must be 'all or nothing'—that, if it did not entirely replace the older methods, it must at any rate take over so much of the business hitherto transacted through them that diplomacy, in the traditional sense of the term, would become a secondary and relatively unimportant factor in international politics. And, though the League itself was slow in acquiring authority, the immediate post-war years certainly witnessed a development of Diplomacy by Conference which for a time put the older methods entirely in the shade.[1] From 1922 onwards, however, a reaction set

[1] Between January 1920 and March 1922 there were no less than eighteen Conferences. Post-war Conferences organised without the technical aid of the League were exposed to all the inconveniences and dangers of the pre-war type of Conference and these were generally intensified by the increased complication of the issues involved. The Genoa Conference of 1922 falls under this heading. The Rapallo agreement, which proved fatal to it, seems to have come about largely through the lack of a central secretariat (see D'Abernon, *The Diary of an Ambassador*, i. 297). For a vivid account of the conditions in a large post-war Conference unprovided with a central organisation see the remarks by M. Poincaré in *Histoire politique, chronique de quinzaine*, iv. 148 ff.

in and the Old Diplomacy began to reassert itself.
Since then it has pursued its course parallel with that
of the League, whose strictly diplomatic activities,
as we have seen, may be said to date from the close of
1924.[1] Hence during the last decade each of the two
systems has been engaged in discovering and settling
down into its appropriate sphere of activity. At the
same time, as was inevitable despite the dreams of the
purists, a subtle process of interpenetration has been
taking place between them. The methods of the Old
Diplomacy have found their way to Geneva,[2] whilst
Geneva in its turn has cast its shadow over the Chancelleries.

But, in the general unsettlement of international

---

[1] See p. 351 above.

[2] One outward and visible sign of this has been the establishment of
'permanent delegations accredited to the League', of which there are no
less than 35 at the present time. Thus the League, as an agency of co-
operation, is in the curious position of being a centre for something like
a diplomatic *corps*, whilst the members of the *corps* are in the still more
curious position of having no government to which to pay their respects.
This is not to say that many of them do not turn their position to excellent use. The same may be said of the so-called Consuls-General maintained in Geneva by certain Powers, notably by the United States. When
the archives are opened it may well be that those of the United States
Consulate will provide the richest material for the historian. Lookers-on,
when they have familiarised themselves with the rules, are in a position
to see most of the game. On the question as to why the states which
are permanent members of the Council do not maintain permanent
delegations at Geneva, see the valedictory remarks of the Hungarian
Permanent Delegate in the *Records of the Fourth Committee*, 1930,
p. 98. Another form in which the spirit of the Old Diplomacy manifests itself in Geneva is in the sphere of social relations, where the
hierarchical elements and other accompaniments of the traditional
system have obtained a certain lodgment. A counter-influence in this
regard has, however, been supplied by the International Labour Office
with its more democratic outlook. Nor must the city of Geneva, with
its strong patrician and plebeian elements, be overlooked in this connexion. The whole Geneva *milieu*, in fact, affords a most interesting
field for study, and such a study would not be so remote from international politics as might be supposed.

politics, this process of adjustment has necessarily been tentative and uncertain. At a time when improvisation has been the order of the day as regards *policies*, it was not to be expected that there should be a clear grasp of *methods*. Thus the conduct of affairs by the Powers whose peoples were sincere in their desire for a better international system has exhibited all the characteristics of a period of transition. Statesmen have been as profuse in professions of loyalty to the League as they have been timid and vacillating in their handling of concrete issues of policy. Indeed, the existence of the League, with its multifarious armoury of diplomatic implements, by increasing the means at their disposal, has afforded them new and up-to-date pretexts for procrastination or evasion. 'Leave it to Geneva' is a formula covering every variety of policy from blank negation or resolute obstruction at one end to whole-hearted co-operation or a powerful initiative at the other.

Thus if we examine the post-war system, as it has shaped itself after close on a generation of trial and error, we find that it is a curious compound of the old and the new, equally unsatisfactory, no doubt, to whole-hearted adherents of either school of opinion. It is the Old Diplomacy—and something more. It is the New Order—and something less. Can we put our finger on that Something?

We may find a clue for the answer to this question if we turn aside for a moment from the problem of method, which has been our main concern throughout these pages, to consider the stuff or substance of international problems in themselves.

The war [recently remarked one of the most experienced of British diplomats] has brought about two great changes

In the first place it has increased the *tempo* of diplomacy, which means a great strain on ambassadors, who are expected to work at lightning speed. The other great change is the institution of the League of Nations, which ought in theory to have relieved an ambassador of a great deal of his work, in as much as it had created a clearing-house for a great many questions, such as minorities, Memel, Danzig and various other matters of that kind. But in point of fact the work of agents and ambassadors has been increased out of all proportion. [1]

In other words, the blending of the older and newer methods has taken place during a period when the problems to which these methods have been applied have become, not in war-time only but once and for all, more *numerous*, more *varied*, more *technical*, more *urgent* and, we may add, more intractable, both in themselves and because of the popular passions liable at any moment to gather around them.[2] What are these new problems which have so greatly increased the work and accentuated the difficulties of those engaged in the conduct of international affairs?

To analyse them in detail would require a separate volume, if not a series of volumes. But, very summarily, we may say that they can be grouped under two heads. There are the problems resulting from the increased importance of public opinion in international politics: and there are the problems resulting from the increased surface of friction through the multiplication of international contacts.

It was no doubt inevitable that, with the progress of democracy, the peoples should insist on playing a larger part in the determination of foreign policy. The problem thus opened out, as has been made clear on

[1] Sir Horace Rumbold in *International Affairs*, September 1935, p. 617.   [2] See p. 138 above.

an earlier page,[1] would have involved serious difficulties of adjustment in any circumstances. But the
difficulty of harmonising the democratic control of
foreign affairs with a far-sighted and consistent policy
calculated to win and to maintain the confidence of
other peoples has been greatly complicated by the
conditions under which the experiment has had to
be conducted. For the conquest of this last stronghold
of oligarchy and special privilege has not taken place
by degrees, as a natural accompaniment of the general
enlargement of the power of the electorate. On the
contrary, it has been precipitated under circumstances
of strain and excitement which have rendered the
voter even less fitted than he would otherwise have
been to face a new and complicated task.

Representative democracy depends for its successful
working above all upon confidence—confidence between the executive and the legislature and between
the legislature and the electorate, confidence between
the group of men at the centre of affairs, whether in
Cabinet or in Parliament or in the executive departments, and the millions of men and women at the
circumference, removed from immediate contact with
day-to-day political happenings, who constitute the
element of public opinion. That confidence has been
built up in the democratic countries of Western
Europe by a process extending over many generations
and it is the force which holds together and propels
the cumbrous, slow-moving but, in the main, surely
directed vehicle of popular government. But in the
sphere of international affairs it is precisely this indispensable element of confidence which has been
lacking. It was destroyed by the events of 1914, events

---

[1] See p. 27 above.

which surpassed not only all the reasonable calculations of the ordinary man but his wildest dreams, his
most fantastic nightmares. The shock of 1914 and the
following years, a shock equivalent to that of the
severest of domestic revolutions, has given its tone to
the public opinion of the post-war generation. It has
created an atmosphere of dull anxiety, of feverish
suspicion, of restless inquisitiveness, which has made
it equally difficult for statesmen either silently to
pursue a long-sighted independent course of their own,
in the best spirit of nineteenth-century diplomacy, or
to carry their peoples with them from stage to stage
of their plans.

It is in these psychological conditions that it
was demanded of statesmen, not simply that they
should conduct foreign affairs with reasonable efficiency but that they should satisfy the hopes and
aspirations that became centred, at the close of the
war, round the name of the League of Nations. For
the very mood of distrust which has weakened the
relationship between the electors and the executive,
while in some it has bred cynicism and indifference,
has led others to desert the familiar ground of reality
and to launch out into romantic flights of political
phantasy. Thus the 'League of Nations movement',
especially in the English-speaking countries, became
a meeting-ground for groups sponsoring schemes and
'ideals' of the most varied kind, the only element
common to them being their divorce from the realities
of the twentieth-century world. Amidst the clamour
of this discordant congregation, scientific students of
public affairs and of the Covenant at first found it hard
to gain a hearing. It was not the appeal to reason but
the inexorable march of events which thinned the

ranks of these so-called 'believers' in the League of Nations and thus enabled men and women of more realistic temper to take their rightful place in the movement. In the case of Great Britain and the British Dominions this process was accompanied, particularly in the years following 1931, by the realisation that a policy based on the collective system was the best and perhaps the only means of enabling the British Commonwealth to hold together in facing the international problems of the post-war world.[1]

But if a policy based upon the League of Nations is to be the element common to the British peoples and, we may add, to the democratic peoples generally, we are faced, under post-war conditions, with a new and very serious difficulty. It is that referred to by Sir Horace Rumbold in the words already cited—the more rapid *tempo* of foreign affairs. Changes in the international situation take place to-day so rapidly that it is impossible for the peoples to keep abreast of them. There was always a time-lag between the situation as revealed in Foreign Office telegrams and the situation as known to the 'man in the street'. But the increased *tempo* of the post-war world has dangerously enlarged the gap between the two and the difficulty has been intensified by the close inter-action which has now been set up between domestic and international affairs. A particular problem in this respect is furnished by the fact that in certain countries, familiarity with the internal conditions of which is of importance in the formation of a general judg-

[1] On this point see the chapter on 'The Empire and the League of Nations' in *The Third British Empire* (1926), by the present writer, and the *Proceedings* of the unofficial Conference on British Commonwealth Relations, held at Toronto in Sept. 1933 (ed. Toynbee: Oxford, 1934), esp. p. 165 ff.

ment on the world-situation, the restraints on the freedom of the press and on the free expression of opinion in speech and in private correspondence have closed some of the most useful channels for the transmission of up-to-date information.

All this creates a peculiar difficulty for the peoples of the British Commonwealth, whose traditional 'common sense' is largely the outcome of leisurely habits in the rumination and digestion of the world's news. Thus the time-lag is apt to operate in different ways in different parts of the Commonwealth. Public opinion in Canada and Australia may be months or even years behindhand in its appreciation of developments in Europe, whilst public opinion in Great Britain may be equally slow in its reaction to events in the Far East or in Africa or even in the United States. Technical means, the discussion of which lies beyond the scope of these pages, may no doubt be adopted to reduce this gap, but it can never be eliminated: for the impact of neighbourhood upon opinion will always be compelling. Regionalism and democracy are, in the last analysis, inseparable. Nothing remains but to strengthen that bond of confidence which, just as it holds together the people of a region and its elected representatives, can and must hold together those representatives themselves in face of the sundering influences of time and space. *Confidence all the time and Conference as often as possible*—there are no other remedies against the wear and tear of distance upon common principles, opinions and policies.

The other standing difficulty with which post-war diplomacy has to cope is the change in the character of the economic system. The war brought the *laissez-faire* period to an abrupt end. It destroyed the con-

fidence on which it had been based and swept away
with it many of the habits and traditions which had
clustered around it. For good or evil, the economic
system of the post-war world is inextricably bound
up with its politics. Business and government continue
to employ separate techniques: but they are now both,
in the fullest sense, 'public affairs'.

With the problems thus opened up this is not the
place to deal. Their influence on the methods of diplomacy from the war years onward has, however, been
profound and lasting. The diplomat of to-day, unlike
the hero of Sir Ernest Satow's pages,[1] needs far more
than a nodding acquaintance with economics, or, to
revive a title which has acquired a new meaning in
these latter days, with *political economy*. Often indeed
he is compelled to be something like a man of business
himself and to become almost as familiar with the
niceties of beef, bacon and vegetables or with the vicissitudes of the exchanges and their management as an
habitué of Smithfield or Covent Garden or a partner in
an accepting house or the Governor of a Central Bank.

Perhaps the best way of bringing home to the reader
the nature and extent of the changes which the twin
factors of Publicity and Business have brought about
in the conduct of the 'old diplomacy' will be to describe
the actual organisation of an important Embassy under
present-day conditions. It will be convenient to use
for this purpose an account which recently appeared
from the pen of a competent witness of the activities
of the French Embassy in Berlin.[2]

[1] See p. 18 above.
[2] Article by M. Camille Loutre in the *Petit Parisien* of January 14,
1935. The translation is slightly abridged in certain passages and the
proper names have been omitted.

The ambassador [we are told] is one of the men of our generation who is best acquainted with Germany not only on the literary side but also as regards the details of her economic life and the vicissitudes of her history. Thus he has conceived of his task in a new spirit. His idea is that the present-day diplomat should no longer be merely a drawing-room personage but also a specialist capable of taking rapid decisions which will be all the surer because they result from the thorough knowledge that is acquired by dint of day to day work.

For the members of his staff the ambassador is before all things an energiser. Always in cordial contact with his colleagues, he throws out ideas, suggests topics for enquiry, coordinates their various activities and sets upon their work the hall-mark of his lively and ever wakeful personality.

This thumbnail sketch of the head of the mission is followed by an account of the different departments of the embassy which reveals how the technique of the League of Nations is being applied to the conduct of diplomacy in individual capitals:

First there is the political section which the ambassador keeps under his own immediate supervision: associated with it is a technical branch which is entrusted to a group of competent specialists. The actual director of the political section is an economic expert who, after spending eight years in the Commercial Relations Department in the French Foreign Office, was brought back to Berlin, where he had once served as Secretary. The place that he occupies in the official scheme testifies to the importance of his special qualifications at a time when the general policy of states is more and more being influenced by economic considerations. His assistant, who holds the rank of First Secretary, came to Berlin from Ankara and his knowledge of Balkan questions is particularly valuable for an understanding of the various aspects of German diplomatic activity in South-Eastern Europe.

But, in addition to the Political Section proper, the Embassy is the home of an elaborate technical organisation. First and foremost in this connexion must be mentioned the Military Attaché and his deputy, both specialists in foreign armies. At a moment when the degree and the pace of German re-armament are exciting passionate interest throughout Europe, the Military Attaché has been both clear-sighted and cool-headed: he is as careful in his ascertainment of facts as he is measured in his judgments upon them when collected. Having held similar posts in London and Tokio he is thoroughly familiar with the diplomatic milieu and was also favourably received in Army circles, where he has many friends. The Naval Attaché comes from the Naval Staff at the Ministry of Marine and the Air Attaché is an aeronautical engineer.

Special rooms in the Embassy are set aside for a Financial Section, the chief of which had for a long time acted as assistant to his predecessor. Like the ambassador himself, with whom he was a class-mate at the University, he has behind him a record of brilliant academic distinction in German studies. For many years past he has devoted himself to a study of the ever darker mysteries of German public and private finance.

On the first floor, in the part of the building belonging to the Consulate, the Commercial Attaché and his assistant are engaged on work which no outsider can appreciate in detail. The increasing complications in which international exchanges are involved through the establishment of virtual state import monopolies and the unsatisfactory working of the clearing-house system constantly provide the Commercial Section of the Embassy with an abundance of fresh problems.

Then follows a brief description of the daily routine in this up-to-date diplomatic establishment:

Every day at 10 A.M. the Ambassador meets the principal members of his staff and discusses with them the questions of the moment, telephoning afterwards to Paris a survey of the principal events and opinions of the day, as they appear from the morning papers. Much information of the same kind comes in from Paris, also over the telephone. Thus the methods of the

Embassy resemble those of the editorial office of a great news-paper. To visit the Registry is to realise how large is the number of reports drawn up for every 'bag' conveyed by special courier to Paris.

The article closes with a reference to the social side of the Embassy's activities—the constant guests, French, German and others, and the 'delicate task of maintaining the indispensable contacts with the German governing circles of the day, in a revolutionary age when the political orthodoxy of yesterday is not necessarily that of tomorrow'.

Here we see how the impact of Business has changed the life of an Embassy in action. The Director of the *Political* Section is an *economic* expert. The inter-penetration between the political and the economic elements in international affairs could not be better illustrated. Cobden and Metternich have come together under the same roof. The system of the Holy Alliance and the system of *laissez-faire* have locked their forces. By the same token, the diplomatic and consular func-tions of the foreign service have become intermingled so as to be practically indistinguishable. This was the case with the U.S.S.R. from the beginning of its official activities in foreign capitals. But what seemed a paradox in 1920 has become an everyday reality in 1935.

One familiar feature in the present-day embassy has, however, been passed over in silence by the French writer. He makes no mention of the Press Officer or Attaché. No doubt the modesty of this official was responsible for this omission in the case in question. But he has become an important personage in the ambassador's family, occupying in the leading foreign capitals a position corresponding to that of the 'News

Department' of the Foreign Office at home.[1]

The problem of fitting League of Nations work into the regular Foreign Office framework has been solved differently in different countries. One expedient is to have a special League of Nations 'section' or 'office'. This is the case at the French Foreign Office, where the 'Head of the Bureau for the League of Nations', who holds the rank of a Minister Plenipotentiary, is also Assistant Director for Political Affairs (in Foreign Office language, Assistant Under-Secretary). In addition there is a political post, that of 'Permanent Representative on the Council of the League of Nations', which is curious in this respect, that it is not necessarily vacated on a change of government. No other country has adopted the present British expedient of having a 'Minister for League of Nations Affairs' side by side with the Foreign Secretary.

Thus we see that, despite the establishment of the League of Nations, the old diplomatic system has not only survived but has passed through a period of rapid development and expansion. This is not due, be it repeated, to abnormal and temporary conditions resulting from the war and the peace treaties. It is due to the general conditions of twentieth-century life, which, so far as can be predicted, are likely to be permanent even when the particular problems of a 'post-war' character have found their solution. It is indeed the conditions of the nineteenth century with its 'private internationalism' and its blindness to the underlying realities of international politics which are likely to strike the future historian as abnormal.

---

[1] The Foreign Office list for 1935 contains the names of 'Financial Advisers' (seconded from the Treasury) in Berlin and Washington, of a 'Press Attaché' in Paris and a 'Press Officer' in Berlin and Rome.

How, then, is the work of carrying on inter-state relations likely to be divided between the League of Nations and the Old Diplomacy? We have already had occasion to refer to this question when dealing with the situation in which the newly created League was placed through the defection of the United States. That defection, disastrous though it seemed, and indeed was, at the time, was nevertheless useful in so far as it brought immediately into view certain under- lying factors which must have revealed themselves sooner or later in any case. In 1920 it became clear that there could be no 'League of Nations policy' on particular issues. The idea of a common policy of the powers belongs to a past age, the age of the Concert. Policies, whether in home and in foreign affairs—the two are, in actual fact indistinguishable—are, in this democratic age, the expression of the popular will: and the sovereign peoples to-day are more alert, more determined to maintain their interests and, above all, more numerous than not only a Talleyrand and a Metternich, but a Bismarck, a Salisbury or a Gort- schakoff could ever have imagined. What did the voice of Prague mean to Metternich or the voice of Warsaw to Bismarck or even the voice of India in foreign affairs to Salisbury? The Little Entente, the Balkan Entente, the less formally organised but none the less real Entente of the Northern States, have come to stay. So too have the factors in international politics represented by Delhi, by Nanking, by Teheran and Bagdad, Cairo and Mecca, by Canberra and Wellington, by Pretoria and even by Addis Ababa. 'It takes all sorts to make a world.' But it is idle to expect that such a world can be induced to march in step. In our domestic concerns we look for no such uniformity.

We are accustomed to the most varied forms of grouping, whether according to affinity or neighbourhood
or material interest. Why should we imagine that a
stricter discipline should be needed in the international
relations of free and independent peoples?

The answer has already been foreshadowed by the
whole development described in these pages. It is
because *inter-state groupings* have hitherto been generally associated with the idea of war, or at least of
defence. In other words, they have been thought of
as being *alliances* or potential alliances. And the word
alliance carries with it the suggestion, not only that
A and B are friends but that C and D are their natural
enemies. It is this idea, the idea of arbitrary friend-
ships and arbitrary enmities, which the League of
Nations system is designed to sweep away. It has never
existed, thanks to the *laissez-faire* tradition, in the
domain of commercial policy. To lower the duty on
French wines in return for freer entry for Lancashire
cottons was never regarded by the old diplomacy as
the first step to an Anglo-French alliance. That kind
of Entente was treated on its merits and not as part
of the sinister game of Power-politics. It is the function
of the League of Nations to enable *all* kinds of inter-
state dealings so to be regarded—to set the peoples
free to handle the problems which concern them on
their merits, whether the group which is interested in
them be small or large, drawn from one neighbourhood
or from many, composed of strong powers or only of
smaller states. The international problems of the post-
war world are no doubt extremely complicated. Regarded in the mass, they seem to defy solution. But
taken one by one and dealt with according to the
technique appropriate to each case, they will yield

to treatment as readily as similar problems in the domestic sphere. There is always a sensible way of dealing with public matters if statesmen and peoples will be sensible enough to look for it. But the statesmen and peoples will not be thus sensible if they have the fear of war ever present in their minds. Indeed it would be senseless for them to be 'sensible' about minor issues of policy to the neglect of the problem of their state's defence or very existence. Thus the first and major function of the League is to eliminate once and for all the fear of war. Once this has been achieved, we shall witness a relaxation of tension which will manifest itself in many different forms. One of these forms will be the appearance in the field of practical politics of many new ideas which have hitherto been confined to the study or to the discussions of learned bodies. Another will be the formation of new groupings in the way suggested above.

But the League has another function. It is, as was suggested already in 1918,[1] that of helping its member states to *discover* 'sensible' ways of dealing with their own affairs. This is, after all, what is meant, and all that is meant, by the familiar words 'the promotion of international co-operation'. The League is a great repository of knowledge and experience and of the practical wisdom derived from close and continuous contact with the public affairs of the modern world. Like a constitutional monarch, it cannot command. But it can wield an ever-present influence. And this influence will, in fact, be all the greater because the elements of which it is compounded do not include either physical force or political power, in the strict sense of the term. In a world at peace the *authority* of

[1] See p. 205 above.

the League, expressed through its various organs, both deliberative and technical, should become a stabilising factor comparable with that of the most revered institutions, be they monarchical or republican, in the life of individual peoples. For it will not only exhort its members to be sensible: it will show them in detail how to be so. Its technical agencies and the conventions and policies worked out by them will be working models for the solution of problems in the most varied fields. This procedure will not give us 'the Parliament of Man'—still less 'the Federation of the World'. But, just because it will not enforce uniformity where it is not felt to be needed, it will maintain the spirit of co-operation which is the only enduring bond between the members of the League, as between the members of the smaller and more intimate League known as the British Commonwealth.

In things necessary, Unity: in things indifferent, Liberty: in all things, Charity.

APPENDIX

THE COVENANT OF THE LEAGUE OF NATIONS

THE HIGH CONTRACTING PARTIES,

In order to promote international co-operation and to achieve international peace and security

by the acceptance of obligations not to resort to war,

by the prescription of open, just and honourable relations between nations,

by the firm establishment of the understandings of international law as the actual rule of conduct among Governments,

and by the maintenance of justice and a scrupulous respect for all treaty obligations in the dealings of organised peoples with one another,

Agree to this Covenant of the League of Nations.

ARTICLE 1

1. The original Members of the League of Nations shall be those of the Signatories which are named in the Annex to this Covenant and also such of those other States named in the Annex as shall accede without reservation to this Covenant. Such accession shall be effected by a Declaration deposited with the Secretariat within two months of the coming into force of the Covenant. Notice thereof shall be sent to all other Members of the League.

2. Any fully self-governing State, Dominion or Colony not named in the Annex may become a Member of the League if its admission is agreed to by two-thirds of the Assembly, provided that it shall give effective guarantees of its sincere intention to observe its international obligations, and shall accept such regulations as may be prescribed by the League in regard to its military, naval and air forces and armaments.

3. Any Member of the League may, after two years' notice of its intention so to do, withdraw from the League, provided that all its international obligations and all its obligations under this Covenant shall have been fulfilled at the time of its withdrawal.

ARTICLE 2

The action of the League under this Covenant shall be effected through the instrumentality of an Assembly and of a Council, with a permanent Secretariat.

ARTICLE 3

1. The Assembly shall consist of Representatives of the Members of the League.

2. The Assembly shall meet at stated intervals and from time to time as occasion may require at the Seat of the League or at such other place as may be decided upon.

3. The Assembly may deal at its meetings with any matter within the sphere of action of the League or affecting the peace of the world.

4. At meetings of the Assembly, each Member of the League shall have one vote, and may have not more than three Representatives.

ARTICLE 4

1. The Council shall consist of Representatives of the Principal Allied and Associated Powers,[1] together with Representatives of four other Members of the League. These four Members of the League shall be selected by the Assembly from time to time in its discretion. Until the appointment of the Representatives of the four Members of the League first selected by the Assembly, Representatives of Belgium, Brazil, Spain and Greece shall be members of the Council.

2. With the approval of the majority of the Assembly, the Council may name additional Members of the League whose Representatives shall always be Members of the Council ; the

---

[1] The Principal Allied and Associated Powers are the following: The United States of America, the British Empire, France, Italy and Japan.

Council with like approval may increase the number of Members of the League to be selected by the Assembly for representation on the Council.

2 *bis*.[1] *The Assembly shall fix by a two-thirds majority the rules dealing with the election of the non-permanent Members of the Council, and particularly such regulations as relate to their term of office and the conditions of re-eligibility.*

3. The Council shall meet from time to time as occasion may require, and at least once a year, at the Seat of the League, or at such other place as may be decided upon.

4. The Council may deal at its meetings with any matter within the sphere of action of the League or affecting the peace of the world.

5. Any Member of the League not represented on the Council shall be invited to send a Representative to sit as a member at any meeting of the Council during the consideration of matters specially affecting the interests of that Member of the League.

6. At meetings of the Council, each Member of the League represented on the Council shall have one vote, and may have not more than one Representative.

ARTICLE 5

1. Except where otherwise expressly provided in this Covenant or by the terms of the present Treaty, decisions at any meeting of the Assembly or of the Council shall require the agreement of all the Members of the League represented at the meeting.

2. All matters of procedure at meetings of the Assembly or of the Council, including the appointment of Committees to investigate particular matters, shall be regulated by the Assembly or by the Council and may be decided by a majority of the Members of the League represented at the meeting.

3. The first meeting of the Assembly and the first meeting of the Council shall be summoned by the President of the United States of America.

[1] This Amendment came into force on July 29, 1926, in accordance with Article 26 of the Covenant.

ARTICLE 6

1. The permanent Secretariat shall be established at the Seat of the League. The Secretariat shall comprise a Secretary-General and such secretaries and staff as may be required.

2. The first Secretary-General shall be the person named in the Annex; thereafter the Secretary-General shall be appointed by the Council with the approval of the majority of the Assembly.

3. The secretaries and staff of the Secretariat shall be appointed by the Secretary-General with the approval of the Council.

4. The Secretary-General shall act in that capacity at all meetings of the Assembly and of the Council.

5.[1] *The expenses of the League shall be borne by the Members of the League in the proportion decided by the Assembly.*

ARTICLE 7

1. The Seat of the League is established at Geneva.

2. The Council may at any time decide that the Seat of the League shall be established elsewhere.

3. All positions under or in connexion with the League, including the Secretariat, shall be open equally to men and women.

4. Representatives of the Members of the League and officials of the League when engaged on the business of the League shall enjoy diplomatic privileges and immunities.

5. The buildings and other property occupied by the League or its officials or by Representatives attending its meetings shall be inviolable.

ARTICLE 8

1. The Members of the League recognise that the maintenance of peace requires the reduction of national armaments to

---

[1] This Amendment came into force on August 13, 1924, in accordance with Article 26 of the Covenant and replaces the following paragraph:

'5. The expenses of the Secretariat shall be borne by the Members of the League in accordance with the apportionment of the expenses of the International Bureau of the Universal Postal Union.'

the lowest point consistent with national safety and the enforcement by common action of international obligations.

2. The Council, taking account of the geographical situation and circumstances of each State, shall formulate plans for such reduction for the consideration and action of the several Governments.

3. Such plans shall be subject to reconsideration and revision at least every ten years.

4. After these plans shall have been adopted by the several Governments, the limits of armaments therein fixed shall not be exceeded without the concurrence of the Council.

5. The Members of the League agree that the manufacture by private enterprise of munitions and implements of war is open to grave objections. The Council shall advise how the evil effects attendant upon such manufacture can be prevented, due regard being had to the necessities of those Members of the League which are not able to manufacture the munitions and implements of war necessary for their safety.

6. The Members of the League undertake to interchange full and frank information as to the scale of their armaments, their military, naval and air programmes and the condition of such of their industries as are adaptable to warlike purposes.

ARTICLE 9

A permanent Commission shall be constituted to advise the Council on the execution of the provisions of Articles 1 and 8 and on military, naval and air questions generally.

ARTICLE 10

The Members of the League undertake to respect and preserve as against external aggression the territorial integrity and existing political independence of all Members of the League. In case of any such aggression or in case of any threat or danger of such aggression the Council shall advise upon the means by which this obligation shall be fulfilled.

ARTICLE 11

1. Any war or threat of war, whether immediately affecting any of the Members of the League or not, is hereby declared

a matter of concern to the whole League, and the League shall take any action that may be deemed wise and effectual to safeguard the peace of nations. In case any such emergency should arise the Secretary-General shall on the request of any Member of the League forthwith summon a meeting of the Council.

2. It is also declared to be the friendly right of each Member of the League to bring to the attention of the Assembly or of the Council any circumstance whatever affecting international relations which threatens to disturb international peace or the good understanding between nations upon which peace depends.

ARTICLE 12 [1]

1. The Members of the League agree that if there should arise between them any dispute likely to lead to a rupture they will submit the matter either to arbitration *or judicial settlement* or to inquiry by the Council, and they agree in no case to resort to war until three months after the award by the arbitrators *or the judicial decision* or the report by the Council.

2. In any case under this Article the award of the arbitrators *or the judicial decision* shall be made within a reasonable time, and the report of the Council shall be made within six months after the submission of the dispute.

ARTICLE 13 [1]

1. The Members of the League agree that whenever any dispute shall arise between them which they recognise to be

---

[1] The Amendments printed in italics relating to these Articles came into force on September 26, 1924, in accordance with Article 26 of the Covenant and replace the following texts:

ARTICLE 12

'The Members of the League agree that if there should arise between them any dispute likely to lead to a rupture they will submit the matter either to arbitration or to inquiry by the Council, and they agree in no case to resort to war until three months after the award by the arbitrators or the report by the Council.

'In any case under this Article the award of the arbitrators shall be made within a reasonable time, and the report of the Council shall be made within six months after the submission of the dispute.'

suitable for submission to arbitration *or judicial settlement*, and which cannot be satisfactorily settled by diplomacy, they will submit the whole subject-matter to arbitration *or judicial settlement*.

2. Disputes as to the interpretation of a treaty, as to any question of international law, as to the existence of any fact which if established would constitute a breach of any international obligation, or as to the extent and nature of the reparation to be made for any such breach, are declared to be among those which are generally suitable for submission to arbitration *or judicial settlement*.

3. *For the consideration of any such dispute, the court to which the case is referred shall be the Permanent Court of International Justice, established in accordance with Article 14, or any tribunal agreed on by the parties to the dispute or stipulated in any convention existing between them.*

4. The Members of the League agree that they will carry out in full good faith any award *or decision* that may be rendered, and that they will not resort to war against a Member of the League which complies therewith. In the event of any failure to carry out such an award *or decision*, the Council shall propose what steps should be taken to give effect thereto.

ARTICLE 13

'The Members of the League agree that whenever any dispute shall arise between them which they recognise to be suitable for submission to arbitration and which cannot be satisfactorily settled by diplomacy, they will submit the whole subject-matter to arbitration.

'Disputes as to the interpretation of a treaty, as to any question of international law, as to the existence of any fact which if established would constitute a breach of any international obligation, or as to the extent and nature of the reparation to be made for any such breach, are declared to be among those which are generally suitable for submission to arbitration.

'For the consideration of any such dispute, the court of arbitration to which the case is referred shall be the court agreed on by the parties to the dispute or stipulated in any convention existing between them.

'The Members of the League agree that they will carry out in full good faith any award that may be rendered and that they will not resort to war against a Member of the League which complies therewith. In the event of any failure to carry out such an award, the Council shall propose what steps should be taken to give effect thereto.'

ARTICLE 14

The Council shall formulate and submit to the Members of the League for adoption plans for the establishment of a Permanent Court of International Justice. The Court shall be competent to hear and determine any dispute of an international character which the parties thereto submit to it. The Court may also give an advisory opinion upon any dispute or question referred to it by the Council or by the Assembly.

ARTICLE 15

1.[1] If there should arise between Members of the League any dispute likely to lead to a rupture, which is not submitted to arbitration *or judicial settlement* in accordance with Article 13, the Members of the League agree that they will submit the matter to the Council. Any party to the dispute may effect such submission by giving notice of the existence of the dispute to the Secretary-General, who will make all necessary arrangements for a full investigation and consideration thereof.

2. For this purpose the parties to the dispute will communicate to the Secretary-General, as promptly as possible, statements of their case with all the relevant facts and papers, and the Council may forthwith direct the publication thereof.

3. The Council shall endeavour to effect a settlement of the dispute, and if such efforts are successful, a statement shall be made public giving such facts and explanations regarding the dispute and the terms of settlement thereof as the Council may deem appropriate.

[1] The Amendment to the first paragraph of this Article came into force on September 26, 1924, in accordance with Article 26 of the Covenant, and replaces the following text:

ARTICLE 15

'If there should arise between Members of the League any dispute likely to lead to a rupture, which is not submitted to arbitration in accordance with Article 13, the Members of the League agree that they will submit the matter to the Council. Any party to the dispute may effect such submission by giving notice of the existence of the dispute to the Secretary-General, who will make all necessary arrangements for a full investigation and consideration thereof.'

4. If the dispute is not thus settled, the Council, either unanimously or by a majority vote, shall make and publish a report containing a statement of the facts of the dispute and the recommendations which are deemed just and proper in regard thereto.

5. Any Member of the League represented on the Council may make public a statement of the facts of the dispute and of its conclusions regarding the same.

6. If a report by the Council is unanimously agreed to by the members thereof other than the Representatives of one or more of the parties to the dispute, the Members of the League agree that they will not go to war with any party to the dispute which complies with the recommendations of the report.

7. If the Council fails to reach a report which is unanimously agreed to by the members thereof, other than the Representatives of one or more of the parties to the dispute, the Members of the League reserve to themselves the right to take such action as they shall consider necessary for the maintenance of right and justice.

8. If the dispute between the parties is claimed by one of them, and is found by the Council, to arise out of a matter which by international law is solely within the domestic jurisdiction of that party, the Council shall so report, and shall make no recommendation as to its settlement.

9. The Council may in any case under this Article refer the dispute to the Assembly. The dispute shall be so referred at the request of either party to the dispute, provided that such request be made within fourteen days after the submission of the dispute to the Council.

10. In any case referred to the Assembly, all the provisions of this Article and of Article 12 relating to the action and powers of the Council shall apply to the action and powers of the Assembly, provided that a report made by the Assembly, if concurred in by the Representatives of those Members of the League represented on the Council and of a majority of the other Members of the League, exclusive in each case of the Representatives of the parties to the dispute, shall have the same force as a report by the Council concurred in by all the

members thereof other than the Representatives of one or more of the parties to the dispute.

ARTICLE 16

1. Should any Member of the League resort to war in disregard of its covenants under Articles 12, 13 or 15, it shall *ipso facto* be deemed to have committed an act of war against all other Members of the League, which hereby undertake immediately to subject it to the severance of all trade or financial relations, the prohibition of all intercourse between their nationals and the nationals of the covenant-breaking State, and the prevention of all financial, commercial or personal intercourse between the nationals of the covenant-breaking State and the nationals of any other State, whether a Member of the League or not.

2. It shall be the duty of the Council in such case to recommend to the several Governments concerned what effective military, naval or air force the Members of the League shall severally contribute to the armed forces to be used to protect the covenants of the League.

3. The Members of the League agree, further, that they will mutually support one another in the financial and economic measures which are taken under this Article, in order to minimise the loss and inconvenience resulting from the above measures, and that they will mutually support one another in resisting any special measures aimed at one of their number by the covenant-breaking State, and that they will take the necessary steps to afford passage through their territory to the forces of any of the Members of the League which are co-operating to protect the covenants of the League.

4. Any Member of the League which has violated any covenant of the League may be declared to be no longer a Member of the League by a vote of the Council concurred in by the Representatives of all the other Members of the League represented thereon.

ARTICLE 17

1. In the event of a dispute between a Member of the League and a State which is not a Member of the League, or between

States not Members of the League, the State or States not Members of the League shall be invited to accept the obligations of membership in the League for the purposes of such dispute, upon such conditions as the Council may deem just. If such invitation is accepted, the provisions of Articles 12 to 16 inclusive shall be applied with such modifications as may be deemed necessary by the Council.

2. Upon such invitation being given the Council shall immediately institute an inquiry into the circumstances of the dispute and recommend such action as may seem best and most effectual in the circumstances.

3. If a State so invited shall refuse to accept the obligations of membership in the League for the purposes of such dispute, and shall resort to war against a Member of the League, the provisions of Article 16 shall be applicable as against the State taking such action.

4. If both parties to the dispute when so invited refuse to accept the obligations of membership in the League for the purposes of such dispute, the Council may take such measures and make such recommendations as will prevent hostilities and will result in the settlement of the dispute.

ARTICLE 18

Every treaty or international engagement entered into hereafter by any Member of the League shall be forthwith registered with the Secretariat and shall as soon as possible be published by it. No such treaty or international engagement shall be binding until so registered.

ARTICLE 19

The Assembly may from time to time advise the reconsideration by Members of the League of treaties which have become inapplicable and the consideration of international conditions whose continuance might endanger the peace of the world.

ARTICLE 20

1. The Members of the League severally agree that this Covenant is accepted as abrogating all obligations or under-

standings *inter se* which are inconsistent with the terms thereof, and solemnly undertake that they will not hereafter enter into any engagements inconsistent with the terms thereof.

2. In case any Member of the League shall, before becoming a Member of the League, have undertaken any obligations inconsistent with the terms of this Covenant, it shall be the duty of such Member to take immediate steps to procure its release from such obligations.

ARTICLE 21

Nothing in this Covenant shall be deemed to affect the validity of international engagements, such as treaties of arbitration or regional understandings like the Monroe Doctrine, for securing the maintenance of peace.

ARTICLE 22

1. To those colonies and territories which as a consequence of the late war have ceased to be under the sovereignty of the States which formerly governed them and which are inhabited by peoples not yet able to stand by themselves under the strenuous conditions of the modern world, there should be applied the principle that the well-being and development of such peoples form a sacred trust of civilisation and that securities for the performance of this trust should be embodied in this Covenant.

2. The best method of giving practical effect to this principle is that the tutelage of such peoples should be entrusted to advanced nations who by reason of their resources, their experience or their geographical position can best undertake this responsibility, and who are willing to accept it, and that this tutelage should be exercised by them as Mandatories on behalf of the League.

3. The character of the mandate must differ according to the stage of the development of the people, the geographical situation of the territory, its economic conditions and other similar circumstances.

4. Certain communities formerly belonging to the Turkish Empire have reached a stage of development where their exist-

ence as independent nations can be provisionally recognised subject to the rendering of administrative advice and assistance by a Mandatory until such time as they are able to stand alone. The wishes of these communities must be a principal consideration in the selection of the Mandatory.

5. Other peoples, especially those of Central Africa, are at such a stage that the Mandatory must be responsible for the administration of the territory under conditions which will guarantee freedom of conscience and religion, subject only to the maintenance of public order and morals, the prohibition of abuses such as the slave trade, the arms traffic and the liquor traffic, and the prevention of the establishment of fortifications or military and naval bases and of military training of the natives for other than police purposes and the defence of territory, and will also secure equal opportunities for the trade and commerce of other Members of the League.

6. There are territories, such as South-West Africa and certain of the South Pacific Islands, which, owing to the sparseness of their population, or their small size, or their remoteness from the centres of civilisation, or their geographical contiguity to the territory of the Mandatory, and other circumstances, can be best administered under the laws of the Mandatory as integral portions of its territory, subject to the safeguards above mentioned in the interests of the indigenous population.

7. In every case of mandate, the Mandatory shall render to the Council an annual report in reference to the territory committed to its charge.

8. The degree of authority, control, or administration to be exercised by the Mandatory shall, if not previously agreed upon by the Members of the League, be explicitly defined in each case by the Council.

9. A permanent Commission shall be constituted to receive and examine the annual reports of the Mandatories and to advise the Council on all matters relating to the observance of the mandates.

ARTICLE 23

Subject to and in accordance with the provisions of international conventions existing or hereafter to be agreed upon, the Members of the League:

- (a) will endeavour to secure and maintain fair and humane conditions of labour for men, women, and children, both in their own countries and in all countries to which their commercial and industrial relations extend, and for that purpose will establish and maintain the necessary international organisations;
- (b) undertake to secure just treatment of the native inhabitants of territories under their control;
- (c) will entrust the League with the general supervision over the execution of agreements with regard to the traffic in women and children, and the traffic in opium and other dangerous drugs;
- (d) will entrust the League with the general supervision of the trade in arms and ammunition with the countries in which the control of this traffic is necessary in the common interest;
- (e) will make provision to secure and maintain freedom of communications and of transit and equitable treatment for the commerce of all Members of the League. In this connexion, the special necessities of the regions devastated during the war of 1914–1918 shall be borne in mind;
- (f) will endeavour to take steps in matters of international concern for the prevention and control of disease.

ARTICLE 24

1. There shall be placed under the direction of the League all international bureaux already established by general treaties if the parties to such treaties consent. All such international bureaux and all commissions for the regulation of matters of international interest hereafter constituted shall be placed under the direction of the League.

2. In all matters of international interest which are regulated by general conventions but which are not placed under the control of international bureaux or commissions, the Secretariat of the League shall, subject to the consent of the

Council and if desired by the parties, collect and distribute all relevant information and shall render any other assistance which may be necessary or desirable.

3. The Council may include as part of the expenses of the Secretariat the expenses of any bureau or commission which is placed under the direction of the League.

ARTICLE 25

The Members of the League agree to encourage and promote the establishment and co-operation of duly authorised voluntary national Red Cross organisations having as purposes the improvement of health, the prevention of disease and the mitigation of suffering throughout the world.

ARTICLE 26

1. Amendments to this Covenant will take effect when ratified by the Members of the League whose Representatives compose the Council and by a majority of the Members of the League whose Representatives compose the Assembly.

2. No such amendments shall bind any Member of the League which signifies its dissent therefrom, but in that case it shall cease to be a Member of the League.

ANNEX

I. *Original Members of the League of Nations, Signatories of the Treaty of Peace*

United States of America
Belgium
Bolivia
Brazil
British Empire
  Canada
  Australia
  South Africa
  New Zealand
  India
China
Cuba
Ecuador
France
Greece
Guatemala

Haiti
Hedjaz
Honduras
Italy
Japan
Liberia
Nicaragua
Panama
Peru
Poland
Portugal
Roumania
Serb-Croat-Slovene State
Siam
Czechoslovakia
Uruguay

States invited to accede to the Covenant

Argentine Republic
Chile
Colombia
Denmark
Netherlands
Norway
Paraguay

Persia
Salvador
Spain
Sweden
Switzerland
Venezuela

II. *First Secretary-General of the League of Nations*
The Hon. Sir JAMES ERIC DRUMMOND, K.C.M.G., C.B.

Members of the League

OCTOBER 22, 1935

Abyssinia	Italy
Afghanistan	Latvia
Albania	Liberia
Argentine Republic	Lithuania
Australia	Luxemburg
Austria	Mexico
Belgium	Netherlands
Bolivia	New Zealand
British Empire	Nicaragua
Bulgaria	Norway
Canada	Panama
Chile	Paraguay [1]
China	Peru
Colombia	Persia
Cuba	Poland
Czechoslovakia	Portugal
Denmark	Salvador
Dominican Republic	Roumania
Ecuador	Siam
Esthonia	South Africa
Finland	Spain
France	Sweden
Greece	Switzerland
Guatemala	Turkey
Haiti	United Socialist Soviet Republics
Honduras	
Hungary	Uruguay
India	Venezuela
Iraq	Yugoslavia
Irish Free State	

[1] Gave notice of withdrawal, Feb. 22, 1935.

2 L

INDEX

THE END

Printed in Great Britain by R. & R. CLARK, LIMITED, *Edinburgh.*